Progress As If Survival Mattered

What is the use of a house if you haven't got a tolerable planet to put it on?—HENRY DAVID THOREAU

Progress As If Survival Mattered

A HANDBOOK

FOR A CONSERVER SOCIETY

BY FRIENDS OF THE EARTH

EDITED BY HUGH NASH

with an introduction by David R. Brower

(with apologies to the Science Council of Canada
and E. F. [Small is Beautiful] Schumacher)

FRIENDS OF THE EARTH · SAN FRANCISCO

Acknowledgments

Friends of the Earth would like to thank the following writers, publications, and publishers for permission to quote from their works. Extracts from these books and articles appear as sidebars and display quotes throughout *Progress As If Survival Mattered,* with author attribution. Copyright to quoted material is retained by the authors, publishers, and periodicals listed here. Material written specifically for *Progress As If Survival Mattered* is copyrighted by Friends of the Earth, Inc. Credit lines appear with graphics and illustrative material and should be considered part of the copyright declaration and acknowledgment statement.

Jack Anderson, "Poison in the Fields" (a syndicated column).

Arthur Ashe (Frank Deford, editor), *Portrait in Motion* (Houghton-Mifflin, 1975; Ballantine Books, 1976).

Orren Beaty, from "Let's Get the Railroads Moving Again!" (*Not Man Apart,* October 1975).

Avrom Bendavid-Val, "Social Economics" (*International Journal of Social Economics,* December 1976).

Murray Bookchin, "Decentralization as Human Scale," adapted from *Our Synthetic Environment* (Harper-Colophon, 1962).

William Bronson, *How to Kill a Golden State* (Doubleday and Company, 1968).

David Brower, "Shall We Burn the Furniture in the Oval Office?" (*Not Man Apart,* April 1975).

Lester Brown, Patricia L. McGrath, and Bruce Stokes, *Twenty-two Dimensions of the Population Problem* (Worldwatch Institute, March 1976).

Wilson Clark, "Innovations in Energy Conservation: Technological Applications" (A paper prepared for the Conservation Foundation).

John Cole, "Letter to a Young Revolutionary" (*Maine Times,* October 31, 1975).

Barry Commoner, *The Poverty of Power* (Alfred Knopf, 1976).

Lewis D. Conta, "Coming: The Real Energy Crisis" (*Mechanical Engineering,* August 1975).

Norman Cousins, "The U.S. and the U.N." (*Saturday Review,* March 6, 1976) The Cousteau Society, "Quiet Violence," a special report.

Jacques Cousteau, "Catch as Catch Can" (*Saturday Review,* August 7, 1976) and "Jonah's Complaint" (*Saturday Review,* June 12, 1976).

Robert R. Curry, "Reinhabiting the Earth: Life Support and the Future Primitive" (A paper presented to The International Symposium on the Recovery of Damaged Ecosystems, 1975).

Raymond Dasmann, "Toward a Dynamic Balance of Man and Nature" (International Union for the Conservation of Nature and Natural Resources, 1975).

William O. Douglas, Dissenting Opinion in *Sierra Club vs. Rogers Morton, etc.* (1972).

Erik P. Eckholm, *Losing Ground* (W.W. Norton, 1976).

The Editors of *The Ecologist, Blueprint for Survival* (Houghton-Mifflin, 1972).

Paul Ehrlich and John Holdren, "Human Population and the Global Environment" *American Scientist,* May–June 1974).

Gil Friend, "Poisoned Cities and Urban Gardens" (*Elements,* January 1976).

John Gofman, "The Technical Approach to Security."

Marshall Goldman, "The Convergence of Environmental Disruption" (*Ecology and Economics,* Prentice-Hall, 1972).

Dennis Hayes, *Energy: The Case for Conservation* (Worldwatch Institute, 1976).

Will Hearst, "The Paper Farmers" (*San Francisco Examiner,* 1976).

Hazel Henderson, "The Decline of Jonesism" (*The*

(Continued on page 318)

Design by David Brower;
Production by Daniel Gridley, San Francisco.

CONTENTS

*In memory of E. F. Schumacher,
Who showed so much of the way.*

Foreword

What kind of country do you want? What kind of world? What kind of neighborhood on a small planet? If you have asked yourself such questions, we think you will like this book. If you haven't, you need it.

The kind of country and world a growing number of people want—and indeed, the kind we all require for sheer survival—will be less populous, more decentralized, less industrial, more agrarian. Our anxiously acquisitive consumer society will give way to a more serenely thrifty conserver society, one which relies most on renewable resources and least on the irreplaceables. Recycling will be taken for granted and planned obsolescence won't. Nuclear proliferation will be viewed in retrospect as a form of temporary insanity. We will stride confidently and lightly along the soft solar energy path so ably scouted out by physicist Amory Lovins. Restless mobility will diminish; people will put down roots and recapture a sense of community. Full employment will be the norm in a sustainable, skill-intensive economy, and indoor pollution where we work, now fifty times higher than outdoors, will no longer be tolerated (and such questions as "Would you rather risk asbestos-caused cancer in five years or be unemployed for five years?" will be judged felonious). Medicine's role in curing disease will shrink as preventive medicine grows and leaves less and less disease to be cured. Corporations will no longer demand the right to dispense cancer to you, or to scrub their pollutants with your lungs. People will turn on TV less and turn on their own senses more, and be better informed of, by, and for the natural world that made them. Parks and wilderness areas will be recognized as legal "persons," as corporations and ships already are, to ensure their permanent and productive survival. Science (and applied science, or technology) will pay more than lip service to elegant solutions; that is, solutions that achieve desired results with the utmost economy of means. (As an archetypically inelegant solution, consider the agitation for space colonization and the fascination of star wars; the truly elegant solution is not to abandon our planet, but, using appropriate technology, to make it increasingly

habitable in ways acceptable to it.) Growthmania will yield to the realization that physical growth is wholesome only during immaturity, and that to continue such growth beyond that point leads to malignancy or other grim devices that keep the planet from being suffocated with a surfeit. The earth will not swarm with life, but be graced with it.

Whatever kind of country and world people decide they want, the next question is, How can they get it? Probably by gaining a new understanding of politics. Politics is democracy's way of handling public business. There is no other. We won't get the kind of country in the kind of world we want unless people take part in the public's business. Unless they embrace politics and people in politics.

Embrace politicians? Yes. Why not? Theirs is, in essence, an honorable calling. When we treat it accordingly, we will deserve politicians who honor their having been called. There is public business to be done. We need to help the men and women who have chosen to undertake it. And from time to time they need our help. The Conserver Society will encourage the Internal Revenue Service to encourage the public to participate in the public's political business.

More than four score and seven years ago Thoreau looked beyond what our fathers had brought forth on this continent and asked a transcendent question: What is the use of a house if you haven't got a tolerable planet to put it on? A growing number of people see that the planet is less and less tolerable because its beauty—and let 'beauty' epitomize all the things that make an environment excellent and the earth a rewarding place to live upon—is being lost more and more rapidly. A slowly growing number of politicians see that there will be no politics at all on a planet that becomes too degraded to support people any longer.

Suppose that one of this growing number of politicians is a presidential candidate and wants to appeal to this growing constituency, to make excellence of environmental quality in fact *the* campaign issue. What kind of platform would such a candidate choose to run on? Or suppose a new political party arose, dedicated, as Friends of the Earth is,

Photo by Suzanne Anderson, from Song of the Earth Spirit
(Friends of the Earth).

to natural law and order. Suppose that party dedicated itself to preserving, restoring, and equitably using the earth and its resources, mineral and living. And suppose it knew that if 'progress' continued to depend upon wiping out irreplaceable resources, such progress could not last long. Imagine, then, a party dedicating itself to timely rethinking and corrective action. What would the platform be like?

Questions like these occurred to us in 1970 and we tried our hand at a voter's guide for environmental protection. It was pretty good. But just about then environmental books became banalized and our co-publisher wandered off into more profitable fields. Early in 1976 we asked ourselves more questions, better ones, and this book is the result. We hoped at first to produce an instant book on the environmental issues of the day, a "platform book," and to challenge candidates in that election to state publicly which of our planks they could stand on and which they feared they would fall between. It is still an appealing idea. We might have helped make the earth's health more of an issue in 1976, and might have nudged some candidates toward realizing that we all needed breatheable air as much as Detroit's lagging engineers needed to build their old air-spoiling cars—perhaps even more so. And that we needed to stop nuclear proliferation, not by lecturing our neighbors, but by cutting it off at the pockets, and cutting it out of any secret desires, right here at home.

Who knows? We might conceivably have encouraged a genuine "environmental candidate" to emerge. Thanks to our sister organization, Les Amis de la Terre, this did happen in France. In the United States, candidates Jerry Brown, Jimmy Carter, and Morris Udall came close enough to keep that contingency feasible. The League of Conservation Voters, founded initially as part of Friends of the Earth and later separated for legal reasons (corporations are not supposed to contribute to political candidates), has been surprisingly successful in giving the environment political weight. So has Environmental Action's Dirty Dozen approach. But no number of preliminary successes will endure if people who know how important the environment is rest on their oars. Or let their powder get wet, or suffer from premature congratulation, or otherwise forget that most of the public must understand why, how, and when before the whole society will let a politician move to spare its environment and save itself. Being human, environmentalists are able to falter, and do.

Our original concept was modified for several reasons. It would be difficult, obviously, to get the book in readers' hands in time to affect the 1976 election campaigns. The cost of publishing was an obstacle. Further, our favorite former co-publisher advised us strongly against tying the book to the 1976 election; the moment the election was over, the book would be yesterday's newspaper. Other possible co-publishers second-guessed our goal and vanished.

The basic idea, although it needed tinkering with, looked as good as ever. As intelligent tinkerers, according to Leopold's Law, we saved all the parts. We would reassemble them as something less ephemeral than a campaign document. An environmental manifesto or credo would obsolesce less. Since the natural laws upon which environmentalism is based can only be perceived, and can never be amended, we thought that a book perceiving those laws well would have lasting value. It could also serve as a yardstick against which to measure the environmental literacy and commitment of a candidate, a party, ourself, and yourself as understanding evolved.

Having determined to proceed, we asked who should write what. We began with what. A few FOE staff members enjoyably weathered brainstorms in a pleasant Pakastani restaurant in San Francisco and selected handfuls of topics. Which brought us to who. Which who? Outside experts, whose knowledge was already proved but whose likelihood of meeting deadlines wasn't, and whose broad philosophy might prove to be temporarily tangential? Or insiders, who share their philosophy with us, are familiar with our deadlines, and who had proved themselves able to dig hard in the fact mines? It is risky to assume that knowledge is acquired more easily than philosophy. We took the risk, and drew upon the talents of FOE officers, members, staff, and advisory counselors. Some of them are recognized authorities in the fields they write about. All care, and all know how to do their homework.

If each author followed his or her own bent, the combined work would lack the coherence a manifesto ought to have. So we recommended a basic chapter outline and suggested that the authors concentrate on what environmentalists believe rather than why. Consequently some parts may read a little the way tablets brought down from a mountain do, but lack divine authentication. We added counterpoint—pertinent material from other sources which, by itself, would make an environmental anthology of lasting value.

The most important challenge to each author was the outlining of feasible, unfrightening, tempting steps toward a sensible goal. It was tough. All environmentalists, it goes without saying, are opposed to evil and in favor of good. If a dam is evil they oppose it. That is a positive action from a river's point of view. But no one should underestimate the difficulty of putting together an appealing series of positive actions. It is easy to trip someone, or to veto, or just to carp and cry. It is hard to get anyone to take a series of steps in a direction you think is right.

It is so hard that the people who put such a series of steps together and stick with them are candidates for hero and should be included in the sequel to John F. Kennedy's book, *Profiles in Courage,* now overdue. The greater the number of needed causes you espouse, the greater the chance of displeasing somebody. Cheap shots are easy. You can positively oppose cancer, heart disease, multiple sclerosis, inflation, unemployment, forest fires, and pneumonoultramicroscopicsilicovolcanokoniosis and never lose a vote. But if you oppose exponential economic growth, however lethal it is, you are not liked by the Conventional Wisdom set. If you take a position for or against abortion or gun control, you divide your constituency and conquer—yourself at the polls.

Conservation organizations, like candidates, have political needs to face. We are aware of the risk to FOE as we try to delineate sound environmental views of the many aspects of society we discuss here. It is perilous to take that risk but more perilous not to. We will pin our faith on your intelligence as a lay citizen who cares. Though you may not share our view in all aspects, we ask you to remember that consensus can be carried too far. It can produce not only a dull world, but also an endangered one. Opinions need to differ. As long as they do, you will know people are alive, awake, not programmed, and still in honest search of truth. And you will remain young in the important sense—still able to listen, ready to change your mind, and willing to avoid being the Practical Man whom Disraeli worried about, who could be counted upon to perpetuate the errors of his ancestors.

Let us propose a grading system. If you agree with, say, seventy-five per cent of what we propose, we'll give you a passing grade, and you can give us one. That's close enough, and qualifies you and us for working together. We probably should.

We freely concede, and think you will, that getting a world to change course will require powerful motivating forces, and we hope to discern them in time. As Dr. Daniel B. Luten (chemist, lecturer on resources, and a FOE director) has said from time to time: Too many people would rather die than change their habits. Almost all of them think the society exists to serve its economy. Too many of them mistake growth for progress. Almost no one understands the extraordinary demands as we now pass from an empty earth to a full one. We have been slow, as we look at the rising population, to ask how dense people can be. We know the planet is lone and finite and that finite things have limits. But we have preferred denying them to facing them. Or we have looked for an escape to some greener colony in space.

People who sense the humor in Dr. Luten's way of put-

ting the vital questions can be cheered. For surely the dawn of new perceptions is breaking. We see that there are better things to do than polarize ourselves. We do not get anywhere by trading epithets, doomsayer versus doommaker, or charging each other with degrees of elitism. We wince at trying to win through intimidation even if the intimidation guidebook sells well. We do not admire the squidlike habit of squirting printer's ink and retreating into the mock security of a different murk. The fatal urge to take care of Number One, whether on one's home lot or one's hemisphere, can be diverted with patience and love, and probably no other way. Before the child in us will give up the lethal toys forged by mindless growth, that child must be offered something else, attractive as well as beneficial.

Our ultimate goal herein is to find an alternative to the most lethal of the Great Powers' toys and to what led the powers to fashion it—to find that alternative before its absence makes all our other hopes academic. Nuclear proliferation is that deadly toy. Nobody wants it. No leading power has lessened the pressure to use it. The Stockholm International Peace Research Institute has predicted that within nine years thirty-five nations will have the capability of making nuclear weapons and nuclear war will be inevitable. Garrett Hardin handles that one: Inevitable? Not if we say no.

No, for example, to the export of nuclear reactors, which the United States is encouraging to help a dying industry, perpetuate a myth, and improve a negative balance of payments. This is tantamount to the export of nuclear weapons capability, as Indira Gandhi quickly proved. (And so, experts and *Time* magazine think, could Israel.) Adding new refinements to the ways nuclear weapons kill (our neutron bomb and Russia's inevitable answer to it), devising multilateral alliances that tip an uneasy balance and increase the desperation of anxious rivals, eases no fateful tensions. Pursuing with a Strangelove gleam a radioactive technology that demonstrates its uncontrollability in ever more disconcerting ways helps no one relax. A new danger develops. The worsening prospect produces a fibrillation of will, a sense of futility or of brave acceptance. People who might have sought a way to safety turn their backs instead. Hope yields to despair. As C. P. Snow admonishes, despair is a sin.

The United States, and we think only the United States, can lead the world back from the nuclear brink to which we led it, with the best of intentions, in the first place. The U.S. can do so, however, only if we step back ourselves and thus persuade other peoples we are to be believed. At this writing we are not stepping back, but rushing forward again, faster than we have been in recent years, protecting our reactor exports, which after all bring us a billion-dollars-plus a crack and let's get the business before someone else does.

Nobody needs that business, and those who think they do ought to try to learn a different trade. The chapters in this book by Amory Lovins identify humanity's nuclear threat and provide the antidote. His theme, first appearing in a letter to *The New York Times* and expanded in the October 1976 *Foreign Affairs,* gaining worldwide attention, has also appeared in *The Unfinished Agenda* (by the Rockefeller Brothers Fund's Environmental Agenda Task Force) and has been augmented in *Soft Energy Paths: Toward a Durable Peace* (Friends of the Earth/Ballinger/Penguin). It is the most important message FOE has yet had a hand in, and we hope it will be understood in governmental, corporate, and public circles. Other chapters in this book can also help people abandon the brink. All of them are intended to help.

People can bring about great changes once they construe the difficult problem to be a challenging opportunity. As an example of such public achievement, consider the National Environmental Policy Act (NEPA). It moved the United States from an old danger to a new safety. One of Mr. Nixon's good deeds was to sign the Act and name Russell Train to oversee it as the first chairman of the Council on Environmental Quality. NEPA became our finest export.

Environmental victories do not, however, stay won by themselves. They require much vigilance and renewed persuasion. The NEPA victory made many enterprising businessmen so uneasy that they set about trying to weaken it without realizing how important it will be to them in the long run if it is kept strong. The first weakening came when Congress, urged on by the oil companies, left NEPA bleeding after the Alaska pipeline controversy, in which Spiro Agnew broke the tie vote in the Senate the wrong way. NEPA requires strengthening if the environment is to remain whole and productive—a requirement as real for corporations as it is for people. It will pay all segments of society well to look searchingly at the social and environmental consequences of a new proposal to alter a piece of the earth. They should also, as NEPA provides, look as hard at the consequences of a fair range of alternatives designed to serve the broad interest instead of the narrow one.

One alternative, rarely considered, can be "Thanks a lot but forget it," coupled with a list of such benefits as would derive from letting things alone—a list that can sometimes be amazingly long. Another alternative is to consider the advantages of exploiting a given resource later on, or more slowly. Alaska's oil, for instance, could be budgeted to last

for the next two or three centuries instead of the next two or three decades. A nation that took from the *Mayflower* until now to get where it is should not rule out, by wiping out, the resources that could get it through another three and a half centuries. Our consideration could well extend to a far-distant future and spare our heirs the need to isolate the nuclear radioactivity generated for our convenience. If Iodine$_{129}$ had been so isolated 300 million years ago at the bottom of the Redwall Limestone formation in the Grand Canyon, it would be safe about now to let it touch living things whose genes should be left intact. It would be fair to do for our genes what our genes have done for us. That way we would not tinker with them. We would revere the miracle in them instead.

Such reverence could let us learn from history, especially from recent, telling history in Alaska. There is a poignant moral in that history, as we in FOE, having been involved in it since we began, can testify. Sadly, we predicted present consequences all too well in our books, *Earth and the Great Weather: The Brooks Range* (1971) and *Cry Crisis! Rehearsal in Alaska* (1974). It is useful to remember the things lost to Alaskans and to all others because, while too many citizens were preoccupied, Congress relaxed its own judgment and ruled out the court's opportunity to check the administrators. This brought a host of evils upon us. Count them:

1) There was a rush to build and use a pipeline that is already seen to be less than safe. Several serious accidents have happened that were curable with difficulty in summer and perhaps may not be curable at all in winter.

2) Those eight hundred miles of pipe can leak badly without detection, endangering wildlife, watersheds, and fisheries.

3) That fragile link crosses fault after fault, as active as any on earth, to reach storm- and earthquake-shaken, tsunami-prone Valdez, a port hazardous in summer and gale-swept in winter.

4) Inadequate tankers, devoid of promised safety in design and vulnerable, like the pipe, to disruptive action, move the oil from Valdez at a rate exceeding what the only legal market can absorb.

5) The brief boom for non-Alaskans, disruptive enough while it lasted, is leading to an economic bust nobody wants.

6) In the suspected Japanese market and presumed American market, people are being dissuaded from treating the oil as precious things ought to be treated; they are being persuaded instead to speed it through tail-pipes and into human lungs that have enough cancer and emphysema already.

7) As for the last great wilderness in the United States:

Alaska's might have belonged to all the generations we can conceive of people who will need wildness in their civilization. It has been split into lesser pieces. Its greatness cannot now be put back together by any number of generations. It was severed wantonly, for profit. Its wildness pours out through the wounds, and the skin shrinks back. Its wholeness and continuity are ended. Your children may not miss what is gone. Like a fully unraveled sweater, what is gone leaves no trace. We cannot measure our own success proudly if it consists of a growing number of things our children will never be allowed to miss.

The unraveling of the earth's heritage of resources can be stopped, we think, by the attitudes and steps our contributors espouse here. People do not have to go on being profligate with resources that are not to be renewed. This is especially true about oil, the unique resource that pervades present-day thinking and that made today's industrial-age euphoria possible. They can stretch it instead, to fuel the transition to other, enduring ways of getting along with the earth. North American oil is but a small part of the recoverable oil left on earth. Although we in the United States are quite capable of using all fossil fuels before our next centennial, we have more admirable capabilities. We could drop out of the lead in the race to see who can make the earth less livable fastest. We would then have a chance of persuading Russia and Japan, or other contenders, from thinking the old race worth the trouble.

Ours was quite a binge. We were not alone in it. The earth's people can still escape the tensions that continuation of the binge will intensify, tensions that threaten the survival of all we or anyone else care about most. We cannot escape by forging on, resolutely and regardless, driven by the unmitigated inertia of outworn habits, until we have forced ourselves over the brink in the "giant step for mankind" no one needs. When you have reached the edge of an abyss, Alwyn Rees said in Wales, the only progressive move you can make is to step backward. A New Zealander whose name escapes me improved upon this retrograde advice with an alternative: turn around, and step forward. Progress, if survival matters, can then become a process that lets people find more joy at less cost to their children and to the earth.

We are grateful to the Science Council of Canada for an overdue insight: on a finite earth a conserver society will outlast and outenjoy a consumer society. We hope that by borrowing this book's title from the Council, we can broaden the acceptance of the Canadian concept. Although we would like to have the Canadians share the ideas we try to synthesize here, we must accept the responsibility for them. Further, it is a good idea to aim at something better than mere survival. As Ivan Illich observes, survival can take place in jail.

So please let our how-to-do-it book be considered a roughish draft of the steps toward, and rewards of, applying conservation conscience to many fields of human activity. There is still an opportunity to treat the earth as if we knew we ought to do this, and we have told ourselves that this book will help discover how.

Take it from there, will you? Tell us about the gaps that you would like to see us try to fill in the next edition. Go even further than that: suggest not only what, but also who, and supplement our supplementary reading. Share your ideas with us as trustingly and hopefully as we share ours with you. And forgive the editors, if you can, for what they did to the unpaid authors, who were given merciless deadlines on the theory that money for production would appear much sooner than it did. If, because of our delay, some of their recommendations have already been realized, credit them for their prescience. You have it in your power to help other recommendations come to pass, and to make this a better book next time.

What kind of country do you want? What kind of world? Filled with a proliferation of the radioactive waste of the old Preempt-the-Resources Game? Or one fulfilling the hope Adlai Stevenson crystallized in Geneva, July 1965, in his last speech:

We travel together, passengers in a little spaceship,
dependent upon its vulnerable reserves of air and soil;
all committed for our safety to its security and peace;
preserved from annihilation only by the care, the work
and, I will say, the love we give our fragile craft.
We cannot maintain it half fortunate, half miserable,
half confident, half despairing, half slave
to the ancient enemies of man, half free
in a liberation of resources undreamed of until this day.
No craft, no crew can travel safely with such vast contradictions.
On their resolution depends the survival of us all.

The resources that can be liberated without being exhausted are human spirit and love. They can bring the resolution.

To preempt or to share?

You can effect the decision. You have the gift. You can pass it on.

David R. Brower, *President*
Friends of the Earth

Berkeley, California, September 4, 1977

That's the first thing to do: start controlling population in affluent white America, where a child born to a white American will use about fifty times the resources of a child born in the black ghetto.

—DAVID BROWER

Population

Projections of current growth rates suggest that Planet Earth's population will double (to eight billion) by the year 2012. But many observers think that unlikely. It would require doubling the amount of food, clothing, shelter, and other necessities in a world already resource-short, polluted, and out of control politically. Humanity is all too likely to have its numbers curtailed by famine, epidemic, war, technological disaster, or an amalgam of them all. But today we still have a choice. Intelligent action can probably still save us. We must seek to limit our numbers by all means available. Indeed, for the noble future that *might* be man's on Earth, we should set a goal of reducing population to a level that the planet's resources can sustain indefinitely at a decent standard of living—perhaps two billion. Americans should take the lead in adopting policies that will bring reduced population. Ultimately, those policies may have to embrace coercion by governments to curb breeding. But coercion can perhaps be avoided by sufficient provision of incentives, education, careers for women other than childbearing, and more widespread availability of the means to limit family size. Incentives should certainly include an improved economic status for all the world's poor and provision for their security in old age. Official persuasion might also include revision of the tax laws, replacing their present pronatalist tendencies with subsidies for childlessness. As a first step, we must certainly banish today's social pressures toward childbearing.

Photo by Paul Almasy, courtesy World Health Organization.

Population

"The population bomb" is a phrase invented nearly a quarter of a century ago by Tom Griessemer and Hugh Moore, who used it to title a pamphlet that described the menace they saw in the growth of human numbers. Medical advances of World War II had helped set population on an unprecedentedly steep climb, and by the pamphlet's publication in 1954, the worldwide increase had already risen to about 1.3 percent a year, or 35 million persons. World population stood at about 2.7 billion.

Two million copies of *The Population Bomb* pamphlet circulated. Its title was recycled when, at David Brower's urging nearly a decade ago, Paul Ehrlich crystalized his own crusade for population restraint into a Sierra Club/Ballantine book. The Ehrlich book sold three million copies in the US and has appeared in five other lands under Friends of the Earth's imprint.

Despite those efforts and many, many more—literary, scientific, and organizational, by legions of dedicated workers—the population bomb is not defused. The globe's population has mushroomed to more than four billion and is exploding at approximately 2 percent, or more than 80 million persons, per year. Even if the growth rate does not continue increasing, we would still, at current rates, have more than eight billion inhabitants on the planet less than 36 years from now, by the year 2012.

Tens, perhaps hundreds, of millions are jobless, inadequately housed, malnourished if not starving. The projected growth of human numbers means that those statistics of agony may be multiplied many times before this century is out. For how can we possibly provide, in slightly more than one generation, as many new dwellings, hospitals, schools, churches, workplaces, and arable acres as today comprise the legacy of all the generations past? Not to mention the problems of energy, resources, and pollution that eight billion human beings would raise. Nor the matter of providing maintenance for all their buildings and machines, those existing today and others yet to be built.

Many observers say such a doubling in the next 36 years is beyond the capability of mankind—that the strain on politics, management, resources, energy, medical facilities, and food distribution (if not food production) makes it certain that growth will soon be curtailed by famine, pestilence, nuclear disaster, social chaos, war, or a combination of them. Population growth will certainly be checked within a generation or so, they say, but checked by resurgence of the death rate rather than by reduction of the birth rate. In the meantime, The Population Institute, which believes population *can* be checked by intelligent action, puts it succinctly: "Whatever your cause, it's a lost cause unless we check the population explosion."

The population problem is really several problems. Perhaps the one that deserves first attention is the problem of rate of growth. Exponential growth has continued so long, and we are already on such a steep part of the growth curve, that human reaction-time may be too slow for us to save ourselves. Can we possibly change humanity's culture patterns of procreation fast enough to reduce growth appreciably before intolerable strain sets in? Perhaps not, but we *must* try.

Next, there is the problem of absolute numbers. Are there already too many passengers aboard Planet Earth? Has the "carrying capacity" of the globe already been surpassed? It seems clear that for the long term, it has. But what is that carrying capacity?

Subordinate to those fundamental problems are others. The problem, for instance, of individual freedom: What constraints are permissible to cope with population pressure? The problem of human distribution: Should migration be restricted or redirected? If so, by whom and how? The problem of feeding hungry nations: Should it be conditional on each nation's population policy? Should we practice the "ethics of the lifeboat," whereby, to conserve supplies for those most likely to survive if helped, we deliberately withhold food aid from today's direst sufferers from famine because their rescue would breed even more hungry mouths (and suffering) in the future?

Each of the population problems raises practical questions, ethical questions, religious questions, and ultimately, political questions.

The Goal:
Balance After Drastic Reduction

What should the United States do?

We must first of all recognize the urgency of the need for worldwide population action, beginning at home. The US per capita use of the world's resources is far greater than that of any other nation and many times—perhaps 50 times—that of most Third World countries. Today, the US has no explicit population policy.

We must resolve to bring the globe's passenger load into

Photo by Dominique Roger, courtesy UNESCO.

lasting balance with its resources, and we in the US must show ourselves willing to go as far as any nation to bring that about.

Few quarrel with the abstract idea of achieving balance between resources and population. Most recognize its inevitability, though some dream of colonies in space to absorb Earth's masses. When one tries to express the goal of balance in terms of numbers, arguments arise. What *is* the globe's ultimate carrying capacity? Some scientists contend that food and all other necessities can be found or synthesized to support a far larger population. Others deny that and point to "the law of the minimum," which will quench growth when the first resource indispensable to growth runs out. The world supply of phosphate fertilizer has been suggested as the vital resource likely to be exhausted first, and that soon. But there are many other weak links, as the Club of Rome's *Limits to Growth* study dramatized.

Although the American Association for the Advancement of Science and the Population Council set a number of formidable thinkers to ponder the question of optimum population, they reached no agreement. Zero Population Growth, Inc., which first set a flat no-growth population curve as its goal, now advocates an unspecified population reduction. Negative Population Growth, Inc., another membership group, has set its goal as one-half the 1970 population of the planet, or less than two billion people, with all nations sharing proportionately in the reduction. NPG contends that a population of that size would be indefinitely sustainable, would be large enough to maintain all the comforts of industrial civilization yet too small to generate its woes.

Our own conviction is that, for both safety and a decent quality of life, the world's population must be vastly reduced. How far depends not only on physical carrying capacity or the law of the minimum, but also on one's social, ethical, and spiritual values. Is a world crowded to its ultimate carrying capacity the kind we want to live in or leave to our posterity? Would such a world provide sufficient privacy? Sufficient individual freedom? How much does one value wilderness?

Assuming the need for drastic reduction, how do we get there from here? At least since Malthus, there has been substantial intellectual advocacy of curbs on growth. For more than 50 years, "family planning" has been promoted. For almost as long, effective contraceptive materials have been available, at least to those who could pay for them.

Until recently nature was able to cope with the pollution generated by the human species. Only in the last generation or so, when both world population and industrial output have soared, has widespread, persistent contamination of the biosphere become a serious problem. As long as human numbers continue to grow, generating new demand for food, other goods, and services, many pollution problems will worsen, despite the most stringent efforts to bring them under control.

As recently as 1950, both North America and Latin America had essentially the same population size, 163 and 168 million respectively. But the difference since then explains why North America emerged as the world's breadbasket while Latin America became a net food importer. While North America's population growth has slowed substantially since the late fifties, that of many Latin American countries has expanded at an explosive 3 percent or more yearly. If North America's 1950 population had expanded at 3 percent per year, it would now be 341 million rather than the actual 236 million. Those additional 105 million people would absorb virtually all the current exportable surpluses, and North America would be struggling to maintain self-sufficiency.

Overgrazing is not new, but its scale and rate of acceleration are. Damage that formerly took place over centuries is now being compressed into years by the fateful arithmetic of population growth. Populations are, in effect, outgrowing the biological systems that sustain them.

Nine-tenths of the people in many of the poorest countries today depend on firewood as their chief source of fuel. And all too often, the growth in human population is outstripping the growth of new trees—not surprising, considering that the average villager needs nearly a ton of firewood a year.

In Colombia, where the birth rate is 40 per thousand and the infant mortality rate is high, one effort to improve health care was to construct in Bogota one of the finest centers anywhere for the care of premature babies. In this facility, the number of infant deaths has been reduced to a European level. Unfortunately, because of the large number of babies born every year, this excellent care cannot be continued after the children leave the hospital. Consequently, almost three-fourths of the infants who receive special treatment die within three months of returning to their parents' homes.

In China, expensive services and sophisticated, exclusive

From the end of World War II, when growth rates began to skyrocket, population limitation has been widely urged. Although there is some evidence that the urging has had some effect in the US, where it has been coupled with easy access to contraceptives and recently to abortion, the growth of numbers worldwide and the overall increase in growth *rate* suggest that mere unofficial advocacy and purely voluntary compliance are far from enough— certainly not enough to stimulate actual reduction in population in the time we have left before population induced catastrophe. What's more, voluntarism guarantees big families for the ignorant, the stupid, and the conscience-less, while it gradually reduces the proportion of people who, in conscience, limit the size of their families.

As discussion at 1974's World Population Conference in Bucharest made clear, many Third World officials believe that "if we take care of the people, population will take care of itself." That is, they believe socio-economic improvement in the have-not nations will automatically bring about a "demographic transition" from high to low birth rates. US, West European, and Japanese experience does suggest some long-range correlation between industrialization and birth-rate reduction. But it is not clear that the transition can occur with anything like the necessary speed.

Moreover, worldwide industrialization on the Western model would soon exhaust the planet's clean air, fresh water, and nonrenewable resources.

So conscious policies of birth control, together with policies to enhance the well-being of the poor, must be pursued simultaneously. In lands where high infant mortality encourages parents to continue childbearing, medical care must be improved. Where children are their parents' only security in old age, social security systems must be instituted. Where sex furnishes the most available entertainment, both substitute pastimes and contraceptives must be provided.

Coercion by many governments will undoubtedly be required at some time in the future, probably sooner than most of us like to think. India instituted a nominal policy of government support for voluntary family planning in 1952, but the growth rate there is now twice what it was then. Today, India is experimenting with incentives and penalties that are indeed coercive. And China has achieved considerable success in curbing births by decreeing late marriages and by stimulating strong social pressures against large families.

Perhaps someday childbearing will be deemed a punishable crime against society unless the parents hold a gov-

facilities are now given low priority. Health care focuses on public sanitation, health education, family planning, and small clinics directed by para-professionals—the so-called barefoot doctors—who provide inexpensive health services that are easily accessible to everyone. This approach, dictated by the inadequacy of traditional health care, has helped lower the death and infant mortality rates. The encouragement of family planning, as a part of overall health service, has led to a dramatic reduction in the birth rate, easing future pressure on health services.

Some 70 million would-be consumers of health care are added to the world's population every year. The immediate economic prospects of poor countries and the long lead times involved in implementing traditional health care strategies suggest that attempts to supply fast growing populations with medical care will fall farther and farther behind demand. A paraprofessional approach to health service should help meet some of the new demand, but few countries can be expected to match China's large scale effort. Unless population growth is slowed, even a paraprofessional approach to health service will be a losing battle.

As the dimensions of the population problem become more apparent, some national political leaders are beginning to respond. Perhaps the most encouraging development over the past year has been the sharp increase in requests from the developing countries for assistance in family planning. The principal aid agencies in this field—the United Nations Fund for Population Activities, the International Planned Parenthood Federation, and the U.S. Agency for International Development—are being overwhelmed with requests for assistance. As of 1976, the principal constraint on efforts to make family planning services available to all who want them is not so much apathy in the developing countries as a lack of financial and technical assistance from the rich countries.

National and international leaders can no longer dodge the peril inherent in continuing rapid population growth or shrug it off with irresponsible optimism. The problem concerns us, but it will concern our children and grandchildren even more. How we respond to the population threat may do more to shape the world in which they will live than anything else we do.

—LESTER BROWN, PATRICIA MCGRATH,
AND BRUCE STOKES

ernment license. Or perhaps all potential parents will be required to use contraceptive chemicals, the governments issuing antidotes to citizens chosen for childbearing.

Steps For Today

To protect ourselves in the US against such far-reaching infringements on liberty, it behooves us to undertake at once such lesser steps as may most surely promote the population decline we need. Certainly, for instance, we must support the Equal Rights Amendment, for it will encourage women to have careers. That need not preclude motherhood, but will perhaps be conducive to smaller families. Further, we should advocate a later marriage age and a longer educational period. We should support all efforts to maintain women's freedom of choice in abortion and make it universally available when contraception fails. We should also support the widest possible availability of voluntary sterilization. Research for better and longer-lasting contraceptives should be encouraged, perhaps supported more heavily by tax money since safety standards have made such research unprofitable for private enterprise. The contraceptives we have now should be made easier to use and more easily available to all sexually active

Photo by Jean Mohr, courtesy UNESCO.

persons of whatever age. Courses in sex education, sexual responsibility, and the global population problem should be taught throughout the educational system so that no child could reach maturity without a clear understanding of the social imperative, of techniques of contraception, and of his or her own obligations.

In addition to urging a clear and explicit statement by the US government that it seeks to reduce the nation's population size, we should promote federal actions to bring that about. Government institutions such as those suggested by the Commission on Population Growth and the American Future—the "Rockefeller Commission," whose report, which went no further than to advocate zero growth in the future, was torpedoed by Richard Nixon—should be created and charged with implementing the reduction policy. Financial support of birth control clinics and contraceptive distribution should be increased. Tax levies that are now pronatalist should be revised to help discourage childbearing if this can be done without injury to the children involved. Indeed, subsidies might be paid to the childless, and adoption should be encouraged. Pronatalist economic practices such as reduced transit fares for children should be discouraged, perhaps by legislation. And if, by legislation, we can require tobacco ads to warn that cigarettes may be unhealthy for the individual, we should be able to legislate that pronatalist advertising is unhealthy for society and should carry a warning.

International migration should be controlled in the interest of reducing the "brain drain" that often hampers education and wise planning in Third World countries, with consequent damage to their population control programs. International aid should be most generous to nations that conduct effective population-control programs. Aid should also be allocated in such a way as to encourage accurate population statistics. The US contribution to the United Nations Fund for Population Activities should be increased, not cut back. And any steps that can be taken to replace the UN with a democratic federal world government, under which the population problem would become much more tractable, deserve support.

Margaret Mead and others have observed that the population explosion demands a worldwide cultural revolution, a new ethic regarding human numbers. In furtherance of the new ethic, we should demand leadership toward a reduced world population by all who run for office. Not only should they promise concrete action after election; they must also help set new social norms and reverse pronatalist peer pressures. They should, for instance, speak out on the advantages of careers for women, later marriage, longer schooling, singleness, and nonparenthood; on the acceptability of abortion to backstop contraception; on the nor-

mality of one-child families; on the right to homosexual practice by consenting adults.

What Will It Cost?

The idea of a shrinking population will raise apprehensions. In a world where the number of men in a nation's army or navy was, till recently, a gauge of power, population reduction may seem an abdication of position; in an economy that has always been able to count more customers year by year, population reduction may appear threatening.

Nuclear arms have long since made sheer numbers almost irrelevant, however, and in any case, the US cannot hope to outdistance China, the USSR, or India in population. As for the economy, population changes will necessarily come so slowly that adjustment to new market conditions need pose no problem. Every industry is already well accustomed to adjusting to fad, fashion, technology, and acts of God much more rapidly than US population is likely to shift from growth to decline. (Gerber's Baby Food, for example, anticipating a continued falling off in the US birth rate, has diversified into insurance for the elderly. Disposable diapers are finding a new market in proliferating old-age homes.) Moreover, growth will almost certainly continue for years even if all the suggestions made in earlier paragraphs were to be adopted tomorrow. Too many young people already stand on the verge of parenthood for instant reversal to be probable.

For centuries to come, population decrease will benefit both the living and coming generations: each individual can share a larger slice of the pie. The labors of those who have gone before us have built a stockpile of resources and of capital goods that can continue to make life easier and more humane if we have the wit and will not to squander it in war. More and more, we can divide and distribute the stock so that none need want materially. More and more, we can divert our economic growth to music and the other arts, sports, science, education, service industries, and the production of fewer but higher-quality material goods.

The result of reducing our population—and the globe's—to some fraction of what it is today can only be a healthier, happier world. It is time we made a determined start toward that goal.

If, by some mischance, we have judged wrong and it is decided in some future generation that renewed growth is desirable, Paul Ehrlich points out that the job of repopulation is one that can be undertaken by unskilled workers who would enjoy their task. Repopulation is altogether too easy. Our task is more difficult, but not impossible unless we choose to make it so.

Cartoon by Don Wright, The Miami News, *winner of the Editorial Category Award in the 1975 Population Cartoon Contest.*

If you travel at all, you need only one eye half open to see that population is the *only* real major issue in the world today. I come back to the States and hear some black people tell me that birth control is some kind of white conspiracy. The Catholic Church says it is a sin, and some blacks say it is cultural genocide. Here are millions of people, *millions*—black mostly, but that is incidental—starving to death in sub-Sahara Africa, and Black Americans and Catholics are telling me they have a *right* to make more babies.

Dick Gregory, whom I greatly admire, is perhaps the best-known black who supports the genocide theory. As I understand it, he believes that we must keep on producing at a higher birthrate to help ourselves politically. But surely, there must be easier ways of stuffing the ballot box. What does it profit blacks if we gain a bigger share of the agony? Is it really an accomplishment if we are the ones who are presiding at the end of the world?

—ARTHUR ASHE

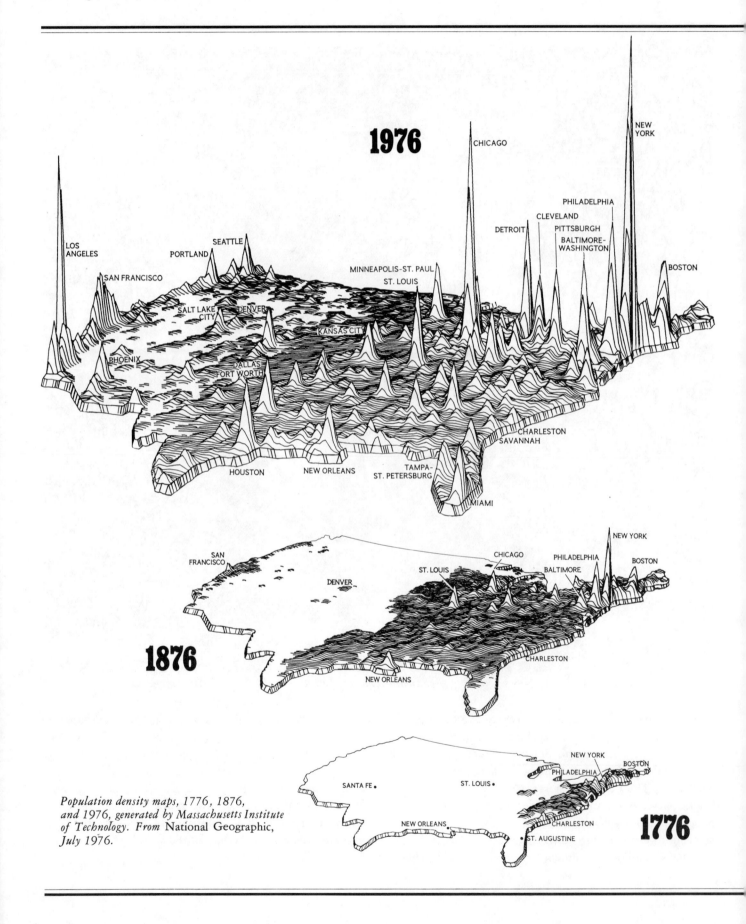

*Population density maps, 1776, 1876,
and 1976, generated by Massachusetts Institute
of Technology. From* National Geographic,
July 1976.

*We use tax incentives to encourage oil exploration; we use them to encourage
the installation of pollution abatement devices; we use them to foster pension
plans. Is there any reason why we should not use them to tackle our most
critical domestic problem—the population crisis?* —SENATOR ROBERT PACKWOOD

The nature of exponential growth is such that limits can be approached with surprising suddenness. The likelihood of overshooting a limit is made even larger by the momentum of human population growth, by the time delays between cause and effect in many environmental systems, and by the fact that some kinds of damage are irreversible by the time they are visible.

The great momentum of human population growth has its origins in deep-seated attitudes toward reproduction and in the age composition of the world's population—37% is under 15 years of age. This means there are far more young people who will soon be reproducing—adding to the population—than there are old people who will soon be dying—subtracting from it. Thus, even if the momentum in attitudes could miraculously be overcome overnight, so that every pair of parents in the world henceforth had only the number of children needed to replace themselves, the imbalance between young and old would cause population to grow for 50 to 70 years more before leveling off. The growth *rate* would be falling during this period, but population would still climb 30% or more during the transition to stability. Under extraordinarily optimistic assumptions about when replacement fertility might *really* become the worldwide norm, one concludes that world population will not stabilize below 8 billion people.

The momentum of population growth manifests itself as a delay between the time when the need to stabilize population is perceived and the time when stabilization is actually accomplished. Forces that are perhaps even more firmly entrenched than those affecting population lend momentum to growth in per capita consumption of materials. These forces create time lags similar to that of population growth in the inevitable transition to stabilized levels of consumption and technological reform. Time delays between the initiation of environmental insults and the appearance of the symptoms compound the predicament because they postpone recognition of the need for any corrective action at all.

The momentum of growth, the time delays between causes and effects, and the irreversibility of many kinds of damage all increase the chances that mankind may temporarily exceed the carrying capacity of the biological environment. Scientific knowledge is not yet adequate to the task of defining that carrying capacity unambiguously, nor can anyone say with assurance how the consequences of overshooting the carrying capacity will manifest themselves. Agricultural failures on a large scale, dramatic loss of fisheries productivity, and epidemic disease initiated by altered environmental conditions are among the possibilities. The evidence presented here concerning the present scale of man's ecological disruption and its rate of increase suggests that such possibilities exist within a time frame measured in decades, rather than centuries.

All of this is not to suggest that the situation is hopeless. The point is rather that the potential for grave damage is real and that prompt and vigorous action to avert or minimize the damage is necessary. Such action should include measures to slow the growth of the global population to zero as rapidly as possible. Success in this endeavor is a necessary but not a sufficient condition for achieving a prosperous yet environmentally sustainable civilization. It will also be necessary to develop and implement programs to alleviate political tensions, render nuclear war impossible, divert flows of resources and energy from wasteful uses in rich countries to necessity-oriented uses in poor ones, reduce the environmental impact and increase the human benefits resulting from each pound of material and gallon of fuel, devise new energy sources, and, ultimately, stabilize civilization's annual throughput of materials and energy.

There are, in short, no easy single-faceted solutions, and no component of the problem can be safely ignored. There is a temptation to "go slow" on population limitation because this component is politically sensitive and operationally difficult, but the temptation must be resisted. The other approaches pose problems, too, and the accomplishments of these approaches will be gradual at best. Ecological disaster will be difficult enough to avoid even if population limitation succeeds; if population growth proceeds unabated the gains of improved technology and stabilized per-capita consumption will be erased, and averting disaster will be impossible.

—PAUL EHRLICH AND JOHN HOLDREN

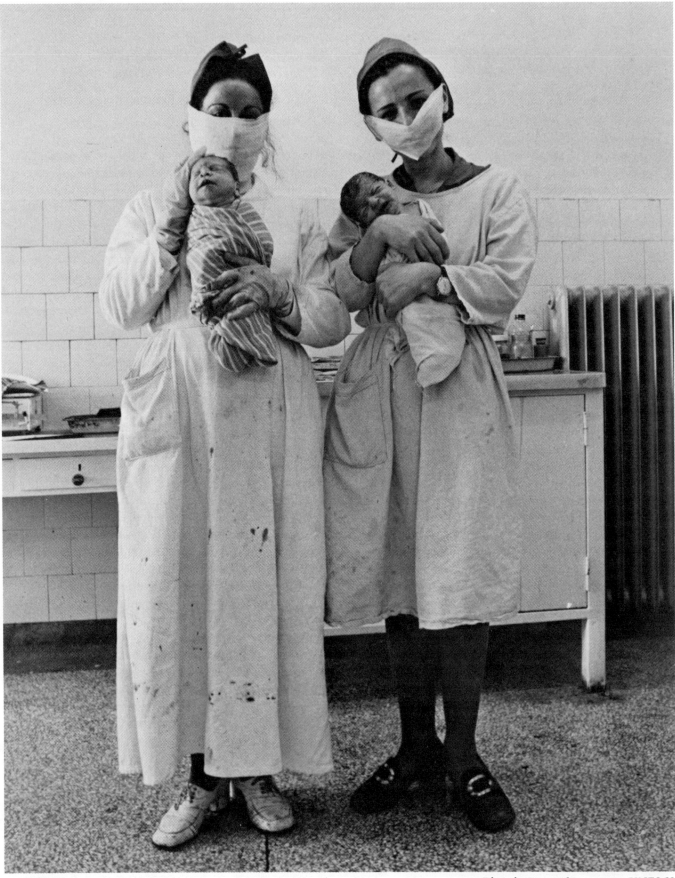

Photo by Joan Liftin, courtesy UNESCO.

Recommended Actions

- ☐ The President should proclaim, and by a joint resolution of both houses, Congress should reaffirm, that population reduction is an essential long-term goal of the United States.

- ☐ In the United Nations and other international forums, and through bilateral diplomacy, the US should seek the earliest and widest possible consensus that population reduction is a crucial goal for the whole human community.

- ☐ The President should appoint a top-level commission to investigate what the carrying capacity of the US may be presumed to be under various reasonable assumptions, and suggest a range of populations within which the optimum population may be presumed to lie.

- ☐ The State Department should encourage other nations to make similar investigations of maximum and optimum population, and the UN should be urged to carry out such investigations for the world as a whole.

- ☐ Congress and the state legislatures should repeal provisions of tax codes that discriminate in favor of parenthood; consideration should be given to a gradual reversal of the bias to discriminate in favor of childlessness and small families.

- ☐ All officials and candidates for office should support the Equal Rights Amendment because, among other reasons, it would help open up to women careers other than motherhood.

- ☐ The Department of Health, Education, and Welfare should promote teaching of population problems and sex education at all educational levels.

- ☐ Appropriate agencies at various levels of government should increase support of contraceptive research, birth control clinics, and the wide distribution of inexpensive contraceptives.

- ☐ Abortions should be freely available, as a right, to women who want them, regardless of age and consent of spouse or parent.

- ☐ Voluntary sterilization of both sexes should be officially encouraged.

- ☐ Opinion-makers in all walks of life should encourage longer schooling, later marriage, and adoption as an alternative to physiological parenthood; we should all help establish new social norms in which singleness is not regarded as inferior to marriage and childlessness is respected no less than parenthood.

- ☐ The US should increase its support of the United Nations Fund for Population Activities.

- ☐ The US should reduce its own infant mortality rates and assist other countries to lower theirs, since, where mortality is high, parents have many children to assure that one or two will reach adulthood.

- ☐ Because the poor tend to look upon children as the only form of security available to them in old age, programs to alleviate poverty and universalize social security should be instituted in the US and encouraged abroad.

As the human population has increased in numbers and become more concentrated, its potential for disrupting the earth's ecosystem has grown. Each additional person, especially in affluent societies, increases the burden on what is, in many areas, an already overburdened environment.

Unlike plagues of the dark ages or contemporary diseases we do not yet understand, the modern plague of overpopulation is soluble by means we have discovered and with resources we possess. What is lacking is not sufficient knowledge of the solution but universal consciousness of the gravity of the problem and education of the billions who are its victims.

—MARTIN LUTHER KING

Each year the US wastes more fuel than most of mankind uses.

—DENIS HAYES

Energy

Official US reaction to the Arab oil embargo is mad. To avoid dependence on foreign sources, we hasten the day when *all* petroleum will be foreign by draining our own dwindling reserves at an accelerated rate. We rely heavily on nuclear power despite its manifest dangers and disadvantages—and despite the fact that we are already beginning to depend on foreign sources of uranium. We rely increasingly on electricity although electricity is an expensive, and for most purposes, an inefficient form of energy. And we, the world's most wastefully lavish users of energy, take seriously dire predictions that the bottom will drop out of our civilization unless we use more and more. A sane energy policy must be based on conservation and end-use efficiency. Countries whose standard of living is fully as high as ours use barely half as much energy per capita—and we used that little ourselves as recently as 1965. Conservation is our best and cheapest short-term "source" of energy. For the long term, we must, and easily can, rely for all energy needs on solar power and solar variants such as wind. During a transition period, our needs can be met by sophisticated fossil-fuel technology applied on a small or intermediate scale. True energy independence, for the individual, consists of being able to tap inexhaustible energy sources locally that no one can monopolize or interrupt. That objective is within reach, but we won't reach it by continuing to rush panic-stricken in the opposite direction.

Photo by Daniel Gridley

Energy

Most Americans eagerly await sound leadership in charting a new course for energy policy—one that uses energy more efficiently, that gets it increasingly from renewable sources, and that obtains energy locally in the quality and at the scale we need.

Such a shift of energy policy does not happen in isolation. It is part of, and reinforced by, many other currents of social change, ranging from a revival of traditional values—thrift, neighborliness, craftsmanship, simplicity—to a reappraisal of the balance between central power (whether governmental or corporate) and local or individual autonomy. In these perceptions, ordinary people are far ahead of the federal government. And as these diverse strivings for change converge, we see more clearly that moving toward a softer energy technology, oriented toward human needs rather than needs of The Economy, will be far more attractive than continuing the ominous and faltering transition to complete dependence on huge and centralized high technologies.

The flaws in present federal energy policy are becoming more obvious every day. We are told that our need for energy will double by about the turn of the century; but at least half the proposed total growth of supply would never reach us. It would be lost earlier in an increasingly inefficient chain of interfuel conversions. We are told, correctly, that we will soon be running out of oil and gas: but the proposed solutions would give us more electrical supply options than we need and still leave us short of oil and gas. We are told that in the year 2000, even with over a thousand huge nuclear reactors, we shall be burning oil and gas one to two times as fast as now, and coal two to three times as fast as now. We are told that we cannot afford oil at $12 a barrel; yet we plunge ahead with plans to produce synthetic gas at the equivalent of $24 a barrel and nuclear electricity at the equivalent of $65–90 a barrel. (New Yorkers are paying the equivalent of $120 a barrel for their electricity right now.) We are told that fossil fuels are too precious to be burned—as we hasten to burn ever vaster mountains of coal under boilers to produce electricity, poach fish, and scrub once-clean air with people's lungs. We are told we shall need 15 times as much electricity in the year 2020 as we do now; yet we already have nearly twice as much electricity as we need for all the end-uses that can take advantage of the high energy quality that is the only justification for making it.

We are told that to make us less dependent on OPEC we must hasten to deplete our domestic resources at practically any cost—a last-fling policy that David Brower calls Strength Through Exhaustion. We are told that the massive disruption of people, land, air, and water that must follow strip-mining of western coal and oil shale is a small price for remote city dwellers to pay for cheap energy. We are told that if oil spills choke off our rich harvests from the sea, or smother our beaches, or (in the Arctic) even plunge the world into starvation by melting the fragile sea ice that governs our weather patterns, it will all have been for our own good. We are told that the waste heat from the power stations we must have in 25 years would suffice to heat the whole freshwater runoff of the lower 48 states by about 30–50°F, and that the fuels used to make that waste heat will be well spent to make America strong and prosperous. We are told that if, as seems fairly likely, emissions from burning fossil fuels cause global climatic changes within the lifetimes of today's children, or if the interaction of human fallibility and malice with nuclear materials destroys our lives or liberties, or if our zealous nuclear salesmanship around the world gives other countries or terrorist groups the means to blow us up, then at least we shall have had lots of energy meanwhile. We are told that we need more electricity with which to help the poor—told by the same utilities that have consistently charged the poor several times as much as big industrial users for the same unit of electricity. We are told that we need more energy with which to feed the starving billions of the Third World—told by the same enterprises whose past activities have so conspicuously failed to address the real causes of poverty at home and abroad. We are told that energy and GNP must forever march in lockstep, even though the energy required to produce a dollar's worth of a good or service varies over a range of tens or hundreds of times depending on what we're buying. We are told that with half as much electricity as now we'd be living in caves—but we used as little as that as recently as 1965. (Most Western Europeans live at least as enjoyable lives as we do on half or one-third as much energy.) We are told that in these cataclysmic, but necessary, changes on the way to Energy Independence, we'll be fully consulted—so long as we don't actually get in the way.

Can We Afford the Future?

The American people have been told many curious things lately by Presidents, on television, in big four-color

ads. In 1977, most people recognize a self-serving fairy tale when they hear one.

Among the most implausible claims made for the rapid growth of big energy technologies is that we can afford them. The capacity to deliver a unit of energy per day to your doorstep requires about ten times as much capital investment with coal-based synthetic fuels, or with many systems to deliver oil and gas from the Arctic or offshore, as with the traditional direct-fuel technologies on which our economy was built. Electrical, especially nuclear, technologies are about *another* tenfold more capital-intensive—so much so that no industrial country can afford to build them on a really big scale. They are (in Monte Canfield's phrase) future technologies whose time has passed.

Specifically, President Ford's ten-year energy program would cost about a trillion of today's dollars, three-quarters of it for electrification. The energy sector in the decade 1976–85 would thus need on average not a quarter, as now, but nearer three-quarters of *all* our net private domestic investment. Two-thirds of all the money we have to spend on social programs, houses, health, education, transport, factories, national parks, and everything else outside the energy sector would go to that sector alone. We couldn't even pay for the things that were supposed to *use* all that energy. And with continuing growth, this unsustainable burden would tend to increase, siphoning off for

the care and feeding of the new money-eating energy technologies most of the money we thought we had earned to spend on other priorities. Already the capital intensity of electrical technologies is bankrupting the utilities and pricing electricity out of the market. The market is trying to tell us something. (The Invisible Fist strikes again!)

Such drains on our scarce resources have important political implications. To divert resources away from other tasks and their weaker constituencies, we would need a strong central authority that could bypass traditional market mechanisms and virtually exercise war-powers allocation (as Senator Jackson has seriously proposed). We would have to concentrate great political and economic power in the hands of a few centralized managers (presumably not elected), and the gigantic investment would require end-use of energy to be nearly optimized—require uses to conform to the needs of the energy source rather than the reverse. As energy-hungry settlement patterns grew more urbanized, political power would shift to the cities and slurbs, which can keep their own turf habitable only by exporting the social costs of centralized energy technologies to the politically weaker minority in the countryside (Appalachia, the Brooks Range, Navajo country, Wyoming). Control over who will have how much energy at which price would become centralized in an elite, politically remote from the people it served and decreasingly accountable to them. Central authorities would have to

> *To maintain independence in petroleum supplies we would need to make a
> Prudhoe Bay strike, or its equivalent in lesser fields, every two years. And at
> current growth rates this interval would be reduced to every year by 1990,
> and about every six months by 2000.*
>
> —LEWIS CONTA

impose big energy facilities and their perceived risks on people who want neither—especially since the utilities who operate the facilities are unwilling to bear the risks themselves. Interregional conflicts would intensify. A divisive form of centrifugal politics—Washington vs. the states, the states vs. towns, towns vs. people—would come to dominate national energy decisions.

The high technologies themselves can be run only by a privileged elite—not an obvious way to stay in tune with the needs of the poor—and cannot be transferred to developing countries without technological dependence, commercial monopoly, and the importation of alien cultural values. The scale and complexity of the big energy technologies, especially the electrical ones, also makes them uniquely vulnerable to accident or malice. A few people become able to turn off a country. Strong social controls must then discourage disruption and perhaps even dissent. With the special dangers of nuclear technologies, pluralism and traditional freedoms must give way to autarchy and repression, all in the name of security and efficiency.

More Affluence With Less Energy

By working backwards from where we might want to be in the long run, we can discover a better path with far lower economic, social, and environmental costs. Its basis is efficient energy use, wringing more social benefit from each unit of primary energy. The improvement we seek here isn't just 10 to 15 percent for good housekeeping; it goes deeper into the structure of the systems we use to turn raw energy to human purposes. Detailed technical analyses have shown that we can *double* our efficiency over the next few decades, saving money and increasing broadly-based employment as a direct result. This would require "technical fixes" that are now economic, use today's (or often 1950's) technologies, and have no significant effect on lifestyles. Doubled efficiency through technical fixes means, for example, driving as much as now but in an efficient car, which can be as big and solid as a modern Mercedes. (People are, in fact, choosing smaller cars,

car-pooling more, riding buses and trains and bicycles, but that sort of change, going beyond a "technical fix," would, of course, *increase* the computed energy and money savings.) With today's level of energy use but doubled efficiency, we could be twice as affluent as now, or with half as much energy, we could (like the British and the Swedes) be as affluent as now. Other combinations are possible; energy is only a means to an end that no two people will choose alike. But conservation, in this sense of doing better with what we have, is so much cheaper, quicker, easier, safer, and more lasting than increasing energy supply that we cannot afford *not* to do it. As Malcolm MacEwen points out, if we can't fill the bathtub because the water keeps running out, we don't need a bigger water heater, we need a plug.

In the long run—say 50 years—we could probably double our efficiency yet again, still saving money and securing jobs in the process, by devoting more attention to the structural evolution of our society: the settlement patterns that make us work to buy a car without which we can't get to work, for example, giving us involuntary traffic when what we wanted was voluntary mobility. But for the next decade or two, we need not all reach a consensus on such long-term changes of values or structures to achieve lifestyles of elegant frugality—not because they are not an important option, but because the "technical fixes" in efficiency without changing lifestyles will keep us busy. We shall be insulating buildings, installing combined cycles and recuperators and heat pumps, making our cars and factories as efficient as those in West Germany (where people are as rich as we are, are more fully employed, and use about three-fifths as much energy). And to make these changes does not require coercive laws, but only adequate information, clearing away needless barriers (such as obsolete building codes and antique mortgage regulations), and applying sound economic principles. Exhortation without these basic measures is only frustrating to people who want to save energy, and its failure is often cited as evidence that people won't conserve: "It won't work, and we know because we haven't tried it."

Once we resolve to use our energy wisely, we can get a

big fraction—approaching half by the turn of the century, essentially 100 percent in about 50 years from now—from renewable, natural energy flows. By using a great variety of soft energy technologies—solar, wind, organic conversion, perhaps geothermal—we can take advantage of their diversity, letting each do what it does best and combining them where they are complementary (as sun and wind often are). Their diversity can match our own pluralism, meeting our basic needs no matter where we live. They draw on the design experience in our own evolution: indeed, the biggest single energy input to the US economy today is not oil, but the sunlight that grows our crops.

Soft energy technologies have two important but often neglected features. First, they match our end-use needs in *scale*, and do not try to recentralize and redistribute energy flows whose original distribution is free. The energy we need is mainly on a house or neighborhood scale; huge blocks of industrial energy (to run those few industrial processes that cannot be scaled down to economic advantage) are only a small part of our total energy budget. We should seek our economies of scale not in huge central units to supply and use energy, but rather in mass-producing small units and in virtually eliminating the overheads caused by distribution costs and losses between centralized sources and consumers. Such distribution overheads account for half your electricity bill. Proper scale can reduce them to essentially zero.

Equally important, soft energy sources must match end-use needs in energy *quality*, supplying energy only in

the quality needed for the task at hand. About 58 percent of our end-use needs are for heat, mainly at low temperatures. Making temperature differences of tens of degrees by burning fuels at thousands of degrees, or rebuilding atoms at millions, wastes both money and fuels when solar collectors (or wind-driven heat pumps) can give us low-temperature heat directly.

Likewise, about 38 percent of our end-use needs are for work—making things move—and the bulk of this (31 percent) that goes to vehicles can, at modern European efficiencies, be met by fuel alcohols economically derived from our current organic wastes with technologies that are already demonstrated. (The industry required would be about seven times the size of a current US microbiological industry—the one that makes our beer and wine—but would replace in function half our refinery capacity.)

About 4 percent of our end-use energy operates industrial electric motors. The other 3 percent of the 38 percent of our energy that does work pumps materials through pipelines. A further 4 percent of our total energy budget includes all other end-use needs *requiring* electricity—lights, electronics, telecommunications, smelting, electrochemistry, welding, electric motors in appliances, electric railways, etc. With efficient use we could meet *all* these electrical needs with industrial cogeneration (generating electricity as a by-product of industrial process steam) and with our present hydroelectric capacity—and so run this country, to our economic advantage, with no central power stations at all! The extreme capital- and resource-intensity

The United States is threatened far more by the hazards of too much energy, too soon, than by the hazards of too little, too late.

The hazards of too much, which have been as widely underestimated as the liabilities of too little have been exaggerated, include diverting financial resources from compelling social needs, making hasty commitments to unproved technologies, and generating environmental and social costs that harm human welfare more than the extra energy improves it.

The higher the level of energy use already attained, the more likely it is that the economic-technological benefits of an additional unit of energy will be outweighed by the social and environmental costs. Mounting evidence suggests that the United States is approaching (if not beyond) the level where further energy growth costs more than it is worth.

Critics of conservation are quick to suggest that what is

implied here is a return to a primitive existence.

In a society that uses its 5,000-pound automobiles for half-mile round trips to the market to fetch a six-pack of beer, consumes the beer in buildings that are overcooled in summer and overheated in winter, and then throws the aluminum cans away at an energy loss equivalent to a third of a gallon of gasoline per six-pack, this "primitive existence" argument strikes me as the most offensive kind of nonsense.

Finally, less energy can mean more employment. The energy-producing industries comprise the most capital-intensive and least labor-intensive major sector of the economy. Accordingly, each dollar of investment capital taken out of energy production and invested in something else, and each personal-consumption dollar saved by reduced energy use and spent elsewhere in the economy, will create more jobs than are lost.

—JOHN HOLDREN

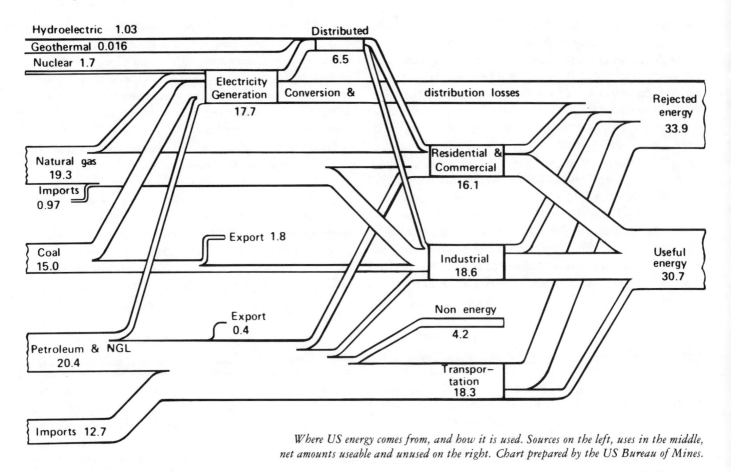

Where US energy comes from, and how it is used. Sources on the left, uses in the middle, net amounts useable and unused on the right. Chart prepared by the US Bureau of Mines.

of all electrical technologies should make us anxious to use electricity only where it is needed. In no industrial country does it appear that additional supplies of electricity could be used to thermodynamic advantage, thus justifying their very high cost in both fuel and money.

Soft Wind, Useful Sun

Recent and continuing work in soft technologies has made great strides. We already have commercially available vertical-axis wind collectors (200 kW capacity) roughly competitive with nuclear power and promising to become much cheaper; the elements of wind systems to make compressed air and pump heat (even better uses than making electricity for a grid); solar heating and cooling systems from 150-odd vendors that are already cheaper than electrical systems and are rapidly coming to compete with direct fuels; elements of systems using solar process heat (today we can make flat-plate collectors that achieve working temperatures approaching 1000°F on a cloudy day in the winter in Scandinavia); systems for converting a wide range of organic wastes into clean fuels; and hybrids between these and similar systems.

Many of these soft technologies are now economic, oth-

ers nearly so. Essentially all are cheaper in the long run than are the high technologies that we would otherwise have to use in their place: the total investment to heat a house entirely with the sun, even in Ontario or Denmark, is far less than to do the same electrically; the total investment to run a car with methanol converted from forestry wastes is less than the investment for synthetic fuels made from coal or oil shale; and so on. This comparative cheapness arises from simplicity, mass production, and virtual elimination of overheads and conversion losses.

The soft technologies have other advantages too. Their lead times are measured in months, not years or decades, and their unit costs are measured in thousands of dollars, not billions. They carry low or (generally) zero risk of technical failure, and are relatively forgiving of imperfect engineering—unlike the high technologies, such as fast breeder reactors and big coal gasification plants, whose success is by no means assured. The soft technologies can be readily adapted to local conditions, skills, and materials, and made on a small as well as a large scale. Their small scale and relatively low energy quality make storage easy. They use no more land than competing high technologies—often less—and do not scar it. Their other environmental impacts are in general minor, well under-

Scientists who know the importance of accurate information can press immediately for the establishment of an enquiry with subpoena power to ascertain from the energy industries the exact state of supplies and reserves in this country. Scientists concerned with the direction of research and the application of scientific knowledge to a technology devoted to human ends can press for a massive project on alternative and environmentally safe forms of energy—solar energy, fusion, other forms. Such a project should be as ambitious as the Manhattan Project or NASA, but there would be no need for secrecy. It would be aimed not at destroying or outdistancing other countries, but at ways to conserve our resources in new technologies. These provide new activities for industries whose present prosperity is based on oil, motor transport and energy-wasting, expensive synthetic materials.

—MARGARET MEAD

stood, and reversible. They have free, freely distributed fuel, independent of cartels, bureaucracies, and strikes. They are inflation-proof. They tend to resist oligopoly. They are flexible, robust, and reliable. They are easy to understand, modify, and repair. If rationally designed, they cannot endanger our health or security even if we make mistakes. They are ample for all our future energy needs so long as the sun shall shine—or rather rise, since modern solar collectors designed for northern climates work very nicely whether it is cloudy or not. Soft energy technologies do not require centralized management, cultural adaptation to foreign values, technical elites to build and operate them, soldiers to guard them, or antitrust lawyers to litigate them. They use standard, widely available skills and components. They rely on a high source potential (that of sunlight exceeds 10,000°F), yet are perfectly matched to the real needs of people for basic functions like heating, cooling, cooking, lighting, and pumping. To the extent that they have conversion losses, nothing depletable or otherwise useful is lost, and any surplus low-temperature heat can be used locally because of the small scale. Soft technologies are based on the main resources of developing countries, especially in the fuel-poor tropics, and are especially well suited to rural eco-development. They help Biharis, Costa Ricans, and Masai—not to mention Austrians, Japanese, and Iranians—more directly than does building reactors in California.

To avoid misunderstanding, soft technology does *not* mean huge solar "farms" in the Arizona desert feeding a pervasive national grid, nor solar-satellite schemes, nor enormous networks of seathermal collectors. These schemes, typical of the main emphasis of ERDA's solar program, are essentially "hard," not soft, technologies, because even though they rely on a renewable source, they do not match most end-use needs in either scale or energy quality. The definition hinges on the technical and sociopolitical *structure* of the energy system, not on the kind or amount of energy used. Cheap silicon or other photovoltaic cells, which might become available in the 1980s, would be a convenient supplement if used on a small scale for purposes requiring electricity, but would become a "hard" technology if centralized and used with elaborate storage schemes to meet most of our energy needs via a huge grid. In any case, photovoltaic cells are not necessary to the conceptual design of a completely soft US energy economy: this can be done using only technologies that are already demonstrated and economic (or very nearly so).

Terrestrial nuclear fusion, a hard technology in all senses, would not be a desirable component of a soft energy system. It can be used to make atomic-bomb materials: indeed, most designs now being considered for fusion reactors would breed plutonium and the like as fuel for fast breeder fission reactors. Fusion will probably be rather dirty—in which case we might use it anyway for lack of perceived alternatives—but if it were clean, we would lack the discipline to use it with enough restraint not to disturb global climate by releasing heat. In this sense the soft technologies are preferable not only because we know they work, but because they limit the amount of mischief we can get into. Finally, fusion is a clever way to do something we don't really want to do, namely to find *yet another* costly, complex, centralized, large-scale, high-technology way to make electricity—all of which goes in the wrong direction.

The Federal Power Commission, in a news release dated Sept. 24, 1974, projected a need for 1.677 million MW of capacity in the contiguous United States by 1993, or an average of 35 1000-MW plants per state. Continuing their projection to the year 2000 would indicate a need for more than 50 such plants per state by that date. Can we have these plants in operation by that time? I believe the answer is clearly no, for at least *three important* reasons:

• The first problem is that of locating acceptable sites, the major criterion being the availability of enormous quantities of cooling water.

• A second major deterrent to the construction of the projected power plants is the enormous *capital* sums that must be raised. Fifty power plants per state plus the required transformer and transmission systems would cost between 1.5 and 2 trillion 1974 dollars. To this must be added the vast sums called for in Project Independence to locate and open new coal and uranium mines and petroleum fields; build shale oil and tar sand conversion plants, and coal gasification, liquification, and desulfurization plants; build fleets of supertankers, and supertanker ports, and finally pay the Arabs for the oil to fill the supertankers. It seems clear that if these needs are met it will be at the expense of nearly all other demands for capital funds outside the energy industries. Anyone who reads the financial pages of the daily newspapers is aware of the difficulties that the utilities are already having with the prob-lem, and of the fact that major construction projects have already been delayed for this reason.

• A third deterrent to the construction of the projected power plants and the concomitant increase in energy supplies is the lack of trained manpower.

A recently released forecast of the AEC indicates that skilled manpower needs for power plants alone will increase from a current 150,000 to over a million by 2000, a greater than six-fold increase. The probability that these trained manpower needs can be met is small indeed.

The problem, of course, is that we have been living for most of this century on an exponential growth curve of electrical energy consumption, and we are approaching the end of our ability to stay on this curve. The fact that we have had a long history of following such a curve does not guarantee a long future.

A major push to utilize solar energy as much and as soon as possible is the most effective single procedure we can use to reduce the growth of electrical load, and thus reduce the need for an unattainable expansion of generating capacity. When energy spokesmen state that solar energy cannot contribute to our energy needs before 1990 or 2000, they are generally referring to the sun as a source of electrical energy. For use as a simple low-temperature heat source the technology is simple and only large-scale commercial application is missing.

Since it is extremely unlikely that utilities will be able to

---

To switch over entirely to living on our energy income would take us about 50 years—about as long as it would take us to do anything else. Indeed, the soft technologies are quicker than the big high technologies because they are vastly simpler and smaller. (Thus even countries like Japan could switch to soft sources at least as quickly and cheaply as they could go nuclear.) To buy the time we need to build this 50-year bridge to our goal, we must use fossil fuels, briefly and sparingly, in special transitional technologies. These should be adaptable to the soft technologies so that we can plug those in as they come along. For example, instead of heating houses with synthetic gas made from coal, a good transitional technique would be to build coal-fired, fluidized-bed gas turbines with district heating and heat pumps. (A complete system of this type, supplying 70 megawatts of electricity and 200 megawatts of heat, is commercially available; it costs half as much as the synthetic-gas plant, including all the district-heating installations, and it uses—cleanly—only two-fifths as much coal.) By building the district-heating system at the right scale, with neighborhood hot-water tanks that are not too big, we can later piggyback onto them neighborhood solar collectors, or wind-driven heat pumps, or waste heat from a local factory or incinerators, or whatever other heat source becomes available. Thus we could marry those urban buildings that can take more backfitted solar collectors than they need with other buildings nearby that cannot be backfitted at all.

By using ingenious, but relatively small and simple, coal technologies (fluidized-bed combustion on all scales, supercritical gas extraction, flash hydrogenation and pyrolysis) we can use a modest, temporary expansion of coal mining to supply our transitional needs for fluid fuels. This supplement and the rapid growth of soft technologies—which several federal assessments show could overtake the highest nuclear estmates during the 1990s—would together make most of the medium-term Arctic and offshore extraction and imports of oil and gas unnecessary. With conservation given a high enough priority, even the coal expansion might not be necessary; and in

continue to raise the capital needed for expansion, government agencies, federal or state, will be increasingly forced to step in and help. This has already happened in New York State. It would be far better for government support to be directed toward helping individual citizens, builders, or industry pay for energy-saving equipment and methods than to invest in new power plants. Subsidies for solar heating panels, for example, would cost far less than the power plants they replace, and would reduce fuel oil consumption much faster and more effectively.

It seems clear that we cannot meet the projected needs for electric energy in the year 2000, and continuing to build buildings and buy equipment and systems based on the assumption that we can will only create exceedingly difficult problems for the years ahead. We can reduce dramatically our need for total energy as well as for electrical energy, but only if we make conservation a new ethic, a new way of life. This will not be a life of privation, but one in which growth is in intellectual and human values, in recreation, and in the enjoyment of a clean and less harried world, rather than in the proliferation of material things which become all too soon a disposal problem. We have been committed for many years to a maximization of the gross national product by an ever increasing flow of materials and energy through the economic system, with little regard for the resulting quality of life. It will not be easy to change, but change we must if we are to leave to our descendants any hope for a good life.

• The major deterrent to change lies in the fact that the political and economic forces which determine our decisions and actions are controlled by short-range influences of the economic marketplace. Our institutions seem unable to respond to long-range problems and needs. The business executive, whether in the automobile industry or the electric utility business, is expected to provide dividends for the stockholders this year, not to solve problems of the year 2000. Political leaders to whom we look for solutions to the very difficult problems we face, must be concerned with the next election, and we have, as a people, a long history of electing candidates who tell us how good it will be during their administrations, and of turning away from leaders who tell us the hard truths about our situation. Our society has never been reluctant to pass the hard problems on to the next generation. Given the choice of guns or butter, we elect both, pay for the butter, and pass the bill for the guns to our children. We are now running out of time, and the energy problem will not wait for our children or grandchildren. If you are under 40, this problem will be on your doorstep before you retire. If my generation doesn't begin to take the drastic steps necessary to bring it under control, you had better start making waves.

—LEWIS D. CONTA

any event, it would not be a massive program entailing irreparable strip mining.

Another element of our transition to a soft energy economy must be the vigorous enforcement of antitrust laws. Giant energy corporations that already control essentially all our fuels must, in the interest of real competition and consumer choice, divest themselves at least horizontally and probably vertically too. It is unhealthy for the equally powerful defense and aerospace contractors, too, to receive such a large share of federal research-and-development funding as they do in preference to the smaller, less formal, and often more innovative workers on softer technologies. Much of the blame here lies with ERDA, which not only tends (over some internal dissent) to push "big science" policies—it may cost $2 million just to respond, when ERDA requests a proposal—but has also defined energy technologies so that they cannot make a major long-term contribution *unless* they are electrified and therefore complex.

We should also consider ways to ensure that technical innovations paid for by the taxpayer are made freely available, especially to developing countries, lest patents and red tape hinder the rapid transfer of appropriate and adaptable technologies to those who need them most. And our research-and-development priorities need a complete overhaul: present emphasis on big high technologies is discouraging good technologists from devoting their careers to anything else.

The immediate steps we need to start moving toward a soft energy path are varied, wide-ranging, and likely to receive wide support from ordinary people, both as applied at home and as a major part of our overseas development program. Much of the action will be at the state or local level, where people can get involved with projects of direct and obvious relevance.

First we must clear away the needless barriers to using energy efficiently. Many people cannot insulate their houses properly because they have bad information, or aren't allowed to by old building codes, or cannot agree with a landlord about who should pay and who should

Over the next few decades we could reduce the energy required to make things by a third, reduce the energy required to run homes and buildings by 40 percent, and reduce transportation needs by 20–40 percent. Aside from the changes in cars and in added recycling, we'll hardly notice the change in energy use except at the bank; for in addition to saving millions of barrels of oil each day we'll save billions of dollars a year.

—LEE SCHIPPER

profit, or can't get finance, or lack economic and psychological incentives, or risk higher property taxes, or have to pay the costs while others reap the benefits. Similar problems—plus lack of expertise in planning conservation measures—dog conservation-minded industrialists. Our fragmentation of government responsibility often makes us spend money at cross-purposes, simultaneously subsidizing energy-wasting practices, energy-producing capacity to fuel them, and users to buy the energy. Our pervasive subsidies to traditional forms of energy make it hard for new ones to compete; indeed, President Ford, while proclaiming the virtues of the free market, wanted a $100 billion slush fund to subsidize those large energy technologies which, for excellent reasons, cannot attract enough capital in the marketplace. One fact alone—that our natural gas is sold for far less than it is worth—distorts our whole energy pricing system. Virtually all our energy prices are fictitious and do not arise from market forces. (Consider gasoline taxes, for example.)

The biggest single step we could take to promote energy efficiency and soft technologies would be to apply the sound economic principles to which we profess devotion. This means giving big users no discount—even perhaps a surcharge—and pricing energy according to the cost of adding a new unit of supply. (There may even be a case for linking gas prices to electricity prices because rapid substitutions of gas for electricity and vice versa can otherwise be so disruptive.) It also means counting all the diseconomies of scale, counting total lifetime costs, and counting the costs of *complete* energy systems—not just a part, like a power station—to perform a given task for a consumer. It also means valuing assets at their replacement cost. It means pricing to take account of the scarcity value of the fossil fuels we have left. It means basing economic decisions on sensitivity to changes in the assumptions. It means not letting anybody unload costs onto someone else; the polluter must pay.

A useful innovation would be to transfer capital to whoever can use it to give society the best value for its money.

For example, a utility could finance a solar heating system or roof insulation, acting as a bank, then be repaid through utility bills at a rate corresponding to the homeowner's rate of return. This would minimize the homeowner's "life-cycle cost"—what he pays over the whole life of his house—but would also help the utility in three important ways: spending at most half as much (for a 100 percent solar heating system) as would be necessary without it, for then the utility would have to build costlier electric capacity instead; turning over the investment several times as fast (because the payback time is much faster than for a power station); and avoiding social obsolescence. This isn't a subsidy; it is a mechanism that gives us a more sensible way to spend society's money for the greatest benefit.

Decentralizing to Fit the Need

We need to focus our energy supply program not on energy or electricity as abstractions, but rather on the nature and scale of the specific end-use functions people need, such as heat at various temperatures, work, light, etc. If we do this we shall find our present direction of development is misguided, for it tries, at great and needless expense, to provide premium fuels and high-grade electricity for purposes that require neither. When we count all the costs and benefits, too, the current stress on huge central facilities linked to vulnerable distribution systems will seem equally irrational, as nearly all our end-use needs are dispersed at small scale (or medium scale, which very few people are thinking about). Of course we already have lots of big power stations and the like, and they will be with us for a long time. The real question, though, is what we should *add* to them—for example, how we shall heat people's houses as the oil and gas runs out. For space heating—about a third of our present end-use energy, and probably half if we used the rest efficiently—it is cheaper to install a soft source than any of the high technologies we would otherwise have to use instead.

Big high technologies demand so much of our money,

First priority in any long-range energy policy must go to conservation, to reducing the demand side of the energy equation by eliminating wasteful practices and improving the efficiency with which energy is produced, delivered and employed. Study after study has shown conservation of existing energy resources to be the most effective and readily available "new source" of supply to meet urgent needs.

—THE NEW YORK TIMES

skill, time, and political will that they effectively foreclose other, more attractive options by diminishing and delaying them until too late. The three components of the soft energy path—end-use efficiency, soft sources, and transitional fossil-fuel technologies—make a coherent whole only if we start them all promptly. Delay in conservation lets wasteful use run on so far that there is no way to catch up. Delay in deploying soft sources, pushing their contribution further into the future, leaves us with no credible fossil-fuel bridge to get to them. Delay in deploying transitional technologies, forcing us to keep using fossil fuels in today's huge, inefficient, dirty plants, would put coal's contributions out of step with our transitional pattern of end-use needs as the oil and gas dwindle. Thus if we are on a soft path, nuclear power is not only unnecessary but a positive encumbrance that keeps us from pursuing our three main tasks at a sufficient priority to make them work together properly. The technologies we must *not* pursue because of what they place beyond our reach are as important as the ones we must explore and embrace.

A more subtle danger of the high technologies is that they lead us into a capital trap. Past major transitions in our energy supply have been smooth because we financed them with cheap fossil fuel, which gave us cheap and plentiful capital. After the present transition—the last in which we shall have cheap fossil fuel—the capital cost of our new energy technologies will typically be 10 to 100 times higher and will stay that way. Thus whatever sort of energy system we now make a transition *to*, the future absence of today's cheap capital will make us stay there for a long time. If the soft and hard paths were equally capital-intensive (which they are not) and if neither had a social or environmental advantage over the other, we would thus still be wise to use our cheap fossil fuels (sparingly) to finance a transition as nearly straight as possible to our ultimate energy-income technologies, because we won't have another chance to get there.

No matter what we do, the era of cheap energy is over. It is silly to try to prolong it artificially, pretending that nothing has happened. If poor people cannot afford properly priced energy, and if we care about equity, then we should make the poor people less poor, not tax everyone to subsidize cheap energy even for the rich. Energy prices are not a good instrument of distributional equity, and we should not ask them to bear the burden of our social conscience when we can discharge it directly. On the other hand, it would be inequitable for energy companies to reap windfall profits from higher prices, and foolish for those revenues to be devoted to new energy technologies that seem economic only because our accounting rules are at variance with good economics or because we offer massive federal subsidies. But the remedy here is in the hands of the same legislators who are trying to keep energy temporarily cheap for us. Constraints can be arranged in myriad ways to suit our practical and ideological convenience. Fear of inequitable and uncontrolled profits is not a good reason to try to maintain our wasteful ways for a few years now so that we can pay a lot more later, after another election or two. That is a false economy for which nobody will thank us. Nor is it beyond our ingenuity to devise ways—whether through direct aid, energy stamps, lifeline rates, or whatever—to make sure that those hardest hit by rising energy prices can still satisfy their basic needs. Indeed, our measures to improve efficiency of energy use should concentrate first on poor people, whose houses are generally the least energy-efficient—a flaw they can least afford. And such measures are an important part of the urban renewal we should do anyway.

Conservation for Jobs

Conservation and soft technologies are among our best paths toward full employment. Overhauling our buildings for energy efficiency would keep the building industry well occupied for years with something better than destroying communities (and, according to the American Institute of Architects, could in 1990 be saving us a third as much energy as we now use for everything). Making soft and

For the designers of these houses, the choice is still open whether to build in energy-saving insulation and soft energy systems, or to use thin walls, electric or gas space-heating, and other wasteful conventional designs—in which case the owners will eventually have to "retrofit" them at great expense, when the cost of energy goes through the roof. It's invest now, or pay later. Photo by Kerry Richardson.

transitional energy hardware (among much else we need) is a fine way to recycle moribund capacity in the auto, defense, and other manufacturing industries. We need insulation, efficient boilers and heat pumps, recycling equipment, control electronics, all the products of our technical sophistication. Some job shifts may require retraining, but many are just a natural progression—as with the fluorescent-light makers now making tubular glass solar collectors, or the metal fabricators and car makers now going into the wind-machine business, or the New England heating-oil dealers who want now to sell solar collectors to their traditional customers. New industries on any scale can be set up where jobs are needed, for the simplicity of the devices we need lets us make them anywhere we like and still have a strong local market. Such low-overhead, labor-intensive investment saves both capital and jobs. In contrast, with a big power station we must invest about a quarter of a million dollars for each job created—about the most capital-intensive major investment in the whole economy. We could make more jobs by investing the capital in practically anything else.

If we don't want to abolish subsidies for traditional energy sources, we might instead consider modest and temporary tax incentives for their softer rivals, which would repay us handsomely. Capital-transfer schemes (e.g., utilities buying insulation or equipment for their customers and being repaid over a period of time via utility bills) are urgently needed to relieve homeowners of the burden of initial investment; they cannot, like utilities, float low-interest bonds and amortize over thirty years. Public-sector demonstration projects on a far larger scale than now would help people to learn what soft systems look like and what they can do. The enormous latent interest in soft technologies and the under-rated initiative and intelligence of the public can be put to work, not least in community and neighborhood projects that increase local pride and self-reliance. The immense resources of our national laboratories can be recycled from mainly nuclear research to the lower-technology but equally exciting and more forgiving soft energy systems; anyone working on their frontiers knows dozens of simple, important questions that nobody now seems to have time or money to answer properly. Much of our federal energy bureaucracy can be recycled too, preferably into smaller chunks. But it does seem likely that some unadaptable people whom time has passed by will have to be reshuffled into positions where their talents can be applied to the narrow engineering questions they love to ask rather than to the broader policy questions they have trouble imagining. And much of the best energy work will continue to be done, as now, by unsung pioneers on the local and state level.

A soft energy path will require strong leadership, but it is in important ways less coercive than the policy we are pursuing now. In a nuclear society, nobody can opt out of

Appliances of sound energy design were built and marketed in this country in the 1940s and 1950s. A home freezer built by the Jacobs Wind Electric Company was equipped with three inches of cork insulation, and used heat exchange coils which contacted food contents directly. This machine was capable of keeping food frozen for a week without power, and used less than 20 percent of the energy required by the average home freezer sold today.

Architect Richard Stein examined one building which used nine million kilowatt-hours of electricity per year; he estimates that "an ample but selective lighting system would permit all office functions to carry on equally well with 11 percent of the kilowatt-hours now consumed."

—WILSON CLARK

nuclear risk, and everyone's lifestyle is shaped inexorably by the political and economic imperatives of the big energy system. But in a soft path, resting on innumerable "micro" consumer choices rather than on what Ivan Illich calls "radical monopoly," everyone will get exactly the costs and benefits of the energy system he or she chooses, and no others, for in decentralized energy systems the costs and benefits are inseparable and cannot be allocated to different times or places. People who want to drive big cars or live in badly insulated houses will be free to do so, and to pay the social costs of doing so. People who want to live where they can walk, bicycle, ride, ski, or skate where they want to go will have the chance. People who don't want the advantages of district heating will be free to reject them— and, if the system is thoughtfully designed, to change their minds later. People can continue to rely on "Big Brother" utilities, or can choose instead to reduce their humiliating (and increasingly costly) dependence on systems they cannot understand or control.

A soft path entails difficult social problems—as does any energy future stretching ahead 50 years. But we have to ask what kinds of social problems we want. There is now ample evidence to suggest that the social changes needed for a "hard" path are less pleasant, less plausible, and less consistent with traditional values than are the social changes that could make a soft path work. This perception is not yet widely shared, for few people have thought hard about the politics of further centralization. But we know instinctively that the centralism and repressiveness of which we have lately had hints are but a small taste of what we could see in an increasingly lopsided battle between insistent federal authority and recalcitrant states or citizens. The conventional wisdom is that while a hard path

involves mainly technical problems, which we have so far been fairly good at solving, a soft path involves mainly social problems, which we haven't, so we should prefer the technical problems. A more realistic view is that a hard path, too, involves unpleasant social changes and problems. We can no longer get away from that. From now on, the most important, difficult, and neglected questions of energy and social policy will not be mainly technical or economic, but rather social and ethical, and hence the right and duty of every citizen to judge if our democracy is to remain healthy.

The essence of the change we need, then, is not technical but political and social and ethical, a change of values and perceptions that is already well under way. It implies technical efforts that would produce a long-term energy strategy greater than the sum of its parts: combining the efficient use of energy with its supply from renewable sources, matching energy supply in scale and quality to the tasks we need to have done, and sparingly using fossil fuels to buy the decades we need to switch to living on our energy income. Such a strategy will not be free of problems. Yet we already know enough about it to be confident that its problems are much more tractable, and more compatible with social diversity and freedom of choice, than are the problems of the centralized high technologies to which present policy would otherwise drive us. And these two paths are mutually exclusive. We must choose one or the other before they diverge much further—and before growing tensions between rich and poor, or growing commitments of the cheap capital made from cheap fossil fuel that we shall not have again, have destroyed the conditions that now make a smooth transition to a soft energy future possible.

With the coming of the industrial age a sizable portion of the land in many parts of the world was cleared at an accelerated pace, thereby modifying the earth's natural capacity for storing and evaporating moisture and for absorbing solar energy. These human-induced modifications of the environment often slightly altered the local climate from what it had been when the land was in its natural state.

Industrialized peoples, with their higher standards of living, rapidly became dependent on the extensive use of energy to turn their wheels, heat their buildings, produce their electricity, and grow, store, and transport their food. Most of the energy liberated was (and still is) derived from fossil fuels—coal, gas, and oil—whose burning is accompanied by the disagreeable by-products that we now call pollution.

One form of such pollution that affects the entire atmosphere is the release of carbon dioxide (CO_2) gas. Even though it makes up a small fraction (less than one one-thousandth) of the gases that comprise the atmosphere, CO_2 is crucial in determining the earth's temperature because it traps some of the earth's heat (to produce the so-called greenhouse effect). Human activities have already raised the CO_2 content in the atmosphere by 10 percent and are estimated to raise it some 25 percent by the year 2000. . . . This could lead to a 1° Celsius (1.8° Fahrenheit) average warming of the earth's surface, which is roughly equivalent to twice the warming that occurred "naturally" in the first half of this century. This 1°C warming could reduce the masses of ice at the poles, and thereby raise the height of the world's oceans, or affect climate in the temperate zones or other latitudes.

If concentrations of CO_2, and perhaps of aerosols, continue to increase, demonstrable climatic changes could occur by the end of this century, if not sooner; recent calculations suggest that if present trends continue, a threshold may soon be reached after which the effects will be unambiguously detectable on a global basis. Problematically, by that point it may be too late to avoid the dangerous consequences of such an occurrence, for *certain proof* of present theories can come only *after* the atmosphere itself has "performed the experiment."

The processes at work in determining climatic change are simply not yet fully understood. Despite the uncertainty in measurements and in theory, estimates must be given and difficult decisions may have to be made on the basis of the available knowledge. In any case, efforts to develop better estimates and models of potential effects will be absolutely necessary to help us reduce the uncertainties in decision-making to a tolerable minimum. Improvement of the quality of these estimates is the responsibility that atmospheric scientists and their funding agents owe to long-range planners, for the climatic effects of human activities are self-evidently the outer limits to growth. The real problem is: If we choose to wait for more certainty before actions are initiated, then can our models be improved in time to prevent an irreversible drift toward a future calamity? And how can we decide how much uncertainty is enough to prevent a policy action based on a climate model? This dilemma rests, metaphorically, in our need to gaze into a very dirty crystal ball; but the tough judgment to be made here is precisely how long we should clean the glass before acting on what we believe we see inside.

—STEPHEN SCHNEIDER

Although I am as guilty as anyone of promoting solar collectors, windplants, and methane generators, I do have grave doubts about the environmental movement's present "white man's eco-technology" approach to solving the world's current problems . . . problems which are largely with us because of earlier white man "solutions" to the world's problems. "Solutions" such as the Industrial Revolution . . . which—if we're honest—we must admit that our plastic-and-aluminum solar collectors, copper-wound windplants, and stainless-steel methane generators are *part of* rather than an alternative *to*.

Perhaps, then, it's time for us to at least question our prevailing love affair with "white man eco-technology" by looking back at what might—for want of a better term—be called *"primitive* eco-technology." And as we conduct this comparison, I ask you to remember—as Bill Coperthwaite, of the Yurt Foundation recently pointed out to me—that the definition of "primitive" is not really "inferior", as we now usually think. "Primitive" derives from "primus" and means "first" or "prime".

Now that's very important to keep in mind. Because it seems to me that, in general—and I want this to be known from now on as Shuttleworth's Law of Something or Other—that, in general, the first and the most basic discoveries and developments in any field are the best. They use the least amount of the most readily available resources, they require the minimum energy input for their manufacture, they last the longest, they work within only a few percentage points of optimum efficiency with minimum care and maintenance, they're recycled the easiest when their useful life is over, and they leave little or no pollution behind when they're gone.

Glass, for instance, is better in all important ways than plastic for containers, windows, lab work, solar collectors, and all the other common uses to which it is put. Glass is made by a relatively low-energy process—at least compared to its "replacement", plastic—and, unlike plastics, which are produced from dwindling petrochemical stocks or increasingly dear foodstuffs, glass is made from silica sand . . . which is one of the most plentiful mineral resources we have.

Glass can be made more shatterproof than plastic. More heat resistant. It doesn't scratch the way plastic does. Unlike the exotic plastic films now being touted for solar collectors, it doesn't age in the sun. It doesn't impart flavor and cancer-causing agents to foods when it's used for storage. And so on.

Another example: No matter what Bucky Fuller says about building houses like airplanes and using aluminum and geodesics for the construction of a minimum-weight dwelling, I still think that basic stone . . . or wood . . . or, most basic of all, earth . . . is awfully hard to beat when it comes to choosing the building material for a house.

Earth is available everywhere you'd really care to live. You don't have to use energy to ship it to your construction site . . . it's already there. You can fabricate an earthen dwelling with only the simplest tools and technology . . . and that home will be naturally warm during the winter and naturally air conditioned in the summer. A properly constructed dirt building will, with minimum care, last hundreds of years almost anywhere on the planet's surface . . . not just in the arid regions, as we usually think.

Unlike an aluminum or plastic dome—or even the more conventional dry-walled, jerry-built frame boxes in which most of us now live—an earthen building deadens sound. Correctly used, earth is windproof, waterproof, and absolutely fireproof. It doesn't give off toxic vapors the way "modern" construction materials do. It *feels* satisfyingly solid. It doesn't wear out.

In short, a home built of earth does exactly what it's supposed to do. It satisfies human wants, needs, and de-

Photo by Stewart Brand.

sires at minimum cost and with minimum trouble. It *works* . . . and works supremely well.

Yet a third example: Many of us—and this includes the folks at *The Mother Earth News* ®—are currently trying to develop "new and better" solar collectors. And we talk about and experiment with and get turned on by flat-plate collectors and vertical-plate flat-plate collectors and parabolic collectors and front surface mirrors for reflectors for collectors and all kinds of other "new and better" solar collectors.

Yet I would like to suggest that the best solar collectors of all—the absolutely most efficient solar converters—have been around for hundreds of thousands of years. We call them trees and vegetation. And they build themselves automatically. They feed us. They shade us. They regulate our micro-climates and play a most important part in regulating the macro-climate. They constantly purify the air. They absorb sound and act as pollution buffers. Shelter and nourish most of the insects, animals, and birds in the world. Warm us in such forms as peat and wood.

Their reeds, thatch, and lumber house us. They supply us with bows and arrows, rifle stocks, axe handles, rope, and other weapons and tools. Their tapa cloth, cotton, linen, etc., clothe us. Their wood and fabric make our sleds, buggies, wagons, automobiles, and airplanes. They are by definition—since *we* have adapted to *them* over thousands of years—absolutely non-polluting and completely recyclable. And, once they've served their useful purpose, they do that recycling all by themselves with no help from us.

We are, in other words, *very* egocentric animals if we grandly think that we are—in any way and by any stretch of the imagination—going to devise any kind of solar energy collection or conversion system that even remotely approaches the total efficiency of vegetation. Our mechanical gadgets may well concentrate more of the sun's warmth into a given area than, say, trees or grass will. But they won't construct themselves automatically in the first place . . . or purify the air . . . or act as noise and pollution buffers . . . or clothe us . . . or repair themselves when they're damaged . . . or recycle themselves automatically when their useful life is over . . . or do any one of a thousand other things that vegetation does for us every day.

Well, the message—at least to me—is clear: "Don't just *do* something, white man . . . *stand* there." It's far easier, you know, to tinker with some external machinery than it is to delve within ourselves and make meaningful changes in the way we view the world.

Perhaps, though, if we'd just open our eyes . . . if we'd humbly accept—as Dave Brower, founder of Friends of the Earth, says—that *everything we really need is already here and we don't have to "improve" on anything* . . . maybe then we'd find that a lot of our "problems" would solve themselves. Or would never have descended on us in the first place.

We wouldn't, for instance, have aerosol cans destroying the ionosphere. Or automobile exhaust eating away at our lungs. Or DDT and other chlorinated hydrocarbons creating cancers in our bodies. Or the so-called "Green Revolution" destroying the world's plant genetic pool. Or cities built for machines instead of people. Or any one of thousands of other "marvels of modern science" with which we're now "blessed".

It is fair to say that—in my mind, at least—"progress" is truly our most important problem. Even to the extent that I have grave reservations about the "progress" of the very ecotechnology that you and I are here today to promote.

I believe, then, that probably *the* single most important thing we eco-freaks can do is to always—first and foremost—evaluate every new development, every new "breakthrough", every new solar collector design, every new windplant, every new aquaculture system we devise against the natural systems they're designed to replace or improve. And we must dispassionately ask ourselves whether or not our "new" and "breakthrough" designs really do improve or replace the natural systems.

And, if we're truthful, I think that, not in 50% of the cases, or 70%, or 85%, or 99% . . . *but virtually 100% of the time our honest answer will have to be "no".*

I suggest, in other words, that our Brave New Eco-Movement is, so far at least, probably no real eco-movement at all. We are still much too preoccupied with taking our machines out into the woods, instead of making a place for the forest in our hearts. We are too intent on finding ways to run our electric toothbrushes and our powered handsaws and our stereo sets on solar or wind energy when, maybe, what we should be doing is remodeling our internal makeup so that we don't *need* electric toothbrushes . . . or powered handsaws . . . or even stereo sets at all.

We cast ourselves out of The Garden thousands of years ago and we daily continue to lock the door behind us.

Until we begin to appreciate the incredible beauty and *rightness* of nature and start fitting ourselves into the naturally occurring scheme of things, in short, instead of constantly trying to bend nature to our irrational, greedy, people-centered desires . . . I don't think we'll have done much that is worthy of the self-proclaimed labels "environmentalist", "ecologist", or even "alternative lifestyle" that we so proudly stick on our chests.

As Pogo quite aptly said, "We have met the enemy and he is, indeed, *us*." When that first inventive caveman struck the first flint-and-stone spark he lit a long, slow fuse which will eventually set off the final thermonuclear holocaust which is destined to destroy this planet. That's just the kind of animal we are and, so far, you and I have done nothing to change our destiny.

Or, to put it another way by paraphrasing a good old saw, "That government is best which governs least": *The only really good technology is no technology at all.*

For, in the larger sense, our technology—even the "white man eco-technology" with which we're now bravely trying to right all mankind's wrongs to the planet—is, in reality, only taxation without representation imposed by an elitist species upon the rest of the natural world. I'm convinced we've got to change that if the planet is to endure.

—JOHN SHUTTLEWORTH

"Dinner Friday at the Smiths', in the Hamptons. They're O.K. on heating oil. How are we on gas?"

Drawing by Alan Dunn; © The New Yorker Magazine, Inc.

In 1975, Americans *wasted* more fossil fuel than was *used* by two-thirds of the world's population. We annually consume more than twice as much fuel as we need to maintain our standard of living. We could lead lives as rich, healthy, and fulfilling—with as much comfort, and with more employment—using less than half of the energy now used.

Neither "accidental" nor "natural," our energy growth rates resulted from conscious decisions. Energy consumption levels have been pushed, pulled, shoved, and kicked upward by every trick and tactic known to the contemporary science of mass marketing. To encourage growth, fuel prices have been kept artificially low and utility rate structures have rewarded waste. Environmental costs and health costs have been ignored.

Roger Sant, Assistant Administrator of the Federal Energy Administration, has argued that a $500 billion investment in energy conservation would save twice as much energy as a comparable investment in new supplies could produce. "Any good businessman would say we ought to do it," according to Sant, until recently himself a businessman. But economic arguments do not constitute the only case for conservation. Additional arguments demonstrate how broad and compelling the case for conservation really is.

Energy conservation by Americans today will allow the earth's limited resource base of high-quality fuels to be "stretched" further. It will enable our children and those in other lands to share in the earth's finite stock of fossil fuels. It will make an especially critical difference to those living in underdeveloped lands where the marginal return per unit of fuel is far greater than in highly developed countries.

Energy conservation will allow a portion of the fossil fuel base to be reserved for non-energy purposes: drugs, lubricants, and other materials. The energy cost of manufacturing such substances from carbon and hydrogen, once our present feedstocks have been exhausted will be astronomical.

Energy conservation will allow us to minimize the environmental degradation associated with all current energy production technologies. The consequences of pollutants such as heavy metal particulates, carcinogenic aromatic hydrocarbons, and various radioactive materials could be terrifying. Energy conservation will allow us to avoid objectionable energy sources while the search for safe, sustainable sources continues. Conservation also decreases the likelihood that we will cross climatological threshholds (e.g., with carbon dioxide production or with regional heat generation), triggering consequences that may be devastating.

Energy conservation will contribute to human health. Much of the fat in our energy diet leads to fat on our bodies. Energy conservation could lead to more exercise, better diets, less pollution, and other indirect benefits to human health.

The security of a modest energy supply is more easily assured than that of an enormous one that depends upon a far-flung network of sources. And an enlightened program of energy conservation will bolster employment levels.

An unequivocally desirable national objective, energy conservation is already among the most widely supported goals in the country. The time has come to translate all those supportive words into supportive action.

Constructing energy-efficient buildings in the first place is easier than upgrading inefficient structures later. Presently all the incentives are geared to keeping down initial costs; inadequate insulation, inefficient equipment, and faulty construction ensue. Attention should instead be fixed on the lifetime costs of new structures.

No insurmountable technical difficulties stand in the way of constructing energy-efficient buildings. But ingrained institutional obstacles should be removed immediately through public policies that place a premium on energy conservation.

Today we use several times as much energy as fuel to produce, process, retail, and prepare food as the food itself contains. None of the energy in the fuel is actually transferred to the food; food energy is all obtained from sunshine. The fuels used in the food system are substitutes for labor, land, capital, rain, and so forth—not for sunshine. In an era when food and fuel are jointly responsible for almost half of our spiraling inflation, the increasing fuel-intensity of the food system deserves close scrutiny.

Sweden, with a product mix very much like that of the U.S. and a very cold climate, might reasonably be expected to consume more energy per unit of GNP, rather than considerably less. Many of the recommendations of this paper—for ample insulation, efficient transportation, and the productive use of waste heat from electrical generation—are already a way of life in Sweden. When one country makes energy go almost twice as far as another country at a similar stage of development, the second country could profitably learn something about efficiency from the first.

Careful energy conservation creates jobs. Of course, no one wants to break rocks. Saving energy should not be used as an excuse to resurrect dreary, unrewarding forms of manual labor, like ditch digging, that are best left to priceless machines. But where human skill, intelligence, or craftsmanship have been replaced by automation, the process should be reversed. Replacing good carpentry by prefabrication plants, cabinet-making by assembly lines, and cobbling by machines that never wore a shoe has become increasingly difficult to justify.

One final point must be made about energy and labor. Though fuels and electricity are the most energy-intensive goods in the economy, the fuel industries and electrical companies provide very little employment per dollar of goods produced. Thus, to the extent that a consumer conserves fuel and spends the money on *anything* else, he will provide more employment as well as use less energy. Capital diverted from nuclear reactors, coal gasification facilities, and petroleum refineries will produce more long-term employment if invested in almost any other enterprise.

A truly well-designed energy conservation program can create a "Snowball Effect" advantageous to the consumer. If the dollars saved by conserving energy are invested in ways that save even more energy, the conservation effect becomes self-multiplying. The bus-to-bicycle savings can be used to plant a home garden; the savings from the home garden can be used to insulate the house, etc. Eventually one may save enough money through energy conservation to purchase a solar collector and, in effect, become an energy producer!

What holds true for the individual in this case also holds true for the nation. National investments and expenditures should be shifted away from areas that require relatively more energy per dollar into areas requiring less. Since there is a direct trade-off between the energy intensity and the labor intensity of expenditures, a shift away from high energy purchases would also reduce unemployment.

If Congress imposes a federal energy conservation tax on fuels and the revenues from this tax are used to build nuclear reactors, coal gasification plants, and highways, the Boomerang Law will prevent any significant energy savings. However, if the revenues from such a tax are instead dedicated to further energy conservation efforts, such as insulating poor people's dwellings and subsidizing public transportation, the Snowball Effect will multiply savings.

Individual actions, though necessary, are not sufficient. A strong national conservation program will come about only if demanded by an aroused and informed citizenry.

The time has come to press our political representatives to change the rules of the game in ways that promote energy conservation—to eliminate tax incentives that encourage the consumption of fuel and other virgin resources, transport rates that discriminate against recycled goods, and utility rate structures that reward energy gluttony.

Policy-makers and consumers alike must learn to recognize and understand the following broad categories of energy conservation strategies: prices, taxes, allocations, incentives, regulations, and exhortation.

1. *Prices* and *taxes* both work to make a source of energy more expensive to the consumer. If the price of gasoline rises rapidly, due to market forces or to increasing taxes, consumers will buy less gasoline.
2. *Allocations* place floors and ceilings on the amount of fuel available to each consumer through, for example, coupon rationing and fuel lifelines.
3. *Incentives* provide the consumer with a positive reward for using less energy. Tax breaks may be offered to homeowners who insulate or to businesses that adopt more energy-efficient processes.
4. *Regulations* take the form of simple legal requirements and prohibitions. Federal legislation could mandate a minimum mileage standard for automobiles, and building codes could be expanded to require strict insulation standards.
5. *Exhortation* is the proclamation of the economic and other advantages of conservation; it ensures that the public is well-informed, and creates a climate of opinion in which energy conservation is seen as desirable and worthwhile. This category encompasses such diverse actions as public education commercials and appliance efficiency labels.

Many conservation programs will involve elements of each of these strategies. The importance of an effective combination cannot be exaggerated. Where there's no will, there's no way.

Above all, the level of future energy consumption must be viewed as a matter of choice. Nothing is binding about the curves that many energy policy studies extrapolate to project future demand. In the past, such curves have tended to become self-fulfilling prophecies. Now they should become "self-undoing prophecies." Every new energy source has costs and risks, and these will grow as energy use levels rise. Our cheapest and best option today is to harness the major portion of our energy budget that we currently waste.
—DENIS HAYES

Recommended Actions

☐ The President should dedicate himself and his administration to a new energy policy based (1) on conservation and end-use efficiency, (2) on sophisticated fossil-fuel technology, as an interim measure, and (3) on decentralized, small-scale power systems drawing energy from renewable sources.

☐ The President should announce the phasing out of all federal nuclear power programs not only for safety reasons, but also because nuclear power plants use up massive amounts of capital badly needed for other social purposes, because electricity can be generated more efficiently by small decentralized plants located near the consumers they serve, and because nuclear technology absorbs talents and resources needed to attain rational energy goals.

☐ Argonne, Brookhaven, Oak Ridge, and other national laboratories should be ordered to turn their attention from nuclear power to conservation techniques, to more efficient combustion of fossil fuels as a transitional technology, and especially to small-scale systems harnessing solar energy and solar variants such as wind; federal funding of other research and development should also reflect these priorities.

☐ Antitrust laws must be strictly enforced in the energy industry, where a few giant corporations that already control most US fossil fuel reserves are buying up uranium reserves and geothermal leases.

☐ All levels of government must review and revise laws, codes, and regulations that impede the efficient use of energy, such as deterrents to the upgrading of existing buildings to make them energy-efficient.

☐ Public Utility Commissions must be encouraged to rationalize electricity rate structures, which now tend to reward wastefulness and penalize thrift and which charge the poor more per unit of electricity than they charge the rich.

Once a bright hope shared by all mankind, including myself, the rash proliferation of atomic-power plants has become one of the ugliest clouds overhanging America.

     —DAVID LILIENTHAL
      (First chairman of the AEC)

Control of the Atom

Peaceful and warlike atoms are not twins, they are one. Fission reactors in commercial power plants produce the stuff of which atomic bombs are made. Proliferation of nuclear power plants in this tinderbox world is an indirect form of nuclear weapons proliferation, and makes a mockery of the Nuclear Nonproliferation Treaty. But the United States still possesses the power to turn civilian nuclear power off, worldwide. Most nuclear installations abroad require US support for their construction, operation, and maintenance. If the US shuts down its own nuclear industry for safety reasons, as it should, the shut-down of nuclear industries in other countries will be a political if not a practical necessity. The US's power to act unilaterally will vanish, however, when nuclear industries in other countries acquire the ability to support themselves unaided. If that is allowed to happen, neither the US nor any other nation will be able to do much on its own initiative to halt nuclear proliferation. We must control the atom in the next few years if we are ever to control it at all.

The control room of the Peachbottom reactor, Virginia.
Photo courtesy of David Comey.

The Atom

The greatest danger to human survival is the splitting of uranium and plutonium atoms—in war, in peace, or in what we thought would be peace but didn't turn out that way, for the atom is the same whether in fist or glove.

The spread of nuclear reactors to make electricity is today the driving force behind the spread of nuclear weapons. Lacking the peace and perfectability needed to coexist with nuclear fission, we who honored the first men to split the atom now race headlong to see who will be the last. Having rejected in our nuclear alchemy the thrust of billions of years' purely chemical evolution, we could negate all that evolution in a few hours, or make it crumble slowly through millenia. If we are not to make the earth all too like the moon, we must now abandon the nuclear experiment, redirect the talent and resources that went into it, and explore primal forces that are more forgiving, more creative, and less likely to destroy us.

Many nuclear advocates deny that the United States can stop nuclear proliferation. They say that if the US does not export nuclear technology, others will—for there is, they claim, no alternative. We might as well get the business and try to use it as a lever to slow the inevitable spread of nuclear weapons to nations and subnational groups in other regions. By this approach, to paraphrase Paul Ylvasaker, we control nuclear proliferation by selling it in an area safely larger than the one we last failed to control it in.

It may seem a fantasy to suggest, with more than 50 power reactors operating today in the US and several hundred operating or planned throughout the world, that the nuclear genie can be put back into its bottle. Yet the genie has only partly emerged—thousands of reactors are proposed a few decades hence, tens of thousands thereafter—and the cork is still in our hands. For at least the next five to ten years, all countries will continue to depend on the US not only for the technical and economic support, but also for the *political* support they need to justify their nuclear programs. Other countries, however great their nuclear ambitions, cannot yet make such support for themselves, but must borrow it. Indeed, the tangible support we lend to other countries' nuclear programs—money, technology, fuel-cycle services—is less important than the political example we provide. For US policy is widely imitated even in the most highly industrialized countries, where public and private divisions over nuclear policy are already deep and growing deeper daily.

Nuclear expansion has been virtually halted by grass-roots opposition in Japan, Holland, and Italy; has been severely impeded in West Germany, Switzerland, Austria, and France; has been slowed and perhaps will soon be stopped in Sweden; has been rejected in Norway and, so far; in Denmark, Australia, and New Zealand; has been widely questioned in Britain, Canada, and (within the scientific community) the USSR; has been opposed in Spain, Brazil, India, Thailand, and elsewhere.

Our current policy toward the technology we have so eagerly pressed on the rest of the world will inevitably help one side of other countries' nuclear disputes and hurt the other. So profound are their own doubts that other countries' nuclear programs could be scuttled virtually everywhere by unilateral US action.

How to Turn Off the Atom

To turn off nuclear power and nuclear proliferation throughout the world would require four prompt, clear statements by the United States:

1. We are abandoning our nascent nuclear power program as unsafe, unreliable, unnecessary, unsociable, and unconscionable; and we are phasing out our support of other countries' nuclear programs.
2. We are redirecting the resources of our nuclear program to a "soft" energy path [defined in chapter on energy]—to a combination of greatly increased end-use efficiency, diverse "soft" supply technologies, and transitional fossil-fuel technologies.
3. We will unreservedly help all other interested countries, both rich and poor, to do the same, adapting the same broad principles to their needs and learning from each other's experience.
4. We shall start to treat non-proliferation, control of civilian fission technology, *and* strategic arms reduction as interrelated parts of the same problem; we shall no longer pretend, while we are asking other nations not to make bombs, that we ourselves feel more secure with bombs than without them.

Nobody can *guarantee* that such an initiative would work. We can, however, see that failure to try could be a shortcut to Armageddon. An atoms-for-bucks program incites an atoms-for-leveling response, now ubiquitous. And many analysts who have carefully studied the European

Connecticut Yankee plant, photo by Tom Zetterstrom.

and world nuclear industry (Professor Irvin Bupp of Howard Business School, for example) are confident that no other country—not even France, Germany, or India—could withstand domestic political pressure and persist with a domestic nuclear power program (let alone nuclear exports) if the United States did not want it to. To these analysts, and to us, the policies just mentioned sound politically irresistible to East and West, North and South alike. Strong anecdotal evidence confirms that this is particularly true in the Soviet bloc. In giving up the export market that our own reactor designs have dominated, we would be demonstrating that this step is motivated by a desire for peace, not for profit. In recognizing that the supposed dichotomy between the peaceful and warlike atom is a fiction, and linking our concerns with both, we would seize our best chance to break the cycle of hypocrisy that has stalled arms control. By reducing pressures on scarce fuels and by helping poor countries to use their most plentiful energy resources, we would be reducing the international tensions that now distract so many countries from sound development and divert them toward nuclear proliferation. (It says much about quasi-civilian nuclear power as a spin-off from military programs that we ever had to have an Atoms for Peace program. Imagine a Sunbeams for Peace

program! Sunbeams have probably not been used for war since the battle of Syracuse.)

It would be the essence of nuclear statesmanship today, then, for the United States not to use its temporary political leverage in ways that would increase its commercial dominance, but rather, in an unprecedented manifestation of reverence for life, to turn off nuclear power and nuclear proliferation everywhere. We could thus turn on policies for energy use, social behavior, and respect for other societies that our grandchildren can live with; but we must stop passing the buck before our clients start passing the bomb. No more important step could be taken to revitalize the American dream.

Dangers by the Numbers

Why should we try to turn off a worldwide industry that we worked hard to establish, for which we had bright hopes only a generation ago, and in which reputable governments and corporations, many following our example, have invested hundreds of billions of dollars, francs, marks, pounds, yen, guilder, kronor, rubles, and lire? What are the problems, more clearly seen now than before, that make it so urgent to draw back from the brink of an irreversible mistake?

1. Nuclear reactors of every type inevitably produce large amounts of toxic and explosive materials. These can be used by governments, factions, terrorist groups, or even individuals, to make weapons of mass destruction. Such misuse can be made more difficult, mainly by repressive measures, but can never be absolutely prevented. Plutonium stolen in one country can be used by another, or by people with no particular country, against a third. Strategic deterrents are useless against the stateless or anonymous terrorist. The next 20 years' planned expansion of the nuclear industry would mean some 20,000 bombs' worth of bomb material being shipped each year as an item of commerce within the same international community that has never been able to stop bank robberies, hijackings, or the heroin traffic. A few decades later the plutonium flow would again have increased enormously with no end in sight, becoming the world's main fuel. Inevitably, despite the best intentions, more reactors must mean the availability to more overwrought people, terrorist groups, and dissatisfied countries, of weapons that combine awesome physical and psychological power.

2. Nuclear facilities store enormous inventories of radioactive materials. These must stay infallibly isolated from living things for geological, or rather theological, periods—up to a hundred million years or so. We have no idea how to guarantee such long-term storage and no idea

Plutonium provides the first rational justification for widespread intelligence gathering against the civilian population. In the past, federal courts have taken a skeptical view of attempts to justify spying on national security grounds, but with the very real threat of nuclear terrorism in the picture, the justification is going to sound very convincing.

—RUSSELL AYRES

whether it can be done at all. Proposed ways to shorten the required time have proved impracticable. Recent research suggests that even tiny escapes of such materials as plutonium, neptunium, and americium may be patient and clever enough to reconcentrate themselves greatly in some biological systems, thus defeating their original dilution. What little we know about ways these materials behave in the environment is far from reassuring.

3. Even if we could contain the wastes in the long run, we could not be sure of containing in the short run the far larger amounts of radioactivity in reactors and other nuclear facilities. A large reactor contains as much radioactiv-

ity as the fallout from several thousand Hiroshima bombs. A large reprocessing plant can contain dozens of times more. A substantial release from either is physically possible and would be an unprecedented catastrophe, killing perhaps as many people as a major war.

4. With such facilities ringing our cities we are more vulnerable to relatively low-technology sabotage by a very few people, or to acts of non-nuclear war, than we are to strategic attack—and we might not even know who did it. Even without sabotage, many experts think, flaws in the facilities' engineering may be so deep and irremediable that public safety is already at risk through random accidents.

5. Nuclear power has basic and unresolved engineering problems in profusion. Yet nuclear safety may be not a mere engineering problem that we can solve by sufficient care, but rather a new kind of problem that we can solve only with infallible people, none of whom is now observable. Nuclear technologists try to be careful, but nobody knows whether they can ever be careful *enough* in a technology where, as Hannes Alfvén puts it, "No acts of God can be permitted." The nuclear industry is building a record of proliferating human error. Quality control is lamentable. Repairing nuclear systems is becoming more and more difficult. This complex and dangerous enterprise appears already to be out of control. It will become even more so if rapid growth, loss of novelty, retirement of dedicated pioneers, commercial pressures, boredom, and routine sloppiness take their historic toll here and abroad.

6. Selective conclusions of the Rasmussen Report are now being given the forced exposure predicted by biographers of nuclear apology. But with respect to this exercise in probability, or any other, however endless its pages, there is no scientific basis for calculating how likely a major accident is (let alone sabotage) or for guaranteeing that its effects will not exceed a particular level. What we do know is that all precautions are, in unknown degree and for fundamental reasons, inherently imperfect. The stakes in that uncertainty are very high.

7. The two sets of experts debating nuclear safety cannot

Of all the changes introduced by man into the household of nature, large-scale nuclear fission is undoubtedly the most dangerous and profound. As a result, ionising radiation has become the most serious agent of pollution of the environment and the greatest threat to man's survival on earth. The attention of the layman, not surprisingly, has been captured by the atom bomb, although there is at least a chance that it may never be used again. The danger to humanity created by the so-called peaceful uses of atomic energy may be much greater.

A new 'dimension' is given also by the fact that while man now can—and does—create radioactive elements, there is nothing he can do to reduce their radioactivity once he has created them. No chemical reaction, no physical interference, only the passage of time reduces the intensity of radiation once it has been set going. Carbon-14 has a half-life of 5900 years, which means that it takes nearly 6000 years for its radioactivity to decline to one-half of what it was before. The half-life of strontium-90 is twenty-eight years. But whatever the length of the half-life, some radiation continues almost indefinitely, and there is nothing that can be done about it, except to try and put the radioactive substance into a safe place.

But what is a safe place, let us say, for the enormous amounts of radioactive waste products created by nuclear reactors? No place on earth can be shown to be safe.

The most massive wastes are, of course, the nuclear reactors themselves after they have become unserviceable.

There is a lot of discussion on the trivial economic question of whether they will last for twenty, twenty-five, or thirty years. No one discusses the humanly vital point that they cannot be dismantled and cannot be shifted but have to be left standing where they are, probably for centuries, perhaps for thousands of years, an active menace to all life, silently leaking radioactivity into air, water and soil. No one has considered the number and location of these satanic mills which will relentlessly accumulate. Earthquakes, of course, are not supposed to happen, nor wars, nor civil disturbances, nor riots like those that infested American cities. Disused nuclear power stations will stand as unsightly monuments to unquiet man's assumption that nothing but tranquillity, from now on, stretches before him, or else—that the future counts as nothing compared with the slightest economic gain now.

No degree of prosperity could justify the accumulation of large amounts of highly toxic substances which nobody knows how to make 'safe' and which remain an incalculable danger to the whole of creation for historical or even geological ages. To do such a thing is a transgression against life itself, a transgression infinitely more serious than any crime ever perpetrated by man. The idea that a civilisation could sustain itself on the basis of such a transgression is an ethical, spiritual, and metaphysical monstrosity. It means conducting the economic affairs of man as if people really did not matter at all.

—E.F. SCHUMACHER

both be right. But there is a fail-safe way to decide with whom to entrust your future. If critics of the nuclear industry are wrong but you believe them, the consequences are not very large. We know from studies by the Energy Policy Project of the Ford Foundation, ERDA, and others, that nuclear growth is unnecessary if we have even a modest energy conservation program. If, on the other hand, defenders of the nuclear industry are wrong but you have believed them, your disbelief will be posthumous.

8. Death, cancer, genetic damage, and contaminated land are the most permanent, but not necessarily the largest, risks that nuclear power imposes. It also has enormous social and political costs. Our peculiar vulnerability to nuclear violence and coercion is starting to edge us towards a garrison state. Wiretapping, infiltration, surveillance, security clearances, computer dossiers, intimidation of dissenters, private armies, checkpoints, armed guards, extended powers of search and arrest—all these would weaken our traditional civil liberties as we tried to protect

ourselves from potentially hostile people in our midst. In a society whose technologies give unprecedented power to the lone fanatic, "unusual" people become a perceived menace. People must be made safe for the technology rather than the reverse. Trying to guess *who* might be potentially threatening can bring about the kinds of political change that our nuclear arsenal was designed to prevent—an efficient and sophisticated police state for the sake of "security."

By making possible catastrophic events that cannot be allowed to happen, we commit ourselves to social engineering that makes us less free. Our civil liberties have been preserved so far, as Russell Ayres points out, to a large extend because we have not yet had to decide whether, for example, we should torture a *suspected* terrorist to try to prevent a threatened nuclear explosion. We have not yet felt the need—not, at least, close to home—to destroy the earth in order to save it.

9. Broad political hazards also arise from our reliance on

Like most people in the West I first heard the name Hiroshima in August, 1945, when I was a small boy at my grandparents' home in rural Manitoba. In the months that followed I read all I could find about this amazing discovery, "atomic energy". The popular awe it inspired, the aura of impressive mystery about it, must have been instrumental in my later decision to major in nuclear physics at university. But what fascinated me was the science and the technology—not their consequences. It did not become clear to me until much later that, at 8:15 am 6 August, 1945, "atomic energy" had killed 200,000 people. The connection between the science and the slaughter was somehow academic, devoid of reality. In due course, as I began collecting popular books on "atomic energy," I acquired a copy of the first Penguin edition of John Hersey's Pulitzer Prize-winning book *Hiroshima*. But I didn't read it. Hiroshima was just a name, a symbol for an event of unparalleled awfulness. I was willing to acknowledge the mythology and leave it at that. I did not want to know the details. I was pretty certain I would not be able to handle them.

This attitude persisted until the middle of 1974, when I began writing a book on nuclear power for Penguin. Within three months I found myself inextricably immersed in the world of nuclear weapons. In the mid-1970s with so many nuclear weapons in so many hands—and by now apparently taken for granted by almost everyone—the thought of Hiroshima came to me with an obsessive resonance. Then, in June this year, one of the world's best-known and most venerable peace organisations, Gensuikin, the Japan Congress against A- and H-Bombs, invited me to be their guest at the Thirtieth Atomic Disaster Anniversary World Conference Against A- and

H-Bombs, to be held in Hiroshima. I was by no means sure that I wanted to know any more than I already did about the consequences of a nuclear explosion on a city: I accepted the invitation with mixed feelings.

For my part, it would have been unthinkable to leave Hiroshima without visiting the Peace Memorial Museum; I made my way there the moment the closing session of the conference concluded. The admission change is trifling—50 yen, when a newspaper costs 70. I found myself almost the only Occidental in the eddying crowd moving slowly past the exhibits. As you step into the first chamber your field of view is filled by a ceiling-high blow-up of a US Air Force photograph, with the official lettering in the lower right-hand corner: "Hiroshima (atomic) strike." The towering cloud, already drifting eastward, casts a black shadow behind it, over what an hour before had been the city of Hiroshima. In the middle of the chamber is a circular enclosure on the floor, perhaps five metres in diameter. Suspended from the ceiling, so that the scale height of 600 metres brings it to your eye level, is a red ball about the size of a billiard ball. Below it, inside the enclosure, is a scale model of Hiroshima after the blast—a wasteland of brownish grey dust, criss-crossed by straight lines where streets had been. Only a few concrete ruins are still standing, except towards the outskirts of the city. The green of the surrounding mountains gives stark emphasis to the lifeless aftermath where the city had been.

Set into the wall beyond the model city is a diorama: three figures, two women and a child, hideously injured, staggering towards you out of a background of raging flames. It is the only exhibit which is anything but matter-of-fact.

—WALT PATTERSON

strategic nuclear weapons. We cannot actually use them without committing bilateral suicide, which an over-stressed leader, in final despair, might wish to achieve for us. This is not a very persuasive deterrent. So we try to prove, by more oblique political gestures, our national willingness to use them. Barred by the very power of our weapons from directly demonstrating our resolve to use that power if necessary, we demonstrate our "credibility"—as Jonathan Schell argues—by fighting non-nuclear wars as theater (just as terrorist atrocities are essentially theater). But since the aim of symbolic-war theater is not to achieve traditional military objectives but rather to score psychological points by presenting the united front of a resolute guarantor, dissident public opin-

ion at home cannot be allowed to belie the image. Demonstrators against such theatrical wars destroy the intended impression of united resolve. Repression or deception—the creation of false images at home in order to influence people to support Executive policy abroad, must therefore substitute for truth and reality. Recent events have painfully emphasized the dangers of contrived consensus.

This political threat will not go away: the military imperatives of having a nuclear weapon to rattle are in conflict with the political imperatives of a free society.

10. The social costs of the atom range even further. Suppose that we determine to protect from geological or social mishaps a greatly expanded store of civilian or military nuclear waste. We shall then need some elite cadre

dedicated to maintaining the most meticulous and vigilant care, continuously and indefinitely. We shall therefore need a rigidly stratified or controlled society to insulate this "technological priesthood" from social unrest. We are committing ourselves in the same way to guard our military bombs forever under rigorous discipline, free from strikes, commercial pressures, and dissent.

Even in making political decisions about nuclear hazards that are disputed, unknown, or unknowable—hazards that depart from everyday experience, are long-term, and cannot be directly sensed—governments are tempted to abandon democratic decision-making and political accountability, even at the cost of their own perceived legitimacy. "Leaving it to the experts" is the easiest course when citizens from diverse walks of life cannot make up their minds or might decide "wrong." Many strategic decisions in the military sphere, too, are now made in secret, by we know not whom, lest public resolution of conflict, the keystone of our political process, somehow give the "wrong" answer. But if the people can choose their President, and can elect those who decide our foreign, fiscal, labor, industrial, scientific, and judicial policies, can they no longer be trusted to choose the technologies that will shape their lives? Is not our government founded not on "we the experts," but on "we the people"?

11. In making ourselves dependent on a vulnerable and demanding technology of unique difficulty and complexity, we are committing ourselves to protect that technology from economic and political risk. If a nuclear accident, here or abroad, or growing public unease and dissent threatened our huge investment and a large part of our electrical supply, would we stifle the dissent and accept the risk, or turn off the country and accept the resulting disruption? Further nuclear growth would face us with such choices in a mere decade or two. And likewise, the more we depend on a nuclear-armed military authority, the more our checked and balanced political institutions must consolidate into a quick-reacting autocracy.

12. Suppose for a moment that the atom presented none of these environmental and social problems. Would the peaceful atom then be a good idea? No. Even then it would exhibit the broader political and economic problems of big, centralized, electrified technology. These problems alone are enough to cause economic and social disintegration. And there are grave logistical problems: the size and complexity of nuclear installations would keep us from building them fast enough to supply our energy wants. Even if we could build reactors fast enough, we would still have too much electricity and too little fluid fuel and low-temperature heat to run our economy properly. We would have committed so much of our scarce resources to a

Inspecting uranium fuel bundles, photo by Samuel Musgrave, Atomic Industrial Forum.

A demonstration against nuclear power in California.
Photo by Tom Turner.

technology extraordinarily demanding of them that we would have foreclosed more attractive options that we should be pursuing instead. For the United States as for other countries—even those as oil-dependent as Japan and Denmark—nuclear power is not only unnecessary but prevents us from doing, until too late, what we should be doing instead.

The Fission-Free Future

Ultimately, to avoid the obvious risk of blowing each other up and the less obvious risk of poisoning ourselves and our social patterns, we shall need a fission-free world where the nearest reactions proceed at a remotely sited, extensively tested spherical reactor 93 million miles away. Ideally, such a world would have no nuclear weapons either—a utopian concept that is worth working hard for. But whether or not we eventually succeed in removing the nuclear sword from over our heads, what are the interim steps that could lay the groundwork for a non-nuclear energy future?

Our nuclear power policies are inseparable from our broader energy and social policies. We cannot abandon nuclear power ourselves, nor expect others to do so, without *at the same time starting to do other things instead that*

make more sense. But we can certainly make it known that we will not enter into new contracts to sell reactors or their technologies abroad, or to provide fuel-cycle services for foreign reactors. We can stop contributing to international programs to develop new kinds of reactors. We can contribute to devising the best ways we can to get out of the nuclear business, civil and military, with the least residual hazard. We can shelve plans for expanding our fuel-cycle facilities, such as reprocessing and enrichment plants, since without a nuclear industry we shall have far better uses for money and skills. We can start to explore for the first time the technical details of phasing out our nuclear program. We can press far harder for strategic arms reduction, recognizing that we can already vaporize everybody so many times over that continuing to make three new hydrogen bombs each day is profligate as well as obscene. We can suspend our work on the strategic cruise missile, an impressive technical achievement that threatens to signal the start of yet another round in the ruinously expensive arms race. We can develop a plan for the orderly closing down of existing nuclear power stations, starting with those closest to cities and those with the most obvious and dangerous technical flaws.

More immediate steps are also needed if we are to retain options needed later and to demonstrate to the world our commitment to a gentler policy. We should, as David Lilienthal recently urged, immediately stop all exports of nuclear technology and equipment (save the tiny fraction used for medical research and other clearly humanitarian needs). We should announce that we plan to phase out existing technical and fuel-cycle support for foreign nuclear programs (except for cooperation in reducing the hazards we have already created). We should insist that the International Atomic Energy Agency stop promoting nuclear power—a task manifestly inconsistent with its more important job of stopping the proliferation of nuclear weapons. We should enforce antitrust and securities laws in the US nuclear industry, and stop the use of taxpayers' and utility customers' money to promote nuclear power at home and abroad.

We should immediately terminate the fast-breeder program, and start to pour its billions of dollars into things we really need. Likewise, we should immediately stop all steps toward a plutonium economy, including construction of new facilities to handle plutonium-bearing fuel: since recycling plutonium and similar materials cannot greatly reduce the total amount of it, we shall not need to recycle it as part of our terminal waste-management programs. Since we shall not need to extract plutonium as a fuel even if it were economic to do so (and we do not yet know whether reprocessing is advisable at all for waste management), we

In 1950, the United States, with 152 million people, depended on foreign sources for more than half of its supplies of only four of the thirteen basic minerals required by a modern industrial society—bauxite, manganese, nickel, and tin. By 1970, potash and zinc had lengthened the list. U.S. Department of the Interior projections indicate that by the end of this century—when the United States population is expected to be 265 million—the country will be primarily dependent on imports for its supply of 12 of the 13 minerals, including iron, chromium, copper, lead, sulfur, and tungsten.

A rise in the price of energy, one of the principal factors in determining the cost of extracting minerals from the earth, can have the effect of reducing economically recoverable reserves. Many assumptions about the future availability of minerals are posited on the availability of vast quantities of cheap energy.

Relying on price increases to expand mineral reserves could prove economically destabilizing. Rather than making the mining of marginal deposits of minerals economically feasible, constantly escalating prices might create a situation in which the cost of minerals exceeds their value to society. If a mineral is readily available only at a price that triggers rampant inflation, availability becomes a largely academic concept.

New technologies—especially recycling, the potential of which has barely been tapped—present opportunities for limited stretching of mineral reserves. Yet the reality that mineral resources have limits is irrefutable, regardless of price and technology. If mined long enough any mineral resource must sooner or later be exhausted. These economic and technical supply problems underscore the importance demand plays in any consideration of the future adequacy of mineral resources.

Population pressure on water supplies is most evident in agriculture, with irrigation needs representing one principal source of future world water demand. Satisfying these needs will prove increasingly difficult in the years ahead because most of the best irrigation sites in the world have already been developed. Irrigated farm land, which expanded by nearly 3 percent per year during the sixties, will be developed more slowly in the future. Indeed, the shortage of fresh water for irrigation will severely constrain efforts to expand world food supplies during the remainder of this century.

As the demand for water in agriculture grows, it is meet-ing vigorous competition for available supplies from efforts to expand energy production. In the northern Great Plains of the United States, ranchers and coal mining interests are waging court battles to determine who will get to use scarce water. Proposed plants to convert coal into natural gas would consume vast amounts of water.

Homo sapiens, a single species, threatens the survival of the countless thousands of plant and animal species through its numbers and activities. The addition of three-quarters of a billion people to the world's population over the last decade has, in many regions, upset the balance between human, plant, and animal life. The very size of the human population is altering natural environments: rural habitats are urbanized, forests are turned into farmland. The chemical wastes from manufacturing and commerce, and the widespread use of pesticides and fertilizers to improve nature's productivity threaten to break the life cycles of many species.

The process of extinction is not solely an aesthetic problem. Many plants and animals are vitally important to human well-being. Plankton form the crucial foundation of the ocean food chain, but oceanic pollution is growing faster than man's ability even to analyze its effects, much less control it.

It is difficult to predict which plants might prove helpful to man in the future. The cinchona tree of Latin America was considered useless until it was discovered that quinine, which can be extracted from it, effectively suppresses malaria.

It is tragically ironic that in many countries where increases in agricultural production are most needed, population growth is even now destroying important native plant species. At a time when millions of dollars are being spent to develop food crops that can be grown in the Andes or in desert environments, the world can little afford the loss of those species that have already adapted to harsh habitats.

The risk to man posed by the extinction of plant and animal species cannot be easily quantified. When extinction is a slow natural process, human beings and the environment can adjust. As more and more species are jeopardized by man's increased numbers and ecologically disruptive activities, the odds mount that the complex web of life that supports man may be dangerously and irrevocably disrupted.

—LESTER BROWN, PATRICIA MCGRATH, AND BRUCE STOKES

Suddenly the message has come across loud and clear: We are living beyond our means. As a people we have developed a life-style that is draining the earth of its priceless and irreplaceable resources without regard for the future of our children and people all around the world.

For far too long Americans regarded ecologists—the scientists who study the relationships between living beings and the environment—as just another breed of prophets of doom. Or they treated ecologists' dire predictions as expressions of exaggerated concern by small groups of stubborn people who cared chiefly about wilderness areas and set their love for natural beauty and for lost, idyllic ways of living above the reasonable necessities of our modern, progressive, industrialized world. But now, unexpectedly, we have discovered tht it is the ecologists who have been facing the realities—the very hard realities of where the wanton and irresponsible use of natural resources in this country has been taking us.

And instead of receiving clarification from our government as to what resources we have and what we can look forward to, we learned with astonishment that our officials were dependent on industry for information about available reserves, information that industry too often treated as a trade secret. Assurances given in one week were taken back the next week, and regulations intended to protect turned out to be based on the vaguest assumptions about the situation. We have had a babel of contending voices, a proliferation of rumors that distract us from the problems that must be met, assertions refuted by further assertions and arguments instead of answers.

All this has been brought home to us by the energy crisis. . . .

Whatever triggered the energy crisis, we can now plainly see the larger, underlying cause. What has been draining our resources, continually raising our demands for more energy, polluting the earth and the air and the water is what we ourselves have been doing every day as a matter of course. The basic trouble is the way our everyday life is organized, the way each family lives.

Of course no one family causes an exorbitant drain on our resources. But when all the simple, convenient and for the most part pleasant things we have and use and discard are multiplied by many millions of users—and by the hundreds of millions more who are longing to become users—it becomes devastatingly clear how the strain on every kind of resource has come about. And it should be clear also that no merely palliative measures, no attempt on our part to become independent of the rest of the world, will solve the problems we face.

It is the life-style of the country—the kind of life each family aspires to and takes for granted as good and desirable—that has placed this incredible burden on the

virgin material if necessary to make up for loss of material in the cycle, then sent on to manufacturers who make finished products of it.

On a routine shopping day, we go to the store with cola bottles, a shampoo bottle, an egg carton, and a bread wrapper in hand. At the store we get our bottle deposits back, refill the shampoo container from a jug with a measured-flow spout, choose bread from a yeasty-smelling assortment of loaves at the bakery counter, and select our eggs from crates. We return home in our eight-year-old, classically designed car that has more than 90,000 miles on the odometer and a lot of life left in it—if the store is too far or our purchases too heavy for walking or the bicycle. We turn on lights powered by municipal or neighborhood solar collectors and distribution systems, and put our purchases away. No wrestling with packaging, no trash to throw out. We cook on a stove that burns methane from our sewage reprocessor. After dinner, we stroll down to the river to watch fishermen test the clean water for trout.

Photo by Philip Evans

world and has brought us—and all other people who share our aspirations—into crisis.

This, then, is the challenge: how to change our life-style.

To meet the challenge we shall need a very widespread understanding of the real nature of the crisis—a crisis that is no passing inconvenience; no mere by-product of the oil-producing countries using the only weapons they have to make themselves heard; no figment of environmentalists' imagined fears; and no by-product of any presently existing system of government, whether free-enterprise, socialist or communist. Our life-style is the outcome of the inventions made during the last 400 years as we have searched for quicker, easier, more mechanized ways of doing things for ever-growing, more demanding populations. It is the outcome of an implicit belief in the existence of unlimited and unfailing resources on our one small planet and an explicit belief that human beings have the right to exploit every kind of resource as they can and will.

Now we must come to terms with reality. We must develop a life-style based on an understanding that the earth's resources are limited and that use of what we have must be combined with conservation. A new life-style also can flow directly from the efforts of science and the capabilities of advanced technology. But fundamentally success will depend on an overriding commitment on the part of every adult and on the willingness of families to educate their children to have very different expectations about a good life.

What does all this mean for individuals and families?

As I see it, it means above all that men and women must inform themselves and must demand to be informed. As individuals, as readers of the press, as viewers of television, as members of every kind of organization, as tenants and homeowners, as producers and consumers, as members of communities, as voters in elections at every level of government, we must firmly demand to be given information—demand that governments obtain and pass on to us, as citizens, enough factual information so that we can intelligently judge national policy and act wisely in making local decisions.

The immediate energy crisis should be enough to alert us to this most pressing of all our needs. The information about our resources that is necessary if we are to make viable plans is not wholly available to us, and no legislation now exists that would ensure its availability. Our response could be simply pessimism, confusion and an attitude of each-man-for-himself. But I do not believe Americans would tolerate such an outcome. Nevertheless, we shall get the kinds of information we need—and the kinds of leadership that can provide firm information—only as we make demands and make our demands heard.

—MARGARET MEAD

How to Get There From Here

Dreaming is one thing, making visions come true is another. We must provide fundamentally sound legislative bases upon which industry can restructure itself in the best interests of the people, and to promote cultural continuity and longevity. Our laws must evolve as we do. The steps in this redirection must be first to eliminate waste wherever possible, then to recycle what wastes we produce.

Eliminating waste is a matter of letting resources' scarcity be reflected in prices, encouraging conservation, and the production of more durable, more reusable goods.

Prices that reflect scarcity are required by the law of supply and demand. We must eliminate artificial advantages for extractive industries. The General Accounting Office recommends that the Mining Law of 1872 be changed to require leases on public lands, and to require detailed exploration, damage-minimization, and land-reclamation plans. Our hard rocks and minerals would be pulled out of the ground more slowly, ensuring that supplies will be available in the future if we needed.

As for fossil fuels, we should eliminate depletion allowances and restrict exploration to safe places. The Gulf of Alaska is one example of an extremely hazardous area that is about to be exploited; grave damage to rich fisheries is unavoidable. That kind of price is simply too high, so exploration should be disallowed. As for land and water, we should tax projects that drain aquifers, tax new low-density urban developments, and grant permanent tax advantages to cropland. And as for timber, we can eliminate *ad valorem* taxes and end the capital gains treatment of profits.

We should encourage conservation by giving loans and temporary tax advantages to urban revitalization projects, to research projects on conservation, and to infant industries that produce conservation-oriented systems. We should end quantity discounts for fossil fuels, electricity, and water.

The ramifications of policies that encourage conservation would be profound. The United States could meet all its new energy needs for the next 25 years, says Denis Hayes, by improving its use of fossil fuels. Industry uses 44 percent of its fossil fuels to produce steam. If the water for

By shifting from a pastoral land-based energy system to a fossil-fuel based economy, the world as a whole has been able to carry an industrial-age population about 25 times greater than could be supported under land-based pastoral systems alone. This is done by short-circuiting energy flow through monocultural food production and fossil-fuel energy-intensive agriculture.

Viewed from the perspective of millenia of future time, the squandering of energy reserves on such short-term frivolities as supersonic transport and snowmobiles in the 20th century will seem unimportant compared with our gross destruction of the carrying capacity of the land. Today's high technology, high fertilization, high erosion land uses will carry a much more significant deficit of potential for carrying capacity to those who may inhabit this planet after us. Our only hope is a radically different land ethic, accommodating understanding of the energy function of life on the planet. The basis for this ethic must be taught as a first priority from pre-school age onward, and should form a criterion for election of responsible political candidates. The basis of the ethic is the fundamental and provable knowledge that all life is merely a temporary restructuring and ordering of energy pathways and that those pathways are completely dependent upon the ability of the land to store and convert solar energy.

—ROBERT CURRY

that steam were preheated, using elementary solar technology, steam output per unit of fossil fuel would be tripled. If the steam was then used to produce electricity first, before its use in industrial processes, more electricity would be produced than the entire industrial sector now uses. A court decision now prevents industry from competing with utilities by selling surplus by-product electricity; that decision should be reversed.

We should save energy by retrofitting buildings with conservation-oriented equipment, such as insulation and windows that open and close. The American Institute of Architects estimates that if we adopted a high-priority national program emphasizing energy-efficient buildings, we could save the equivalent of more than 12.5 million barrels of oil per day by 1990.

Conservation of metals and minerals will, in part, be a by-product of high prices for materials and energy. Many short-lived or wasteful products will price themselves out of the market. After the economy has adjusted somewhat to these forces, further conservation can be achieved by systematically encouraging production of durable products. The law against nonreturnable bottles has decreased beverage costs in Oregon without affecting sales. Similar bans could be imposed on nondurable goods. Tax discounts could be given for repairs, especially in housing. Incentives and funding could be granted to cities to establish sewage treatment facilities that recycle detoxified water and use treated sewage as a source of methane and fertilizer.

When we have a good start on conserving, we can begin encouraging recycling programs. It is imperative that we design them to prevent dependence on a continuing stream of waste; cities that have sunk capital into facilities that burn wastes as a source of energy are subsidizing waste. Instead, we should concentrate on means of recovering the materials in the waste, then perhaps derive energy from the residue.

A major step would be to end discrimination in freight rates against scrap and used materials. Some recovery industries would become financially feasible immediately, even accounting for high labor costs. To develop others, it would be necessary to grant seed money and temporary tax advantages. Once the industries were established, these incentives should be withdrawn; market conditions would ensure their survival.

Such measures as these will necessitate relocating people who work in industries that now rely on continued exploitation of scarce resources. This is a task that must be done sooner or later in any case. To solve the problem, unions could establish mutually-funded national communication networks that match displaced workers with openings in industries that must grow to balance the production-reclamation system. Construction workers will retrofit buildings with insulation and windows that open. Machinists will manufacture recycling and heat-reclamation equipment. Machine operators will produce electricity from industrial steam. Semi-skilled workers will rip unholstry out of car bodies to facilitate recycling. Unskilled workers will sort and wash bottles. There will be abundant jobs in growing industries, and smart unions will take advantage of the opportunity to broaden their bases. Where unions fail, governments could establish similar placement services.

Within 25 or 30 years, we could redirect our society toward dynamic equilibrium in its use of resources. If we use our resources sparingly, if we design reusable and durable products, if we use energy efficiently, and if we recover the materials in articles that cannot be repaired, we could minimize our dependence on infusions of raw materials. Then we would have designed a pattern of cultural longevity and continuity.

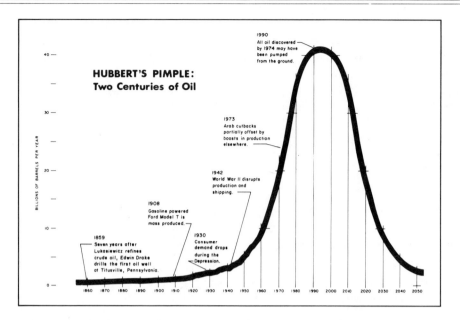

It is difficult for people living now, who have become accustomed to the steady exponential growth in the consumption of energy from the fossil fuels, to realize how transitory the fossil-fuel epoch will eventually prove to be when it is viewed over a longer span of human history. The situation can better be seen in the perspective of some 10,000 years, half before the present and half afterward. On such a scale the complete cycle of the exploitation of the world's fossil fuels will be seen to encompass perhaps 1,300 years, with the principal segment of the cycle (defined as the period during which all but the first 10 percent and the last 10 percent of the fuels are extracted and burned) covering only about 300 years. . . .

Little of the organic material produced before the Cambrian period, which began about 600 million years ago, has been preserved. During the past 600 million years, however, some of the organic materials that did not immediately decay have been buried under a great thickness of sedimentary sands, muds and limes. These are the fossil fuels: coal, oil shale, petroleum and natural gas, which are rich in energy stored up chemically from the sunshine of the past 600 million years. The process is still continuing, but probably at about the same rate as in the past; the accumulation during the next million years will probably be a six-hundredth of the amount built up thus far.

Industrialization has of course withdrawn the deposits in this energy bank with increasing rapidity. In the case of coal, for example, the world's consumption during the past 110 years has been about 19 times greater than it was during the preceding seven centuries. The increasing magnitude of the rate of withdrawal can also be seen in the fact that the amount of coal produced and consumed since 1940 is approximately equal to the total consumption up to that time.

Petroleum and related products were not extracted in significant amounts before 1880. Since then production has increased at a nearly constant exponential rate. During the 80-year period from 1890 through 1970 the average rate of increase has been 6.94 percent per year, with a doubling period of 10 years. The cumulative production until the end of 1969 amounted to 227 billion (227×10^9) barrels, or 9.5 trillion U.S. gallons. Once again the period that encompasses most of the production is notably brief.

[Even] Unlimited resources of energy [theoretically available using breeder reactors, deuterium fusion, and other exotic sources], however, do not imply an unlimited number of power plants. It is as true of power plants or automobiles as it is of biological populations that the earth cannot sustain any physical growth for more than a few tens of successive doublings. Because of this impossibility the exponential rates of industrial and population growth that have prevailed during the past century and a half must soon cease. Although the forthcoming period of stability poses no insuperable physical or biological difficulties, it can hardly fail to force a major revision of those aspects of our current social and economic thinking that stem from the assumption that the growth rates that have characterized this temporary period can somehow be made permanent.

—M. KING HUBBERT

The forests of America have been relentlessly plundered ever since Europeans invaded the western hemisphere 500 years ago. The destruction continues almost unabated today—despite the contrary impression that slick, nationally circulated tree-farm propaganda seeks to promote.

In 1970, the most recent year for which we have statistics, 48 billion board feet of softwood timber was removed from the US's commercial forest land. But we grew only 40 billion board feet. That same year, removals from the national forests were 12.7 billion board feet, but growth was only 8.6 billion board feet.

The timber industry's campaign to increase cutting on the national forests is evidence that the long-predicted wood famine has finally arrived. Even worse is the growing evidence that for the past 25 years, the Forest Service has been yielding to this pressure by greatly increasing the sale of timber and is now grossly mismanaging the national forests.

In looking at a well-managed forest, one will observe that it is fully stocked with trees of all sizes and ages. It will be obvious that the land is growing about all the timber it can and that most of the growth is valuable older trees. It will be evident that no erosion is taking place. Roads will be stable and attractive: they will look laid on the land rather than cut into it. the soil will be intact; the forest floor will be covered with leaf litter and other vegetative matter in various stages of growth or decomposition. This absorbent layer holds rain and melting snow while it soaks down into the ground through animal burrows, pores such as wormholes, channels dug by ants, and tracks left by decaying roots of past generations of vegetation. The forest becomes a vast reservoir of water that gradually seeps down through the earth and comes out in springs—clear, cool water. This is how the forest stabilizes stream flow, and this is what is referred to when one reads of the forest protecting watersheds.

One also observes in the well-managed forest that there are frequent small openings stocked with herbs and browse—food close to shelter for wildlife. Finally, one observes that such a forest stays beautiful and will continue to serve our recreational needs as long as it is so managed.

Good forestry means limiting the cutting of timber to the amount that can be removed annually in perpetuity. Good forestry involves cutting selectively where it is consistent with the biological requirements of the species involved. In other cases, good forestry involves keeping the cuts no larger than necessary to meet the biological requirements of the species. Good forestry keeps the full range of naturally occurring species of plants and animals. And—very important—good forestry allows a generous proportion of trees to reach full maturity before being cut.

This is not the way our federal forests are being managed. The annual cut on our national forests has been increased from 5.6 billion board feet in 1950 to more than 14.8 billion board feet in 1969. The forests are not bigger than they were, nor are they being more efficiently managed. They are simply being cut faster and faster. And these cuts have been justified by a long and dismal series of rationalizations by the timber industry and the Forest Service.

Forest statistics are gathered by sampling techniques, and the people who collect the data do not see the results of their work. The information is forwarded to a computer center, where it is processed and delivered to still others. Management decisions get further and further away from people actually familiar with the particular forest. Basic decisions of how much and which timber to sell are now based on rules and regulations emanating from Washington and depending on data-processing printouts.

The practicing forester has lost touch, and the forests are run by bureaucrats who are closer to industry than to the living forests they control.

In the Douglas fir region, both the Forest Service and the BLM are selling timber under one standard of measurement while estimating future yields under another. The minimum-sized tree counted in present inventories of standing timber measures 12 inches in diameter, and its volume is calculated to an 8-inch diameter at the treetop. (In the case of the BLM, trees below that size are included in sales but are not counted.) Estimates of future yields, however, which are used for calculating allowable cuts, include minimum-sized trees only 7 inches in diameter measured to a 5-inch top. The difference in volume between these two standards of measurement in a second-growth stand will be about 40 percent of the total; the second "crop" will be 40 percent smaller than the first.

So while the BLM says it is selling timber in annual amounts that will never decline, there will actually be a decline of as much as 40 percent in the sustained yield, once the present forests (which have taken centuries to mature) have been liquidated. The next stand will be smaller and much less valuable. The Forest Service makes use of the same rationalization, but in a more involved way.

The Monongahela decision was one result of the rising tide of dissatisfaction with Forest Service policy. A number of environmental groups had sued to prevent a particular

"Happy?"

Drawing by Edward Koren; © *The New Yorker Magazine, Inc.*

timber sale on the grounds that under the original enabling legislation, clearcutting was plainly illegal. In 1973, the court agreed. Federal judge Robert Maxwell ruled that the Organic Act of 1897 implicitly forbade clearcutting and that the Forest Service was guilty of "an unwarranted intrusion into timber policy. . . . an exclusive area of Congressional province. A court order followed that enjoined the Forest Service from contracting for timber sales under the authority of the Organic Act of 1897 to allow cutting in the Monongahela National Forest (and, by extension, anywhere else) of (1) trees which are not dead, matured, or large growth; (2) trees which have not been previously marked; or (3) trees which will not be removed.

What then is the effect of the Monongahela decision? It should result in lengthening rotations generally. It will probably thereby reduce the allowable cut for the present in many instances, but not the sustained yield, which will usually be improved. It will improve the quality and value of timber sold, now and in the future. The Monongahela decision should generally reduce the adverse effects of logging on the national forests.

By requiring the removal of timber that has been cut, the decision will require far better utilization of timber, particularly in the West, where about 14 percent of the timber cut is abandoned in the woods.

The Forest Service will have to mark the timber which is to be cut, which in turn means it will have to put foresters in the woods where they can really practice the art of forestry. It may prevent even-aged management in many situations, but will not stop the Forest Service from practicing even-age silviculture entirely. The Service can create openings in the forest of sufficient size to favor regeneration of shade-intolerant species, but generally it will not be able to clearcut areas large enough to keep track of the inventory by aerial mapping. The Forest Service will have to give up tree farming and go back to practicing forestry.

With regard to private forest lands, we must recognize that good forestry is not a lucrative business. It never was and never will be; it takes longer than a man lives to grow high-quality timber, longer than anyone can wait for a return on investment. It takes from 75 to 150 years to maximize growth of timber in sizes useful for lumber and plywood. It takes twice that long to grow high-quality wood such as we use for fine furniture and musical instruments. The large spruce trees in Alaska, now being cut and shipped to Japan for piano sounding-boards, for guitars, and for exquisite Japanese residential panelling, are often as much as 1,000 years old.

Owners of timberland, confronted with the choice between a high income for themselves or an even higher income for their heirs, will nearly always choose the former. Few of us can afford to be philanthropists. Firms with large investments will always do what they must to obtain the highest possible rate of return on investment, and this decision means growing low-quality timber and cutting trees as soon as they become marketable instead of letting them grow to achieve high quality.

The forester, on the other hand, if he loves the forest and has not confused his role with that of the businessman, will resist the temptation to maximize income and will be more concerned with a wide range of environmental factors. He will want to restrict removal to those trees that can be spared for the sake of improving the health and vigor of the forest. He will want to keep trees growing until they reach their highest value, and he will recognize that maintaining a high inventory of marketable trees is an absolute necessity if the forest is to be managed for recreation, watershed, and wildlife, as well as for the forest industry's raw materials.

For these reasons we require a clear separation of responsibility between the forester and the businessman. The forester alone should have responsibility for the forest. It is quite properly the role of the businessman to make what profit he can from the timber the forester makes available. But the businessman should not be able to set policy or production goals for the forester. Otherwise, forestry cannot be properly practiced.

A satisfactory program for state regulation of forestry on private lands consists essentially of the following:

A law requiring that foresters be licensed and that it be unlawful to practice without a license. The licensing board should comprise people from a cross-section of fields related to managing wild lands. These include aquatic biology, entomology, forest ecology, geology, hydrology, mycology, ornithology, plant and animal ecology, pathology, soil science, and wildlife biology.

There must be no exemptions for foresters who are employed by lumber companies; corporations are frequently the worst offenders.

There should be a sustained-yield law. The best way to achieve this goal is to require states to identify all commercial forest lands and require that all owners file timber-management plans prepared by a licensed forester, with the state division of forestry. A sustained-yield law should include the provisions I have characterized as good forestry: actually practicing sustained-yield, selection management, long rotations, and maximizing diversity of species. A sustained-yield law should establish the precautions necessary to protect the soil from accelerated erosion and leaching of nutrients. These precautions should include

standards for design and construction of logging roads, skid trails and landings, and regulation of the kind and size of logging equipment.

Standing timber should be exempt from *ad valorem* taxes, except for timber cut and removed during the tax year. It is neither fair nor reasonable to require good forest practices on private land unless property taxes on forest land are consistent with those on other properties providing similar net income.

Inheritance and gift taxes should be modified to allow a family to pass a small forest from generation to generation without forcing the family to liquidate immature and unmerchantable timber.

The citizen's right to sue must be preserved. Fifty years of experience with regulatory agencies teaches us that they tend to serve the industries they are intended to regulate, unless they are made accountable by the courts. This is the very essence of our check-and-balance system.

Finally, state laws should emphasize enforcement of water-quality standards for streams originating in or flowing through lands on which logging has occurred. Standards should specify that the water not contain more than normal amounts of suspended matter and nutrients; streams should be monitored regularly to assure that the standards have been met.

—GORDON ROBINSON

Recommended Actions

☐ The President should proclaim that good husbandry of the nation's natural resources is a national goal and a special mission of the Departments of Agriculture and of the Interior.

☐ The President should appoint Secretaries of Agriculture and of the Interior who are personally committed to stewardship (as opposed to exploitation) of the land and its resources.

☐ The Secretary of Agriculture should order the Forest Service to pay more than lip service to sustained-yield forestry and to cater less to commercial timber interests.

☐ The Secretary should also dedicate his department to the maintenance and rebuilding of topsoil and its fertility.

☐ The Secretary of the Interior should instruct the Bureau of Land Management (and other agencies under his jurisdiction) to put land to its best use (or non-use), not necessarily to the use most profitable to entrepreneurs.

☐ The Bureau of Reclamation, the Corps of Engineers, and other water resource agencies should be diverted from damming and ditching to erosion control, aquifer recharging, and water conservation.

☐ An appropriate committee of Congress should draft a totally new mining law ensuring that mining claims in the public domain be leased, not given away, that leaseholders pay royalties to the US Treasury on the minerals extracted, and that the land be reclaimed at the mine operators' expense when mining operations cease.

☐ Congress should repeal all special tax advantages now enjoyed by the extractive industries since these indirect subsidies keep prices artificially low and consumption artificially high.

☐ The President and other opinion-makers should rekindle pride in the traditional American virtue of thrift.

☐ The federal, state, and local governments should buy recycled materials for their own use to the greatest extent possible.

☐ The federal and state governments should support recycling research, and through tax incentives and other inducements, should help recycling industries get established.

☐ All levels of government should require that new government buildings be energy-efficient and economical in their use of materials, and wherever possible, should upgrade the energy efficiency of existing government buildings.

☐ Tax policies should reward the owners of commercial, industrial, and residential property who retrofit energy-efficient equipment such as insulation and openable windows.

☐ Tax policies should also reward owners who help minimize the need for new construction by maintaining existing properties in good repair or rehabilitating rundown properties.

☐ Throwaway containers, a symbol of our wasteful use of resources, should be banned nationally by act of Congress.

☐ The administration should investigate ways to discourage or prohibit excess packaging.

☐ All levels of government should oppose low-density housing developments and settlement patterns, which waste both energy and resources.

☐ Manufacturers of durable goods should be required to design them for easy maintenance and repair, and ultimately, for easy recycling.

☐ The Interstate Commerce Commission should immediately revise rail freight rates that discriminate against recycled materials.

Jobs and the Environment

The case for energy conservation so ably advocated by Amory Lovins in "The Road Not Taken?" (*Foreign Affairs,* October, 1976) was promptly disputed within the federal energy bureaucracy on the basis that more energy is needed to fuel economic growth and a growing economy is needed to produce jobs. Both premises are unsound: there is no one-to-one relationship between energy consumption and GNP, nor does a growth economy necessarily produce more jobs. Sweden, for example, uses only one-half as much energy per capita to match our standard of living, and unemployment in Puerto Rico rose from 13 to 40 percent between 1950 and 1975, a period during which Puerto Rico's GNP increased from $755 million to $7 billion. Burning up energy doesn't necessarily stimulate the economy and economic growth doesn't necessarily benefit the labor force. Environmentalists who believe in energy conservation and a sustainable-state economy are nevertheless accused at times of being job destroyers. This charge isn't merely wide of the mark, it's the opposite of true. As of mid-1976, about 20,000 jobs had been lost because obsolescent industrial plants couldn't meet air or water pollution standards. Those 20,000 jobs matter, and environmentalists are concerned about them. But the same pollution laws and regulations that cost 20,000 jobs created about 1,000,000 new jobs in a brand new pollution-control industry. And that's just the beginning. Think of the jobs involved, for instance, in retrofitting existing buildings with adequate insulation (which, by its nature, is a non-automatable undertaking). In any event, creating jobs at the expense of the environment is the wrong way to create jobs. An anti-ecological advertisement once prompted David Brower to remark that there wouldn't be corporate profits made on a dead planet. There wouldn't be any Help Wanted signs hanging there either. Hereafter, four articles on saving jobs by saving the environment.

Jobs

Philosophically, there is no reason to see any conflict between jobs and environmental protection. Environmental quality should be just one more goal of production and industry.

Both the environmental movement and the labor movement must keep in mind the ecological principle that there can be no division between the natural and the social environment.

Over the summer, solar heating and wind-powered electrical generating equipment were installed at the Walter and May Reuther Family Education Center at Black Lake, Michigan. We expect to make a substantial saving on our fuel and energy costs by installing this still-experimental technology.

Our solar heating and windmill project is a small example of how the United Auto Workers and its members have long been active in the environmental field, not necessarily because of moral conviction or love of trees but because working people, and those others not lucky enough to have jobs, suffer from the worst conditions.

The elimination of pollutants in the plant has always been a goal of the labor movement. The growth of the environmental movement has focused attention on the long-term health effects of occupational chemical exposures and has spurred a new effort on the part of many unions, including the UAW. We have included new safeguards in our contracts, trained safety and health committeemen and expanded our professional staff in spite of difficult economic times. But the problems go beyond what labor can achieve in collective bargaining, or solely with its own forces in the political area.

It is the responsibility of the environmental movement to become involved in the issue of the environment inside the workplace.

Unless the environmental movement takes up this commitment, it will be hard to enlist the interest of working people in what appears to many of them as the much less immediate health problems of the general environment.

There is one very clear parallel between in-plant and community environmental standards—the industry response. First, an industry will claim it can't comply with a proposed standard because the technology to do so does not exist. Next the industry will claim that the cost will drive it out of business. Finally, companies announce that they can and will comply but that it will cost everyone plenty. The idea that businesses will be driven to bank-ruptcy if strict environmental standards are adopted is the same tired line that has been brought up again and again since workers first organized to improve working conditions. It was brought up when child labor was eliminated, when the minimum wage was introduced, when Social Security and Unemployment Insurance were developed. The fact is, as I will discuss later, that some analysts feel that environmental regulations can have a positive economic result.

This serious economic situation creates a greater need that environmentalists and planners take into account the loss of jobs and the need for adequate compensation, retraining, and other safeguards for workers whose jobs are threatened by regulation. If this is not done, our efforts together to improve the environment both inside and outside the plants will suffer a serious setback.

There is some evidence that governmental regulations in the area of environment should be a stimulus, rather than a block, to industrial development. A study by the MIT Center for Policy Alternatives was presented to a Senate hearing on the impact of federal regulations on the American consumer and businessman. The study examined the impact of health and safety regulations on the automotive, chemical, textile, consumer electronics, and computer industries in four Western European countries and Japan. The study found two positive results of such regulation. To quote the authors:

"What had been seen is that environmental regulations, by forcing firms to implement product or process changes, often-times shock them out of a rather inflexible production system and thereby provide the catalyst which is necessary for innovation to occur." The second point was that compliance with regulations "provided a demand not only for increased production of abatement technologies, but also [for] development of new and improved techniques."

Lately, we have learned not to trust the predictions of government economists, but they have done some studies of the effects of general environmental control. One study, quoted by the National Commission on Materials Policy in 1973, stated that "Over the 1972-80 period, pollution control and compensatory macroeconomic policy measures are expected to raise the US unemployment rate by 0.3 percent, raise the average rate of inflation by 0.26 percent," and have similar small negative impacts on investment and balance of trade. These figures are tiny compared to the economic hardships produced by the Ford Administration economic policies.

In hard times or in certain localities, there are few alternative jobs and workers are forced to bear the burden of economic dislocation. Legislation to protect workers from damages suffered in plant shutdowns or layoffs resulting from environmental regulation or other causes would be a practical, substantial step towards controlling and distributing the burden of change. It would free workers from the fear, skillfully played upon by environment-ravaging employers, that vigorous action to protect the environment must mean loss of jobs.

We cannot aim at solving environmental problems by simply introducing an environmental ethic into our society or by changing attitudes. This goal implies instead that we must work concurrently on the environment, on the conditions in the places where people work, on providing jobs, and on developing the services needed to maintain health.

—LEONARD WOODCOCK

Economic Justice

This year, in order to satisfy the requirements of Federal laws, Americans will spend $17 billion to clean up or prevent air and water pollution. That amounts to $80 for every man, woman and child in the country.

We could do a lot of other things with that money.

The $17 billion we will spend on pollution control this year could send 83,677 lucky youngsters off to four years at Harvard with a color TV in the back seat of their Mercedes 450 SL, and $50 a week in spending money in their pockets. After paying room, board, and tuition, they'd still have enough left for four years in medical school. Every night for all eight of those years, they could have a steak or lobster dinner in virtually any restaurant they chose. And for the last four of those years—after they reached 21—they could, in addition, have two martinis before dinner and a cognac after.

Instead, we're going to spend the money on cleaning up our air and water.

In the real world, of course, that $17 billion would not simply be lying around, waiting to be spent on luxuries or medical school educations. But it would be available to us in various forms—in hundreds of dollars for some people, in pennies for others. It would mean larger profits for some industries, freeing capital for new investment or for distribution to stockholders. If automobiles did not have to be equipped with emissions controls, they would cost less. If the pulp and paper industry did not have such a formidable problem with water pollution, their products could be cheaper—thus reducing the cost of many things we buy from magazines to packaged cereals. If our cities and towns did not have to spend so much on sewage treatment, our taxes could be lower—or we could devote more public funds to the people at the bottom of our economic ladder. Finally, if the most pollution-prone industries—especially paper, metal finishing, electric utilities, chemicals, and iron and steel—did not have to invest so much in control

equipment, they might be able to sell their goods at lower prices, sell more of them and, hence, need to employ more workers.

Thus, there *are* real possibilities for conflict between environmental protection, economic justice, and jobs. And as you have often heard—from some governmental officials, as well as from many business executives—these conflicts make it necessary for us to go slow on environmental protection. We're trying to go too far, too fast, they say.

Well . . . it's possible, of course, to go too far, too fast in *any* line of endeavor, including—to cite some examples that have crossed my desk from time to time—the filling-in of wetlands, the strip-mining of coal, the depletion of our domestic oil and gas, and the manufacture of cancer-causing chemicals.

Extremism in the pursuit of environmental clean-up could indeed slow our economy. But it hasn't happened yet. Indeed, the evidence is that environmental regulation has created jobs that otherwise would not exist. Our current recession—from which, hopefully, we are now recovering—was not caused by environmental regulations, or the cost of pollution control. It was caused by a number of factors, but mainly by a sudden, sharp increase in the price of oil. Even if there had been no environmental regulations whatever, we would have suffered a substantial economic setback. Environmental regulations did nothing to cause the long lines at gas stations a while back, nor the sudden loss of consumer confidence that led to deferred purchases and widespread layoffs. Industry itself, nervous about energy prices and slackening demand, postponed expansion plans, began using stockpiled materials instead of buying new, and waited to see what would happen.

In the recession economy of 1974 and 1975, environmental regulations *forced* expenditures that would not otherwise have been made. They put people to work: according to several studies that the Council on Environmen-

The trans-Alaska pipeline brought thousands of jobs north, along with tens of thousands of workers and long lines at hiring halls like the one above in Fairbanks. Photo by Jim Kowalsky.

tal Quality and the Environmental Protection Agency commissioned, about one million people are employed today as a result of the environmental clean-up regulations established over the past 10 years. This includes jobs directly involved in pollution-abatement, as well as the induced jobs necessary to service the former. Directly and indirectly, every billion dollars of environmental spending employs—depending on the nature of the expenditure—between 40,000 and 80,000 people. Some of these people, it is true, would have had jobs in any case, since most of the money spent on environmental clean-up would have been spent elsewhere without the environmental regulations. We figure, though, that 300,000 people who are working today would be out of jobs if it weren't for those regulations.

Obviously, that's good for America. So is the better health that pollution-control expenditures protect—not only for us, but for our children and their children. We spend billions of dollars annually for health care—much of it necessitated by exposure to pollutants in our air and water. And this figure, huge as it is, does not include the costs of lost time and of incalculable human suffering.

Environmental regulations have also led to the creation of a new environmental industry. It's young now, and still relatively small—but indications are that it will remain a permanent fixture on the American economic scene. Some well-known corporations have gotten into the field in a substantial way. After figuring out ways to control its own pollutants, for example, Dow Chemical formed a subsidiary to sell its experience and processes to other companies. In reporting earnings results for the first quarter of 1976, the president of UOP, Inc., singled out the company's two environment-related divisions for special mention as "important contributors to profits." Engelhard Industries, of Newark, developed a catalyst to reduce pollution in auto exhausts years ago; they couldn't sell their idea to the auto companies. Then, with the almost unanimous passage by Congress of the Clean Air Act, Engelhard found itself with a bonanza on its hands; its catalytic converter market, I understand, totalled over $800 million last year, and were expected to double in 1976, to $1.7 billion. A substantial part of that sum goes to the steel industry, since catalytic converters are now one of the principal uses for stainless steel in the U.S. The converter is a brand-new product—and it has created brand-new jobs, including many on auto-assembly lines all over the U.S.

Despite such evidence that environment-related investments have been a bright spot in an otherwise gloomy economy, many business and government officials have continued to argue that such spending hampers the economy. Thus I have found it interesting to note that during the most rapid growth in pollution-control expenditures in our history, first-quarter earnings for a number of major corporations—including some in pollution-prone industries—have jumped quite sharply.

First-quarter profits for the International Paper Co. in 1976, for example, were $63.5 million, up 35 percent from the same period of 1975, and those for Allied Chemical, up 25 per cent. The Chrysler Corporation reported profits of $72 million—the company's second-best performance for a first quarter in history. And I was particularly interested in the performance of the DuPont Corporation—not only because I am an alumnus, but because a senior official of the Corporation recently lambasted my arguments in a speech. DuPont's first quarter profits—get this—were up 600 percent from the same quarter of 1975. Although these marked percentage increases result primarily from comparison with the low level of profits in the first quarter of the year before, the absolute profit levels of most of these companies are near their historic highs.

In reciting these profit-increases, I don't want to leave the impression that I'm critical of healthy profits. I'm all for them. But what particularly interests me about the sudden recovery of corporate earnings is this: environmental regulations have not been relaxed since 1975—in fact, the reverse is true—and corporations have had to spend more on pollution-control in each succeeding year since 1970. If pollution-control spending hurts economic growth, it is not obvious from an analysis of the sudden profit increases.

Decades ago, American companies began developing a new industry based on providing cool air to consumers. We call it the air-conditioning industry. Virtually everyone here, I suspect, lives in an air-conditioned home or apartment, drives an air-conditioned car, and works in an air-conditioned office. The manufacture of equipment to provide cool air has become a major source of profits, dividends, and jobs. Never have I heard any industrial leader, economist, or banker refer to the air-conditioning industry as non-productive.

And yet now, when a new industry—formed to manufacture, operate, and maintain equipment to produce *clean* air—comes along, it is termed "nonproductive"—even though it, too, offers investment opportunities, profits, and jobs.

So far, the amount of unemployment caused by environmental restrictions has been minor. Since 1971, EPA—which operates an "early warning system" to

Unemployment line in San Francisco, 1976. Photo by Emilio Mercado/Jeroboam, Inc.

monitor the impact of its regulations on jobs—has learned of 76 plant-closings affecting 16,500 workers—about fifteen-thousandths of one percent of the labor force. I do not want to minimize these losses. If your job was one of the 16,500, it's cold comfort to be told that as a result of environmental regulations, there are at least 300,000 additional jobs in the U.S. than there otherwise would have been.

In every pollution industry, requirements to clean up will hit smaller and older plants especially hard. Larger firms, with better access to capital and to top-flight engineering talent, can often devise their own pollution-control technology—sometimes even making a profit in the process, as they recover valuable chemicals, minerals, and materials that used to be thrown out. Several paper companies have done well in this respect. Some time ago, the Chairman of Hanes Dye and Finishing testified that "cleaning up our stacks and neutralizing our liquids was expensive, but in the balance we have actually made money on our pollution control efforts." Smaller companies, on the other hand, are usually forced to buy standard technology which, typically, costs more per unit of volume and is not tailored to meet the needs of a specific plant. Some of the smaller, older plants in the paper industry are only marginally profitable now, and the extra investment required for pollution control could make the difference between staying open and closing their doors.

Such potential failures—and the unemployment they might entail—must seriously concern us in every case, no matter how small the firm. It is important to recognize, however, that for the country as a whole, the shutting

Photo by Kerry Richardson.

down of an operation in one place doesn't necessarily mean the loss of the jobs involved. Increased production and more jobs will probably be created in a more modern plant elsewhere. In some cases, the magnitude of prospective unemployment may warrant a relaxation or postponing of pollution controls.

But such relaxations must be the rare exception, not the rule, for every such exception invites attempts by some members of industry to escape pollution-abatement by pleading economic disaster. We have embarked on a course of environmental clean-up, and we should go ahead with it until we get the job done. We are, after all, talking about the air we breathe and the water we drink.

And if any sector of our society has recognized the utter seriousness and practicality of environmental protection, it is labor. Workers are more vulnerable to health problems caused by pollution than the typical American, for industrial pollutants are concentrated in the workplace. The workplace, indeed, requires concentrated scrutiny, for it has often given us the first indication of potentially broader problems. Almost every pollutant that has proven to be a hazard in the workplace has gone on to become a full-blown community problem—as witness, asbestos and vinyl chloride. Cleaning up the working environment will add costs to the products produced—costs that must be passed on to the consumer. But certainly that is only just, since

the worker is bearing those costs now. If the proper safeguards had been installed at the Life Sciences plant at Hopewell, Virginia, the price of Kepone might have been substantially higher than its normal selling price.

But look what has happened as a result of inadequate safeguards: a number of workers appear to have suffered severe and permanent nerve disorders; oyster-fishing was halted for a time in the James River, and tests on Kepone levels in crabs as far north as Maryland and Delaware are now being conducted to determine if they are safe for human consumption; for a time, the municipal sewage-treatment system of Hopewell was knocked out, because Kepone destroyed its biological base; and the Commonwealth of Virginia, which initially issued reassuring statements about the modest harm done, has now joined in a multi-million dollar suit against Life Sciences and Allied Chemical.

A pesticide that costs that much to produce—not only in terms of economic impact, but also in terms of human health—perhaps *should* be priced out of the market, *even* at the expense of jobs.

We are in a difficult transition period, one that challenges our traditional view of cost. It has been said that there is no free lunch. There is no free pollution, either. Until recently, you and I have been subsidizing without complaint those companies that have been discharging their wastes into our air and water. The price of a product should be calculated to include safeguards to human health and the disposal of waste, as well as the cost of materials, labor, capital equipment, and distribution. Such expansion of our economics of pricing would undoubtedly raise prices; why shouldn't the product that causes the pollution bear the cost of cleaning it up? And since it is usually more difficult and expensive to correct a mistake than to avoid it in the first place, why shouldn't decision-makers be required to build into their decisions the means for avoiding environmental degradation?

This is what the National Environmental Policy Act, and the much-maligned environmental impact statement, are all about. They require any Federal project-manager to take a look at *all* the costs of his project—not only the concrete and steel and labor, but also the environmental expenses—and determine whether the benefits exceed the costs. In addition, the law requires the project-manager to explore alternatives: is there any better, more cost-efficient way of getting the same job done? These questions, indeed, may force a look at the most fundamental question: is the job worth doing at all?

Over the next quarter-century, I think this new, comprehensive, long-range way of looking at environmental costs will be extended to all facets of decision-making, and will lead to a significant restructuring of the types of projects we undertake. We have been running on underpriced energy for a century now, and we have been using it and other natural resources in a wasteful fashion. Despite all the talk about conserving energy and recycling materials, and the logic of such a course, too little conserving and re-cycling are being done. But probably the most wasteful thing we do is to forego the talents and productive capacity of millions of unemployed.

As energy prices keep going up, and as we start running into serious shortages of some natural materials, and as we face up to putting our large numbers of unemployed to work, I think we shall see a shift to a technology that will put man rather than the machine at the center of industrial economics. To employ, to conserve, and to recycle will be the battle-cry of the future.

Some of our proposed capital-intensive projects are already getting a more comprehensive scrutiny than ever before. The Kaiparowits electrical generating plant in Southern Utah is a good example. As you probably know, two of the utility companies sponsoring the project have bowed out. There has been speculation that environmentalists' objections killed the project, and there is considerable bitterness in Utah about its cancellation.

In fact, it appears that *economics*, pure and simple, killed the project. Environmental safeguards would have added roughly $600 million to its costs, and that is a sizeable sum. But the project was based on the electrical companies' assumptions that power demand in Southern California and Arizona would increase at the rate of 4.5 to 11 percent per year, for the years 1975-1980.

The actual rate of increase in power demand now forecast for California by some highly qualified analysts is only 1.4 percent—one-third the lowest projection, and about one-eighth the highest. It's noteworthy that the two utility companies announced their withdrawal only one day before they would have had to go before the California public service commission to justify their rates. I have a hunch that the costs of the Kaiparowits project, coupled with the lower rate of increase in energy demand, would have made that electricity the most expensive in the United States.

Whatever the truth of this matter, I was most struck by one fact: The Kaiparowits project, costing $3.5 billion, would have created 3,135 jobs for people in Utah after it went into full operation. That works out to $1,116,000 for every job.

We can and we must weigh these costs, too—and I think our new environmental consciousness will help us do so. I think the environmental age will bring all of us humans—machinists, bird-watchers, Wall Street brokers, inner-city residents, truck-drivers, teachers, and astronauts—back into touch with a central fact of man's continuing existence: we remain dependent on our earth. We can manipulate it, convert its resources to our own benefit, and use our ingenuity to improve the quality of all our lives. But we can go too far, too fast—and one of the basic principles of ecology is that the symptoms of damage to an ecosystem do not show up until that damage is irreversible.

We must renew our sense of dependence upon the earth and learn to use it wisely, for the air, the water, the soil and the sun are the ultimate sources of all our wealth. Whatever temporary conflicts there may be between environmentalists and labor union members, I hope you will join us—for ultimately, a concern for the environment is inseparable from a concern for jobs, communities, and economic justice.

—Russell Peterson

Jobs Putting Things Back Together

Latter-day timber barons are apparently unwilling to be as responsible for the environment and society in which they live as the rest of us must be, under the National Environmental Policy Act. They are putting their employees up to some rather ugly demonstrations, which seem aimed at frightening the new governor [of California], his officers, the legislature, the courts, and the public.

The company officials are like people described by Dr. Dan Luten, "who would rather die than change their habits." It is all too easy to infer that they will not change their habit of cutting down virgin redwood stands, unique to California, until they have cut the last of them, or have severely impaired what they cannot reach yet.

Since they are going to have to change their habits eventually, it makes sense to have them change those habits now, while we still have some chance to save the vestige they left us of what should have been a great Redwood National Park.

We are in sympathy with the straits of the unemployed

Photo by Karen R. Preuss/Jeroboam, Inc.

loggers, but before we let sympathy be an easy route to expedience, let us consider who else needs some sympathy.

Not, for one, former Governor Reagan, famous for his "Once you've seen one redwood you've seen them all." That was long ago appropriately countered with "Once you've seen one redwood *stump*, you've seen them all."

Neither statement is true, of course, as anyone would know who has recently flown over the thousands of unnecessary redwood stumps that mark the boundary of the pitifully thin line of Redwood Creek giants finally included in Redwood National Park. You can be excused for the rage you feel at the vindictive logging, or call it the preemptive logging, that put those great trees down and out, precluding forever, for us and all who follow us, the chance to see what that park should have been.

You can be excused for feeling that the people who let this happen should be locked up for the grand larceny against the future they took part in. You wonder what

would have happened if a lot of people had not sat on their hands, or been defensive—if they had paid attention and had been bold enough. You could wonder, too, what might have happened if former Governor Reagan had appointed Claire Dedrick as his Resource Secretary instead of Norman B. ("Ike") Livermore, Jr., whose feeling toward redwoods (if not toward Sierra wilderness, which he worked courageously to save) was conditioned by his having been an officer of Pacific Lumber Company for so long. You wonder what might have happened had Martin Litton been appointed—the man who more than anyone else was trying to get the National Park Service, the Save-the-Redwoods League, and the Sierra Club to listen to what he knew about where the finest redwoods were for a national park. The Sierra Club listened.

How much sympathy should go to an industry that won't change its ways, or workers who won't change theirs, until something had been destroyed that belongs to all the future, and not really to them?

Dick Cavett once asked a conservationist appearing on his show how he responded to the charge that saving the environment was putting people out of work. But Mr. Cavett then said something like: "No, I can answer that question myself. I suppose a lot of furnace tenders were put out of work when they closed Dachau." He apologized to his audience for having stumbled into so brutal an answer, but perhaps he needn't have. War makes brutal jobs, and we have ended unemployment that way more than once. Pollution makes jobs. Napalm-making makes jobs and, as a friend has observed, takes the furnace to the people. Dumping asbestos into Lake Superior makes jobs. Making teratogenic herbicides like 2,4,5-T makes jobs. Making reactors makes jobs, and Henry Kissinger's proposal to make still more reactors and, Johnny Appleseed-like, to plant them in various and sundry countries we seek favors from, would make jobs. Putting a multi-billion-dollar Trident base in the Hood Canal would make jobs. Making bigger, faster, fuel gulping cars and airplanes makes jobs. Anything else?

Yes. Trying to put a tiny fragment of ecosystem back together can make jobs, and is doing just that in a tiny national park in Australia. Trouble is, they aren't succeeding. They are finding out that just as you can't put Humpty Dumpty together again, or unscramble an egg, or make pancakes in a toaster, you cannot put a whole web of life back together once you have taken it apart. It takes God to do that, and He requires, we understand, a generous allowance of time to accomplish it.

Closer at hand, there are nevertheless many jobs in trying as best we can to put a forest back together, in letting men do carefully what machines do recklessly, as if they were all thumbs, or bulldozers in a China shop. There are tiny good examples, such as what people can do in a commune when they set about healing a piece of earth instead of ripping it up. And there are big examples, such as in Boeing's learning how to survive nicely, even better, without an SST business, and in what this nation did in getting some twelve million men and women out of wartime work and into peaceful jobs in a few months of assiduous manpower retraining.

Elsewhere in these pages are suggested lists of jobs that need doing, that are indeed needed so much that there should be federal and state financial support for retraining and reëquipping unemployed loggers and logging industries to accomplish them. There are substitutes for over-mechanized, over-energy-intensive timber operations. There are substitutes for the hundreds of thousands of unrestocked or poorly restocked forest lands that earlier

cut-and-get-out loggers bequeathed their descendants—loggers as well as all the rest of us. Indeed, there are substitutes for wasteful use of lumber, as any Italian stone mason will tell you. And those Italian substitutes, travelers to Rome note, last a great deal longer than wood.

There are no substitutes for the last intact virgin redwood stands, and there are no substitutes, in this crowded world, for acting responsibly toward the society and the environment in which we live, and in which we hope thousands of future generations of people and other live things will be living. Enjoyably, we hope. With a chance to see more than one two-thousand-year-old redwood, and to see it in the right setting.

We would not expect the President, in a fuel shortage, to burn the furniture in the Oval Office to keep the fireplace going in some other part of the house that is lent him. Logging company presidents, please copy.

—DAVID BROWER

The Environment Behind The Economy

I start with this simple premise: a strong and healthy economy cannot exist within an unhealthy environment, just as only a strong economy can enable us to achieve that healthy environment.

Corporate and governmental decisions that result in real unemployment rates of more than 10 per cent have inflicted massive personal tragedy on millions of American workers and their families. At the same time, such economic dislocation has, to a degree, dulled the momentum of our struggle to clean-up the environment.

Today, as the result of a number of developments including the emergency tax cut enacted by the Congress over President Ford's objection, we are experiencing a recovery. But the official jobless figure offered by the Ford Administration of 7.5 per cent is far below the true level of unemployment because the government does not count discouraged and part-time workers.

Our experts and those of the AFL-CIO now estimate that more than nine million people in this country are unemployed. The true jobless rate is close to 10.5 per cent. Within this horrible economic context, the concern of the individual worker for his or her job has probably never been as important. The tremendous insecurity among workers resulting from the Nixon-Ford recession is something those in corporate boardrooms are quite aware of and ready to turn to their advantage.

Environmental blackmail has been going on for years. But it is in times such as these that the corporate tactic of trying to make workers and communities choose between jobs or ending pollution can be most effective. It's frequently a false conflict, but to a worker confronted with the loss of wages, health care benefits and pension rights, it can seem very real.

If we had a full employment economy in America today, corporate polluters would have a far more difficult time with environmental blackmail. The Union Carbide's, the Allied Chemical's, the U.S. Steel's and the General Motors's would be far less successful in selling the myth that workers must sacrifice their jobs if we are to have a clean environment.

I believe in a full employment economy—the kind of economy that the Hawkins-Humphrey bill seeks to achieve—the GM's and the GE's are going to have a much harder time practicing their environmental blackmail. Both the labor movement and the environmental movement would benefit. This is an area in which a coalition is not only possible, but in fact probable.

There is another such area in which a strong alliance between working people and environmentalists must occur and that is the fight against in-plant pollution. Jobs may be the key issue facing the labor movement right now, but just as pressing is the fight to protect the health and safety of those who are employed. It is the responsibility of the environmental movement to become even more involved in the issue of the environment inside the workplace.

Objective, independent scientific research has proven the existence of health problems which until now workers could only suspect. We in the labor movement are glad for that help. But workers need allies in the political fight to set better standards for workplace contaminants. We need the political muscle of the environmental movement to help us counteract corporate efforts to weaken occupational health and safety legislation and regulations. We need your help in our fight against the under-funding and under-enforcement of the safety and health programs which do exist.

Put simply, there wasn't much scientific interest in studying PCB's as long as they were destroying the health of workers. When they showed up in fish and eagles, though, then suddenly it becomes worthy of intensive scientific investigation. It is exactly this kind of double standard that angers those of us in the labor movement so much.

The elimination of pollutants in the plant has always been a goal of the labor movement. The growth of the environmental movement has focused attention on the long-term effects of occupational chemical exposures and has spurred new effort on the part of many unions, including the UAW.

Here again, as in the drive for full employment, I think workers and environmentalists can create a strong alliance that will benefit everyone. In order for many of the chemicals to get into our air, our streams and ultimately our bodies, they first appear in heavy and toxic amounts in industrial plants.

I have been very encouraged by the support many environmentalists have evidenced for the Toxic Substances Control Bill now before the Congress. They have been among the most effective and outspoken supporters of that crucial legislation, which would mandate testing of all potentially toxic chemicals and regulate their manufacture, usage and disposal. In addition, that Bill would protect employees against corporate retaliation if they "blow the whistle" on hazardous conditions. If it is finally enacted, and I strongly hope it will be, the government will finally have a chance to control toxic substances *before* they are introduced into the workplace and, ultimately, into the general environment. The alliance between environmentalists, labor unions, consumer and community groups backing the Bill is an excellent beginning toward a stronger, continuing effort to clean up in-plant pollution as well as out-of-plant pollution.

The people who are opposed to that alliance and who are doing what they can to put it on the skids use the same approach on workplace health and safety that they employ on environmental controls. The corporate executive's message to workers who complain about health and safety conditions often is: keep quiet or we'll have to shut down. The reality is that they seldom do shut down, and when plant closures do occur that are attributed to safety enforcement, closer investigation often reveals that the operation was old, outmoded and unprofitable for other reasons. Yet to a worker worried about losing his or her job, health and safety blackmail can have the same devastating effect as environmental blackmail.

OSHA enforcement of safety and health legislation has aroused great whimpering from companies which would like to take us back to the 1800's. But the statistics show few plant closures because of OSHA enforcement. Similarly, the Environmental Protection Agency reported in a letter sent to Labor Secretary William Usery on April 12 of this year that since January, 1971, only 76 industrial plant closings or curtailments involving 25 or more jobs have occurred for which pollution control was cited as even a significant factor. These closings of plants of all types, including foundries, have involved 16,500 jobs.

The National Employment Priorities Act, also called the Mondale-Ford Bill, is a step in the right direction. The Bill would require that a business intending to close or transfer a large portion of the operations of an establishment give written advance notice of its intent. The notice is to include the reasons for closing, the extent of the potential unemployment, the economic circumstances of the establishment and the concern, and plans to alleviate the economic loss to affected employees. Upon request of affected employees, an investigation of the circumstances of the closing or transfer would be made by the government. A report would be made on the economic justification for the closing or transfer, the potential economic losses, and recommendations for alleviating the losses or making unnecessary the closing or transfer.

Federal adjustment assistance to workers under the Act would include income, pension and health benefit maintenance, as well as job placement, retraining and relocation assistance. Communities could also receive benefits. For the business, technical and financial assistance would be offered to head off the shutdown.

However, if the proposed closing or transfer of operations is found to be unjustified, or if the business establishment refuses to accept assistance which would make shutdown unnecessary, then certain federal tax benefits including the investment tax credit, the foreign tax credit and the treatment of some expenses for tax purposes would be withdrawn for up to ten years.

It is a widely accepted principle—although one all too often ignored in practice—that the burdens and sacrifices required by an action taken in the service of the interests of the whole society should be shared equitably by *all* who benefit from that action. They should not be allowed to fall disproportionately upon *some* who are innocent victims of it. Certainly, purification of the environment is in the interests of all citizens. All of us will ultimately pay in increased taxes and often, unfortunately, in higher prices for steps taken publicly and privately to avoid, eliminate or reduce pollution. Increased taxes and higher prices will also be paid by the workers who stand to lose their jobs, temporarily or permanently, as a result of plant shutdowns resulting from environmental problems. They and their families should not be asked, in addition, to pay with loss of income and valuable fringe benefit protections.

Many labor unions have supported environmental legislation. To be credible the environmental movement must also push hard to prevent the costs of pollution control from falling on the victims and avoid the implied view that factory workers are partners in pollution with the corporations. The ecological principles which link jobs and the environment dictate that there can be no one-dimensional solution.

I'm sure most of us here are familiar with the annual listing of the so-called "Dirty Dozen"—the 12 Congressmen whom Environmental Action rates as having horrible environmental records. I took this year's list of the Dirty Dozen and compared their voting records on labor issues. They were, without exception, terrible.

The UAW publishes congressional voting records on 20 key issues, ranging from public service jobs to aid to education. On those labor issues, the Dirty Dozen had five members who voted against labor on 95 per cent or more of those issues. Another six voted against labor on 75 per cent or more of the issues. The best the Dirty Dozen could muster was Rep. White, a Texas Democrat who only voted against labor 50 per cent of the time.

Clearly, in addition to fighting similar battles with the same corporations, workers and environmentalists have good reason to wage political war jointly on the many political foes we both have on Capitol Hill, and in state and local government as well.

We will hear from many prominent environmental experts and I'm sure those of us in the labor movement will learn a great deal. I hope, too, that all of us will remember that workers are people, too. They and their unions care about the environment. And they are usually the first to suffer when it's polluted.

Workers want the Chesapeake Bay to be saved, and the San Francisco Bay, too. In their precious time off, they'd like to be able to fish in clean water or walk in the redwoods. When they drink water, they want it to be clean. When they eat, they don't want a chemical feast fouling their food. I'm sure most think furs look better on their original owners than on the shoulders of Scarsdale socialites. They don't want the land they hunt and hike in to disappear under water backed up by unnecessary dams.

These aren't just idle thoughts. The Conservation Department of the UAW, which Odessa Komer directs, has put our union's political power to work on many of these issues. For years, we fought against unsafe nuclear power plant development, spending thousands of dollars in court suits and organizing actions. We've strongly opposed the Concorde SST. We've joined public interest groups in the fight to fund mass transit programs and divert public funds to mass transit from the Highway Trust Fund. We strongly believe America must wean itself from too great a dependence on the automobile and must develop a more balanced transportation system.

We've not only advocated energy conservation, but have begun implementing such programs ourselves. Instead of tilting at windmills, the UAW is building them. In 1975, wind-powered electrical generating equipment was installed here at our Family Education Center. Solar heating equipment was also installed. We expect to make a substantial saving on our energy costs, as well as demonstrating new sources of energy.

We in the UAW are proud of our commitment to environmental issues. Many other unions have reason to be proud as well. My good friend Cesar Chavez and the members of the United Farm Workers played the pivotal role in forcing regulation of many pesticides. The United Mine Workers urged enactment of strip mining legislation. The Oil, Chemical and Atomic Workers has pioneered in the effort to bring toxic chemicals, such as asbestos and mercury under control. The Steelworkers have fought to control smelter emissions.

Not all of these efforts have been as effective or successful as we would hope, but they clearly again point the way to the many concerns the labor and environmental movements have in common. I have asked tonight for your consideration and support of full employment legislation, for a new alliance to fight workplace pollution, for help in passing legislation that would help limit environmental blackmail, and for political action to elect pro-worker and pro-environment candidates.

These potential areas of mutual interest are not an end, but rather a beginning. I look forward to the task we all have of defining the fight for environmental and economic justice.

—LEONARD WOODCOCK

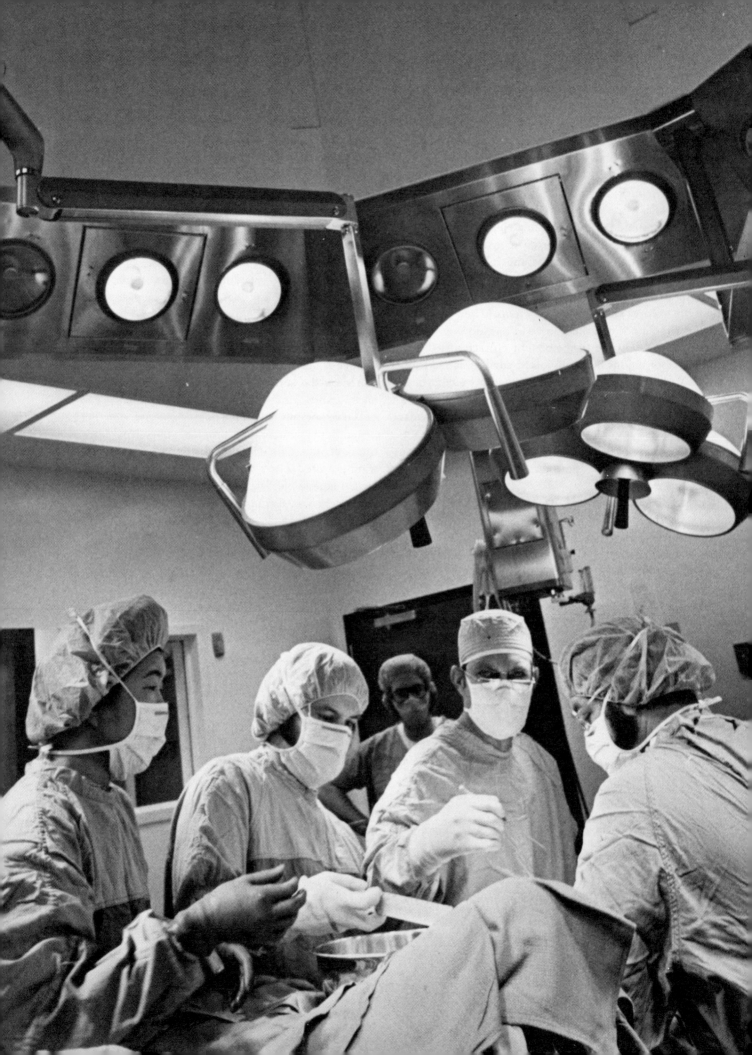

*A now apparently standard response by certain sectors of industry to at-
tempts by regulatory agencies to promulgate standards limiting environmental and occupational exposure to chemical carcinogens is to forecast, generally
on the basis of procured reports, major economic disruption and unemployment attendant on compliance.*

—SAMUEL EPSTEIN, M.D.

Public Health

Medical practitioners have traditionally gone to heroic lengths
to cure sick people, but have done relatively little to keep healthy
people well. This was inevitable in medicine's early days, when little or
nothing was known about the causes of disease; there wasn't much a
doctor could do but wait for people to get sick, then do his best to
cure them. But much more is now known about the causes of disease,
and preventive medicine should at last begin to come into its own. We
are learning that many causes of disease are environmental: air, water,
and soil pollution, toxic chemicals, natural and man-made radioactivity, and stresses caused by noise and overcrowding, to name some of
the most familiar. Restoration of the environment to ecological health
would be a form of preventive medicine whose importance can hardly
be overstated. It would not be enough to eliminate pollution and
stresses in the general environment, however. Many farm and industrial workers are exposed to far greater concentrations of toxic pollutants at the workplace than the law permits the general public to be
exposed to. This double standard should be eliminated at once. Until
environmental hazards are eliminated, health workers will continue to
be burdened unnecessarily with the care of millions of Americans
whose illnesses were not only foreseeable, but also preventable.

Health

The practice of medicine in the United States is almost entirely remedial. Diseases that little or nothing has been done to prevent are treated only after their symptoms become acute. The illogic of this is self-evident. Remedial medicine will always be needed, of course, but its need ought to be a sign of *preventive* medicine's limitations, not its almost total absence.

Preventive medicine should not be equated with innoculations and vaccinations. These are certainly crucial preventive measures, but the potential scope of disease prevention is much broader. So broad, indeed, that it far transcends any strictly medical approach.

"For more than a century," Ivan Illich says, "analysis of disease trends has shown that the environment is the primary determinant of the state of general health of any population." That being so, it follows that improving environmental quality is the most promising of public health measures.

Environmental Health Hazards

Overpopulation is a health hazard. Industry, expanding to meet the growing "needs" of a growing population, pollutes air, water, and soil. Maldistribution of population aggravates problems; overcrowding causes stress, and stress exacerbates maladies such as peptic ulcers, high blood pressure, migraine headaches, and insomnia.

Air quality has improved since passage of the Clean Air Act amendments of 1972. But according to the Council on Environmental Quality, more than half of our air quality control regions were unable to meet mandated standards in 1975. Pollution abatement is subject to the law of diminishing returns: at the beginning, great improvement can be bought at modest cost; later, it costs a lot to produce a modest improvement. So we cannot be complacent about progress to date. The easiest and cheapest gains have already been made. We must be prepared for polluters to dig in their heels, insisting that the results already achieved are good enough and that further abatement measures would not be "cost-effective." Their insistence will convince many who have always heard that the business of this country is business. The trouble is, even low levels of pollution may be lethal to particularly susceptible people. If equal protection under the law means anything, we cannot let polluters off the hook at the expense of the most helpless members of our society: infants, the elderly, and the chronically ill. Nothing less than state-of-the-art pollution abatement is morally acceptable in the long run.

Some pollutants, such as mercury, arsenic, and organophosphates, inhibit the activity of essential enzymes. Other pollutants combine with cell constituents and interfere with bodily processes. Carbon monoxide, for example—the greatest non-particulate pollutant of urban air—combines with hemoglobin and slows the uptake of oxygen by red blood cells. Oxygen deficiency caused by carbon monoxide poisoning affects respiration and the functioning of heart and brain. People with heart or lung diseases, or anemia, are especially vulnerable. And overexposure of pregnant women may cause congenital defects in their children. Still other pollutants trigger dangerous responses in the body; carbon tetrachloride, for instance, can cause massive discharges of epinephrine and result in liver damage.

Many thousands of man-made chemical compounds not found in nature are introduced into the environment every year without the slightest assurance that they are safe. Synergistic effects, which cause two or more compounds to be far more toxic in combination than they are separately, aggravate the danger. More testing would help, but no testing program can give complete assurance of safety because the number of possibly synergistic combinations approaches infinity. To compound the difficulty, ill effects may not become apparent for decades after first exposure. We can certainly live without any more man-made molecules; it is by no means certain, however, that all of those we invent can be lived with.

Pollution can severely damage fetuses and infants because they have fewer cells and early cell injury can later affect large areas of the body. Young animals are more seriously affected than adults by fluoride, ozone, sulfur dioxide, lead, and mercury. The elderly are also highly susceptible. The lungs of older people lose some of their elasticity and ability to withstand disease. Respiratory and cardiovascular diseases, most common in the aged, make people of all ages less able to tolerate the stresses imposed by pollution. Assessments of pollution health hazards must recognize the special vulnerability of high-risk groups such as these.

Minorities and the poor are largely the victims of pollution caused by middle- and upper-class citizens—not that middle- and upper-class citizens want it that way, that's just the way it works. Pollution is a function of consumption,

"Air clean enough for you today?"

and families with incomes of more than $16,000 a year consume almost twice as much electricity and natural gas as families with incomes of less than $7,000; the well-to-do also use almost five times as much gasoline. Air pollution hits hardest those who are least responsible for it and least able to do anything about it.

Cancer On The Rise

Only three major causes of death have increased recently: homicide, cirrhosis of the liver, and cancer. Twenty-five percent of all Americans will develop some form of cancer, and cancer causes 20 percent of our deaths. Cancer death rates increased about 1 percent a year after

1933—until 1975, when the increase for the first seven months was about 3 percent.

Dr. Samuel Epstein, who is responsible for pioneering work in this field, found that occupational exposures are a prime cause of cancer. Occupational exposures are responsible for lung cancer, asbestosis, and pleural mesotheliomas in asbestos workers; for lung cancer in uranium and coke-oven workers; for bladder cancer in aniline dye and rubber workers; for sinus cancer in woodworkers; for cancer of the pancreas and lymphomas in organic chemists; for angiosarcoma of the liver and other forms of cancer in polyvinyl chloride workers. Fifty percent of asbestos insulation workers die of cancer, and 30 percent of all premature deaths among uranium miners are

Union Oil refinery, Rodeo, California, 1975. Photo by Kerry Richardson.

caused by lung cancer. Other high-risk occupations are in the petrochemical, smelting, and steel industries.

"There is now a growing consensus that the majority of human cancers are environmental in origin," says Dr. Epstein, "and that they are hence ultimately preventable."

We now combat cancer with what Dr. Lewis Thomas calls "halfway technology." We try to deal with cancer after it is firmly entrenched and a threat to life. Even if an infallible cure existed, *preventing* cancer would be infinitely preferable to curing it. And the prevention of thousands upon thousands of cancers requires only that we clean up our grossly polluted workplace environments. But industrial leaders and government officials seem indifferent to that shining opportunity. The secretary of Asbestos Workers Union Local 16 in San Francisco found that 42 of the 74 deaths among his local's membership between 1967 and 1975 were caused by asbestosis or cancer—between 20 and 28 years *after* a British government study had conclusively linked cancer with asbestos inhalation. While morbid statistics like these pile up, work goes on as usual in

workplace environments that are virtually guaranteed to shorten industrial workers' lives. Yet the Occupational Safety and Health Administration in early 1976 postponed the adoption of new safety standards until after that fall's presidential election. It seems that industrial safety is controversial.

OSHA, Ozone, Etc.

The Occupational Health and Safety Act of 1970 states that its aim is to "assure so far as possible every working man and woman in the nation safe and healthful working conditions and to preserve our human resources." But farm workers are exposed to insecticides, herbicides, rodenticides, nematocides, fungicides, soil sterilizers, growth regulators, fumigants, solvents, and other toxic chemicals. Many such agricultural chemicals are inadequately tested for their potential danger to exposed workers, and where special precautions are required, they are all too often neglected. The industrialization of agricul-

Environmentally induced illnesses take many forms. Horrifying but egalitarian, they spare none; the rich and poor alike are potential victims. No respecter of age, sex, or social status, cancer now ranks as one of the most feared killers in industrial societies.

To meet burgeoning food needs, governments in many regions are damming rivers and expanding irrigation facilities, despite the certainty that schistosomiasis will spread. The disease, which shortens the lives of its victims, is almost incurable. In many nations it is already epidemic. In Egypt, at least 15 million people, two of every five persons, are infected with the parasite.

Dust, sulfur dioxide, and other by-products of the burning of fossil fuels have been directly linked to illness and death. A recent study conducted in Nashville, Tennessee, showed that the incidence of heart disease in polluted areas was nearly double the normal rate. A similar study of non-cigaret smokers in California indicated that men who live in cities die of lung cancer over three times as often as their counterparts in relatively unpolluted rural areas.

The final story on environmental illnesses has yet to be written. The effects of increased exposure to carcinogenic chemicals may not show up in death statistics for 20 years. A U.S. National Academy of Sciences report suggests that, as a result of this delay, serious environmental hazards could go undetected for many years and then appear in mortality statistics with dramatic suddenness.

—LESTER BROWN, PATRICIA MCGRATH, AND
BRUCE STOKES

ture also subjects farm workers to many of the environmental insults endured by factory workers.

An ozone layer in the stratosphere filters out ultraviolet radiation, preventing it from reaching the earth in dangerous amounts. There is now considerable evidence that fluorocarbons released from aerosol spray cans are reacting chemically with the ozone layer and depleting it. Continued use of fluorocarbons might cause from 42,000 to 300,000 additional cases of skin cancer a year in the United States alone, according to one estimate.

High-flying supersonic jets are another threat to the ozone layer. The infamous SSTs are also worse producers of noise and air pollution than subsonic jets. The Concorde, for example, produces five times as much oxides of nitrogen and 12 times as much carbon monoxide and hydrocarbons as the 747. Even if it were economical and efficient, the SST should be permanently grounded as a public health measure.

Nitrates from treated sewage effluents, animal wastes, and runoff from land fertilized with chemicals are con-

verted into nitrites by intestinal bacteria. Nitrites cause serious oxygen depletion in the body.

Airborne mercury from chemical plants or pesticide sprays becomes a dangerous pollutant when it settles on bodies of water. Bacteria convert mercury to methyl mercury, a compound easily absorbed by organisms in the food chain. Methyl mercury destroys brain cells, and since it can cross the placenta, it can damage fetuses.

Polychlorinated biphenyls (PCBs) were introduced in the US in 1930, but the damage they do was undetected for nearly four decades. Like DDT, PCBs degrade very slowly and accumulate in fatty tissues. PCBs affect the liver and interfere with enzyme activity. They can also disturb the central nervous system, affect the heart and blood vessels, and cause physical deformities. The Environmental Protection Agency issued waste-disposal restrictions in early 1972 designed to keep PCB levels low. Nevertheless, EPA's Office of Toxic Substances estimates that at least 4.5 million kilograms of PCBs are dumped into the environment each year. Many fish in the Great Lakes are

Seemingly innocuous compounds present in the atmosphere can often have dramatic, unforeseen side effects, particularly when they are present in large quantities. One bizarre example is the recently discovered effect that chlorofluorocarbons (CFCs) have on the atmosphere's ozone layer.

Ozone is a gas continuously created by sunlight in the stratosphere. It not only absorbs most of the ultraviolet radiation of the sun, but also controls the temperature of the stratosphere—and thus indirectly affects the climate at the earth's surface. Removal or substantial reduction of the ozone layer would likely lead to enormous increases in the rate of skin cancer in humans and largely unknown but generally destructive effects in other animals and plants. A National Academy of Sciences publication reported that studies of the effects of a simulated 50 percent decrease in ozone showed that for some species of plants growth decreased from 20 to 50 percent, chlorophyll content declined 10 to 30 percent, and degenerative changes in cell structures occurred. Harmful mutations increased seven- to twentyfold in some preliminary experiments.

But chlorofluorocarbons may not be the only culprits. Equally perplexing is the recent discovery that the atmosphere contains large amounts of ozone-destroying chlorine atoms in the form of carbon tetrachloride (CCl_4), a compound that has been used for years as a household cleaner. Thus, CCl_4 might turn out to be just as serious a threat to the ozone layer as the CFCs. The important question is, Where did so much CCl_4 come from and how will its future concentration change relative to that of the CFCs?

Another speculation is that the chlorine compound chloroform may be associated with the purification of drinking water or sewage treatment; both processes often use chlorine. If chloroform could get to the stratosphere and destroy ozone, then the populations of all countries will be confronted with a serious long-term dilemma. If improvement of living and health standards for the growing billions, especially in less developed countries, is to be accomplished and maintained—and I have no doubt that this is an essential international goal—then a massive effort to upgrade water and sewage purification everywhere is imperative. However, since this could entail a huge increase in the use of chlorine (which in water may react chemically to produce chloroform), there arises the question of potential ozone depletion, which could endanger life on the entire planet.

There is some hard evidence connecting the increased usage of nitrogen fertilizer to an increase in the production of the gas nitrous oxide (N_2O), otherwise known as laughing gas, in the soil. It is known that N_2O can destroy ozone; therefore, when fertilizer-produced N_2O works its way up into the stratosphere, it, too, can reduce our protective shield against ultraviolet radiation. The most difficult question is, How great are these effects? Preliminary calculations suggest that they could be enormous, although there are still great uncertainties to be cleared up. Moreover, industrially produced fertilizer is the key ingredient in modern scientific farming, and, indeed, its use is projected to increase by hundreds of percent in the next twenty-five years. Thus, a discovery and warning that a great increase in fertilizer use could ultimately destroy part of the ozone shield would, if heeded, dash hopes that the developing countries could achieve self-sufficiency in food production soon. Such a discovery could be a staggering blow to those who are counting on expanded use of this particular technology to solve one important aspect of the world predicament.

—Stephen Schneider

---

badly contaminated, as are fish in the Hudson, Milwaukee, and Ohio Rivers.

Radiation and Noise

Radiation damage to cellular DNA can kill the cell or cause a mutation. If sperm or ovum cells are damaged, the damage is genetic and will be passed on to subsequent generations. Radiation damage to a fetus at a crucial stage of organ development can cause congenital abnormalities. Exposure to radiation increases the likelihood of cancer and leukemia.

Man-made sources of radiation include the testing (or use) of nuclear weapons, nuclear power plants and associated facilities, nuclear powered ships, and radioisotopes used in industry, agriculture, medicine, and scientific research. Plutonium 239, a by-product of nuclear power plants and the material of which atomic bombs are made, is the most virulent of carcinogens; it decays very slowly and remains lethal for hundreds of thousands of years.

Our world is brim-full of noise-makers: motor vehicles, construction equipment, aircraft, lawnmowers, chainsaws, factory and farm machinery, motorcycles, trail bikes, snowmobiles, hydroplanes, dune buggies. . . . Noise has subtle but decisive effects on physical and mental well-being. It contributes to adrenal enlargements, coronary problems, ulcers, and nervous disorders. Noise creates stress, even when we resolutely banish it from our consciousness, and stress aggravates almost all ailments. People need reasonable quiet for psychological equilibrium, so silence should not be regarded as a luxury.

Nearly all processed and packaged foods in this country are adulterated. A Ralph Nader study group revealed in 1970 that less than half the more than 2,000 food additives then in use—artificial flavorings, colorings, texturizers, preservatives, and what have you—had been tested for safety. Exertions to detoxify such chemical additives may overstress the liver, kidneys, and spleen. Additives such as sulfur dioxide, sodium nitrate, and food colorings interfere with the normal functioning of enzymes and vitamins.

Countless other environmental hazards menace human health, but those mentioned here are enough to outline the problem and suggest some remedies.

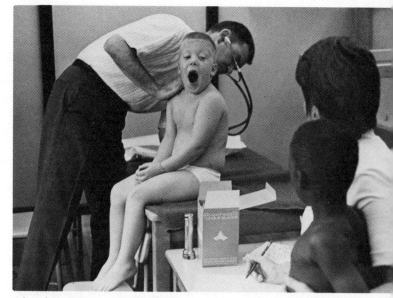

Photo by Karen R. Preuss/Jeroboam, Inc.

Healthier People in a Clean World

An ecologically sick environment is an unhealthy environment to live in. Restoring the environment to health would be the form of preventive medicine that would do the most good for the greatest number in the shortest time. Ecologically benign ways of meeting man's material needs do exist, and the Appropriate Technology movement can discover many more. Modern man need not become unmodern, but he *must* stop poisoning the environment with wastes of a concentration or a character unknown in the natural world.

Clean air and water, uncontaminated soils, and reduced levels of noise and man-made radioactivity cannot be achieved overnight. But the further we progress toward those goals, the more we will be rewarded by major improvements in public health. Cleaning up the general outdoor environment will be of limited benefit, however, if workplace environments remain unhealthy and unsafe. Some industry spokesmen insist that by working where they do, workers tacitly accept any risks associated with the job. There are several troubles with this. For one, industry has seldom been completely candid about the risks its employees are exposed to. For another, workers aware of the risks may face an agonizing choice between known health hazards and the known hazards of unemployment. If workplace environmental hazards were inherent and unavoidable, it'd be a somewhat different matter. But they're not; their non-abatement merely increases the profits of those whose risks are purely financial.

Farming has traditionally been exempted from many of the safety regulations haphazardly applied to other vocations. This seemed reasonable when the family farm was

the archetype, perhaps; but in the era of huge agribusiness farms, exemption from health and safety regulations is one more subsidy for the rich at the expense of the poor.

If our external environments were all we could hope for, we might still suffer unnecessarily from faulty *interior* environments. The Food and Drug Administration has permitted (pending further tests) continued consumption of food colorings found to cause cancer in laboratory animals. Our current practice reflects the philosophy that food additives and pharmaceuticals are presumed safe until proved to be otherwise. This philosophy has blighted many lives and ended many others. The burden of proof should not rest on the consumer—or even the government—to prove products dangerous; instead, the burden of proof must be placed on the manufacturer to show that his product is safe. No one should be permitted to market a product whose safety is merely assumed and whose possible dangers have not even been investigated. If this means that the deluge of untested new chemical compounds slows to a trickle, no doubt the chemical companies and their customers will manage to survive. It is by no means certain, on the other hand, that either the companies or their customers can long survive if the random introduction of countless untested chemicals continues.

Even if our exterior and interior environments were all satisfactory, we would still find ourselves paradoxically unsatisfied. It isn't enough that every place will barely do; we need islands of excellence that far exceed minimum environmental standards. For the nation as a whole, that need can best be met by preserving and enlarging park, recreation, and wilderness areas. But the need is particularly acute within cities, where environments are often hard to

They picnic on exquisitely packaged food from a portable icebox by a polluted stream and go on to spend the night at a park which is a menace to public health and morals. Just before dozing off on an air mattress, beneath a nylon tent, amid the stench of decaying refuse, they may reflect vaguely on the curious unevenness of their blessings. Is this, indeed, the American genius?

—JOHN KENNETH GALBRAITH

raise above borderline levels and where exceptional stresses threaten physical and mental health. It must therefore become national policy to vastly increase the quantity and quality of urban parklands.

Cleaning the Cities

It is impossible to imagine a healthy environment unless population and population density are controlled. Ways of stabilizing population at a sustainable level and of securing a better distribution of population are discussed in chapters on decentralization and population. We merely remind you here that these matters profoundly affect public health and safety.

Cities are the worst polluted areas, and their worst polluter is the automobile. Exhaust fumes are responsible for about 60 percent of all air pollution, and as much as 90 percent in some urban areas. The federal and state governments should therefore support municipalities that seek to limit or eliminate the use of private cars in central cities. Among alternative modes of transportation, priority should be given to the most energy- and resource-efficient, notably walking, bicycling, jitneys, buses, and trolleys.

En route to a pollution-free environment, several principles must be kept in mind:

* Pollution must be controlled at the source, the only place where it is concentrated enough to be dealt with. Dispersal techniques such as the use of tall smokestacks are a fraud: they merely redistribute the same total amount of pollution so that close-by people get less of it and far-off people get more.
* Where air quality is better than EPA standards, the rule must be that the air is not to be degraded at all. Otherwise, polluting industries have an incentive to lo-

cate factories where the air is best and standards can be met with minimal abatement costs.
* Polluters must pay. Enforcement has too often been lax or absent. Fines have been set so low that a polluter saves money by continuing to defy the law. Penalties must be realistic and enforcement must be strict. Better in principle than fines are taxes based on the type and amount of emissions, rewarding good performance and penalizing bad. Such laws in West Germany have been remarkably successful in maintaining air and water quality in the heavily industrial Ruhr Valley.

A healthy environment is the foundation upon which public health must rest. Without it, medical practitioners can only palliate illnesses that should have been prevented.

"This is the man who ate the steak that came from the steer that nibbled the grass that grew in the field where roamed the cat that caught the bird that ate the fish that fed on the bug that floated around in the oil slick."

Drawing by J. B. Handelsman; © *The New Yorker Magazine, Inc.*

There is no quiet place in the white man's cities. No place to hear the leaves of spring or the rustle of insects' wings. . . .
—CHIEF SEALTH

Thanks to the progress of medicine, many great health hazards have been eradicated. Some of the remaining problems of how to defend ourselves against disease producers will undoubtedly be solved in the future, but there will always remain one great threat to man: his own kind.

Modern society has progressed dramatically in terms of technological advances, but this has been at the cost of human mental and physical well-being. Pollution of all kinds—noise, air, water, overpopulation—plague us, and the world literature on the consequences of such developments is enormous.

We have defined stress as the "nonspecific response of the body to any demand," and this would mean essentially that all living beings are constantly under stress. Anything, whether pleasant or unpleasant, that speeds up the intensity of life causes a temporary increase in stress. Stress does not consist merely of damage, but also of adaptation to damage, irrespective of what causes the wear and tear.

Our research has determined that when man is confronted with a stress-producing agent (a stressor), no matter what the particular irritant is, he undergoes a triphasic reaction called the "general adaptation syndrome." This consists of 1) the phase of alarm, during which the body is put on the alert and summons its defensive forces to combat the stressor, 2) the stage of resistance, where the body maintains its fight against the irritant, and 3) the stage of exhaustion, when, unable to resist attack any longer, the body finally gives in to disease and/or death. There is considerable evidence that the body's adaptive potential is finite; although adaptation can be acquired and sometimes maintained for long periods, constant exposure to any stressors leads to the inevitable breakdown of resistance.

Although the public makes a clear distinction between the "annoyance" caused by pollution and its ability to affect health, science understands that the difference is merely one of degree, because any kind of annoyance, if sufficiently intense and prolonged, will adversely influence mental and physical well-being.

Furthermore, even the distinction between mental and physical health is somewhat artificial and arbitrary, as proven by the very existence of "psychosomatic medicine." No modern physician will doubt that mental stress can give rise to such tangible and objective physical morbid changes as peptic ulcers, high blood pressure, migraine headaches, insomnia, or acute cardiac death.

We know that pollution can induce:

—the diseases known to result from stress;
—biochemical changes (mostly those characteristic of excessive stress) in the constitution of the body's tissues and fluids;
—varying degrees of nervous derangements, from simple sleeplessness to emotional upsets and even epileptiform convulsions;
—cardiovascular changes, such as hypertension, sometimes conducive to heart disease;
—gastrointestinal ulcers;
—interference with the normal sexual cycle of females;
—embryonic malformation or still birth, when applied during certain stages of pregnancy.

Some of the results of the stress encountered in daily life can be treated with standard medicines, others cannot. In order to meet the social stresses of our time, suggestions have been made for better laws or more severe law enforcement, arms limitation, and so on. To counteract the effects of mental distress people try out various techniques which claim to eradicate the ill effects, or at least help us to cope with them. This is why so many people turn to psychotherapy, Transcendental Meditation, the use of ginseng—the number of remedies and psychologic techniques grows every day. When nothing seems to work, some find an outlet for their energy only in violence, drugs, or alcohol, thus creating still another problem for society. To my mind, the root of the problem lies in the lack of a proper code of motivation that gives our lives a purpose which we can respect. I have tried to introduce a behavioral code called "altruistic egoism", which I described in my book *Stress Without Distress*. Based on scientific laws rather than absolute faith in traditional values, I think this could help people with their constant desire to find worthwhile goals and improve the quality of life.

Yet wouldn't it be better if we could find a way to prevent the distress of life, rather than find means to help us deal with a hostile world? I believe that this should be our highest priority in formulating the policies of governments to meet the stresses of modern civilization.

—HANS SELYE

Of approximately two million known chemical compounds, only 6,000 have undergone laboratory tests for carcinogenicity. Of those that have been tested, between ten and 16 percent have produced cancer in animals. Therefore, our current situation is not unlike having 20,000 suspected criminals walking the streets while our doors are unlocked.

Carefully controlled laboratory experiments with animals and statistical correlations in selected groups of humans and in society at large have revealed a great deal about the origins of cancer. Probably the most startling revelation of all is that between 75 and 90 percent of all cancers are related to environmental factors. The term "environmental," in this case, encompasses substances in the food we eat, the air we breathe, and the water we drink, as well as our personal habits, occupations and lifestyles.

Today, the workplace environment unfortunately continues to be the primary laboratory in which the carcinogenicity to humans of certain substances is first revealed.

It has been discovered that virtually every substance (with the notable exception of arsenic) which is carcinogenic to man also causes cancer in animals. This has allowed scientists to identify suspected carcinogens which, although their potential danger is not as clearly established as it would be from direct observation among humans, should be treated with extreme suspicion and caution.

More than any other type of cancer, lung cancer—which in the overwhelming majority of cases is attributable to cigarette smoking—is responsible for the rapid rise in the incidence of cancer in the United States over the past fifty years. In this century the occurrence of several types of cancer, including cancer of the esophagus, prostate, and intestinal tract has remained fairly stable, and cancers of the stomach and uterus have actually declined significantly. Lung cancer, on the other hand, has soared among men (from a rate of about 2 cases per 100,000 population in 1930 to over 50 cases per 100,000 today) and is beginning to rise steeply among women as well.

Despite growing awareness that cancer is largely an environmental disease, scientific testing (and hence meaningful regulation) of chemicals in our environment has lagged far behind. Nevertheless, about 22 chemical substances are generally conceded to be human carcinogens, and a much larger number—about 1,500, according to data from the National Institute for Occupational Health and Safety—are under suspicion.

Vinyl chloride came to public attention in 1974 when several workers who had handled the substance for long periods began developing angiosarcoma, a rare and invariably fatal type of liver cancer. Polyvinyl chloride, which is manufactured from vinyl chloride, is one of the most common plastics in use today, found in everything from toys to food wrappings.

Several pesticides in the chlorinated hydrocarbon family—DDT, Aldrin, Dieldrin, chlordane and heptachlor—have been banned or suspended by the Environmental Protection Agency because they cause cancer in laboratory animals. However, virtually all living Americans still have residues of these chemicals in their bodies. Whether they are dangerous levels is not known. It is worth mentioning that pesticide industry spokesmen and scientists launched a vicious attack of ridicule and vituperation against the late Dr. Rachel Carson when she suggested over a decade ago that some of the chlorinated hydrocarbons should be banned.

The carcinogenic potential of a number of food additives is currently being hotly disputed, with public interest groups and independent researchers often calling for controls on the basis of disturbing but inconclusive tests, and the food industry calling for more testing and a go-slow approach. In the past, the Food and Drug Administration has tended to take industry's side.

Despite many uncertainties about the relationship between diet and cancer, the patterns of cancer incidence in different nations with distinct eating habits are good evidence that dietary customs do affect cancer incidence. The Japanese, who eat considerable amounts of salted fish (containing nitrosamines) and pickled vegetables and like many foods charcoal-broiled, have an incidence of stomach cancer six times higher than Americans.

It is well established that air pollution aggravates, often

seriously, respiratory diseases such as emphysema. It is also possible that air pollution acts as a cocarcinogen; in fact, Pike and a number of colleagues from the University of Southern California suggest that cigarette smoking may help convert low-level carcinogens in the air to their most destructive forms.

Acute side effects of drugs are relatively easy to determine and are generally eliminated, or at least discovered and made known to the potential user before a new drug is brought on the market. Long-term side effects, including cancer, are much more difficult to determine and, in the case of many drugs, remain largely unknown. Cancer-causing properties of several common drugs have been demonstrated, however, even though in some cases more than a shadow of a doubt remains.

The main cancer research arm of the federal government is the National Cancer Institute, which has an annual budget of over $750 million. (Only a small fraction of this is spent on research on environmental carcinogens and on preventive approaches—a particularly sore point with the Institute's critics.)

Unfortunately, the FDA has been, at best, a rather sleepy watchdog. It has let a number of substances go by without testing them adequately for carcinogenicity, even though the substances should have been regarded with extreme suspicion. A good example is acrylonitrile, a chemical substance which is similar in its molecular structure to vinyl chloride. The FDA has given "interim" approval to a number of plastic beverage bottles made from acrylonitrile monomers without performing itself, or requiring of the manufacturer, any long-term feeding studies on the substance.

The agency is allowed to approve substances without premarket testing if they are Generally Recognized As Safe (GRAS) or if they were on the market prior to 1958 and 1960, when separate amendments strengthening the Food, Drug and Cosmetic Act were passed. However, it must remove any approved substance from the market if new evidence shows that it is unsafe. The FDA's testing program for GRAS substances and those which have been judged acceptable by default is almost ludicrously behind schedule. Its review of color additives, which was to have been completed by 1962, is still not completed in 1976.

The agency's stumblebum performance has been well documented by Ralph Nader and other consumer spokesmen and amply criticized by consumers, environmentalists and some members of Congress, but to little effect. Its problem, according to many observers, is that it is far too

much under the influence of the food, drug and chemical industries—the result of decades of pressure from these interests with very little counterpressure from consumer and environmental organizations.

The Nuclear Regulatory Commission is responsible for setting radiation standards and for acting as a watchdog over the nation's nuclear power industry. The NRC was formed out of the old AEC and its record is generally an improvement over that compiled by its predecessor, which winked at serious violations of its own safety standards and seemed obsessed with promoting nuclear power. The NRC is, nevertheless, attempting to steer the nation toward a "plutonium economy", which would leave us dependent on one of the most explosive and carcinogenic substances known to man. A recent NRDC lawsuit has set back the agency's plans.

It is time that we forced our regulatory agencies to take a much tougher stance against proven and suspected carcinogens in the environment. Even with existing laws, controls over cancer-causing substances could be considerably more effective than they are today. New laws requiring better premarket testing of chemicals and more comprehensive regulation of toxic substances would, if properly drafted and implemented, be enormously helpful.

Finally, we must face the fact that the "chemical revolution" of the past fifty years appears to be one of the chief factors behind the rapid rise in the incidence of cancer. And we may only be seeing the tip of the iceberg, because most of the suspected chemical carcinogens did not come into widespread use until after World War II. Ominously, the rate of cancer incidence increased 2 percent last year after rising at a rate of about 1 percent per year for many years. There is no obvious reason why we cannot have a high standard of living without dwelling amid a chemical minefield of cancer-causing agents.

More than any other disease, cancer gives rise to a feeling of hopelessness in all of us, tempting us to throw up our hands and ask, "What can I do?" But if 8 out of every 10 cancer cases are attributable to environmental factors, then it is obvious that cancer is not, except in a minority of cases, inevitable.

Therefore, while we continue to search for a cure, the best remedy is still the oldest one: preventive medicine.

—From the *Newsletter* of the
Natural Resources Defense Council,
Summer 1976

The sense of helplessness, the sense of not knowing, the fright, the confusion, the notion that there's a "juggernaut" or "combine," makes it extremely difficult for one to develop one's own innate capacity for growth, for self-healing. Survival becomes the goal, not aliveness.
                                                           —LEONARD DUHL, M.D.

I wish to comment on the misapprehension that medicine has already developed into a full-fledged science, and having matured to this state has already run out of its string. What I hope to persuade you to is, instead, the view that medicine is still the most immature and undeveloped, and, on balance, most unaccomplished of sciences, with a long, long way to go still ahead.

Preventive medicine is being urged on us, from all sides, as though we'd never heard of it, nor ever hankered for it to become, some day, a reality. And if you fail to prevent disease, through some unspecified oversight, then early detection is the thing; if you can check the progress of glaucoma or cervical cancer by early detection, why not do the same for coronary disease, arthritis, diabetes, stroke and all the rest? This has become the public expectation, and it is our misfortune not to have been sufficiently candid about the impossibility of such an expectation, at this state of our knowledge.

We must be careful, in my opinion, not to make promises about preventive medicine as we should have been (but weren't) about curative medicine in the past quarter-century.

For, if the truth be told, we are still at a very early, primitive stage in the development of medical science. There should be nothing shocking or unnerving about this statement. On the contrary, it ought to provide a source for the greatest optimism about the future. It is not that the science has not been getting anywhere, or is stuck somehow; there are the most convincing sorts of evidence that it is moving, and getting ready to move faster and more productively. But it has to be said that it is just at its beginnings, and most of its new world lies still ahead.

It is often said that as medicine becomes more of a science, the costs of care become higher and higher, but the truth is just the opposite. When the science is really far enough advanced so that the resulting technology can deal directly and decisively with an underlying disease mechanism, the costs go down. The more effective the medical technology, the simpler it is, and the cheaper.

The cost is at its highest, and the technology at its most complex, when we are only halfway along.

We are only halfway, or less than that distance, in our understanding of the causative mechanisms in heart dis-

ease, cancer, stroke, nephritis, arthritis, schizophrenia and the others, and what we have for therapy is, correspondingly, a halfway technology, costing enormous sums of money and involving high complexity.

Fifteen years ago, when the biological revolution was just getting under way, things were still quiet and relatively inactive in medicine. Now, the new information is coming in cascades, and it is filled with meaning and astonishment for all of us. And it should not need mentioning that the greatest part of this information has come out of laboratories engaged in the fundamental biological sciences—from the fields of immunology, bacteriophage and microbial genetics, cell biology, membrane structure and physiology, neurophysiology and molecular biology.

Moreover, it is my belief that we are just at the beginning of this.

What is likely to come of this, in the best of possible worlds? Eventually, if all goes reasonably well, nothing less than the control of human disease. If not the outright elimination of disease, at the least a technological capacity to turn it around and govern it when it occurs.

This does not mean as much as it sounds like meaning. It has nothing at all to do with death, beyond the prevention of premature death. No matter how skilled we become at controlling or abolishing the last of our major diseases, we will still die, and probably die by the same, unalterable genetic clock, as always. We will still grow old, although aging will not be the incapacitating and humiliating disorder that it is for most of us, sooner or later, these days.

So things will be significantly better, and the health care system will be very much less a drain on the public purse. But not Utopia. We will still have our other anxieties, our neuroses, our fears of meaninglessness, our problems with each other. We will still be compelled to stare at famine and death on our television screens, trying to think up new excuses. Coping once and for all with organic disease will not solve any of these, but perhaps it is safe to say that we will be somewhat better at constructing a workable society if we are, at least, physically healthy. Given enough time and patience, and enough good luck in the science, that objective, limited as it may be, is within our grasp.

                                                           —LEWIS THOMAS

Lewis Thomas, president of the Sloan-Kettering Cancer Center in New York, has publicly confessed that he is less intelligent than his liver. If he were consciously in control of hepatic decisions for his own body, Dr. Thomas would expect to make a mess of things. He feels the same way about all his working parts: "They are better off without my intervention, whatever they do." Autonomic systems, he concludes, are best left autonomous. It is refreshing to find a major scientist and medical man who feels humility before his liver.

It has not always been so. We have inherited a long tradition which proclaims the superiority of human mentality over all systems which lack consciousness. When the human brain reached a level of evolutionary development permitting it to understand some of the processes going on in the world, it promptly began to manage and manipulate those processes in the service of what it took to be human advantage. With hindsight acquired through several thousands of years of human experience, we are now in a position to see that the brain, in its pride and power, has made some colossal errors.

Acting in ignorance, we have discovered that we can significantly alter genetic structures without even trying to do so, merely as an accidental byproduct of some of our other engineering endeavors. A recent article in *Science* examines scores of environmental mutagenic hazards, from aspirin to X-rays, and proposes an elaborate and sophisticated screening procedure to find out what we are doing to our poor, battered genetic heritage. Science, arriving late as usual, is now needed to uncover the effects of accidental engineering because it has not been able to inform engineers of the meaning of their actions in advance. The "engineers" in this case include the medical profession, cosmetic and pharmaceutical manufacturers, agricultural experts, military leaders, pesticide salesmen, and other such practical public servants who do not characteristically consult scientific journals before going to work in the morning. Even if they did, they would find pitifully little information there about the genetic implications of their activities. Nobody knows what is going on, but everybody keeps busy.

Humans have not proved to be the world's most clever livers, but merely the most powerful. Intelligence and even wisdom reside in the evolved workings of many natural systems which lack both our consciousness and our addiction to meddling. If we were really clever livers—that is, clever at the business of living—we would nourish our own minds upon the principles we are able to discover at work in the natural systems around us, and those within us.

—JOSEPH MEEKER

Recommended Actions

☐ The Administration should propose legislation to establish a National Institute for Preventive Medicine.

☐ Congress should enact a law to control toxic substances; the law must require manufacturers to prove the safety of new chemical compounds before marketing them.

☐ Congress should enact a law to curb pollution by taxing polluters in proportion to the amount they pollute.

☐ Anti-pollution laws should be more strictly enforced, and to this end, the budget of the Environmental Protection Agency should be increased.

☐ Congress should mandate that workplace environments meet the same pollution standards that apply elsewhere.

☐ An appropriate committee of Congress should hold hearings to determine why the Occupational Health and Safety Act has been less effective than it should, proposing corrective amendments.

☐ A committee of Congress should investigate the inadequacy of the Food and Drug Administration's protection of consumers.

☐ The Environmental Protection Agency should set noise-pollution standards and strictly enforce them.

☐ Congress should ban supersonic transport planes from US airspace because of associated health hazards (among other things).

☐ Aerosol cans with fluorocarbon propellants should be banned because of their effect on the ozone layer.

☐ Federal and state governments should support municipal initiatives to limit or ban the use of private automobiles in high-density urban areas.

☐ Cities, with federal and state encouragement and support, must create more urban parks for the physical and mental well-being of their residents.

☐ For ways of reducing health hazards associated with maldistribution of population, see the chapter on decentralization and human settlements.

☐ For ways of reducing the health hazards of man-made radioactivity, see the chapter on control of the atom.

... agriculture, still the greatest single activity of man on earth. ...

—E.F. Schumacher

Agriculture, Food, and Nutrition

Amid the technicolored marvels of the American supermarket, the links between agriculture, food, and nutrition fall away. American nutrition is increasingly a branch of industrial chemistry. The newest of American foods are manmade objects to which nutrition can be added. And American agriculture, once a handicraft, is rapidly becoming a large-scale corporate enterprise managed not by sons of the soil but by captains of commerce. That we have gone so far so fast in breaking the chain that binds together earth and the nourishment of man is astonishing. That we should fail to reverse the trend is unthinkable. For the system that supports our curiously baroque food supply has been built upon an unsustainable illusion: that the natural flow of energy and materials in the biosphere can be interrupted indefinitely—with impunity. Mechanized, energy-intensive, chemicals-dependent American agriculture makes inefficient use of two finite and dwindling resources: fossil fuels and arable land. Yields per man-hour are high, but yields per acre or per unit of energy input are not. Contemporary US-style agriculture is inappropriate even for the US under current and future conditions; for Third World countries to mimic US agricultural technology would be suicidal.

Vet rice agriculture in Mali.
Photo courtesy of the International Labour Office.

Agriculture

Human life depends on some half-a-hundred known nutrients. These, along with nutrients as yet unknown, are acquirable through the ingestion of enough of the right kinds of foods. The production of enough of the right kinds of foods depends very largely on the intentional culture of plants and animals. (Of all human food, some three quarters comes from crop land.) But in the American marketplace, the smells of field and farmyard seem remote. The abundance is dazzling; the produce seasonless, but earth's foods do not predominate here. The aisles are lined with tens of hundreds of "food products" turned out for "fun" (ours) and profit (theirs) by scores of food "manufacturers"—part of the largest single industry in the US.

It is a questionable abundance this system has produced. Food has often been treated like a somewhat inferior raw material that, in the search for profit, is steamed, smashed, extruded, teased, toasted, prodded, and—above all—extended. The resulting "product," its nutritional qualities destroyed, is then patched up by food scientists in the hope that it may once more be capable of sustaining life.

Virtually all processing reduces food's nutritional value. Some losses are tolerable—in canning and freezing produce, for example—since food and its nutrients that would otherwise go to waste are thereby saved and made available out of season. But it is a fair generality that the more a food is processed, the less nutrients it contains. Processing has this overall degrading effect because it eliminates vitamins and minerals—by removal as in refining, or by destruction as in high-heat processing—and because it dilutes the remaining nutrients by adding cheap fillers: water, fats, starches, sugars. Foods so degraded cannot be reconstituted nutritionally for the same reasons that a "complete" food cannot be fabricated de novo: because (1) there is no certainty that every nutrient essential for man has been identified, and (2) even if all essentials had been identified, it is not known at what level and in what sorts of contexts many nutrients ought to be restored. Given unlimited funds, unlimited energy supplies, and lots of time, mankind could probably learn to restore to food what we have taken out. We might do this if it were either necessary or rational to do so. Clearly it is neither.

After the subtractives come the additives, accidental and intentional. Some come unbidden from the universal contamination of the food producing environment—pesticides, PCBs, PBBs, chemicals like machinery cleaners and sterilants left over from processing—and are not meant to turn up in the food. But in addition to these inadvertent contaminants, an increasing number of novel chemicals are entering the food supply because someone put them there deliberately. The average American consumed three pounds of intentional additives in 1966, five pounds in 1971, and an estimated nine pounds in 1976, a 200 percent increase in ten years. Even if each additive had been thoroughly tested for known hazards—chronic toxicity, carcinogenicity, mutagenicity, teratogenicity—which each has not, their sheer number and the quantities in which they are entering the human diet would indicate an unacceptable level of risk. For hazards as yet unimagined cannot be tested for at all. And it is universally acknowledged that *there is no way of accounting for the interactions of these chemicals*—with each other, with other ingredients of the foods they inhabit, with other foods in the diet, with other chemicals in the environment, with the diversity of human biochemistries and human states of health.

Unmolested foods may also contain unsafe components; rhubarb leaves can kill. But unless it is argued that all risk is acceptable so long as some risk is unavoidable, that fact is not a rational defense of additives, especially when the benefits to the consumer from the most abundantly used additives are so frivolous. Could the possible risk of cancer from the ingestion of Red #2 be rationally weighed against the benefit of a richer brown devil's food cake? (Fortunately, the FDA decided that it could not.)

Most additives are not used, as is often claimed, to protect perishable foods from spoilage. America, with more refrigerators per capita than any other country, also has more additives per capita. More than 90 percent of the additives now in use (both by weight and by value) are not preservatives. They are colors, flavors, emulsifiers, stabilizers, texturizers, and nutrients designed to replace the colors, flavors, textures, and nutrients destroyed by processing. Additives have also made possible whole new families of food inventions: fake fruit juices, mock eggs, imitation bacon, and mock plastic puddings in plastic containers.

"Progress" in Preparing Foods

Until now, food processing has seemed an inevitable accompaniment to "progress," an investment in the continued growth of the food industry. Since the total amount of food an individual can consume is limited by nature

A typical breakfast cereal, which you buy for 69 cents, brings you 12 cents worth of advertising, three cents worth of grain, and about seven cents of cardboard box.

(even for individuals willing to tolerate obesity), a stabilizing population threatened the food industry with zero economic growth. Profits could be increased only by developing substitute foods that used cheaper raw materials or through the addition to raw produce of a benefit, real or imagined, for which the customer could be led by advertising to pay a premium. The food objects this system has created—fruitless jams, imitation margarines, low-calorie whipped creams, cholesterol-free eggs, nutrient-free diet cookies and the rest—are not merely nutritionally disastrous and toxicologically questionable, they are ecologically irresponsible. Food is being degraded, nutrition comprised, and energy wasted.

The system that moves food from farms and laboratories to the stove tops of America is absurdly energy-intensive. Food processing and related industries are sixth among major industrial groups in the US in energy use. Indeed, the total food system utilizes in production, transportation, processing, and storage, roughly ten units of energy for every unit of energy represented by the food itself. For every calorie eaten in the US, in other words, ten calories of fossil fuel have been consumed. Yet unlike the production of steel or aluminum, food production ought logically to be an energy-yielding activity.

To understand why this is so, it is necessary to understand how agriculture and food systems are supposed to work. All human foods that are not laboratory produced are either plants or plant-consumers (i.e., animals). Plants are autotrophs, or self-nourishers. Given the right elements (carbon, oxygen, hydrogen, nitrogen, and a dozen or so minerals), plants can make their own foodstuffs, vita-

mins, proteins, fats, carbohydrates. Man, like other animals, is a heterotroph. He depends on plants to construct for him many of the complex organic molecules necessary for life. And in order to hunt out, consume, digest, and degrade those substances, then to reconstruct their parts into tissues of his own, man needs energy.

The energy man lives on is solar energy, transduced by plants into substances solid enough to sink the teeth into. Through photosynthesis, plants capture in chemical form some portion of that inexhaustible energy store that streams in daily from outer space, thus providing energy for their own metabolism (including the manufacture of proteins and oils) as well as for the growth and maintenance of man and other animals. In his turn, man degrades plant substance, extracting its energy and releasing back to the environment water, carbon dioxide, and nitrogen so that the cycle can begin again.

All life is ultimately dependent upon the green pigment chlorophyll, the actual compound in plants that uses photons of light energy to transmute water and carbon dioxide into carbohydrate. Man's dependence on this leafy pigment is so profound that it has been called the "green thralldom." Modern man, however, is much more conscious of his dependence upon the sunlight stored in the bodies of ancient plants and animals and transformed over time into petrochemicals. Like industrial progress, agricultural progress has come to be dependent on such fossil fuels. Thus modern crop plants depend for their productivity not only on incoming solar energy, but on fossil solar energy converted into nitrogen fertilizers, pesticides, herbicides, and irrigation, plus tractors, combines, and other farm machinery and the fuel that propels them. US yields

The California Aqueduct. Photo courtesy of the California Department of Water Resources.

sions will be made closer to the people affected by them. There will be a better chance to do things right.

Revamping the financing of transportation will create local options so that local needs can be met in the most appropriate way. Revamping transportation regulations will let each mode find its own level, and the rates charged customers will reflect the true, unsubsidized cost of providing service.

Control by one company of production for competing modes should be outlawed. General Motors, for example, should be required to divest itself of either its auto, bus, or locomotive divisions.

Changes in regulations can put more cargo onto carriers that will deliver it most economically, and changes in the same direction are needed for passenger transportation. Travelers and commuters must be coaxed out of cars and airplanes and won back to trains, buses, and mass transit.

American trains should be brought up to the quality of European, Canadian, and Japanese trains. Run-of-the-mill trains abroad give better service than ours, and elite trains far surpass anything we have. First-class trains in Europe and Japan provide comfortable accommodations and good meals; some also offer businessmen office equipment, telephones, and stenographers. Parents can even obtain baby-sitters.

The salesmanship as well as the service of Amtrak seems lacking. Entertainment aboard would help make passenger trains more attractive. Holiday specials—such as ski trains between Boston and New Hampshire or New York and Vermont, or tour trains to other popular holiday areas— are naturals and ski trains, at least, used to be common. Arranging for passengers either to bring their cars along piggy-back on flat cars or to rent autos at their destinations

at a discount, as part of a package deal, are other obvious promotions.

But train rides won't be comfortable, much less enjoyable, if our roadbeds aren't improved. They are so rough and poorly kept up that even on our best passenger train, the Metroliner, one sways more wildly than on an ordinary train in Europe; and our potentially fastest train, the New York to Boston Turbotrain, uses only a fraction of its design speed, going no faster than conventional equipment. Train travel should be fast and restful. But freight doesn't care about smooth rides and railroads have seemingly cared about nothing but freight, so roadbeds have been allowed to deteriorate. If train patrons are to become regulars, they must be given tolerably comfortable service.

The federal government should participate in repairing and upgrading roadbeds. A program on the model of the Civilian Conservation Corps could employ people to work on the roadbeds. (The Army Corps of Engineers is another institution that could be used; roadbed improvement would be better work for the Corps than damming wild rivers.) Or a system of low-interest federal loans could be provided to railroads to improve their roadbeds, with penalties for railroads that do not. It may eventually be necessary to nationalize the roadbeds, with their signal systems and field facilities, in order to upgrade them. If so, fine. Virtually all the world's railroads outside the US are government-owned, and nationalization would put railroad rights-of-way on an equal footing with highways, airports, and navigable waterways. Arguments about nationalization are beside the main point, however, which is repair. Arguments are bound to be fierce; nevertheless, they must not be allowed to delay the work.

Repair of roadbeds—leveling bad grades, loosening

Freight hauling is vital in a major industrial and heavy agricultural nation like ours. Railroads can do the job better, more reliably, with less air pollution, and with better fuel-use efficiency than any other mode of transport. With Amtrak's new, more reliable and comfortable passenger equipment now being built, trains can obtain the higher load factors that will make railroads the most energy-efficient transporter of people as well as freight. Both accomplishments are possible using existing facilities. Little, if any, additional land would have to be ripped from fields and forests or cities and towns to build new freeways or truckways. . . .

Since 1920, governments in this country at all levels have spent about $400 billion on transportation. Railroads

have received less than one percent of that money. The federal government provides as much as a billion dollars a year in support of air travel and much more for building and maintaining highways.

On the bright side, there's substantial evidence that Americans . . . will patronize good [rail] service when it is provided. Surprising ridership increases are being realized on clean, reliable trains operated at relatively slow speeds. The French Turbotrains operating between Chicago and Detroit, which achieve an overall average of only 50 mph and do not exceed 70 mph, drew 90 percent more passengers in June of 1975 than in the same month of 1974.

—ORREN BEATY

Photo by Peeter Vilms/Jeroboam, Inc.

A few years ago several conservation-environment groups and the United Auto Workers issued a joint statement declaring that the conventional, reciprocating, internal-combustion, Otto-cycle engine had to go. Hardly anyone listened, and since the untimely death of Walter Reuther, the union hasn't uttered anything like it.

One after the other, various technologies have been touted prematurely as the alternative panacea to the conventional ICE: diesel, wankel, gas-turbine, Rankine- and Stirling-cycle steam engines, flywheels and electric motors, and engines powered by propane, methane, hydrogen, and other exotic fuels. Perhaps, some day, one of them will emerge as *the* engine of the future, but I doubt it.

Given the different demands of the long-haul heavy trucker, the inner-city deliveryman, and the suburban family, there does not and probably never will exist an engine equally well suited to these tasks. If you didn't have to worry about noxious emissions and fuel consumption, the old ICE is about as good a compromise as any. That's why it has come to dominate the market. But if Henry Ford, Louis Chevrolet, and the other automotive pioneers had had to cope with EPA, ERDA, FEA, and the other regulators of today, you can bet there would be a different kind of propulsion system in the family heap.

If we are to come to grips with the demands for cleaner and thriftier engines that are capable of meeting the operating and transportation needs of myriad interests, we are going to have to drop the notion of a single solution and start looking to a range of engines for different purposes.

tight curves, smoothing bumps, and the continuous-welding of all track used by passenger trains—should be a major goal of the new Administration. It is a more modest goal than the moon, one achievable earlier than wiping out poverty (which railroad jobs would help to do), and its benefits would last a century or more if we took good care of them.

Bringing our trains up to the standards of the USSR's or Japan's or Europe's would require very hard work; to make them *better* would be a great goal, one with patriotism to fuel it and usefulness besides. We must begin soon. If we don't, costs will escalate as resources dwindle and scarcity drives prices up.

It will take time to wean Americans from the automobile, so we must now mitigate its consequences.

The Interstate Highway System should be declared complete, and no new segments built.

A miles-per-gallon standard for cars should be set—in the mid-20s at first, moving upwards over the years—with penalties for manufacturers who fail to meet it. Such penalties should be matched with financial aid to companies that exceed the standard. The Environmental Protection Agency already publishes figures on fuel economy for most cars on the market; EPA's testing should be expanded and refined.

Better fuel economy can come about through refinements in engine design, including alternatives to the internal combustion engine that should be vigorously pursued; through limiting car weight; by banning automatic transmissions (except on cars specially prepared for handicapped people); by restricting auto air conditioning to climates where it is a near-necessity, and by making radial tires standard equipment.

Existing cars can be used better. No car should travel in

Assuming, for the sake of brevity, that I am right, that it is at least desirable if not altogether imperative that we develop several kinds of engines, the question arises: Why isn't that being done?

There are several reasons.

First, because there is no single engine that could corner the same diverse market that is dominated by the ICE. Consider the diesel. It gets more miles out of cheaper fuel and is cheaper to maintain, but Mercedes Benz still builds more gasoline-fueled, ICE-powered cars for the larger market that wants something quicker and more powerful. And because diesel engines are not produced in such great numbers, they are more expensive to buy. If a single manufacturer tried dropping the ICE in favor of any other engine, it would find itself with a tiny share of the market. And it would be prohibitively expensive to tool up for a wide range of engines that would blanket the markets. It would be possible to phase over, one engine at a time, but it is cheaper, easier, and safer not to.

Second, compare the automobile and aircraft industries. For a long time, airplanes have been powered by engines made by companies other than the ones who make the airframes. So, when the engine makers found a better engine, the turbojet took most of the market away from the ICE. (For cost and other reasons, most small, light planes are still powered by propellored ICEs.) On the other hand, the auto makers build their own engines, a not unprofitable sideline. Because of the complexity of the ICE in its advanced stage of development, it is prohibitively expensive for anyone to tool up to meet the competition of the established auto makers. By sticking with the ICE, the car makers effectively shut out any would-be competition. If, however, Detroit decided that, say, the gas turbine was the way to go, immediately Detroit would lose its technological edge to those companies who have more experience with turbine engines, and the profits to be made from putting powerplants under Chevrolet hoods would go, not to GM's shareholders, but to those of a company like United Aircraft.

Third, there is no compelling reason for the auto makers to drop the reciprocating ICE. So long as Congress and the American public accept the wisdom of Detroit (allowing here and there for a little foot-dragging and pettifoggery), we are stuck with the old ICE. There are limits as to how clean those engines will run, and on how little fuel, and in some respects we are closing on those limits fast. The Otto-cycle engine is inherently inefficient, both mechanically and thermally, and it has taken several decades of wizardry and tinkering to make the old four-banger what it is today. But there soon will come a time when you can't get another MPG or one less GPM out of it.

The impetus for making the switchover to cleaner and better engines is going to have to come from outside the auto industry. No one else, perhaps, is competent to decide which ways to go, but it would be possible for the government to set down a long-range schedule of emission and consumption goals so that even Detroit would get the message. It will not be easy, but nothing worth having ever is.

—GARY SOUCIE

commute traffic that isn't as nearly full as its owner's generosity and sense of community can make it. And there should be inducements to car pooling: toll-free or restricted-access lanes on freeways and bridges have been tried successfully in Boston, San Francisco, and elsewhere.

Cars can be made to last longer and get their best performance by proud and loving mechanics, but craftsmanship has left most dealers' service divisions. Detroit would prefer that repairmen bolt on new parts, throw out the old, and never mind the quality of the work. This country still produces craftsmen of cars and could produce many more.

Craftsmanship is also gone from Detroit. It is not possible on the assembly line. Henry Ford's invention may be responsible for more human misery than any other modern, above-ground industrial institution. The assembly line should be replaced by group assembly shops of the kind Saab uses in Sweden: crews of six or eight or ten are given quotas for certain phases of car-building—engine assembly, let's say—but are free to divide the work and working time any way they like.

Whatever changes are possible in Detroit or the internal combustion engine, no more appropriate engineering is possible than the human foot's and no more elegant technology than the bicycle, ski, or shoe. The cyclist who uses two rather than four wheels and leg muscles rather than hydrocarbons to get to work or do errands should be able to deduct the bike's expenses from taxes as one can on one's car. And cyclists shouldn't have to be ever-wary of the heedless motorist or rampaging taxi; bike routes, bike lanes, even bicycle-only streets, would give cyclists greater safety and convenience. Walking in the city should be pleasant, too; walkways and car-free districts should be established soon, and people should be encouraged to walk, not drive, in town.

Photo by Peter Gerba/Jeroboam, Inc.

Ivan Illich says social progress should go at a bicycle's pace. We agree.

Urban mass transit should replace automobiles in commuting, but there is the big question to be faced of what form such transit systems should take. The most advanced new rapid transit system, the Bay Area Rapid Transit District (BART) serving San Francisco and environs, has not been a success. It cost billions of dollars to build, its fares have risen as fast as the Public Utilities Commission would allow, and its service isn't anything like its planners hoped for. At any given moment, 40 percent of its gear is in the repair shop, down with everything from broken windows to gremlins in the control apparatus. BART's computerized control systems (with token human back-up) is infamous for opening doors at 80 miles per hour but not at station stops.

Many lessons can be learned from BART. Lessons about making contractors accountable. Lessons about deploying high technology with which there has been no previous experience. Lessons about optimistic projections and their probable fate (BART's enabling legislation directed it to operate on revenues from fares, which it can't seem to do). Even lessons about prematurely giving up on current solutions to continuing problems: in the late 1950s, hundreds of thousands of dollars were spent tearing up tracks of the old Key System, which covered the same "catchment basin" as BART, and in the 1960s, hundreds of millions were spent laying BART's tracks down, very often where Key tracks had been.

BART *is* about twice as energy-efficient as the average electric commuter train operating in 1970 (leaving out the energy costs of building each), and it is not without redeeming qualities, many of them. The stations are clean, the trains smooth and quiet. Some day BART's bugs will be ironed out, we trust, and it will provide reliably superior transportation.

Meanwhile, transit planners will look closely at BART and its sister-system in Washington, D.C., which has similar equipment without such intricate control technology.

We do not expect many new programs like BART. Instead, less aggressively "advanced" technology will more often replace the auto. Suburbs and central cities that are connected by rail lines should put commuter trains on them. (The trains feeding into Manhattan are an example to be improved upon.) Toronto achieved commuter rail service only two years after it was first proposed, a success to be emulated elsewhere. The upgrading of long-haul passenger trains will have obvious spin-off benefits for commuter trains.

Where rails don't exist and cities don't want to go the BART route, available funds may be spent on commuter

Photo by British Aircraft Corporation.

and intracity bus service. It is essential to rehumanize our cities by giving everyone access to clean, safe, regular, and convenient public transit, whether by bus, subway, or above-ground trains.

To woo commuters back onto buses, there should be buses-only lanes on freeways and bridges; buses zipping by while you are stalled in bumper-to-bumper traffic are a strangely moving sight. Fare structures should be set so that it costs more to drive than to ride.

Saving Energy Aloft

To improve the fuel economy of air service, a hard look at CAB policy is needed—and with it, the adoption of a US policy withholding landing rights from the Anglo-French *Concorde* and its Russian sister in sprints, the Tu-144. When an SST is developed that uses no more fuel per passenger-mile than a standard jumbo jet, is as safe and no noisier, then perhaps we should consider lifting the ban. Until then, we should renounce SSTs as an aberration, a mistake. Our renunciation will have important symbolic value, as did Congress's vote to shelve the American SST in 1971; it will signal our commitment to lowering the energy-intensiveness of transportation.

The CAB restrictions on fare competition among airlines should be lifted. Price competition would reduce overscheduling; under present conditions, frequency of flights is one of the few things an airline can brag about.

If the marketplace does not eliminate under-utilized flights, the CAB should order the amalgamation of flights

---

During the last few years, promoters of development have come to admit that cars, as operated now, are inefficient. This inefficiency is blamed on the fact that modern vehicles are designed for private ownership, not for the public good. In fact, modern personnel transport is inefficient not because an individual capsule rather than a cabin is the model for the largest number of vehicles, or because these vehicles are now owned by their drivers. It is inefficient because of the obsessive identification of higher speed with better transport.

That motor traffic limits the right to walk, not that more people drive Chevies than Fords, constitutes radical monopoly. What cars do to people by virtue of this radical monopoly is quite distinct from and independent of what they do by burning gasoline that could be transformed into food in a crowded world. It is also distinct from automotive manslaughter. . . . The radical monopoly cars establish is destructive in a special way. Cars create distance. Speedy vehicles of all kinds render space scarce. . . . Even if planes and buses could run as nonpolluting, nondepleting public services, their inhuman velocities would degrade man's innate mobility and force him to spend more time for the sake of travel.

Commuter transport brings us negative returns when it admits, anywhere in the system, speeds much above those reached on a bicycle. Once the barrier of bicycle velocity is broken at any point in the system, the total per capita monthly time spent at the service of the travel industry [as stalled in traffic jams, waiting for connections, or recovering from accidents] increases.

Transportation above bicycle speeds demands power inputs from the environment. Velocity translates directly into power, and soon power needs increase exponentially. In the United States, 22 percent of the energy converted drives vehicles, and another 10 percent keeps roads open for them. The amount of energy is comparable to the total energy—except for domestic heating—required for the combined economies of India and China.

—Ivan Illich

A BART station. Photo by Peter Gerba/Jeroboam, Inc.

that are going half empty and deny route applications that duplicate train and bus service. The goal should be to fly fewer, but larger, fuller, and more efficient planes on fewer routes. If three airlines were flying partly full between Cincinnati and Dallas, for example, the CAB should order that there be only one flight in any given hour, a wide-body jumbo jet that would be nearly full. A smaller back-up plane might also be indicated in case there weren't enough passengers to load the big one to near-capacity. The three airlines could take turns supplying the plane and crew. Passengers would still be able to buy tickets from any of the three, and accountants could divide the proceeds later. This kind of cooperation is foreshadowed by most airlines' acceptance of each other's tickets in lieu of cash from travelers who change their plans.

Alternatively, license to fly between any two points might be granted on an exclusive basis to a single carrier. There is precious little genuine competition anyway, and with an exclusive franchise, it would be to an airline's advantage to rationalize operations. The CAB would be responsible for seeing that the public was well served. Licenses to fly a given route might be for a period of three years, revokable for cause, and renewable if the operator had performed well.

All the advances we can achieve in technology, finance, regulation, scheduling, and competition will be to no avail if the public is not kept informed about how best to use the transportation facilities at its disposal. Most Americans know where their local bus service goes and how convenient it is for them. Most do *not* know how it compares for convenience and economy with their own cars. They don't know how much better sense buses or trains make than planes or cars for longer trips. The facts haven't been "sold" to them.

Most traveler education can take the form of conventional advertising. But education about transportation should begin in schools. Many states have driver education requirements; these classes should not so much introduce students to the joys of automobilemania as place autos in their proper context and steer students toward walking, bicycling, and patronizing more energy-efficient carriers.

In every area of transportation there is room for technological improvement. We need a continual evaluation of the various tools that inventors and engineers want to place at our disposal, and part of our long-term transportation planning should be an office of technology assessment. When something better comes along, it should be put to work to increase efficiency and reduce waste.

Recommended Actions

☐ The President should declare it to be an objective of his Administration to begin decentralizing the nation's settlement patterns, which would eliminate the need for much travel; for recommended actions leading to decentralization, see the chapter on decentralization of human settlements.

☐ The President should make "Is This Trip Necessary?" a watchword throughout the federal government and commend the slogan to private citizens as well.

☐ The President and other opinion-makers should use their influence to convert us to a nation of walkers and bicyclists who, wherever practicable, *prefer* to get places under their own power.

☐ The President should inform the country of the need to phase out the auto era, and propose to Congress that the US help finance highway projects only in cases where a clear social need has been convincingly demonstrated.

☐ The President should ask Congress to end the Highway Trust Fund and the Airport Trust Fund.

☐ The President should appoint a commission to study ways in which improved communications, including better postal service, might substitute for travel.

☐ Declaring it imperative that the US have unsurpassed rail service, the President should call top railroad executives and other authorities together to discuss with him how this can be achieved.

☐ Congress should withdraw all direct and indirect subsidies to energy- and resource-intensive modes of transportation such as airplanes, autos, and long-haul trucks; consideration should be given to subsidizing energy-efficient modes such as walking, bicycling, buses, railroads, and barges.

☐ Congress should ban supersonic transports from US airspace as an egregious example of energy-intensive transportation.

☐ Congress should reorganize the Interstate Commerce Commission and the Civil Aeronautics Board, and give them a mandate to minimize the amount of energy wasted in flying empty airline seats around, for example, or in miles driven empty by trucks that could be loaded.

☐ Congress should establish a miles-per-gallon standard for cars and raise the standard as rapidly as developing technology permits.

☐ Municipal governments must discourage the private car, creating car-free zones and improving mass transit systems.

☐ Cities and towns should do everything possible to promote car pooling, which amounts to mini mass transit.

☐ Officials at all levels should do whatever they can to popularize walking and bicycling, the most environmentally benign (and healthy) way of getting about.

Parklands have been torn, cities have been shattered and rich agricultural lands have been invaded in the process of building the widely heralded and anxiously awaited 12,500-mile California Freeway System. Of the total, 2177 miles are part of the federal interstate system, ninety percent of which is paid for by Uncle Sam. The balance is financed on a fifty-fifty basis by the state and federal governments. The interstate system, like California's freeway system, is a toll-free network, the reason being that only a little more than one fifth of it will carry enough traffic to pay for itself out of toll revenue. What has been boasted as "the biggest construction project in history" is without doubt the largest boondoggle in history, too.

Perhaps the most telling indictment of the highway program is the fact that there is not one mile in a hundred that can be considered anything more than a means to an end. You will find no romance, no beauty, no majesty. There will be no sentimental ballad written for Interstate 5. Where in the freeway system can one find that element of nobility characteristic of man's great works of the past?

In a moment of madness, California State's Division of Highways proposed in 1956 to name a section of new highway in Contra Costa County the "John Muir Freeway," in honor of the great conservationist and founder of the Sierra Club. Naming a freeway for John Muir is about as appropriate as naming a saloon for Carrie Nation.

—WILLIAM BRONSON

The first thing needed is a federal Clean Air Act with teeth. That means diregarding the whimpers of the American automobile lobby, which has been telling us for years that the industry would be technologically unable to meet the 1975 emissions standards—when all the while, three foreign manufacturers (Honda, Mazda, and the Mercedes Benz diesel) were meeting the 1977 standards. The US auto industry has repeatedly made "bad judgments" in its hunt for short term profits; thinking—incorrectly—that the growing appeal of small foreign cars was just a fad, thinking—perhaps more correctly—that it could weasel out of cleaning up what comes out of Detroit-made tailpipes.

Beyond bad judgments, it has consciously misrepresented the feasibility and impact of meeting clean air standards. *Environment* magazine (November 1975) reported the results of a Ford Motor Company-financed study, conducted by Cal Tech's Jet Propulsion Laboratory, which stated that "strict air pollution limits set by the 1970 Clean Air Act *can* be met even while fuel economy is *improved*" (emphasis added). *Environment* adds, "Just as the JPL's results were being released, Ford and the other three US auto manufacturers sponsored joint ads in all 1800 US daily newspapers, making claims directly contrary to those of the Lab study and calling for easing of federal regulation of the industry."

It's time that the auto industry, along with other industries, be held fully accountable for their products. That accountability might take the form of steeply graduated taxes on pollution which could have the double effect of improving the market position of those companies that cleaned up their acts, as well as encouraging consumers to favor less polluting products. Those who criticize this approach, saying it would increase the prices we pay for goods, must understand that we are paying for pollution anyway. The costs—health and property costs—though they are borne by us all, are "assigned" to no one and hence easily ignored. In fact, economist K. William Kapp estimates that pollution-related costs would account for 15 percent of all business costs if these costs were not externalized.

Second, effective urban mass transit systems are needed. These systems should be free so that they are accessible to the poor and provide an incentive *not* to use private transportation. According to a draft report from the Congressional Office of Technology Assessment (OTA), "Total elimination of the transit fare would cause a 60-80 percent increase in transit ridership. . . . A free fare transit fleet could be funded by a 50 percent increase in the price of gasoline." Such a price increase would itself contribute to increased ridership, as well as to greatly reduced transport energy use. If it remains unsubsidized, the spiralling rate

Photo by Emilio Mercado/Jeroboam, Inc.

structure of mass transit systems will only serve to encourage commuters to return to the use of private cars, as happened in New York City in response to the recent 43 percent fare increase there. Transportation subsidies are nothing new: private autos are subsidized by public expenditures for road systems, as well as the invisible subsidy the environment (and our bodies) provide by absorbing toxic wastes.

Third, building and using electric vehicles should be encouraged, as recently introduced federal legislation attempts to do. Electric vehicles are not pollution free, as is often claimed, but the pollution generated to provide them with power is more readily controllable, coming from a single source far from the urban center, than pollution emanating from millions of individual, inefficient engines. They use less energy than internal combustion vehicles, a result of both a higher basic efficiency and the fact that an electric car does not idle, but shuts off while you wait for a light. They are quieter than conventional vehicles and can be powered by renewable solar and wind energy resources, as these become economically competitive over the coming years.

Electric vehicles might be exempted from downtown traffic bans, but there is an even better way to approach that problem. Amsterdam has been experimenting with a cooperative electric car utility. Rather than having individuals own their own cars and leave them parked, idle, on the streets for most of the day, cooperative ownership permits far more efficient use of vehicles. People pay a flat fee to join the cooperative and receive a magnetically coded car-key. When members need a car, they go to the nearest charging terminal (there will be 15 by the end of the year), insert the key in a computer unit, select a destination—probably another charging station—and drive away the first car sitting at the charging rail. The member is automatically billed four cents a minute until the car is returned to a terminal and is encouraged to keep the car only when it is in use. Clearly, with such a system, a far smaller number of vehicles could handle in-town loads of shoppers and business trips, while reducing traffic congestion.

A more basic response to the problem of reducing travel-related air pollution would be reducing the very need to travel. Automobiles and the like are an "efficient" way to get around in our society because our society is designed for the automobile. People once lived near their workplaces and near their merchants: we now have industrial communities, business communities, residential communities, retail communities, educational communities, recreational communities, all "connected" (read: "separated") by highways and roads. Lured by the "freedom" of the automobile, we have made ourselves completely dependent on it.   —GIL FRIEND

We are reaching the end of technological fixes, each of which gives rise to new, and often more severe problems. It is time that we get back to looking at the land, water, and life on which our future depends, and the way in which people interact with these elements.

—RAYMOND DASMANN

Science and Technology

Early scientific discoveries were so basic they were hard to misapply. It would be hard to do much mischief with the simple knowledge that all elements are composed of atoms, for example, but it's dreadfully easy to go wrong when you know that atoms can be smashed and rearranged in ways unknown to nature. Modern, big science is not only risky, it's also highly centralized, incredibly costly, and largely incomprehensible to non-scientists. A change is in order, and to see what kind of change we want, we might try turning big science inside out. The technology we would come up with would be relatively risk-free, decentralized, inexpensive, comprehensible to ordinary citizens, and hence controllable by them. This sounds like a description of Appropriate Technology, which is gaining ground in both developed and undeveloped countries. Of course, big science won't shrivel up and disappear. It must be brought under more effective control. As a step in this direction, courses in the vocabulary and methods of science should be required in high school and college, and should be available in institutions that offer adult education. Science students should also be required to take courses in the effective communication of technical material in a non-technical manner. After we have taken these steps to demystify science, we can take further steps to democratize it.

Science

Science and technology have captivated the American polity since the days of Jefferson and Franklin. In those simpler times, statesmen could also be inventors and experimenters: Franklin with his kite, and Jefferson with his gadgets at Monticello. Today, politicians and scientists have become so specialized in their respective pursuits that communication between them has become difficult—and the evaluation of science policy by the public, even more so. Nevertheless, the optimistic Prometheanism of our science shapes our lives and institutions to an ever-greater degree.

Consider the impact of Sputnik on a whole generation of Americans. We were appalled when it was demonstrated that we hadn't got into space firstest with the mostest, so we mobilized; science education became a priority, aerospace became the surefire career. Our curiosity was directed away from more serious, if mundane, problems. We were knee-deep in garbage, firing rockets at the moon. Only now are we beginning to wonder whether we can afford guns *and* butter *and* NASA.

Lessons like that take time to sink in. We are not in the habit of questioning the beneficence of science, so we assent to an orthodoxy of expertise. We overlook the fact that expertise is often sold to the highest bidder and frequently emerges somewhat the less objective from such transactions.

We cling to the concept of science's objectivity because we must. We yearn for there to be some pure truths—provable, replicable facts to believe in above the subjective mess of sociopolitics. Many of us place more faith in the scientist's lack of bias than some scientists do themselves. Hear what Stephen Schneider has to say in his preface to *The Genesis Strategy:* "I have been unable to avoid injecting my own personal philosophies into some of the discussions, particularly those addressing the question of whether present scientific evidence justifies immediate action. Realizing that total objectivity is impossible, I have tried . . . to state my biases openly and to help the reader separate personal or political philosophy from scientific opinions."

Would that such attitudes were more prevalent. Establishment Science has become so abstracted in purposing to be value-free that it has wished horrors on us. The dispassionate development of the power of the atom, whether for war or peace, is such a good illustration of this problem that it has become a cliché.

The fathers of the bomb were honored because of the mystique, the patriarchy, and the finance of large-scale science. As it stands now, certain kinds of knowledge are inevitably the province of the elites who by talent or good fortune manage to work their way through years of specialized academic discipline and then find support for their ongoing research. Not surprisingly, the market is often defense; that's where the big bucks are in the national budget.

The gulf between scientist and citizen, then, grows ever wider. We wind up taking on faith that the tools and ideas that scientists produce are value-free and ipso facto worth developing.

Maybe a few of us ignorant outsiders are willing to ask questions like "What price are we willing to pay for what knowledge?" or "What if we simply don't do it?" But in this age of technological hubris, we're still blowing in the wind. Science has tooled itself up into a juggernaut and gathered a lot of impetus.

Once we've paid for the big labs and institutes, once we've financed the universities that produce the priesthoods that run the labs, once the obscurity of classification is drawn around, the juggernaut heads downhill. The religion of objectivity gains momentum, taking over the study of society—once the province of poets, philosophers, and historians—and turning it into sociology, demography, and psychology: give us enough rats and enough paper to graph their behavior on and we can lever the world into predictability. (If we simplify it enough, maybe we really *can*.)

One mustn't be too hard on the hard scientists, because, as Schneider's honesty demonstrates, science is mutable—depending on the scientist, the scale he or she is operating on, and his or her awareness of social concerns.

What Limits to Measuring?

A more cautious, more responsible public attitude toward science, while desirable, will be difficult to arouse. A wealth of invention, native and borrowed, has enabled the US to develop its vast resources quickly, to settle a continent in a few hundred years, to become the richest country in the world, and to arm itself to the teeth against all contenders for superpower status. Can we begin to question those accomplishments and the attitudes that spawned them?

America has been built on a grand scale and so has its science. Science has come to mean a man on the moon, a

Nobody can really believe that conservation can be effective if we have 10 per cent or less of the country in protected areas and the rest of the country is wide open to exploitation. To be meaningful we need begin to restore conditions in which conservation will be a way of life for most people, where it will be a partner in development activities, where agriculturally productive land and natural areas are interspersed and the village forest is as important as the village field. In other words we need restore some of the old partnership with nature that once existed throughout Africa. In the old days the partnership existed without people being aware of it. Now, with more people, we need a more conscious partnership. Some so-called "primitive" groups of people today still have it. We could all learn from them.

—RAYMOND DASMANN

cure for cancer, and the Green Revolution. Our social policies are statistically analyzed, our welfare is phrased in cost/benefit terms. Our pollution has been weighed, mass spectrographed, and proclaimed an investment opportunity. Quantification, sometimes necessary, is always seductive. Putting numerical values on anything—triumph or disaster—makes it more comprehensible, less affecting.

Quantification aside, we've got to find ways for the public to assess the value judgments implicit in scientific and technological developments before they get under way (and rapidly out of control). We as taxpayers are bankrolling the bombs and missiles and cyclotrons and rat cancers

and experiments that watch what terminal syphilis does to people or observe whether a plutonium injection will hasten death. Perhaps one reason why we still feel that science has been an unalloyed blessing is that the typical non-scientific education communicates this message: that we probably couldn't understand the issues around science if we tried, and that we would therefore be unqualified to participate in decision-making.

So education is part of the problem, both for the scientist and the non-scientist. Non-scientists feel no need to master the vocabulary and concepts of science any more than most Americans feel the need to learn a second lan-

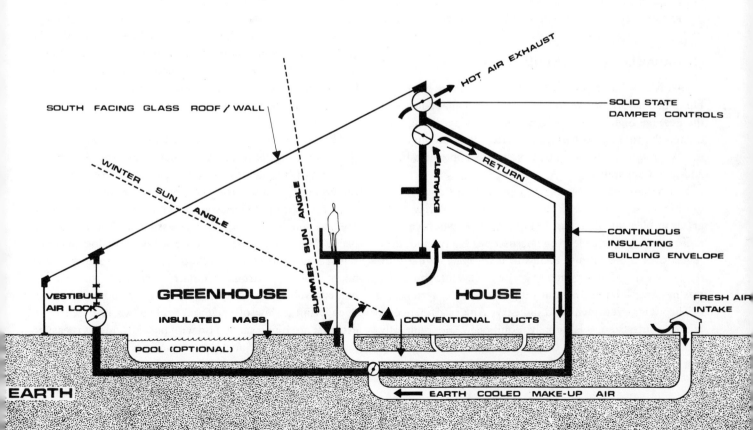

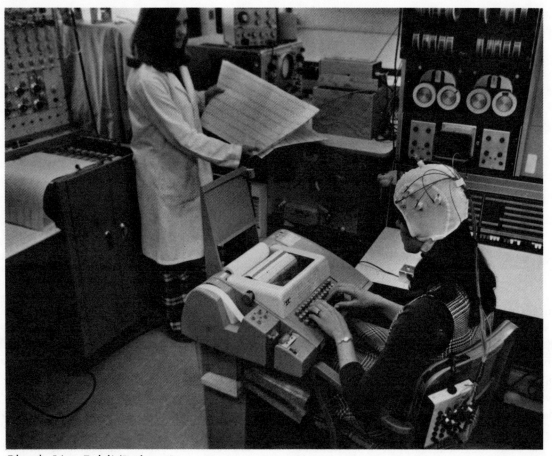

Photo by Liane Enkelis/Jeroboam, Inc.

guage. Scientists are all too often sequestered (or remove themselves) from society; too often they become narrowed in their disciplines and head for the labs, perhaps never to participate directly in the communities their work affects.

Quantum Leaps in Scientific Gear

Lavoisier's laboratory was little more than a hearth. Fleming's laboratory would be considered inadequate by the average high school biology teacher today. Fermi conducted the first controlled nuclear reaction in an olive barrel. We might even look upon Newton's apple as a bit of god-given apparatus.

Since then there have been quantum leaps in the elaboration (and cost) of the tools of science. Perhaps the greatest blessing that has resulted is that wherever the radio telescopes and electron microscopes are trained, they reveal ever more infinite realms to investigate. What they really reveal is that we'll never know it all. Unfortunately, this has engendered precious little humility.

Through government and industry, America finances a highly centralized, elaborately equipped, and generally short-term goal-oriented science. "Respectable" research is conducted primarily by three sorts of institutions: universities, national labs, and free enterprise think tanks. Because of a shrinking economy, subsidies for university research—particularly the sort that addresses long-range questions and promises no immediate breakthrough or fiscal benefit—are becoming scarcer. If we are to continue to finance academic research, we should permit it to take a longer view; we should encourage interdisciplinary approaches and leave immediate-return R&D to private industry.

There may be some initial difficulty in reconciling this need for long-term research that addresses big, broad questions (the planet's carrying capacity, for example, or the amount of abuse the ecosphere can endure) with the need for more public participation in setting priorities for science and technology and assessing their possible impacts. Without first opening up a better dialog between science and the citizen, public scrutiny of some projects might result in curtailing inquiry that seems to lack immediate value. Newspapers preside over an annual event: uncovering a slew of seemingly ridiculous research projects that are being carried on with public funds. It is easy to make a mockery of abstruse scientific pursuits to a public that prefers to regard science as a good gray monolith and does not wish to be troubled with the details.

If our science is to be democratized, then the citizen must begin to take some responsibility for thinking about it, not seek sweet oblivion by letting Werner or J. Robert or Jonas do it. We could all use a better understanding of the scientific method and vocabulary, and this is something we should demand of our educational systems and the news media. If we could develop this understanding and an awareness that there are more scientific styles than just the western style, then we'd begin to be in a position to evaluate and make trade-offs.

Do we want to feed people, do we want to be able to incinerate them all twice, or do we want to see golf balls whacked across the lunar landscape? (There are still a lot of people who refuse to believe that the last ever happened; some diehards of the flat-earth ilk steadfastly cling to the conviction that NASA is a film studio in Utah. While this extreme disbelief may strike us as funny, it illuminates the need for scientists to make what they're doing more comprehensible and not seek the showy accomplishment of a media blitz or the refuge of an ivory tower.)

Only when the dialog between scientist and citizen has begun in earnest can the importance of long-range projects be justified in human terms. When that dialog begins, science may begin to serve people better, and with their consent. Universities and research institutes should be able to pursue some lofty abstractions, but they also need to become much more responsive to their locales. Greater citizen participation in scientific and technological decision-making might well lead to some scaling down of research, demystification of science, and humanization of its goals.

Congress has established an Office of Technology Assessment, which has a citizen's advisory council. This acknowledgement that some technological innovations have far more sweeping influence on the public than legislation ever can is long overdue. Legislators often wind up cleaning up technological messes which—given a more democratic, better informed planning process—might never have been made. Perhaps the people who are to endure the impacts or enjoy the benefits of publicly financed (or tacitly condoned) technologies should be allowed to ask that question: "What if we simply don't do it?" Perhaps they should be given the benefit of knowledgeable counsel on the pros and cons of proposed developments that would affect them. And (without any perhaps this time) their answers should be heeded and acted upon.

Needless to say, some scientists are beginning to worry that they won't be able to *pioneer* if their work is to be subject to public scrutiny. There is a tendency on the part of such scientists to look down on non-scientists. This at-

titude is exemplified by Dixy Lee Ray, former head of the late Atomic Energy Commission, who dealt with non-scientists as children, uninformed and quaking in their boots at the thought of a world wired up to nuclear energy—a world with more than enough plutonium to add a touch of whimsy to the evolutionary process through random mutations. Some scientists wish we would have more faith in their particular judgments and overlook the value questions. But what are we to do when the experts are obviously deadlocked, as they have been for years now on nuclear power?

Hexachlorophene sources. Photo by Ron Scherl.

Here is a political question rather than a political proposal: How can we encourage a more benign, more accessible science—a science which understands that all new technology raises value questions that must be answered before the technology, for better or worse, is turned loose?

Our Goals Should Lead Our Work

Do we want better, more costly scrubbers on ever-higher "beauty tubes" or do we want homesteads that are energy self-sufficient? Do we want more kidney machines or do we want to create working conditions and settlement patterns that promote healthy kidneys in healthy bodies?

Some of the answers to those questions will be provided by the rapidly developing Appropriate Technology movement. AT is the application of science and engineering to local problems in ways that are simple and affordable. It includes things like village water purification systems, solar collectors, windmills, modest agricultural equipment. (One AT networker recently described the invention of the shovel in a remote village in India.) It also makes possible the devolution of large-scale manufacturing processes that are currently highly centralized, such as steel and glass furnaces. More importantly, Appropriate Technology is the concrete expression of a decentralist philosophy. Its

To challenge "endless" scientific and technological progress amounts to a kind of secular heresy. Yet thermodynamic limits, limits to knowledge, and practical limits to the use of technology are clearly discernible; the end of the scientific and technological frontier (and thus compound-interest material growth as well) may be visible.

At some point even the most ordinary technological solutions become physically self-contradictory. For example, no matter how ingenious our technology, we cannot use coastal waters both for extensive mining or petroleum production and for mariculture; we cannot reap greater production from farmlands and still strip mine the coal underneath them; we cannot continually expand energy production without eventually cutting into the room we need to grow food or supply our other necessities; and so forth. In sum, the thermodynamic costs attached to technological fixes seem to be becoming more and more onerous, and at some point in the not-too-distant future we are likely to be unwilling or unable to pay them.

The substitution of one ever-more-efficient form of technology for another cannot continue forever, and we have already reached the limits of technological scale in many areas. Indeed, expenditures in research and development reveal diminishing returns. The millions spent by modern physicists compare unfavorably with the modest budgets of the great turn-of-the-century experimental scientists (to say nothing of Isaac Newton). In effect, the better our current technology, the harder it is likely to be to improve on it.

Even if we were to assume that ways of evading the thermodynamic limits more or less indefinitely can readily be found and that necessity always proves to be the mother of invention, the feasibility of continued technological growth is not assured. For one thing, the management burden thrown on our decision-makers and institutional machinery by continued growth will be enormous and will extend across the board. The rates of growth now prevailing require us to double our capital stock, our capacity to control pollution, our agricultural productivity, and so on every 15 to 30 years. Since we already start from a very high absolute level, especially in the "developed" nations, the increment of new construction and new invention required will be staggering.

Technology cannot be implemented in a vacuum. Something like the ecological "law of the minimum," which states that the factor in least supply governs the rate of growth in the system as a whole, applies to social systems as well as ecosystems, and technological fixes cannot run ahead of our ability to plan, construct, fund, and man them—as engineers who examine the macro problem and not just isolated projects readily admit.

Our ability to achieve the requisite level of planning effectiveness is especially doubtful. In the first place, we cannot foresee with certainty what the consequences of our technological acts are likely to be. As Weinberg points out, virtually none of the critical decisions we confront can be made scientifically. For example, no certain answers to such "trans-scientific" questions as the risks attached to nuclear energy or to the use of certain chemicals can be found in advance. The only way to determine the risks empirically is to run an experiment on the population at large, and such decisions must therefore be made by prudent men—that is, politically.

Not only must we reach and carry out decisions more

ideas are neatly explained in E.F. Schumacher's *Small Is Beautiful*. (Schumacher is rightly regarded as a founder of the movement, although he acknowledges a debt to Gandhi for his description of an appropriate scale of production and technology: "not mass production but production by the masses.")

It is perhaps more meaningful to think of AT as ideas rather than a collection of cheap, non-destructive tools. The tools themselves will have to be developed everywhere by the people who will use them, but technical advisers will be helpful. AT is almost like re-inventing the wheel, except that it involves the invention of many different kinds of wheels for thousands of different uses. It is the creation of tools that can help people in developing countries to lead better lives without paying the price of massive cultural disruption that follows the centralization of production. It is a way of enabling people in industrialized countries to detach themselves from central systems and reclaim a measure of self-reliance and control of their own lives. It may catch on faster in the developing world, because here, in the developed countries, it means that we'll have to change our lives enough to be able to do some real, honest-to-god, healthy physical work.

Since Appropriate Technology in all its possible applications is still a nascent body of thought, it's not surprising that a lot of information necessary to users of it is either nonexistent or not yet taught in high schools, colleges, and universities. Consider the plight of the young farmer who would like to learn organic methods at a state agricultural college. In all likelihood, he or she will be disappointed

quickly than in the past, but we must also be very sure that our decisions and actions are the right ones, for we may not get much of a second chance. Indeed, the growing vulnerability of a highly technological society to accident and error is probably our most intractable management prob-

Drawing by Niculae Asciu; © The New Yorker Magazine, Inc.

lem. The main cause for concern is, of course, some of the especially dangerous technologies we are beginning to employ.

To count on perfect design, perfect skill, perfect efficiency, or perfect reliability in any human enterprise is folly. In addition, all man's works, no matter how perfect as self-contained engineering creations, are still vulnerable to earthquake, storm, drought, and other acts of God, and some of these are bound to happen in just the wrong place at just the wrong time. Nevertheless, we seem headed toward a society in which nothing less than perfect planning and management will do.

Even massive amounts of money, enormous effort, and supreme technological cleverness can never guarantee accident-free operation of our technological devices, and it is indeed strange that technologists—who discovered the infamous Murphy's Law, which states that "if something can possibly go wrong, it will"—should so often assume to the contrary that they can make their creations invulnerable to acts of God or fool-proof in normal operations.

To proceed on the assumption that we can achieve standards of perfection hitherto unattained may be to fall victim to the overweening pride preceding self-destruction that the Greeks called hubris.

The days of "muddling through" in a basically laissez-faire socio-economic system are over. Indeed, to ask only whether continued technological growth is possible without also asking whether it is humanly desirable is to evade the most important question. Yet all-too-many who talk glibly about "exponential technological growth" virtually ignore the social and political consequences of modern technology.

In a crowded world where only the most exquisite care will avoid the collapse of the technological Leviathan we are well on the way to creating, the grip of planning and social control will of necessity become more and more complete. Accidents cannot be permitted, much less individual behavior that deviates from technological imperatives.

We must ask ourselves, therefore, if continued technological growth will not merely serve to replace the so-called tyranny of nature with a potentially even more odious tyranny of man. Discussions of technological growth as a response to our environmental predicament that do not take such political and social issues into consideration are fatally defective. —WILLIAM OPHULS

because agribusiness calls the tune, or because what little applicable research there is is scattered and beyond the pale of academe. As a consequence of this lag in the educational system, much of the information needed has to be dug out and passed on by the individuals who need it. While the existence of such networks is a good thing, surely our institutions could begin to acknowledge the importance of Appropriate Technology and abet its development and dissemination.

Another possibly beneficial consequence of this academic neglect is that there are now a number of individuals and small, non-profit organizations conducting fairly rigorous (albeit scaled-down) scientific research, much of it having to do with decentralized approaches to energy and food production, housing, and health. Rene-

gade scientists, engineers, and amateurs are taking upon themselves the responsibility of researching local alternatives. This is true to the classic mode of invention, which is rarely accomplished in large establishments.

While this sort of innovative research is currently most likely to be financed by philanthropy or the inventors themselves, the government might try to figure out ways to help without requiring that the innovators also be skilled grantsmen. Imagine what could be accomplished if the cost of a single B-1 bomber were scattered across the country in the form of $2,500 no-strings-attached grants to help finance the development of aquaculture projects, roof gardens, windmills, solar collectors, companion-planting experiments, pedal-powered workshops, and the like. No doubt many such projects would fail, but that's usually the case with experimentation regardless of the scale on which it is carried out. And the value of a few successes would be tremendous.

The advantages of encouraging small-scale basic research into alternative methods of food and energy production, energy conservation, housing, and transportation are the promotion of diversity and the creation of greater opportunities for public participation in the discovery process. At the very least, such approaches would spare us the trauma of huge financial commitments to single-option crash programs (like nuclear power, disneylandish rapid transit systems, and fossil-fueled agricultural revolutions) which all too often do crash—and increasingly have the potential to take whole regions down with them when they go.

Deciding how funding for conventional, high-technology, academic research and for Appropriate Technology should be apportioned should be up to the taxpayers. Decisions should be based on the clearest information possible as to the relative merits (and impacts) of the alternatives. This suggests a whole new set of processes for budgeting, and would probably involve a regionalization of federal spending and a localization of state spending. It would require that elected officials seek suggestions from representative groups of citizens—and that means a statistically valid sample of the people, not just Kiwanis or Junior League members appointed by the mayor. These citizens should have access to experts, generalists, and proponents acting in an advisory (and adversary) capacity.

All this may sound drastic, but is it really that drastic to trust *ourselves* with the responsibility to make sensible decisions about the developments that will shape our lives?

Science Serves Humanity: Humanity Returns the Serve

The so-called "hard" sciences do not study mankind, but their practitioners act as if they know what is good for mankind. A scientist's motivation is often based upon untested assumptions about human needs and satisfactions, perhaps derived from his personal or family experiences, from his early education, or from popular views of what constitutes human welfare. These views are sometimes utilitarian, usually quite practical, and often rather shallow: people need relief from physical discomfort, satisfaction of their desires, convenience, wealth, and ease. The scientist who serves humanity seems to believe that his knowledge of the world should be employed to manipulate the world to serve such widely-felt needs.

Humanity, of course, shows appreciation for the scientist's efforts, and bolsters his personal identity with such good things as professorships, tenure, salary increases, awards, or maybe even a Nobel Prize. Everybody seems to win. Humanity's desires are satisfied through the efforts of scientists, and the scientists are rewarded by praise and status.

Such services to humanity, unfortunately, are often disservices to the world and to the overall well-being of mankind. Land and resources that are "developed" by scientific technology are usually destroyed in the process. Human tensions mount as human environments become more cluttered with mechanisms designed to make life easier. It begins to seem possible that the Chinese philosopher Chuang-Tzu may have been right when he observed: "He who develops mankind injures life."

Physicists who formulated the theories necessary for energy development and industrial growth have served humanity, but they have also influenced the rapid depletion of natural resources and have provided the world with levels of air, water and radiation pollution unknown in any previous period of history. Those scientists who have served humanity through agriculture have developed new crop strains, increased productivity, brought us the Green Revolution, and disrupted nearly every agricultural pattern of land use that had been developed empirically over the several thousand years of agricultural history preceding their influence. Scientists who developed an atomic bomb to end the suffering of World War II contributed generously to the psychological and political chaos of life in a nuclear era. Very few areas of scientific inquiry are free of damaging consequences which arise from their technological applications.

The good intentions of scientists over the past few centuries have produced far too many destructive and unacceptable results. We resemble the highly-skilled disciplinary Brahmans of the Indian fable who found the bones of a dead lion in the forest, and decided to apply their scientific scholarship by reconstructing it. One knew how to

If God had meant for us to fly, He would have made our bones as hollow as our heads.

The trouble is that the human brain often seeks power before it seeks understanding. It is customary to say that scientists discover how things work before engineers step in to apply scientific knowledge for human benefit, but unfortunately that sequence is usually reversed. Genetic engineering is a good example. Some ten or twelve thousand years ago humans became genetic engineers when they discovered the techniques of plant and animal domestication. No knowledge of the principles of natural selection was needed to discover the human advantage of selective breeding which produced early cattle, sheep, and goats. Minor behavioral modifications were probably achieved first to assure tractability and to enforce the dependence of animals upon their human mentors. Later, it proved possible to modify also the anatomy and physiology of some animals for meat production, more abundant reproduction, and for hauling human loads. Anthropologists make much of the "revolution" which occurred with the advent of human pastoralism based upon domesticated animals, suggesting that at last mankind then emerged from the ranks of animals and began to achieve the supremacy over nature that was our destiny. They neglect to point out, however, that only about a dozen species of the

million or more on the planet have proved susceptible to domestication during ten thousand years of trying, and that those species which have suffered domestication have not been deeply moved by the experience. Two or three generations without human intervention would largely unravel the work of ten millenia. Domestication, genetically speaking, is only skin deep.

Genetic engineering messed up the lives of billions of animals before scientists such as Darwin and Mendel came along to examine the principles which made it all possible. A little has been learned since Darwin about the influence of genetic modification upon species phylogeny, but as usual this information is lagging far behind the sophisticated techniques of practitioners who spend their days influencing genes. We remain now as we were ten thousand years ago: it is easier to do something than it is to know what we're doing. Very great knowledge is needed to understand any natural system or process; only rudimentary knowledge is required to alter or manipulate them. In the history of human civilization, engineering has generally come much too early and science has come much too late.

—JOSEPH MEEKER

assemble the skeleton, another knew how to create the skin and flesh and blood, and the third said he could give it life. The fourth companion, who was not a scientist but merely a man of sense, objected, reminding the others that if you create a lion he will probably kill you. The scholars argued that their accomplishment would amount to a scientific breakthrough for all mankind, and would of course be good for their reputations. The man of sense prudently climbed a convenient tree. When the lion was brought to

life, it rose up and ate the three scientists. The story concludes in verse:

Scholarship is less than sense;
Therefore seek intelligence:
Senseless scholars in their pride
Made a lion; then they died.

Science has served humanity's self-indulgent whims during the honeymoon of the industrial era, but now a more stable relationship is needed if the marriage is to endure. Technological applications of scientific theories are increasingly suspect because of their often unforeseen and unacceptable consequences, and because many have discovered that they do not in fact improve human life or the natural environment in significant ways. Humanity's most valuable cultural achievement grew from societies that knew nothing about automobiles, petroleum by-products, electrical energy, nuclear reactors, bacteriology, or the many other sophisticated offspring of the mating between science and technology.

New admiration has arisen for ways of life that are free of technological science. Increasing numbers of people are studying and experimenting with Oriental and primitive religions, with the social lives of hunting/gathering peoples, with agricultural communes, with personal crafts, and with interpersonal relationships, all of which offer alternatives to the shallowness of technological society. This is not mere escapism, but an affirmative search for ways of living which satisfy the deep human needs which science has deliberately neglected.

Non-technological cultures, past or present, still need *science*. They must have accurate and detailed knowledge of natural things and processes. Carleton Coon has estimated that most successful Eskimo hunters have more precise and complete knowledge of the tundra environment than any professor with a Ph.D. in arctic biology. The Sahelian natives may know better the ecology of arid lands than do agricultural experts trained in great European universities. When scientific knowledge is integrated with the total social, psychological, and cultural life of a people, it is able to serve real human needs and to adapt human life better to its natural environments.

The human mind needs vast and complex scientific knowledge of the world, but it also needs more than that. It needs challenge, perhaps even danger, as well as the security and convenience that technology offers. It needs those close social ties with other humans which come through love, family closeness and friendship. It needs joy and it enjoys beauty. And it needs what is known as identity, or a sense of the self. Identity is acquired through both scientific and spiritual knowledge of the *otherness* of the world, and through understanding of the meaning of the self in relation to all that otherness.

And what does the world need from the human mind? Not much, it seems. All that is required of us or any other species is that we learn to adapt to our environmental circumstances. The reward for success is merely more life, and the penalty for failure is extinction. The human mind is our best means toward winning more life, providing we can get it all together.

—JOSEPH W. MEEKER

Recommended Actions

☐ The President should appoint science advisors familiar with the theory and practice of Appropriate Technology, and should be wary of multi-billion-dollar Big Science proposals.

☐ Congress, too, should be suspicious of grandiose research and development schemes that too often do more for the national ego than the national welfare.

☐ The President or Congress should charge an appropriate agency of the executive branch with responsibility to dispense grants in support of small-scale, decentralized research into various facets of Appropriate Technology.

☐ Citizens' panels should be empowered to recommend how research grants should be allocated in their regions.

☐ Educators should also require (or strongly encourage) science students to take courses in the effective communication of technical material to non-technical readers (and technologists in other fields of specialization).

☐ Cross-sectional panels of citizens (perhaps chosen like jurors) should be empowered to assess proposed technological developments in their localities, reporting their findings to politicians and the public.

☐ Educators and officials concerned with education at all levels of government should work to make the methods and vocabulary of science part of the required curriculum for all students.

SOLAR ENERGY

SOLAR COLLECTORS capture the sun's radiant energy for heating household water. A flat-plate collector on the southern roof daily heats 120 gallons of water to temperatures above 140°. A small electric water heater provides a back-up on cloudy days.

A "BOTTLE WALL" in the southern window of the bathroom employs the principle of "thermal lag" to store the sun's energy to moderate internal temperatures.

A SOLAR OVEN warms and cooks food produced in the vegetable garden, in the animal yard, and breads from the kitchen.

FOOD RAISING

DOMESTICATED BEES produce honey and pollinate vegetable crops and fruit trees. An observation hive provides an inside view of the honey bee's life.

A VEGETABLE GARDEN, based on labor saving and environmentally sound techniques of food raising, yields produce enough for the family of four.

AN AQUACULTURE POND tests the feasibility of raising fish as a supplementary protein source.

A ROOF TOP GARDEN utilizes otherwise nonproductive space for raising vegetables in light weight planters.

ORNAMENTAL CROPS demonstrate how food can be produced by planting a landscape of dwarf fruit trees, herbs, and edible flowering foliage.

A GREENHOUSE provides a warm protective environment for germinating seeds and raising tomatoes and cucumbers in the winter.

INSECTS are controlled using biological and cultural methods of pest management. No synthetic pesticides are used.

RABBITS AND CHICKENS, housed in sanitary pens on the cool north side of the house, provide a dependable source of high quality protein. Much of their diet is raised on the premises, and their wastes are recycled to the soil.

A KITCHEN PANTRY provides storage for garden surpluses preserved by canning, pickling, and drying.

WASTE RECYCLING

HUMANS

THE CLIVUS MULTRUM waterless toilet converts human excrement into a pathogenically safe soil conditioner for use on fruit trees and ornamental crops. The process conserves water and recycles nutrients.

SOLID WASTES, such as glass, aluminum, tin, and newspaper, are sorted into bins and delivered to neighborhood recycling centers.

HOUSEHOLD WASTE WATER from wash basins and the shower is filtered, mixed with human urine, and reused as a garden irrigation water rich in nutrients.

COMPOSTING wastes and returning their nutrients to the soil is a central theme in the Integral House. A variety of biological systems transform garden, animal and kitchen wastes into a valuable soil amendment.

Drawing by Andrea Thrams, courtesy of the Farallones Institute.

Our scientists and technologists have learned to compound substances unknown to nature. Against many of them, nature is virtually defenceless. There are no natural agents to attack and break them down. It is as if aborigines were suddenly attacked with machine-gun fire: their bows and arrows are of no avail. These substances, unknown to nature, owe their almost magical effectiveness precisely to nature's defencelessness—and that accounts also for their dangerous ecological impact. It is only in the last twenty years or so that they have made their appearance *in bulk*. Because they have no natural enemies, they tend to accumulate, and the long-term consequences of this accumulation are in many cases known to be extremely dangerous, and in other cases totally unpredictable.

Scientific or technological 'solutions' which poison the environment or degrade the social structure and man himself are of no benefit, no matter how brilliantly conceived or how great their superficial attraction. Ever bigger machines, entailing ever bigger concentrations of economic power and exerting ever greater violence against the environment, do not represent progress: they are a denial of wisdom. Wisdom demands a new orientation of science and technology toward the organic, the gentle, the non-violent, the elegant and beautiful.

Man cannot live without science and technology any more than he can live against nature. What needs the most careful consideration, however, is the *direction* of scientific research. We cannot leave this to the scientists alone. As Einstein himself said, "almost all scientists are economically completely dependent" and "the number of scientists who possess a sense of social responsibility is so small" that they cannot determine the direction of research. The latter dictum applies, no doubt, to all specialists, and the task therefore falls to the intelligent layman, to people like those who form the National Society for Clean Air and other, similar societies concerned with *conservation*. They must work on public opinion, so that the politicians, depending on public opinion, will free themselves from the thraldom of economism and attend to the things that really matter. What matters, as I said, is the *direction* of research, that the direction should be towards non-violence rather than violence; towards an harmonious cooperation with nature rather than a warfare against nature; towards the noiseless, low-energy, elegant, and economical solutions normally applied in nature rather than the noisy, high-energy, brutal, wasteful, and clumsy solutions of our present-day sciences.

Nature always, so to speak, knows where and when to stop. Greater even than the mystery of natural growth is the mystery of the natural cessation of growth. There is measure in all natural things—in their size, speed, or violence. As a result, the system of nature, of which man is a part, tends to be self-balancing, self-adjusting, self-cleansing. Not so with technology, or perhaps I should say: not so with man dominated by technology and specialization. Technology recognizes no self-limiting principle—in terms, for instance, of size, speed, or violence. It therefore does not possess the virtues of being self-balancing, self-adjusting, and self-cleansing. In the subtle system of nature, technology, and in particular the super-technology of the modern world, acts like a foreign body, and there are now numerous signs of rejection.

The type of work which modern technology is most successful in reducing or even eliminating is skillful, productive work of human hands, in touch with real materials of one kind or another. In an advanced industrial society, such work has become exceedingly rare, and to make a decent living by doing such work has become virtually impossible. A great part of the modern neurosis may be due to this very fact; for the human being, defined by Thomas Aquinas as a being with brains and hands, enjoys nothing more than to be creatively, usefully, productively engaged with both his hands and his brains. Today, a person has to be wealthy to be able to enjoy this simple thing, this very great luxury: he has to be able to afford space and good tools; he has to be lucky enough to find a good teacher and plenty of free time to learn and practice. He really has to be rich enough not to need a job; for the number of jobs that would be satisfactory in these respects is very small indeed.

We may say, therefore, that modern technology has deprived man of the kind of work that he enjoys most, creative, useful work with hands and brains, and given him plenty of work of a fragmented kind, most of which he does not enjoy at all. It has multiplied the number of people who are exceedingly busy doing a kind of work which, if it is productive at all, is so only in an indirect or 'roundabout' way, and much of which would not be necessary at all if technology were rather less modern. Karl Marx appears to have foreseen much of this when he wrote: "They want production to be limited to useful things, but they forget that the production of too many useful things results in too many useless people", to which we might add: particularly when the processes of production are joyless and boring. All this confirms our suspicion that modern technology, the way it has developed, is developing, and promises further to develop, is showing an increasingly inhuman face, and that we might do well to take stock and reconsider our goals.

As Ghandi said, the poor of the world cannot be helped by mass production, only by production by the masses. The system of *mass production,* based on sophisticated, highly capital-intensive, high energy-input dependent, and human labour-saving technology, presupposes that you are already rich, for a great deal of capital investment is needed to establish one single workplace. The system of *production by the masses* mobilizes the priceless resources which are possessed by all human beings, their clever brains and skillful hands, *and supports them with first-class tools.* The technology of *mass production* is inherently violent, ecologically damaging, self-defeating in terms of non-renewable resources, and stultifying for the human person. The technology of *production by the masses*, making use of the best of modern knowledge and experience, is conducive to decentralization, compatible with the laws of ecology, gentle in its use of scarce resources, and designed to serve the human person instead of making him the servant of machines. I have named it *intermediate technology* to signify that it is vastly superior to the primitive technology of bygone ages but at the same time much simpler, cheaper, and freer than the super-technology of the rich. One can also call it self-help technology, or democratic or people's technology—a technology to which everybody can gain admittance and which is not reserved to those already rich and powerful.

It is my experience that it is rather more difficult to recapture directness and simplicity than to advance in the direction of ever more sophistication and complexity. Any third-rate engineer or researcher can increase complexity; but it takes a certain flair of real insight to make things simple again. And this insight does not come easily to people who have allowed themselves to become alienated from real, productive work and from the self-balancing system of nature, which never fails to recognize measure and limitation. Any activity which fails to recognize a self-limiting principle is of the devil.

It is widely accepted that politics is too important a matter to be left to experts. Today, the main content of politics is economics, and the main content of economics is technology. If politics cannot be left to the experts, neither can economics and technology.

I have no doubt that it is possible to give a new direction to technological development, a direction that shall lead it back to the real needs of man, and that also means: *to the actual size of man.* Man is small, and, therefore, small is beautiful. To go for giantism is to go for self-destruction. And what is the cost of a reorientation? We might remind ourselves that to calculate the cost of survival is perverse. No doubt, a price has to be paid for anything worth while: to redirect technology so that it serves man instead of destroying him requires primarily an effort of the imagination and an abandonment of fear.

The idea of intermediate technology does not imply simply a 'going back' in history to methods now out-dated;

Photo by Suzanne Arms/Jeroboam, Inc.

although a systematic study of methods employed in the developed countries, say, a hundred years ago could indeed yield highly suggestive results. It is too often assumed that the achievement of western science, pure and applied, lies mainly in the apparatus and machinery that have been developed from it, and that a rejection of the apparatus and machinery would be tantamount to a rejection of science. This is an excessively superficial view. The real achievement lies in the accumulation of precise knowledge, and this knowledge can be applied in a great variety of ways, of which the current application in modern industry is only one. The development of an intermediate technology, therefore, means a genuine forward movement into new territory, where the enormous cost and complication of production methods for the sake of labour saving and job elimination is avoided and technology is made appropriate for labour-surplus societies.

—E.F. SCHUMACHER

From an economic point of view, the central concept of wisdom is permanence. We must study the economics of permanence. Nothing makes economic sense unless its continuance for a long time can be projected.

—E.F. SCHUMACHER

Readings in Economics

Conventional American economic theory assumes that natural resources are inexhaustible and that perpetual economic growth is possible, desirable, and indeed, essential. Based on these premises, conventional economics is innately anti-ecological. Fortunately, there is a new breed of economic thinkers who are in closer touch with reality. They hold that a steady-state economy is essential in a finite world, and that economics, like everything else, is subject to physical laws (in particular, to the Second Law of Thermodynamics). We offer here some writings by thinkers of this persuasion. Any legislator who fails to heed the steady-state economists does himself a disservice; any President who fails to heed them does the nation a disservice.

A Steady-State Economy

A steady-state economy (SSE) is defined by four characteristics: a constant population of human bodies; a constant population of artifacts ("extentions" of human bodies); the two populations or stocks are maintained constant at chosen levels that are sufficient for a good life and sustainable for a long future; the rate of throughput of matter-energy by which the two stocks are maintained (i.e., the entropic flow of matter-energy from mines and wells to garbage dumps and environmental sinks) is reduced to the lowest feasible level.

The only things held constant are the two physical stocks: population and total artifact inventory. Knowledge, goodness, information, technology, design and mix of artifacts, genetic characteristics of population, distribution of wealth, etc., are *not* held constant. Progress in the SSE takes the form of qualitative improvement rather than quantitative increase. The goal of technical progress in particular becomes two-fold: to maintain the physical stocks with the least throughput cost (depletion and pollution); and to design, allocate and distribute the constant stock of physical artifacts so as to maximize the service (want-satisfying capacity) of the stock. The concept of GNP is irrelevant to the SSE. A reduction of throughput, other things equal, would imply a lower GNP, which is totally acceptable. If GNP decreases when efficiency increases, then that is a problem for the concept of GNP, not for the SSE.

The standard, somewhat ponderous, definition of economics found in the textbooks is "the study of the allocation of scarce means among competing ends where the object of the allocation is the maximization of the attainment of those ends". In other words, how to do the best with what you've got. But that definition has the virtue of emphasizing the fact that economics is about ends and means. The problem with conventional economics is that it focuses only on the middle of the ends-means spectrum where limits are not apparent. If we expand our vision to the whole ends-means spectrum and include ultimate means and ultimate ends as well, limits become visible. This is illustrated in the following diagram.

From this diagram economic growth can be defined as the creation of ever more intermediate means for the purpose of satisfying ever more intermediate ends. Orthodox growth economics recognizes that individual resources might be limited, but does not recognize any general scarcity of all resources together. The orthodox dogma is that technology can always substitute new resources for old, without limit. Since intermediate means have grown over the last century it is taken as empirically verified that

Ends-Means Spectrum

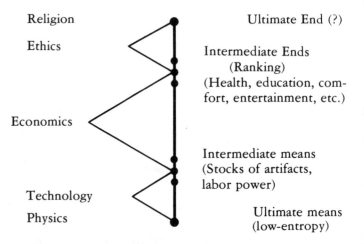

Religion
Ethics

Economics

Technology
Physics

Ultimate End (?)

Intermediate Ends
(Ranking)
(Health, education, comfort, entertainment, etc.)

Intermediate means
(Stocks of artifacts, labor power)

Ultimate means
(low-entropy)

technology is a limitless source of means. A longer run empiricism would reveal that man has lived in a near SSE throughout most of his history and that the growing industrial economy is an aberration, not a norm. But more of that later.

Growth economists also recognize that any single intermediate end or want can be satisfied for any given individual. But new wants keep emerging (and new people as well) so the aggregate of all wants is held to be insatiable, or infinite in number, if not in intensity. So the growth economists' vision is one of continuous growth in intermediate means, which requires continual growth in throughput, with no limits in sight.

A consideration of the ultimate poles of the ends-means spectrum, however, gives us a different perspective. It forces us to raise two questions: (1) What precisely are our ultimate means, and are they limited in ways that cannot be overcome by technology? (2) What is the nature of the Ultimate End, and is it such that, beyond a certain point, further accumulation of intermediate means (people and artifacts) not only fails to serve the Ultimate End but actually renders a disservice? It will be argued below that the answer to both questions is yes. The nature of ultimate means limits the *possibility* of growth, and the nature of the ultimate end limits *desirability* of growth. Moreover the interaction of possibility and desirability provides the *economic* limit to growth.

The branch of physics known as thermodynamics teaches us that the ultimate means is low-entropy matter-energy. Economist Nicholas Georgescu-Roegen (*The Entropy Law and the Economic Process*) has drawn some important implications from this fact. We have two sources of low-entropy: terrestrial stocks of concentrated minerals, and the solar flow of sunlight. In materials, low-entropy means structure, concentration, order. Dispersed, randomly scattered molecules of any material are useless (high entropy). In energy, low entropy means the capacity to do work, or concentrated, relatively high temperature energy. Energy dispersed in equilibrium temperature with general environmental sinks is useless (high entropy). The terrestrial source of low entropy is obviously limited in total amount, though the rate at which we use it up is largely subject to our choice. The solar source is practically unlimited in total amount, but strictly limited in its rate of arrival to earth for use. Both sources of ultimate means are limited—one in total amount, the other in rate of use.

There is an enormous disproportion in the total amounts of the two sources: if all the earth's fossil fuels could be burned up, they would only provide the energy equivalent of a few weeks of sunlight. The sun is expected to shine for another five billion years or so. This raises a cosmically embarrassing economic question. If the solar source is so vastly more abundant, why have we over the last two centuries shifted the physical base of our economy from overwhelming dependence on solar energy and renewable resources, to overwhelming dependence on non-renewable terrestrial minerals? An important part of the answer is that terrestrial stocks can, for a while at least, be used up at a rate of man's own choosing—i.e., rapidly. Solar energy and renewable resource usage is limited by the fixed solar flux, and the natural rates of growth of plants and animals. This provides a natural constraint on economic growth. But growth can be speeded up for a time at least by consuming geological capital—by running down the reserves of terrestrial low entropy. If the object is growth, then it can be achieved most easily by using up terrestrial stocks rapidly. As population and per capita consumption grow beyond the capacity of renewable resources and solar energy to support, then we have all the more pressure to rely on terrestrial stocks, or geological capital.

The difficulty is two-fold. First, we will run out of terrestrial sources eventually. Second, *even if we never ran out* we still would face problems of ecological imbalance caused by a growing throughput of matter-energy. Mankind is the only species that lives beyond the budget of solar income. The whole biosphere has evolved as a complex system around the fixed point of a given solar flux. Now man, in escaping the common constraint, has got

badly out of balance with the rest of the biosphere and runs the considerable danger of destroying or at least inhibiting the complex life support systems that all life and wealth depend on. As stocks of people and artifacts have grown, the throughput has had to grow also, implying more depletion and more pollution. Natural biogeochemical cycles become overloaded. Exotic substances are produced and thrown wholesale into the biosphere—substances with which we have had no evolutionary experience, and which are consequently nearly always disruptive.

But are we not giving insufficient credit to technology in claiming that ultimate means are limited? Is technology not itself a limitless resource? All technologies, nature's as well as man's, run on an entropy gradient—i.e., the total entropy of the outputs of the process must always be greater than the total entropy of inputs. Otherwise we would have a process that violates the second law of thermodynamics, and so far no such process has been observed. Technology uses up low entropy. If low entropy sources are limited then so is technology. It is ironic to be told by growth boosters that technology is freeing man from dependence on resources. It has done nearly the opposite. Modern technology has made us ever more dependent on the *scarcer* of the two sources of ultimate means. The entropy law tells us that when technology increases order in one part of the universe it must produce an even greater amount of disorder somewhere else. If that "somewhere else" is the sun (as it is for nature's technology and man's traditional preindustrial technologies), we need not worry. If "somewhere else" is on the earth then we had better pay close attention. The throughput flow maintains or increases the order within the human economy, but at the cost of creating greater disorder in the rest of the natural world, as a result of depletion and pollution. There is a limit to how much disorder can be produced in the rest of the biosphere and still have it function well enough to support the human subsystem.

Although man's technology cannot overcome these limits it could achieve a better accommodation to them, and could work more in harmony with nature's technology than it has in the past. In so doing it may be that welfare can increase forever, even though physical stocks are constant. But this improved accommodation cannot be achieved in a growth context, in an economy that would rather maximize throughput than reduce it. It requires the framework of a SSE.

From these considerations about ultimate means, I conclude that there are limits to the possibility of continued growth and that a SSE will sooner or later become necessary. And likely sooner when we consider the growing evidence of ecosystem disruption.

The gross national product includes air pollution and advertising for cigarettes, and ambulances to clear our highways of carnage. It counts special locks for our doors, and jails for the people who break them. The gross national product includes the destruction of the redwoods and the death of Lake Superior. It grows with the production of napalm and missiles and nuclear warheads, and it even includes research on the improved dissemination of bubonic plague. The gross national product swells with equipment for the police to put down riots in our cities; and though it is not diminished by the damage these riots do, still it goes up as slums are rebuilt on their ashes. It includes Whitman's rifle and Speck's knife, and the broadcasting of television programs which glorify violence to sell goods to our children.

—Robert Kennedy

Let us turn now to a consideration of the Ultimate End and the limits it imposes on the desirability of growth. What is the Ultimate End? The fact that one does not know the answer is no excuse for not raising the question, because certainly it is *the* question for all of us. Only a kind of minimum answer to such a maximum question would be likely to command consensus. As a minimum answer, let me suggest that whatever the ultimate end is, it presupposes a respect for, and the survival of, the evolutionary process through which God has bestowed upon us the gift of self-conscious life. Whatever human values are put in first place, their further realization requires the survival of human beings. It may be a noble thing to sacrifice the remaining years of one's own personal life to a higher cause, but to sacrifice the whole evolutionary process to some "higher cause" is surely fanaticism. This minimum answer begs many questions: Survival and evolution of life in what direction? To what extent should the evolutionary process be influenced by man and to what extent should it be left spontaneous? I leave these questions aside. The only point is that survival must rank very high in the ends hierarchy and consequently any growth that is made possible only by the creation of means that threaten survival should be strictly limited. Is the further growth made possible by the development of breeder reactors and multi-ton quantities of plutonium really desirable? The distinguished Committee of Inquiry on the Plutonium Economy of the National Council of Churches believes that it is not desirable, and I certainly agree. Others disagree on this specific question. But surely *some* kinds of growth are limited by their undesirability, even though they may be possible. But what about growth per se? Are *all* kinds of physical growth subject to desirability limits? Is there such a thing as "enough" in the material realm, and is enough better than

"more than enough"? Certainly all organic needs can be satiated, and to go beyond enough is harmful. The only want that seems insatiable is the want for distinction, the desire to be in some way superior to one's neighbors. The main avenue of distinction in our society is to have a larger income than the next fellow and to spend more. The only way for everyone to earn more is to have aggregate growth. But that is the rub. If everyone earns more then where is the distinction? It is possible for everyone's *absolute* income to increase, but not for everyone's *relative* income to increase. To the extent that it is higher relative income that is important, growth becomes useless. As E. J. Mishan has expressed it,

In its extreme form—and as affluence rises we draw closer to it—only relative income matters. A man would then prefer a 5% reduction in his own income accompanied by a 10% reduction in the income of others, to a 25% increase in both his income and the income of others. . . . The more this attitude prevails—and the ethos of our society actively promotes it—the more futile is the objective of economic growth for society as a whole. For it is obvious that over time everyone cannot become relatively better off ("Growth and Anti-Growth: What are the Issues?" *Challenge*, May/June, 1973, p. 30).

So even if one's ultimate end is merely to have more than his neighbor, aggregate growth is limited in its capacity to satisfy that end. If one's concept of the Ultimate End is more noble than winning one more round in the materialistic rat race to keep up with the Joneses, then aggregate economic growth is even less able to serve it. It is as futile as the arms race—if each side achieves the capacity to annihilate the other side twenty times over instead of only ten times over, nothing has really changed, except that a lot more resources have been absolutely wasted without altering relative positions.

I conclude that growth beyond some point becomes undesirable, even if still possible. Therefore a SSE becomes desirable.

The actual point at which economic growth should stop is determined by the interaction of desirability and possibility limits. We do not satisfy ends in any random order. We satisfy our most pressing needs first. We do not use our low entropy means in any random order. We use the highest grade and most accessible resources first. This elementary rule of sensible behavior underlies the law of diminishing marginal benefit, and the law of increasing marginal cost. As growth continues, at some point the curve of falling marginal benefits of growth will intersect the curve of rising marginal costs. At that point growth should cease. Growth economists would not deny the logic, but would rightly object that the analysis is too static. Technology shifts the whole cost curve downward. New wants can push the whole benefits curve upward. Looked at statically the curves have opposite slopes and will certainly intersect. But considered dynamically, technical and psychological change will push the curves apart so fast that, although they still intersect, their intersection will forever remain far ahead of us. That is the faith of the growth economist.

But our consideration of ultimate means and the ultimate end has raised insuperable problems for the growth economist. Technology is limited in its ability to lower costs. Technology uses up ultimate means and cannot create them. New wants in affluent societies tend to be relative wants of distinction, and aggregate growth cannot make everyone relatively better off. Growth can of course continue to make some people relatively better off, but then the price of continuing growth would be increasing inequality. The nature of ultimate means limits the downward shift of the cost curve. The nature of the ultimate end limits the upward shift of the benefits curve. The curves shift but the domain in which they can shift is limited.

I think the case for the necessity and desirability of the SSE must be admitted. But we have not said when. Maybe it won't be necessary for another thousand years. Maybe we can grow for a long time yet. Maybe we have not yet reached the optimum size?

Even if we have not yet reached the optimum size, we should still learn to live in a SSE so that we could remain at the optimum once we got there, rather than grow through it. If we achieve a SSE at one level we are not forever frozen at that level. If we later discover that a larger or smaller stock would be better we can either grow or decline to the preferred level, at which we would again be

stable. (Growth or decline would then be a temporary adjustment process, and not a norm.) I believe, however, that we have passed the optimum and will in the future probably have to reduce population and per capita consumption. But the issue of optimum level is very difficult to handle, because a number of related questions must be answered simultaneously: (1) What size population do we want, (2) living at what level of per capita resource consumption, (3) for how long, and (4) on the basis of what kinds of technology? Also we must ask whether the level we choose for the U.S. should be generalizable to the world as a whole. With 6% of the world's people we now consume in the U.S. about 30% of the world's annual production of non-renewable resources. To generalize the U.S. standard of per capita consumption to the entire world requires a six-fold increase in current resource throughput. In addition, to supply the rest of the world with the average per capita "standing crop" of industrial metals already embodied in the existing artifacts in the ten richest nations, would require more than 60 years' world production of these metals

Copyright 1965 Jules Feiffer, Courtesy Publishers-Hall Syndicate.

at 1970 rates (Harrison Brown, "Human Materials Production as a Process in the Biosphere," *Scientific American*, Sept. 1970). The ecological disruption caused by the next six-fold increase will be much greater per unit of resource produced because of diminishing returns. Even technological optimists like Dr. Alvin Weinberg recognize the heat limit to energy use.

Man was increasing his production of energy by about 5% per year: within 200 years at this rate he would be producing as much energy as he receives from the sun. Obviously, long before that time man would have to come to terms with global climatological limits imposed on his production of energy. Although it is difficult to estimate just how soon we shall have to adjust the world's energy policies to take this limit into account, it might well be as little as 30 to 50 years. (*Science,* 18 Oct. 1974)

These considerations make me doubt very strongly that present U.S. levels of living are generalizable, either to the world as a whole, or to very many future generations. Attempts at such generalization are likely to embrace unacceptable techologies. So I think the sooner we move to a SSE, the better.

A SSE is not a panacea. Even a SSE will not last forever, nor will it overcome diminishing returns and the entropy law. But it will permit our economy to die gracefully of old age rather than prematurely from the cancer of growth-mania.

Given that continuous growth is neither feasible nor desirable, how can we stop it, how can we achieve a SSE without enormous disruption? The difficult part is mustering the political will to do it. The technical problems are small by comparison. People often overestimate the technical problems because they identify a SSE with a failed growth economy. A situation of non-growth can come about in two ways: as the success of steady-state policies, or as the failure of growth policies. Non-growth resulting from the failure of a growth economy is chaotic beyond repair. But that is a shortcoming of the growth economy, not the SSE. The fact that airplanes fall from the air if they stand still does not mean that a helicopter cannot stand still.

In an effort to stimulate discussion on policies for attaining a SSE I have suggested three institutions which seem to me to provide the necessary control with the minimum sacrifice of individual freedom (c.f., H. E. Daly, ed., *Toward a Steady-State Economy,* W. H. Freeman Co., San Francisco 1973). First we need a *distributist institution* which would limit the range of inequality to some functionally justifiable degree. This could be accomplished by setting minimum income and maximum income and wealth limits for individuals and families, and a maximum size for corporations. Since aggregate growth can no longer be appealed to as the "solution" to poverty, we must face the distribution issue directly. The maximum and minimum define a range within which inequality is legitimate, and beyond which it is not. The exact numbers are of secondary importance, but let me suggest a minimum of $7,000 and a maximum of $70,000 on income.

Second, aggregate depletion of each of the basic minerals would be limited by *depletion quotas*, to be auctioned, in conveniently divisible units by the government. The resource market would become two-tiered. First the government, as a monopolist, auctions the limited quota rights to many buyers. Resource buyers having purchased their quota rights then confront many resource sellers in a competitive resource market. The competitive price in the resource market will tend to equal the average cost of the marginal producer. More efficient producers will earn differential rents, but the pure scarcity rent resulting from the quotas will have been captured in the depletion quota auction market by the government monopoly. The total price of the resource (quota price plus price to owner) will be raised as a result of the quotas. All products using these resources become more expensive. Higher resource prices will force more efficient and frugal use of resources by both producers and consumers. But the windfall rent arising from higher resource prices is captured by the government and becomes public income—a partial realization of Henry George's single tax on rent. It would not be a "single tax", but it would permit the elimination of some other taxes whose effects cause greater resource distortions. Allocative efficiency is improved to the extent that a rent tax, or in this case its equivalent in the form of auctioned quotas, replaces, say an income or a sales tax. But the major advantage is that higher resources prices result in increased efficiency, while the quotas directly limit depletion (increase conservation), and indirectly limit pollution. Pollution is limited in two ways, first because it is simply the other end of the throughput from depletion, so that limiting the input to the pipeline naturally limits the output. Second, higher prices will induce more recycling, and will push technology toward greater reliance on the abundant solar source and away from excessive use of the scarce terrestrial source of low entropy. The revenue from the depletion quota auction can be used to help finance the minimum income part of the distributist institution, thus offsetting the regressive effect on income distribution of the higher resource prices. Higher prices on basic resources are absolutely necessary and any plan that refuses to face up to this is worthless. Back in 1925 economist John Ise made the point in these words:

> Preposterous as it may seem at first blush, it is probably true that, even if all the timber in the United States, or all the oil or gas or anthracite, were owned by an absolute monopoly, entirely free of public control, prices to consumers would be fixed lower than the long-run interests of the public would justify. Pragmatically this means that all efforts on the part of the government to keep down the prices of lumber, oil, gas, or anthracite are contrary to the public interest; that the government should be trying to keep prices up rather than down (*American Economic Review,* June 1925, p. 284).

Ise also went on to suggest a general principle of resource pricing: that non-renewable resources be priced at the cost of the nearest renewable substitute. Thus virgin timber should cost at least as much per board foot as re-planted timber; petroleum should be priced at its Btu equivalent of sugar or wood alcohol, assuming that they are the closest renewable alternatives. If no renewable substitutes exist, then the price merely reflects the purely ethical judgment of how fast the resources should be used up— i.e., how important are future wants relative to present wants. Renewable resources are assumed to be exploited on a sustained yield basis and priced accordingly. These principles could be used in setting the aggregate quota amounts to be auctioned. For renewables the quota should be set at an amount equivalent to some reasonable calculation of maximum sustainable yield. For non-renewables with renewable substitutes the quota should be set so that the resulting price of the non-renewable resource is at least as high as the price of its renewable substitute. For non-renewables with no close renewable substitute the quota reflects a purely ethical judgment concerning the relative importance of present versus future wants.

In addition to Ise's rules, which deal only with depletion costs, one must be sure that the quotas are low enough to prevent excessive pollution and ecological disruption. Pragmatically quotas would probably be set near existing extraction levels initially. The first task would be to stabilize, to get off the growth path. Later we could gradually reduce quotas to a more sustainable level, if present flows proved too high. Resources in abundant supply and whose use is not environmentally disruptive would have generous quotas and hence relatively low prices.

Depletion quotas would capture the increasing scarcity rents, but would not require expropriation of resource owners. Quotas are clearly against the interests of resource owners, but not unjustly so, since rent is by definition unearned income resulting from a price in excess of the minimum supply price. Additionally, incentive to new exploration could be provided by a system of cash bounties for actual discoveries, or by a public enterprise, since geologic exploration has many characteristics of a natural monopoly.

The remaining institution in our model must provide a mechanism of population control. A stationary population can be achieved by various means that are consistent with the first two institutions. My own favorite is the *transferrable birth license scheme*, first proposed by Kenneth Boulding. But, important as it is, for this occasion I will treat population control as a separate issue and not try to argue for a specific plan, since the depletion quota and distributist institutions could function with a wide range of population control programs, and in no way require the transferrable license scheme (For a defense of transferrable licenses, see H. Daly, *op cit.;* and David Heer, "Marketable Licenses for Babies: Boulding's Proposal Revisited", *Social Biology*, Spring 1975).

Two distinct questions must be asked about these proposed institutions for achieving a SSE. First, would they work if people accepted the goal of a SSE, and, say, voted these institutions into effect? Second, would people ever accept either the steady state idea, or these particular institutions? I have tried to show that the answer to the first question is probably "yes". Let the critic find the flaw— better yet let him suggest an improvement. The answer to the second question is clearly "no" in 1976. But in the future the mounting costs of our failing growth economy will make a SSE look better and better. The sooner we realize this the less we will suffer.   —HERMAN E. DALY

The Convergence of Environmental Disruption

Most conservationists and social critics are unaware that the USSR has environmental disruption that is as extensive and severe as ours. Most of us have been so distressed by our own environmental disruption that we lack the emotional energy to worry about anyone else's difficulties. Yet before we can find a solution to the environmental disruption in our own country, it is necessary to explain why it is that a socialist or communist country like the USSR finds itself abusing the environment in the same way, and to the same degree, that we abuse it. This is especially important for those who have come to believe as basic doctrine that it is capitalism and private greed that are the root causes of environmental disruption. Undoubtedly private enterprise and the profit motive account for a good portion of the environmental disruption that we encounter in this country. However, a study of pollution in the Soviet Union suggests that abolishing private property will not necessarily mean an end to environmental disruption. In some ways, state ownership of the country's productive resources may actually exacerbate rather than ameliorate the situation.

Comparing pollution in the United States and in the

USSR is something like a game. Any depressing story that can be told about an incident in the United States can be matched by a horror story from the USSR. For example, there have been hundreds of fish-kill incidents in both countries. Rivers and lakes from Maine to California have had such incidents. In the USSR, effluent from the Chernorechensk Chemical Plant near Dzerzhinsk killed almost all the fish life in the Oka River in 1965 because of uncontrolled dumping. Factories along major rivers such as the Volga, Ob, Yenesei, Ural, and Northern Dvina have committed similar offenses, and these rivers are considered to be highly polluted. There is not one river in the Ukraine whose natural state has been preserved. The Molognaia River in the Ukraine and many other rivers throughout the country are officially reported as dead. How dangerous this can be is illustrated by what happened in Sverdlovsk in 1965. A careless smoker threw his cigarette into the Iset River and, like the Cuyahoga in Cleveland, the Iset caught fire.

Sixty-five percent of all the factories in the largest Soviet republic, the Russian Soviet Federated Socialist Republic (RSFSR), discharge their waste without bothering to clean it up. But factories are not the only ones responsible for the poor quality of the water. Mines, oil wells, and ships freely dump their waste and ballast into the nearest body of water. Added to this industrial waste is the sewage of many Russian cities.

The misuse of air resources in the USSR is not very different from the misuse of water. Despite the fact that the Russians at present produce less than one-tenth the number of cars each year that we produce in the United States, most Soviet cities have air pollution. It can be quite serious, especially when the city is situated in a valley or a hilly region. In the hilly cities of Armenia, the established health norms for carbon monoxide are often exceeded. Similarly Magnitogorsk, Alma Ata, and Chelyabinsk, with their metallurgical industries, frequently have a dark blue cap over them. Like Los Angeles, Tbilisi, the capital of the Republic of Georgia, has smog almost 6 months of the year. Nor is air pollution limited to hilly regions. Leningrad has 40 percent fewer clear daylight hours than the nearby town of Pavlovsk.

Of all the factories that emit harmful wastes through their stacks, only 14 percent were reported in 1968 to have fully equipped air-cleaning devices. Another 26 percent had some treatment equipment. Even so, there are frequent complaints that such equipment is either operating improperly or of no use.

Because the relative impact of environmental disruption is a difficult thing to measure, it is somewhat meaningless to say that the Russians are more affected than we are, or vice versa. But what should be of interest is an attempt to ascertain why it is that pollution exists in a state-owned, centrally planned economy like that of the Soviet Union. Despite the fact that our economies differ, many if not all of the usual economic explanations for pollution in the non-Communist world also hold for the Soviet Union. The Russians, too, have been unable to adjust their accounting system so that each enterprise pays not only its direct costs of production for labor, raw materials, and equipment but also its social costs of production arising from such by-products as dirty air and water. If the factory were charged for these social costs and had to take them into account when trying to make a profit on its operations, presumably factories would throw off less waste and would reuse or recycle their air and water. However, the precise social cost of such waste is difficult to measure and allocate under the best of circumstances, be it in the United States or the USSR. (In the Ruhr Valley in Germany, industries and municipalities are charged for the water they consume and discharge, but their system has shortcomings.)

In addition, almost everyone in the world regards air and water as free goods. Thus, even if it were always technologically feasible, it would still be awkward ideologically to charge for something that "belongs to everyone," particularly in a Communist society. For a variety of reasons, therefore, air and water in the USSR are treated as free or undervalued goods. When anything is free, there is a tendency to consume it without regard for future consequences. But with water and air, as with free love, there is a limit to the amount available to be consumed, and after a time there is the risk of exhaustion. We saw an illustration of this principle in the use of water for irrigation. Since water was treated virtually as a free good, the Russians did not care how much water they lost through unlined canals or how much water they used to irrigate the soil.

Similarly, the Russians have not been able to create clear lines of authority and responsibility for enforcing pollution-control regulations. As in the United States, various Russian agencies, from the Ministry of Agriculture to the Ministry of Public Health, have some but not ultimate say in coping with the problem. Frequently when an agency does attempt to enforce a law, the polluter will deliberately choose to break the law. As we saw at Lake Baikal, this is especially tempting when the penalty for breaking the law is only $55 a time, while the cost of eliminating the effluent may be in the millions of dollars.

The Russians also have to contend with an increase in population growth and the concentration of much of this increase in urban areas. In addition, this larger population has been the beneficiary of an increase in the quantity and complexity of production that accompanies industrialization. As a result, not only is each individual in the Soviet Union, as in the United States, provided with more goods to consume, but the resulting products, such as plastics and detergents, are more exotic and less easily disposed of than goods of an earlier, less complicated age.

Like their fellow inhabitants of the world, the Russians have to contend with something even more ominous than the Malthusian Principle. Malthus observed that the population increased at a geometric rate but that food production grew at only an arithmetic rate. If he really wants to be dismal, the economist of today has more to worry about. It is true that the population seems to be increasing at accelerated rates, but, whereas food production at least continues to increase, our air, water, and soil supplies are relatively constant. They can be renewed, just as crops can be replanted, but, for the most part, they cannot be expanded. In the long run, this "Doomsday Principle" may prove to be of more consequence than the Malthusian doctrine. With time and pollution we may simply run out of fresh air and water.

In addition to the factors which confront all the people of the earth, regardless of their social or economic system, there are some reasons for polluting which seem to be peculiar to a socialist country such as the Soviet Union in its present state of economic development. First of all, state officials in the .Soviet Union are judged almost entirely by how much they are able to increase their region's economic growth. Thus, government officials are not likely to be promoted if they decide to act as impartial referees between contending factions on questions of pollution. State officials identify with the polluters, not the conservationists, because the polluters will increase economic growth and the prosperity of the region while the antipolluters want to divert resources away from increased production. There is almost a political as well as an economic imperative to devour idle resources. The limnologists at Lake Baikal fear no one so much as the voracious Gosplan (State Planning) officials and their allies in the regional government offices. These officials do not have to face a voting constituency which might reflect the conservation point of view, such as the League of Women Voters or the Sierra Club in this country. It is true that there are outspoken conservationists in the USSR who are often supported by the Soviet press, but for the most part they do not have a vote. Thus the lime smelters continued to smoke away behind the resort area of Kislovodsk even though critics in *Izvestiia, Literaturnaya Gazeta, Sovetskaia Rossiia, Trud,* and *Krokodil* protested long and loud.

Until July 1967, all raw materials in the ground were treated by the Russians as free goods. As a result, whenever the mine operator or oil driller had exploited the

Photo by Eileen Christelow/Jeroboam, Inc.

most accessible oil and ore, he moved on to a new site where the average variable costs were lower. This has resulted in very low recovery rates and the discarding of large quantities of salvageable materials, which increase the amount of waste to be disposed of.

As we have seen, it is as hard for the Russians as it is for us to include social costs in factory-pricing calculations. However, not only do they have to worry about social cost accounting, they also are unable to reflect all the private cost considerations. Because there is no private ownership of land, there are no private property owners to protest the abuse of various resources.

The Russians, however, under their existing system, now only have to worry about accounting for social costs,

Above all, you must work to see that this turbulent time of transition is not exploited by the dinosaur bureaucracies and multi-national corporations; they will still attempt to satisfy their greeds even as they stagger to the tarpits.

The degree of their avarice will grow in direction relation to the vacuum of alternatives. If there is no post-industrial design forthcoming, the industrial giants will exploit their own. It is up to you, the young revolutionaries, to produce the post-industrial patterns, to live them, to do battle on their behalf, to create careers of equilibrium, to germinate the institutions that will flower even as your children.

—JOHN COLE

they lack the first line of protection that would come from balancing private costs and private benefits.

The power of the state to make fundamental changes may be so great that irreversible changes may frequently be inflicted on the environment without anyone's realizing what is happening until it is too late. This seems to be the best explanation of the meteorological disruption that is taking place in Siberia. It is easier for an all-powerful organism like the state than for a group of private entrepreneurs to build the reservoirs and reverse the rivers. Private enterprises can cause their own havoc, as our dust bowl experience or our use of certain pesticides or sedatives indicates, but in the absence of private business or property interests the state's powers can be much more far-reaching in scope. In an age of rampant technology, where the consequences of one's actions are not always fully anticipated, even well-intentioned programs can have disastrous effects on the environmental status quo.

Amidst all these problems, there are some things the Russians do very well. For example, the Russians have the power to prevent the production of various products. Thus, the Soviet Union is the only country in the world that does not put ethyl lead in most of the gasoline it produces. This may be due to technical lag as much as to considerations of health, but the result is considerably more lead-free gasoline. Similarly, the Russians have not permitted as much emphasis on consumer-goods production as we have in the West. Consequently there is less waste to discard. Russian consumers may be somewhat less enthusiastic about this than the ecologists and conservationists, but in the USSR there are no disposable bottles or disposable diapers to worry about. It also happens that, because labor costs are low relative to the price of goods, more emphasis is placed on prolonging the life of various products. In other words it is worthwhile to use labor to pick up bottles and collect junk. No one would intentionally abandon his car on a Moscow street, as 70,000 people did in New York City in 1970. Even if a Russian car is

twenty years old, it is still valuable. Because of the price relationships that exist in the USSR, the junkman can still make a profit. This facilitates the recycling process, which ecologists tell us is the ultimate solution to environmental disruption.

It should also be remembered that, while not all Russian laws are observed, the Russians do have an effective law enforcement system which they have periodically brought to bear in the past. Similarly, they have the power to set aside land for use as natural preserves. The lack of private land ownership makes this a much easier process to implement than in the United States. As of 1969, the Soviet Government had set aside eighty such preserves, encompassing nearly 65,000 square kilometers.

Again because they own all the utilities as well as most of the buildings, the Russians have stressed the installation of centrally supplied steam. Thus, heating and hot water are provided by central stations, and this makes possible more efficient combustion and better smoke control than would be achieved if each building were to provide heat and hot water for itself. Although some American cities have similar systems, this approach is something we should know more about.

In sum, if the study of environmental disruption in the Soviet Union demonstrates anything, it shows that not private enterprise but industrialization is the primary cause of environmental disruption. This suggests that state ownership of all the productive resources is not a cure-all. The replacement of private greed by public greed is not much of an improvement. Currently the proposals for the solution of environmental disruption seem to be no more advanced in the USSR than they are in the United States. One thing does seem clear, however, and that is that, unless the Russians change their ways, there seems little reason to believe that a strong centralized and planned economy has any notable advantages over other economic systems in solving environmental disruption.

—MARSHALL GOLDMAN

Production in Service To Life

The idea of unlimited economic growth, more and more until everybody is saturated with wealth, needs to be seriously questioned on at least two counts: the availability of basic resources and, alternatively or additionally, the capacity of the environment to cope with the degree of interference implied.

It is only necessary to assert that something would reduce the 'standard of living', and every debate is instantly closed. That soul-destroying, meaningless, mechanical, monotonous, moronic work is an insult to human nature which must necessarily and inevitably produce either escapism or aggression, and that no amount of 'bread and circuses' can compensate for the damage done—these are facts which are neither denied nor acknowledged but are met with an unbreakable conspiracy of silence—because to deny them would be too obviously absurd and to acknowledge them would condemn the central preoccupation of modern society as a crime against humanity.

It is hardly an exaggeration to say that, with increasing affluence, economics has moved into the very centre of public concern, and economic performance, economic growth, economic expansion, and so forth have become the abiding interest, if not the obsession, of all modern societies. In the current vocabulary of condemnation there are few words as final and conclusive as the word 'uneconomic'. If an activity has been branded as uneconomic, its right to existence is not merely questioned but energetically denied. Anything that is found to be an impediment to economic growth is a shameful thing, and if people cling to it, they are thought of as either saboteurs or fools. Call a thing immoral or ugly, soul-destroying or a degradation of man, a peril to the peace of the world or to the well-being of future generations; as long as you have not shown it to be 'uneconomic' you have not really questioned its right to exist, grow, and prosper.

But what does it *mean* when we say something is uneconomic? . . . The answer to this question cannot be in doubt: something is uneconomic when it fails to earn an adequate profit in terms of money. The method of economics does not, and cannot, produce any other meaning.

The judgement of economics, in other words, is an extremely *fragmentary* judgement; out of the large number of aspects which in real life have to be seen and judged together before a decision can be taken, economics supplies only one—whether a thing yields a money profit *to those who undertake it* or not.

Do not overlook the words 'to those who undertake it'. It is a great error to assume, for instance, that the methodology of economics is normally applied to determine whether an activity carried on by a group within society yields a profit to society as a whole. Even nationalised industries are not considered from this more comprehensive point of view. Every one of them is given a financial target—which is, in fact, an obligation—and is expected to pursue this target without regard to any damage it might be inflicting on other parts of the economy.

Economics, moreover, deals with goods in accordance with their market value and not in accordance with what they really are. The same rules and criteria are applied to primary goods, which man has to win from nature, and secondary goods, which presuppose the existence of primary goods and are manufactured from them. All goods are treated the same, because the point of view is fundamentally that of private profit-making, and this means that it is inherent in the methodology of economics *to ignore man's dependence on the natural world.*

To press non-economic values into the framework of the economic calculus, economists use the method of cost/ benefit analysis. This is generally thought to be an enlightened and progressive development, as it is at least an attempt to take account of costs and benefits which might otherwise be disregarded altogether. In fact, however, it is a procedure by which the higher is reduced to the level of the lower and the priceless is given a price. It can therefore never serve to clarify the situation and lead to an enlightened decision. All it can do is lead to self-deception or the deception of others; for to undertake to measure the immeasurable is absurd and constitutes but an elaborate method of moving from preconceived notions to foregone conclusions; all one has to do to obtain the desired results is to impute suitable values to the immeasurable costs and benefits. The logical absurdity, however, is not the greatest fault of the undertaking: what is worse, and destructive of civilization, is the pretence that everything has a price or, in other words, that money is the highest of all values.

Having established by his purely quantitative methods that the Gross National Product of a country has risen by, say, five percent, the economist-turned-econometrician is unwilling, and generally unable, to face the question of whether this is to be taken as a good thing or a bad thing. He would lose all his certainties if he even entertained such a question: Growth of GNP must be a good thing, irrespective of what has grown and who, if anyone, has benefited. The idea that there could be pathological growth, unhealthy growth, disruptive or destructive growth is to him a perverse idea which must not be allowed to surface.

It is of course true that quality is much more difficult to 'handle' than quantity, just as the exercise of judgment is a higher function than the ability to count and calculate. Quantitative differences can be more easily grasped and certainly more easily defined than qualitative differences; their concreteness is beguiling and gives them the appearance of scientific precision, even when this precision has been purchased by the suppression of vital differences of quality. The great majority of economists is still pursuing the absurd ideal of making their 'science' as scientific and precise as physics, as if there were no qualitative difference between mindless atoms and men made in the image of God.

There is universal agreement that a fundamental source of wealth is human labour. Now, the modern economist has been brought up to consider 'labour' or work as little more than a necessary evil. From the point of view of the employer, it is in any case simply an item of cost, to be reduced to a minimum if it cannot be eliminated altogether, say, by automation. From the point of view of the workman, it is a 'disutility'; to work is to make a sacrifice of one's leisure and comfort, and wages are a kind of compensation for the sacrifice. Hence the ideal from the point of view of the employer is to have output without employees, and the ideal from the point of view of the employee is to have income without employment.

While the materialist is mainly interested in goods, the Buddhist is mainly interested in liberation. But Buddhism is 'The Middle Way' and therefore in no way antagonistic to physical well-being. It is not wealth that stands in the way of liberation but the attachment to wealth; not the enjoyment of pleasurable things but the craving for them. The keynote of Buddhist economics, therefore, is simplicity and non-violence. From an economist's point of view, the marvel of the Buddhist way of life is the utter rationality of its pattern—amazingly small means leading to extraordinarily satisfactory results.

For the modern economist this is very difficult to understand. He is used to measuring the 'standard of living' by the amount of annual consumption, assuming all the time that a man who consumes more is 'better off' than a man who consumes less. A Buddhist economist would consider this approach excessively irrational: since consumption is merely a means to human well-being, the aim should be to obtain the maximum of well-being with the minimum of consumption.

Buddhist economics is the systematic study of how to attain given ends with the minimum means.

The economics of giantism and automation is a left-over of nineteenth-century conditions and nineteenth-century thinking and it is totally incapable of solving any of the real problems of today. An entirely new system of thought is needed, a system based on attention to people, and not primarily attention to goods—(the goods will look after themselves!). It could be summed up in the phrase, 'production by the masses, rather than mass production'.

What is the meaning of democracy, freedom, human dignity, standard of living, self-realisation, fulfillment? Is it a matter of goods, or of people? Of course it is a matter of people. But people can be themselves only in small comprehensible groups. Therefore we must learn to think in terms of an articulated structure that can cope with a multiplicity of small-scale units. If economic thinking cannot grasp this it is useless. If it cannot get beyond its vast abstractions, the national income, the rate of growth, capital/output ratio, input-output analysis, labour mobility, capital accumulation; if it cannot get beyond all this and make contact with the human realities of poverty, frustration, alienation, despair, breakdown, crime, escapism, stress, congestion, ugliness, and spiritual death, then let us scrap economics and start afresh.

When I first began to travel the world, visiting rich and poor countries alike, I was tempted to formulate the first law of economics as follows: 'The amount of real leisure a society enjoys tends to be in inverse proportion to the amount of labour-saving machinery it employs.' It might be a good idea for the professors of economics to put this proposition into their examination papers and ask their pupils to discuss it. However that may be, the evidence is very strong indeed. If you go from easy-going England to, say, Germany or the United States, you find that people there live under much more strain than here. And if you move to a country like Burma, which is very near to the bottom of the league table of industrial progress, you find that people have an enormous amount of leisure really to enjoy themselves. Of course, as there is so much less labour-saving machinery to help them, they 'accomplish' much less than we do; but that is a different point. The fact remains that the burden of living rests much more lightly on their shoulders than on ours.

The strength of the idea of private enterprise lies in its terrifying simplicity. It suggests that the totality of life can be reduced to one aspect—profits. The businessman, as a private individual, may still be interested in other aspects of life—perhaps even in goodness, truth and beauty—but *as a businessman* he concerns himself only with profits.

Everything becomes crystal clear after you have reduced reality to one—one only—of its thousand aspects. You know what to do—whatever produces profits; you know what to avoid—whatever reduces them or makes a loss. And there is at the same time a perfect measuring rod for the degree of success or failure. Let no one befog the issue

One good example to show that small is more beautiful is the nation of Norway. The Norwegian economy is based on small units of production, and by 1980, this country will have the highest per capita income of any nation in the world. The Japanese government is catching on and has announced that their national growth rate will not be allowed to exceed 3% per annum hereafter. In America the exciting area of development is the California government of Jerry Brown. Brown represents a growing synthesis which both the conservatives and the radicals accept—that government needs to be scaled down from large to small.

—BOB SCHWARTZ

by asking whether a particular action is conducive to the wealth and well-being of society, whether it leads to moral, aesthetic, or cultural enrichment. Simply find out whether it pays; simply investigate whether there is an alternative that pays better. If there is, choose the alternative.

It is no accident that successful businessmen are often astonishingly primitive; they live in a world made primitive by this process of reduction. They fit into this simplified version of the world and are satisfied with it. And when the real world occasionally makes its existence known and attempts to force upon their attention a different one of its facets, one not provided for in their philosophy, they tend to become quite helpless and confused. They feel exposed to incalculable dangers and 'unsound' forces and freely predict general disaster. As a result, their judgements on actions dictated by a more comprehensive outlook on the meaning and purpose of life are generally quite worthless.

General evidence of material progress would suggest that the *modern* private enterprise system is—or has been—the most perfect instrument for the pursuit of personal enrichment. The *modern* private enterprise system ingeniously employs the human urges of greed and envy as its motive power, but manages to overcome the most blatant deficiencies of *laissez-faire* by means of Keynesian economic management, a bit of redistributive taxation, and the 'countervailing power' of the trade unions.

Can such a system conceivably deal with the problems we are now having to face? The answer is self-evident: greed and envy demand continuous and limitless economic growth of a material kind, without proper regard for conservation, and this type of growth cannot possibly fit into a finite environment. We must therefore study the essential nature of the private enterprise system and the possibilities of evolving an alternative system which might fit the new situation.

We shrink back from the truth if we believe that the destructive forces of the modern world can be 'brought under control' simply by mobilizing more resources—of wealth, education, and research—to fight pollution, to preserve wildlife, to discover new sources of energy, and to arrive at more effective agreements on peaceful coexistence. Needless to say, wealth, education, research, and many other things are needed for any civilization, but what is most needed today is a revision of the ends which these means are meant to serve. And this implies, above all else, the development of a life-style which accords to material things their proper, legitimate place, which is secondary and not primary.

The 'logic of production' is neither the logic of life nor that of society. It is a small and subservient part of both. The destructive forces unleashed by it cannot be brought under control, unless the 'logic of production' itself is brought under control—so that destructive forces cease to be unleashed. It is of little use trying to suppress terrorism if the production of deadly devices continues to be deemed a legitimate employment of man's creative powers. Nor can the fight against pollution be successful if the patterns of production and consumption continue to be of a scale, a complexity, and a degree of violence which, as is becoming more and more apparent, do not fit into the laws of the universe, to which man is just as much subject as the rest of creation. Equally, the chance of mitigating the rate of resource depletion or of bringing harmony into the relationships between those in possession of wealth and power and those without is non-existent as long as there is no idea anywhere of enough being good and more-than-enough being evil.

—E.F. SCHUMACHER

From *The Poverty of Power*

When engineers want to test the strength of a mechanical system, they stress it until it breaks and thereby reveals where it is weakest. The energy crisis is such an "engineering test" of the economic system. The stress it has imposed on that system is the threatened shortage of energy—the inevitable result of our short-sighted dependence on non-renewable and technically unreliable sources of energy, and our grossly inefficient ways of using it. Modern production technology has transmuted that stress into a shortage of capital and jobs. This is an ominous metamorphosis, for it signifies that the economic system is unable to regenerate the essential resource—capital—which is crucial to its continued operation, or to serve the people in whose name it was created. What is now threatened is the economic system itself. This may be the true price of power.

Another reason why the capitalist economy is unable to meet many social needs is that it is based on the exchange of *commodities*—privately owned goods that are produced for profitable exchange in the marketplace. In the energy sector what is produced is oil, coal, and uranium; power plants, furnaces, and air-conditioners; automobiles, trucks, and airplanes. The *social need* is for a system that efficiently applies energy toward a suitable task, but this need is met solely by thrusting these commodities into the marketplace and hoping for the best. A furnace is not manufactured and sold as the manufacturer's most effective contribution to the social need that people's homes shall be maintained at 70° in the winter. If the manufacturer's purpose were defined by that thermodynamic task, then what would be sold would not necessarily be a furnace at all, but perhaps a heat pump or a solar collector. In the absence of such a task-oriented, *social* motivation, we have been provided with the wrong kinds of heating and cooling devices, the wrong kinds of automobiles and freight carriers, the wrong kinds of power plants, the wrong kinds of fuels. No society, however wise or disciplined, can readily make a rational *system* for the efficient production and use of energy out of such inappropriate ingredients. These goods have not been foisted on us out of malice, or even—in most cases—out of personal greed. These inappropriate, wasteful, and sometimes harmful commodities have been produced and sold as the logical embodiment of the accepted principle which in a capitalist economy governs what is produced—the maximization of profit.

A distinguished journalist, John B. Oakes, of the *New York Times*, has written movingly about the deepening anguish of America: "[H]ave our concepts of government and society kept pace with the technological progress of mankind?" He then describes what we must do to confront that question:

> The new era requires new leadership, new creativity, a willingness to evaluate new ideas and new concepts and new relationships with the kind of courage and conscience that our history and our heritage have bestowed upon us.

We will not know how best to answer this question until we have the collective courage to ask it; we will not have the "willingness to evaluate new ideas" until we have the wisdom to evaluate old ones.

Here we come to the end of the blind, mindless chain of events that transformed the technologies of agricultural and industrial production and reorganized transportation; that increased the output of the production system, but increased even more its appetite for capital, energy, and other resources; that eliminated jobs and degraded the environment; that concentrated the physical power of energy and the social power of the resultant wealth into ever fewer, larger corporations; that has fed this power on a diet of unemployment and poverty. Here is the basic fault that has spawned the environmental crisis and the energy crisis, and that threatens—if no remedy is found—to engulf us in the wreckage of a crumbling economic system.

Now all this has culminated in the ignominious confession of those who hold the power: That the capitalist economic system which has loudly proclaimed itself the best means of assuring a rising standard of living for the people of the United States, can now survive, if at all, only by reducing that standard. The powerful have confessed to the poverty of their power.

No one can escape the momentous consequences of this confession. No one can escape the duty to understand the origin of this historic default and to transform it from a threat to social progress into a signal for a new advance.

—Barry Commoner

Drawing by Ann Kelley.

Society of Stability

The principal defect of the industrial way of life with its ethos of expansion is that it is not sustainable. Its termination within the lifetime of someone born today is inevitable—unless it continues to be sustained for a while longer by an entrenched minority at the cost of imposing great suffering on the rest of mankind. We can be certain, however, that sooner or later it will end (only the precise time and circumstances are in doubt), and that it will do so in one of two ways: either against our will, in a succession of famines, epidemics, social crises, and wars, or in the way we want it to—because we wish to create a society that will not impose hardship and cruelty upon our children—in a succession of thoughtful, humane, and measured changes.

Radical change is both necessary and inevitable because the present increases in human numbers and per capita consumption, by disrupting ecosystems and depleting resources, are undermining the very foundations of survival.

Our task is to create a society that is sustainable and will give the fullest possible satisfaction to its members. Such a society by definition would depend not on expansion but on stability. This does not mean to say that it would be stagnant; indeed, it could well afford more variety than does the state of uniformity that at present is being imposed by the pursuit of technological efficiency.

The extent to which we are simplifying ecosystems and destroying natural controls so that we are forced to provide technological substitutes is a real cost against society and should be accounted as one. At the moment, however, we merely add up the value of mining operations, factories, and the like, and that of cleaning up the mess whenever we attempt to do so, and conclude that we have never been better off.

In many ways the stable society, with its diversity of physical and social environments, would provide considerable scope for human skill and ingenuity. Indeed, if we are capable of ensuring a relatively smooth transition to it, we can be optimistic about providing our children with a way of life psychologically, intellectually, and esthetically more satisfying than the present one. And we can be confident that it will be sustainable, as ours cannot be, so that the legacy of despair we are about to leave them may at the last minute be changed to one of hope.   —THE ECOLOGIST

Population and Inflation

During the seventies a new source of long-term inflation has begun to emerge. World demand for goods and services has expanded at about 4 percent per year from 1950 to 1975, nearly tripling during this 25 year span. About half of all production gains were absorbed by population growth, which averaged close to 2 percent per year during this period, and about half by increases in per capita consumption. Meanwhile, it has become increasingly difficult, for a combination of economic and political reasons, to expand the supply of many strategic goods commensurately. The result has been scarcity-induced inflation. The impact of these conditions on the price and availability of such essential resources as food and energy has become dramatically evident during the seventies.

Those who suffer most under the burden of scarcity-induced inflation are the poor, whether in the *barriadas* of Lima or the slums of Naples. Worsening inflation means that those living at subsistence level find themselves in-creasingly unable to make ends meet. When the price of grain triples, families that already spend 60 percent of their income on food can only eat less.

With four billion consumers already on the scene and 200,000 more being added each day, scarcity-induced inflationary pressures may grow chronic. Indeed, inflation poses one of the most difficult challenges that political leaders will face in the years ahead. What they must now realize is that, without a marked slowdown in population growth, inflation simply may not be manageable.

During the mid-seventies recession, over 17 million workers, the highest number in forty years, were unemployed in eighteen industrialized European countries, North America, Japan, Australia, and New Zealand. The continuously expanding corps of jobless is becoming a grave social onus. In many developing countries, entrants into the job market outnumber new jobs by two to one, thus creating levels of unemployment and underemployment far greater than ever before experienced anywhere.

Economists estimate that for every 1 percent growth in the labor force, a 3 percent rate of economic growth is required to generate jobs. With current technology, countries experiencing a 3 percent rate of population growth therefore require a 9 percent rate of economic growth just to maintain employment at its current level. Attaining full employment would require an even faster rate of economic expansion. But economic growth rates have been falling during the seventies rather than rising; fewer jobs are being created even while the number of potential workers is climbing at an unprecedented rate.

In Latin America, the first region to experience rapid population growth, the number of unemployed tripled in the fifteen years from 1950 to 1965, climbing from 2.9 million to 8.8 million. The rate of visible unemployment went from less than 6 percent to over 11 percent during this period. Available data indicate that the tide of the unemployed is continuing to swell.

India's labor force is projected to increase from 210 million to 273 million during the seventies. Already plagued with widespread unemployment and underemployment, India is now beleaguered by 100,000 new entrants into the labor force each week. According to economist Harry T. Oshima, at least 15 percent of the labor force is jobless in Pakistan, Sri Lanka, Malaysia, and the Philippines. One-third of Bangladesh's available manpower may be unemployed. Indonesia's working-age population is growing by an estimated 1.8 million annually: one-fourth of the nation's potential labor force may now be out of work.

Looking at the developing nations as a whole, the International Labor Office (ILO) estimates that 24.7 percent of the total labor force was either unemployed or underemployed in 1970. The comparable figure for 1980 is expected to rise to 29.5 percent. Yet, the labor force in the less developed nations is projected by the ILO to expand by 91 percent between 1970 and the end of the century, nearly doubling within the span of a single generation. The labor force in the more developed regions is expected to increase by only 33 percent during this period.

Further aggravating the problem, the number of persons requiring non-agricultural employment in developing economies will increase from 342 million in 1970 to a projected 1,091 million in the year 2000, a staggering increase of 219 percent in one generation. Few, if any, developing countries have the kind of investment capital needed to generate new jobs at such a fast pace.

—LESTER BROWN, PATRICIA MCGRATH,
AND BRUCE STOKES

Toward a Human Economics

The evolution of our global household earth is approaching a crisis on whose resolution man's very survival may depend, a crisis whose dimensions are indicated by current rates of population expansion, runaway industrial growth, and environmental pollution, with their attendant threats of famine, war and biological collapse.

This evolution, however, has not been determined solely by inexorable laws of nature, but by the human will operating within nature. Man has shaped his destiny through a history of decisions for which he is responsible; he can change the course of that destiny by new conscious decisions, by a new exertion of will. To begin with, he requires a new vision.

Basic to our function as economists is the description and analysis of economic processes as we observe them in operation. Increasingly over the last two hundred years, the economists have been called upon, and have undertaken, not merely to analyze, theorize, describe and measure the economic scene, but also to advise, to plan, and to take an active part in the conduct of affairs. The power of the economists, and therewith their responsibility, has become very great indeed.

In the past, production has been regarded as a benefit. But production also entails costs that have only recently become apparent. Production necessarily drains our finite stock of raw materials and energy, while it floods the equally finite capacity of our ecosystem with the wastes of its processes. The economist's traditional measure of national and social health has been growth. But continued industrial growth in areas already highly industrialized is a short-term value only; present production continues to grow at the expense of future production, and at the expense of the delicate and evermore threatened environment.

The reality that our system is finite and that no expenditure of energy is free, confronts us with a moral decision at every point in the economic process, in planning and development and production. What do we need to make? What are the real, long-term costs of production, and who is required to pay them? What is truly in the interests of man, not in the present only, but as a continuing species? Even the clear formulation from the economist's perspective of the choices before us is an ethical task, not a purely analytical one, and economists ought to accept these ethical implications of their work.

We call upon our fellow economists to embrace their role in the management of our earth home, and to join the efforts of other scientists and planners, indeed, of other men and women in all areas of thought and endeavor, to ensure the survival of man. The science of economics, like other fields of inquiry in search of precision and objectivity, has tended in the last century increasingly to isolate its domain from others. But the time when economists could fruitfully work in isolation is gone.

We must have a new economics whose purpose is the husbanding of resources and the achievement of rational control over the development and application of technology to serve real human needs rather than expanding profits, warfare, or national prestige. We must have an economics of survival, still more, of hope—theory and vision of a global economy based on justice, which would make possible the equitable distribution of the earth's wealth among its people, present and future.

It is clear that we can no longer usefully consider apparently separate national economies apart from their relations to the larger global system. But economists can do more than measure and describe the complex interrelations among economic entities; we can work actively for a new order of priorities that transcends the narrow interests of national sovereignty and serves instead the interests of the world community. We must replace the ideal of growth, which has served as a substitute for equitable distribution of wealth, with a more humane vision in which production and consumption are subordinated to the goals of survival and justice.

Currently, a minority of the earth's people enjoy an inordinate share of resources and industrial capacity. These industrial economies, capitalist and socialist alike, must find ways to cooperate with developing economies to correct the imbalance, without pursuing ideological or imperialist competition, and without exploiting the people they propose to aid. In order to achieve equitable distribution of wealth throughout the world, the people of the

People who live in the inner city suffer from high fuel costs, pollution, and the effects of inhumane economics; they, too will benefit from the environmentally-sound economics of stability and sustainability. Drawing by Ann Kelley.

industrialized countries must relinquish what now seems an unbounded right to consume whatever resources are available to them, and we as economists must play a role in the reshaping of human values toward this end. The accidents of history and geography must no longer serve as rationale for injustice.

The task for economists is therefore an extremely novel and difficult one. Many people now look at the available data—the trends of population growth, pollution, resource depletion, and social upheaval—and lose hope. We have already passed the point of no return toward our rendezvous with disaster, they say gloomily; nothing can be done. But despair is a position we must reject. The moral imperative is for us to create a new vision, to make a road to survival through a treacherous country where there are no roads. At the present moment, man possesses the wealth and the technology not only to save himself for a very long future, but to make for himself and for all his children a world in which it is possible to live with dignity and hope and comfort; but he must decide to do it. We call on economists to join in framing the new vision that will enable man to use his wealth in his own interests, disagreeing, perhaps, on details of method and policy, but agreeing emphatically on the goals of survival and justice.

—Drafted by Nicholas Georgescu-Roegen, aided by Kenneth Boulding and Herman Daly, and signed by more than 200 economists

Why the GNP Is Not The Best Measure of Production

Much of the blame for our predicament has been heaped on our economic system and its social and political ramifications. This, however, is somewhat like blaming the car for the gasoline shortage. The origin of the problem lies, rather, in having made the attainment of ever-increasing material consumption our sole open-ended national goal. Obviously, *any* system or nation seeking infinitely increasing production in a finite world is bound to show, sooner or later, the unmistakable symptoms of its impending self-destruction.

We have made economics, which reflects only a tiny wedge of the truth of the "real world", the principal determinant in decision-making, and therefore have come to measure everything in terms of money, ascribing secondary importance to other terms of measurement, and least importance to criteria that cannot be quantified at all. This is tragic, because most of the really important things cannot be measured, and certainly not in terms of money; they relate to levels of natural existence or human experience far above that.

Extensive, mathematically sophisticated, and esoteric economic calculations might demonstrate, for example, that one machine will cost less than 100 workers in a certain production process, and therefore should be substituted for them. Who are we, who don't know the difference between a second derivative and semi-log paper, to argue? But does one measure the "cost" of a worker, perhaps a craftsman, a fellow citizen and member of society, by the same yardstick used to measure a piece of machinery, a common product? To whom does one machine cost less than 100 workers? For how long? By what measurement that makes any sense at all? And as for the piece of machinery, are not the loss of the human skills it replaces and its dehumanizing impact on those who operate it to be considered a part of *its* cost?

Obviously, if there is a diminishing quantity of resources, and our demands upon them grow from astronomical to even more astronomical each year, and all the while worldwide competition for them heightens and becomes more aggressive, prices are going to rise, not a little bit, not cyclically, but a great deal, steadily. That's not permitted in economic theory, so economists grasp at the slightest hesitation in the trend to show that everything is going to be O.K. after all.

We urgently need to study means of reorganizing agriculture and other critical industries in ways that minimize the use of energy, capital, and other material inputs, instead of maximizing their use, as is presently the case. The objective would be to attain adequate levels of production using the technologies most viable in the long run, probably labor-intensive and on a small enterprise basis, rather than seeking only to maximize short-run output or profits.

Too many people are in jobs destructive to the human spirit, and too few have an opportunity for creative work. The statistics do not show this, they could not possibly do so, but it is nevertheless the *real* problem with employment and work today, and it is getting worse. If human satisfaction in work is made a consideration above, or even equal to, simple production efficiency in the generation of workplaces, many creative and productive work opportunities previously precluded by production maximization economics will become available, and what is today called unemployment will take care of itself.

The costs of production, however wasteful the product or production process might be, are not taxed; only profits are, and it is left pretty much to the producer to decide which costs are necessary. This is equivalent to taxing individuals not in accordance with income, but in accordance with what they report as left (their "profits") after they have decided what costs are necessary to enable them to do whatever they declare themselves to be doing, whether or not there is any value to anyone else in what they do, and whether or not it is done in the least-cost way. Is it not strange that the cost of delivering raw materials to a factory or a product to your door is not taxed, but the expense you might incur commuting to work or driving to the store to pick up that same product is taxed? We have been taught that the costs of producing products are legitimate, the costs of producing our own satisfactions are not.

The engine that drives production maximization is dissatisfaction, coupled with the promise that products can relieve it. But products can never relieve it, because if they delivered on the promise we would no longer feel impelled to strive for ever higher incomes so that we can buy ever more products. If we did not feel deprived, Madison Avenue would be considered a failure, as it would in fact be, and the entire economic superstructure based on this deprivation-driven production maximization would collapse. Since this has been the path *we* have taken to what we have called our "development", it is what we have tried to transfer to "underdeveloped" countries so that they can get to where we are.

Let there be no mistake or euphemistic distortion about it: generally speaking, our international development efforts have been based on the notion that we can increase human satisfaction by generating feelings of deprivation, teaching that these can be relieved by the agencies of a "modern" economy and the products they bring, and then showing how to go about it. But our own experience has shown that this cannot work. You can teach people to make more and more products; and you can industrialize a country; and you can urbanize a country; and you can destroy its culture and social cohesion in the process of "modernizing" it; and you can make it dependent upon the vagaries of the international market for its viability—all this and more has been and is being done to "underdeveloped" countries—but you can never increase general human satisfaction this way because *dissatisfaction* is what makes it work and keeps it running.

Since making and selling products is but one small part of a culture, and serves social development only in a limited way, particularly in countries traditionally not product-oriented, the notion of teaching, encouraging, even forcing foreign nations to redirect all energies to production and consumption at a faster and ever-increasing rate and calling that "development assistance" is worse than an absurdity. We are always busy trying to "modernize" the agriculture of product-poor countries. We drive people off the farms; build highways; bring in tractors that make them dependent upon us and the world for parts, fertilizers, chemical poisons, and whatnot; teach them to work in factories instead of their extended households during the slow season; destroy family and community life; disrupt religious cycles; pollute and destroy the countryside; create an army of unemployed urban squatters; and in general turn all but the already rich and powerful into miserable unsatisfied production maximizers and product consumers. And for what? So that they can earn the foreign exchange to buy the things they need to support such a system? To increase their agricultural yield which now becomes dependent on foreign inputs and totters when the price of oil rises? To buy the products, including ours, that we have taught them to feel deprived without? The consequence of this "development" is to obliterate ways of life much older than ours. . . .

No nation or government could possibly suggest to another how it should develop. If a government cannot figure that out for itself, it must be completely out of touch with its people, to whom it would do well to turn for advice rather than turning to foreign "experts", the vast majority of whom have never even participated in development planning in their own countries. The drive, means, and plan for development *must* come from within a nation,

rooted in the many facets of its cultural essence, building upon what was already there in all areas of human activity, and relying upon its own resources. If asked, we *may* be able to help others design better tools from local materials; achieve better health and nutrition within their environments; even make better basic products for local consumption to increase self-reliance; and, of course, always stand ready to provide disaster relief if at all possible. There is a valid distinction between lending a brotherly hand and meddling.

The confusion between the amount of money made (GNP) and the value of the national economic product has deep and disquieting moral as well as practical implications. J.K. Galbraith pointed out many years ago that to strive for growth in money terms (GNP) alone is to declare that it is legitimate to be concerned with *how much* is produced, to the exclusion of concern with the actual value of *what* is produced. Thus, an appliance made in a shabby manner, deceptively or otherwise sold at an unfair profit, requiring many supplements for its effective operation, wasteful of resources, needing constant repairs, and wearing out quickly will result in the making of more money, i.e. will contribute more to the GNP, than a well-made, effective, and durable version sold at a fair profit. Similarly, the destruction of or failure to build an adequate mass transit system leads to more cars, more gas stations, more auto accessories, more auto repairs, more auto insurance, more parking lots, more highways and road repairs—in short, much much more GNP— while creating much more pollution and perhaps human misery, and in the end providing much worse transit effectiveness than would have been the case with a proper public system. Those products employing lead, asbestos, vinyl chloride, poison chemicals, and other lethal or dangerous materials in their manufacture contribute more to the GNP than safe alternatives, the production and use of which do not require regulation enforcement, litigation, lobbying, and precautionary procedures, or medical treatment for victims. Selling a part of the harvest abroad, where it will fetch higher profits while driving up prices and depriving segments of society of adequate diets domestically, will produce a higher GNP than will a policy of national nutritional self-sufficiency. In general, the more wasteful, inept, shortsighted, duplicative, uncoordinated, given to malfunction, nondurable, unfair, and inflationary our products and production techniques, the greater will be the GNP.

The present GNP concept makes sense as the principal means of assessing the economy only if the sole purpose of the economy is to facilitate the making of money.

—AVROM BENDAVID-VAL

Markets and Abundance

This paper is the tale of a quest for the relationships among growth, equity, and various economic distributive systems. It began some time ago with the question: is a non-growing economy likely to be an equitable one? That question evolved to: is a non-growing economy consistent with capitalism? As we shall see, that question led, to my own surprise, to still a third question: is capitalism consistent with equity?

For some time now I have been searching for a theory that explains the dynamics of the distribution of social goods and bads. I have found few theories but many conclusions that must have been drawn from unexpressed theories. The most often-voiced conclusion is that an end to material growth will worsen distributional inequities.

The assumption behind this argument seems both reasonable and simple. Material growth leads to an abundance of things to be distributed. Abundance of anything makes equitable distribution more likely, because it is a natural human trait to be generous with something you have a lot of, and stingy with something scarce.

If we define "abundance" as *per capita* availability, then population growth automatically decreases the abundance of unexpandable natural resources, such as land, fresh water, clean air, petroleum and ore deposits. Population growth may add to the abundance of manufactured goods by adding to the labor force, but since labor is rarely the limiting factor in production these days, the net effect of population growth on per capita abundance of manufactured goods is also negative. Thus, according to the theory, population growth, by creating two kinds of scarcity, is doubly a cause of inequity.

Capital growth increases the abundance of manufactured goods, and if capital grows faster than population, everyone may appear to be richer.

The other result of capital growth is a diminishing abundance of natural resources. Factories and machines use land, air, water, energy and ores, and the richness in manufactured wealth they produce is inevitably accompanied by an impoverishment in natural wealth. And since the manufactured wealth is ultimately derived from irreplaceable natural resources, as they become more depleted, eventually even manufactured wealth will be threatened by capital growth.

This analysis leads us to the opposite conclusion from the one we started with. Continued material growth may create a temporary illusion of abundance and equity, but in the long run it will worsen distributional equality by in-creasing scarcity, first of natural resources, then of manufactured ones.

According to this theory of distributional dynamics, the steady-state society, while it may not improve distributional equity, at least will keep it from getting worse quite so fast. That is comforting news, but we need a more positive conclusion upon which to base a design for a sustainable state. Let us press on and examine the basic distribution mechanism of the Western world, the market system.

Another problematic theory: The free market

The ideal distribution of society's scarce resources, according to Western economic theory, is attained through the decentralized market system. We need to take a fairly extended excursion into the theory of this system and a hard look at how it works in practice to understand how the free market does or does not fit into the design of a sustainable state.

If at any time the demand for any item on the market is higher than the supply of that item, its price will rise. The higher price causes two automatic responses. On the supply side, higher price stimulates more profit and thus more production of the scarce item. On the demand side, higher price causes some prospective purchasers to buy something else instead, or to do without. Thus supply rises and demand falls until the initial imbalance is corrected. At that point supply equals demand, the price is stable, and the system is in equilibrium. The market adjustment mechanisms also work in the opposite direction; a supply higher than demand causes prices to fall, causing, on the supply side, a cutback in production, and on the demand side, more customers, attracted by the bargain price.

The beauty of the system is in its self-regulating mechanism. No one needs to plan or control anything. Price acts as a signal to tell both consumers and producers about a relative scarcity or oversupply, and then consumers and producers, acting in their own best interests, correct the imbalance by producing or consuming more or less, whatever is required.

That is the theory, and it is a very appealing one. If you imagine a centralized planning bureaucracy trying to control prices, production, and consumption without the market system, you begin to understand why there are often long queues and barren store counters in the Soviet Union. It would seem that decentralized allocation decisions are ideally suited for a society that emphasizes long-term stability. After all, their very function is to maintain a stable and optimal equilibrium.

However, if we look not at the theory but at the way real

The monopolists denounce a "planned economy" as heresy. But what they really oppose is not planning—for the most part our economy is already shaped by a handful of officials. Raw materials are used or abused, prices are set and profits are maintained not by the operation of free market forces, but by the bureaucrats of the corporate structure. What the monopolists object to is any measure of planning for the public good instead of private profits. What they say is that we are restricting free enterprise; what they mean is that they want unrestricted power to manipulate an unfree enterprise system.

—GEORGE MCGOVERN

markets work, some problems appear. These problems are so well known and so often discussed that one must believe they are intrinsic, not accidental, flaws in the market system. For instance:

* Response on the supply side to a changing price, especially a higher one, rarely can be instantaneous. Producers may have to perceive the higher price long enough to believe it, decide to expand capacity, obtain financing, build new machines or factories, and hire new workers before a larger supply actually appears on the market. This response delay may not be as long as it would be in a centrally-planned economy, but it may easily be several years, especially in complex, high-technology productive processes. Delays in a feedback response may actually destabilize a system by causing over-adjustments and oscillations. (If you have ever tried to adjust the temperature of a shower with a very long pipe between the faucets and the showerhead, you have experienced these oscillations.) Long response delays also mean that the market is always somewhat behind the times. This basic defect can be countered somewhat by the addition of some sort of planning activity that *supplements* the backward-looking price signal with additional information gained from looking ahead. If this oracle is perfect and if everyone trusts it, the system will be stabilized. If the oracle takes the form of rumor-prone futures markets, small signals may be amplified into large ones, and the system is further destabilized.

* A more complete representation of the market system would include the constraints of cost and income. If the price of an item ever falls below the marginal cost to the producer of making it, he will shut down. If the price ever equals (or even approaches) the total income of a consumer, he will stop buying. . . . Thus cost and income act as two walls limiting the regulatory capability of the system.

* The "cost" that influences profits and the expansion de-

cision of suppliers is only the perceived immediate cost to the supplier. Since the system is competitive, each supplier is effectively rewarded for cutting costs (and thus continuing to realize a profit at price levels that shut down his competitors). A very effective way to cut costs is to transfer them to other parts of the system; release pollution that must be cleaned up by public agencies, convince the government to subsidize exploration for new oil wells, fail to install capital that would increase worker safety, create toxic waste products that must be safeguarded by future generations. These "externalities," as they are called, are widely recognized as basic faults of the market system. They result in prices that are lower than true total costs; this false price information induces consumers to buy products that they actually, in the total sense, can't afford.

* A common complaint about the market system is that it is blind to considerations of equity. The elegant market allocation mechanisms may result in maximum overall "efficiency," but one may ask whether that efficient allocation is "fair," whether it results in maximum satisfaction of real human needs, whether it properly rewards real productive contributions to society. . . .

How Does the Market Really Distribute The Means of Production?

Critics have observed the real market allocating grain to some people to feed cattle to feed fancy purebred dogs, while other people can't afford to buy grain to feed their children. They see the market rewarding with a pittance the man who works all day in the field to produce that grain, while greatly enriching the man who does nothing more than buy it and hold it off the market until the price is right. Two questions are raised by these observations. First, is the market system really rewarding productive efficiency, as it must to function well?

Second, even if it is, would a society that allocates its output that way be stable, and would it be one we would like to live in?

To answer that question, I am going to use two nearly-perfect market systems as examples: dairy farms in Vermont and wheat farms in the Punjab of Northern India. I became involved with these two agricultural systems independently and under circumstances that had nothing to do with market investigations. I was trying to analyze two problems raised by government officials in the two widely-distant areas. Why is the number of dairy farmers in Vermont decreasing so precipitously? Why is the rural-urban migration rate in the Punjab so high? To my surprise, the answers to both those questions turned out to be quite similar, and both of them could be traced back to the operation of the free market.

The Vermont and Punjab agricultural economies both consist of many small-scale producers, and their product is undifferentiable (one farm's milk or wheat is essentially indistinguishable from another farm's milk or wheat). There has been some governmental interference in each system, but in each case the effect seems to have been to enhance, not impede, market function.

In Vermont the number of dairy farms has decreased from 22,000 in 1950 to 6,000 in 1975. The average number of cows per farm has tripled over the same period. One farmer can handle such a large number of cows either by hiring labor or by mechanizing everything from milking to manure handling. Vermont farmers have followed the second option; the average value of farm machinery has increased (in real dollars) from $20,000 in 1962 to $37,000 in 1973, and the average indebtedness per farm has increased since 1950 by a factor of six.

Vermont farmers are not at all happy with these changes, and neither are non-farming Vermonters. The farmers complain of the back-breaking debt loads, of the increasingly tight management needed to make ends meet, of the high risk of bankruptcy, and of the impossibility of a young new farmer raising an estimated $250,000 to start in business. With few exceptions, the only young farmers in Vermont are sons of old farmers, who have inherited their farms or received low-interest, start-up financing from their fathers. Non-farmers in Vermont are unhappy with the trend away from dairy farming for both economic and aesthetic reasons. Economically, although the total dairy income to the state in real dollars is about the same as it ever was, it now supports far fewer people. Much of the money flows out again, to bankers, feed distributors, and tractor factories in other states. Aesthetically, Vermonters like the look of dairy farms. Over the last 25 years, 2 million acres of dairy farm, amounting to 30% of the

state's area, have been converted to something else—typically scrub forest, recreation developments, or shopping centers, none of which, according to opinion polls, especially appeal to Vermonters.

Many factors are blamed for the decline of the dairy industry in Vermont. Some say the trouble is the burdensome property tax that hits farmers especially hard. Others blame rising land prices, or avaricious developers, or higher prices of midwestern grain, which is fed to Vermont cows. Philip Budzik and I undertook a study of Vermont farm economics to see which of these factors was actually causing the problem. All of them were indeed involved, but none was very important. The real problem was the perfect functioning of the market mechanism.

Vermont milk goes to a market called the "Boston milkshed," where the total demand for milk, the average real price, and the total supply have not varied significantly in twenty years. In a fixed market like this, the effect of competition is very clear. The real cost of producing one gallon of milk has risen steadily over this period. Since the price (in constant dollars) has been constant, the profit per gallon must be falling. To maintain a constant income, every farmer must then produce more gallons of milk. But demand is constant; no more gallons will be bought. So for every farmer who successfully expands his production, another must decrease his. For every farmer who successfully maintains or expands his income, another finds his income decreasing. And almost without exception, it is the larger farmer who expands and the small farmer who is squeezed out.

One might think that the main problem in the Vermont dairy system is the constant demand for milk. If the market could expand in some way, then all the farmers could get rich together instead of some forcing others out. However, in my second example, wheat in the Punjab, the market is by no means saturated, yet the same process is occurring.

The Punjab is one of the great success stories of the Green Revolution. From 1960 to 1968 wheat production in one district there increased by 300%. At the same time, the price of wheat doubled, indicating a strongly rising demand. In such booming circumstances everyone in the district benefited but some more than others. Wages for landless laborers doubled, but the price of farm land quadrupled, as did the income of landholders. The distribution of land followed a pattern similar to the one I have already described in Vermont. Farms of 20 acres or more expanded in area by an average of 9% in 12 years, by buying out smaller farms. The proportion of landless laborers in the male work force increased from 9.2% to 19.8% (in a period of net emigration). In the Punjab wheat market, demand is not fixed—all of India's burgeoning population must be fed. But there is one fixed factor at the center of competition, and that is land. Arable land in the Punjab is essentially all occupied. If any farmer expands his land holdings, he must do so by buying from another farmer. And, as in Vermont, it is the large farmers who are expanding and the small farmers who are selling out and leaving for the city.

Checking the Vermont statistics in detail, one finds that the average herd size per farm increased from 32 to 53 from 1960 to 1973, and is still rising rapidly. The number of 20-cow-or-less herds dropped from over 3,000 to about 200. Yet there is *no* indication that small herds are less efficient than large ones. In fact in 1973 the total cost of producing a hundredweight of milk was *less* for small (32-cow average) farms than for medium-size (57-cow average) farms, and still less than for large (115-cow average) farms. Small farms spent less per hundredweight on labor, fertilizer, trucking, and interest, and slightly more on utilities and gas and oil. The two major costs of running a dairy farm—feed and capital purchases—were almost exactly equal (per hundredweight of product) across all farm sizes.

The same kind of message can be gleaned from the less detailed Punjab statistics. The small farms selling out to large neighbors are not less efficient in terms of total cost per unit of product. They do tend to be less efficient in output per man-hour, but far more efficient in output per acre or per dollar of capital investment. But the scarcest resources in India are land and capital, not man-hours.

Why are these two market systems moving toward larger productive units when there is no economic reason for doing so?

Big farms (or factories) are more likely to get loans for expansion than small ones. That fact may stem initially from the supposition within loaning organizations that economies of scale make bigger units better investments. Vermont farm loan agencies have been known to declare publicly that farms with less than 50 cows are, in their view, simply not viable. It is also true that bigger units generally possess more social power, contacts, collateral, information, and political strength. That is certainly the case in both the Punjab and Vermont. This allows large farms to grow preferentially, primarily because they are large, not because they are more efficient.

As some producers expand, they decrease the number of their competitors. This need not always happen, but it *must* happen in any market where the productive sector is up against any kind of limit. In Vermont the limit is total demand; in India the limit is land; in both cases the limit means that an increase in one farm's size must be bought by decreasing another farm's size (or eliminating it entirely). . . .

Farm expansion in Vermont and the Punjab are both relatively recent phenomena. For at least a century, both of these systems possessed all the characteristics that I have said might cause farm size to expand: a competitive market system, an intrinsic limit to the market, and a credit advantage to larger farms. But farms didn't expand, because of another limit; no farmer, even with a big family, could handle very many cows or harvest very much wheat. Labor could be hired, but there is also a limit to how much labor can be managed effectively. Only recently have new capital-intensive technologies permitted farmers to expand their operation without hiring many more laborers. Of course, those technologies are first adopted and are always more accessible to farms that are already large, that can get credit for new machinery, that can take risks.

This little exercise indicates that in at least two examples the market system has a flaw that not only balloons productive units far beyond their most efficient size, but that could lead to the destruction of the market system. That hasn't happened yet in the Vermont dairy or Punjabi wheat markets, although they seem to be moving rapidly in that direction. I would hesitate to generalize to other markets, but the evidence seems overwhelming. The market system is already gone for computers, and automobiles, and petroleum. John Kenneth Galbraith claims that 50% of the American economy has already entered the oligopolistic category. One wonders why more notice hasn't been taken of this self-destructive characteristic of the competitive market system. But my theme here is equity, and although monopolies have highly inequitable consequences, I believe that there are equity problems in the competitive market long before it evolves into a monopoly.

In the Punjab, Vermont, and most other places, farmers expand not by hiring more laborers, but by replacing laborers with machines. This choice is sometimes justified by economic calculation, but often the economic gain is not that clear. I suspect that farmers are attracted to machines for two nonquantifiable but very real reasons; machines reduce hassle and they increase status. It is easier to be boss of a machine than boss of a man, and the neighbors admire you more for it.

So as productive units expand, labor costs decrease while capital costs increase. The distribution of the *means of production,* wealth, farms, or factories, necessarily becomes more unequal as the size of productive units increases. And the distribution of *income* also becomes more uneven. The costs of milk production are as high as they have ever been. But these costs are no longer paid to thousands of farmers or farm laborers in Vermont. Instead they go to tractor producers, oil companies, chemical plants, and especially bankers. In effect, the increasing bigness of productive units is producing an allocation of both wealth and income from the relatively poor to the relatively rich. . . . Of course some of that reallocation does go to laborers in tractor factories, oil refineries and banks, but these units are also increasing in size, replacing labor with capital, and returning more of their income to the owners of capital. It's happening in Vermont and the Punjab, in Detroit and Houston, in Tokyo and Tehran.

Is the Free Market Consistent With The Sustainable State?

As the balance of production shifts from labor to capital, causing more uneven distribution of income, the demand side of the market may be disrupted, as the income wall moves inward for some consumers. At the extreme, as in the poorer regions of India, a large fraction of the population has so little income that it is excluded even from the markets of necessities such as grain. Under such circumstances price does not reflect real demand, farmers have no incentive to produce more, and the only outlet for

the system is conflict. But even before things get that bad . . . market demand reflects more and more the desires of the rich instead of the needs of the poor.

The market system, as I have described it, is inherently inequitable and unstable. It is certainly not consistent with a social system dedicated to sustainability. That does not mean, however, that we need to discard the idea of decentralized economic allocation entirely. What we need to do is understand better the strengths and weaknesses of the market system and look for ways to emphasize the strengths while eliminating the weaknesses. As Joan Robinson has said, "a pricing system based on supply and demand, though a bad master, may be a useful servant."

The market's tendency to generate inefficiency and inequity, the weakness I have explored in this paper, arises directly from the competitive character of market interactions. The market rewards successful competitors with the means for further successful competition. If the market is limited, and if technology permits the substitution of capital for labor, the competition is enhanced. The competition need not be ethical or even very efficient, it need only

Photo by David Powers/Jeroboam, Inc.

permit one producer to expand faster than another.

Two possible approaches might correct this deficiency. One would be to design a system that rewards cooperation instead of competition. That is what various socialist and communist movements have tried to do, with varying degrees of success. Cooperation seems to work better on a small scale than a large one, but I am looking for decentralized solutions, so a new sort of small-scale socialism might be a good design for a sustainable state. It would have to be a long-term solution, however, because it would require deep changes in values, education, and nearly every institution in our society, and such changes would take generations to implement.

The second approach is to accept competition, but to interrupt or continually counteract its undesirable effects. Several methods for doing this have already been instituted, weakly, in our society. Some examples are the progressive income tax, antitrust legislation, and various legal or social sanctions against certain ways of doing business. We could use more of these constraints, more vigorously enforced.

A more direct correction, applied to a central and easily measurable part of the system, would be a limit on the size of productive units. I have simulated the detailed effects of such a limit in only one case, dairy farming in Vermont. The limit there can be applied in many ways, on acreage, on number of cows, or on total milk production per farm. The latter seems most desirable. When a production limit is combined with protective zoning for agricultural land and financing aid for young farmers, the number of farmers

in Vermont stabilizes, and milk price is essentially unchanged.

In addition to, or in place of, limits on size of productive units, the sustainable state could impose upper as well as lower limits upon both income and wealth.

A steady-state society will automatically make the attainment of equity easier by limiting the population and capital growth that create physical scarcity. These limits will also tend to decrease the inequitable effect of capital-intensive technologies. But fixed population and stabilized material standards of living will also automatically limit markets, intensifying competition. Therefore, if a steady-state economy is to utilize a stable market system, it must incorporate an effective redistribution mechanism. This mechanism could be an upper limit on the size of productive units, or upper and lower limits on personal wealth and income, or some combination of these.

There is no question that the thoughts and policies posed here conflict with some freedoms that many of us have come to believe are important; freedom to make a profit, freedom to conduct our own business our own way, freedom to gain and wield power, freedom to grow. At the same time, a sustainable state that deliberately interferes with these freedoms would release others that we have forgotten about: freedom to define and create meaningful, dignified employment; freedom from want; freedom from the gainers and wielders of power; freedom from the pressures of growth. The real question is what kinds of freedoms do we want—what kind of society do we want?

—DONELLA MEADOWS

The Common Interests That Unite Us

With the post-World War II miracle of production, it was not long before the postwar backlog of consumer demand had been caught up with, and yet the capacity to produce went right on climbing. To absorb the output, it became necessary to stimulate and create markets for more and more of everything.

In part, this was accomplished by bringing more and more people into the mainstream of the market who had never been there before—large minority segments of our own population at home and comparable blocs in the developing nations throughout the world. But to a great extent it involved developing a pattern of greater consump-

tion among previous consumers. The manipulation of consumer demand involved pushing out new models of everything and discarding the old to make room for the new. It became a tremendously wasteful pattern—a fact that was not overlooked by those concerned with protecting the environment.

Before we proceed to project ourselves from this history into the third century, there is one other piece of the picture puzzle that needs to be put into place—the political interface with the economic realities. The political myths and misconceptions about the nature of our economy are myriad. We refer to our economy in various ways. We call

Smog is damaging the flora in Sequoia and Death Valley, and we mentioned the Anaconda problem at Glacier Park earlier.

Legal action should be taken against such outside causes of injury to parks, as was done for the Devils Hole pupfish, which survives only in a remote Nevada spring that is part of Death Valley National Monument. The spring was being drained by nearby wells of ranchers and subdividers until they were stopped by a Park Service lawsuit. Some sheriff's cars in Nevada sported "Kill The Pupfish" bumper stickers, but the Supreme Court ruled in favor of the fish.

Interpretation

Interpretation is an important function of the Park Service, but is one of the first services to suffer from budget cuts. In spite of budgetary restrictions, however, the Park Service has been expanding its valuable environmental education programs.

The preservation role of the parks must be emphasized in interpretive programs, which should be used to explain ecological concepts to a largely urban population (especially school children). Ranger-led overnight camping trips could provide an unforgettable experience for visitors afraid to set out on their own. Shuttlebus systems in parks can be used to expand interpretive services to captive audiences. Park buildings should demonstrate needed soft technologies, like solar heating and cooling.

Parks have an important role in explaining environmental problems. A good job of this is being done on the shuttle service in the Everglades' Shark Valley, where the effects of the diversion of the park's water supplies are obvious. Not so in Mesa Verde, where the bus to Wetherill Mesa has a view of the pollution emitted by a

The Berry Glen cut in Prairie Creek watershed, California. The Lady Bird Johnson Grove of Redwood National Park is on the right; the edge of the clear cut roughly follows the park boundary. Photo by Homer Gasquet.

Four Corners power plant but rangers aren't allowed to discuss it.

Wilderness

David Brower has said: "Wilderness is the bank for the genetic variability of the earth. We're wiping out that reserve at a frightening rate. We should draw a line right now. Whatever is wild, leave it wild. . . . Living diversity is the thing we're preserving."

The Wilderness Act provides for federal lands to be set aside by Congress, after study by the managing agency and public hearings, to be left in a wild state, not vulnerable to administrative whims. This landmark act set the precedent for public involvement in public land management decisions, and Congress has often passed citizens' wilderness proposals larger than the agencies'.

Only four small units of the National Park System have had areas protected under the Wilderness Act. The Department of the Interior has tried in the past to thwart the intent of the Wilderness Act, omitting "wilderness enclaves" and large "management zones" around the boundaries and roads. Conservationists are asking that about three million acres more than the Park Service proposes be designated as wilderness. Burying utility lines along roads could further increase the eligible acreage. The Park Ser-

vice has recommended *no* wilderness for some parks such as White Sands and Mammoth Cave (where conservationists want both caverns and the surface in wilderness) and has ignored others such as Acadia and Virgin Islands. Concessioners in Mammoth Cave and other parks have mounted media campaigns against wilderness designations in "their" parks even though existing facilities wouldn't be affected. Fortunately, both the Park Service wilderness recommendations and public support are increasing year by year.

Although more than 12 million acres have been established as wilderness in national forests, the Forest Service has avoided wilderness designation in crucial areas by establishing stricter criteria than the law requires, or even by logging and road building in de facto wilderness. Environmentalists have had to force the Forest Service even to study many potential wilderness areas, including *all* those in eastern forests. The clause allowing mineral entry and mining in wilderness areas administered by the Forest Service must be repealed if these areas are to remain wild.

Half a million acres of national wildlife refuges have been designated as wilderness, but action is still awaited on over 100 federal refuges. The Interior Department has maintained that public domain administered by the Bureau of Land Management, which includes two-thirds of our public lands, is not eligible for wilderness designation.

Conservationists disputed this, and new legislation requires all roadless BLM land to be studied for protection under the Wilderness Act by 1991.

Parks Under Seige

Coast redwoods are the tallest living things; the tallest remaining tree measures 367 feet. The northern California coast from Big Sur to Oregon was once a fern-carpeted redwood cathedral, but fewer than 5 percent of the giants still stand.

The redwoods once were mostly in public ownership. But logging companies and speculators gained control, often through fraudulent means, and began a demolition of the monarchs—some of which were alive when Christ was born. A Redwood National Park was authorized in 1968 after decades of battling, but its boundaries were based on political rather than ecological considerations. The park is now little more than a parkway, although it is preserving many miles of coastline.

We and the earth are once again paying the price of not protecting *complete* watersheds and ecosystems. The Redwood Creek "worm," a half-mile wide strip "protecting" the tallest trees in the world, is becoming an anomaly surrounded by devastation. Farther south, at Bull Creek, a similar situation caused floods and landslides that devastated a state redwood park.

Redwood loggers, so vocal in their opposition to environmentalists, are sawing off the branches they sit on. If cutting continues, old-growth trees will be gone in a decade and their children (like ours) will be left with a landscape capable of supporting neither a logging nor a tourist industry. Remaining virgin redwood stands and the park's watersheds must be protected. A bill to double the size of Redwood National Park has been introduced but has gotten nowhere. The reason given is the price—but many times the needed funds could be available if certain unneeded and destructive dam projects were halted. California's New Melones, Auburn, and Warm Springs come to mind as candidates. A program of reforesting and repairing wasted lands could nurse the redwood logging industry along into the twentieth century.

Across the continent at the southern tip of Florida lie the Everglades. Here the tropics meet the temperate zone and produce one of the country's broadest spectrums of life. The heart of the region is a river with nearly no gradient flowing slowly from Lake Okeechobee to Florida Bay and the Gulf of Mexico, 100 miles to the south. Everglades National Park, a seemingly endless expanse of sawgrass dotted with forested islands called hammocks, together with Big Cypress National Preserve, protects a portion of this river as it flows through mangrove swamps and exceptionally productive estuaries.

The Everglades were dying and are still threatened. Water essential to this ecosystem has been diverted for urban water supplies and agriculture. Land speculators trying to subdivide swamps divert water away from the 'Glades directly into the sea. Two large corporations, Context and Aerojet (General Tire), recently began diverting water away from Taylor Slough, the park's most popular area.

More than "just the park" is ruined when fresh water is diverted and salt water creeps further inland. Salt now threatens the water supplies both for agriculture and for Miami. Wild areas west of the park are being developed. These are estuarine breeding grounds essential to a multi-million-dollar seafood industry.

Many areas being altered by commercial interests were originally to be part of Everglades National Park, but were deleted. Powerful pressures to delete and drain more of the park still continue. Farmers covet the park to make up for farmlands lost to suburbia. Big Cypress has finally been remade a preserve, but more federal, state, and local action is needed to protect the other water supplies by expanding the park and creating recreation areas and preserves adjoining it. Otherwise, the Everglades will continue to dry up; this amazing display of animal and plant life, already severely damaged, will be decimated.

Starting in 1971, Tenneco, Johns-Manville, Pfizer, Cyprus Industrial Minerals, and American Borate have strip-mined for borates and talc (minerals that are plentiful elsewhere) in Death Valley National Monument. They exploit a loophole intended to allow "single-blanket jackass prospectors" to remain in the Monument. Tenneco even staked out world-famous Zabriskie Point, refraining from stripping it only in the face of outraged public protest. The Park Service has been outspoken in defense of Death Valley, but the Interior Department and Ford administration hamstrung the Service and refused to fulfill what environmentalists believed was a "legal duty to stop this official vandalism." Legislation to prohibit new mining claims in Death Valley, Glacier Bay, and the four other parks where mineral entry was permitted, passed in 1976, but the future of existing mines and claims is yet to be resolved.

A related problem is mineral *leasing* in recreation areas and preserves. The Park Service and Bureau of Land Management granted uranium leases to Exxon in a portion of the Grand Canyon that is in Lake Mead National Recreation Area and under study for wilderness protection and addition to the park. Environmentalists threatened legal action and the leases were cancelled. Offshore drilling threatens some parks, and oil wells along the border of Theodore Roosevelt National Memorial Park, in the North Dakota Badlands, are drilled at an angle to remove the oil underlying it. Resource exploitation of Park Service lands is being promoted by other agencies of government. Legislation is needed to close numerous loopholes that have accumulated to the benefit of special interests. Private inholdings in parks are subdivided, logged, and mined because funds to buy them are not forthcoming.

Reservoirs should not be allowed to inundate parts of parks. This was done in Yosemite, almost happened in Grand Canyon and Dinosaur, and is now occurring in Bandelier and Rainbow Bridge National Monuments. In the latter, the reservoir called Lake Powell is being allowed to flood the base of the world's largest natural bridge despite congressional promises to the contrary. Existing dams that compromise parks, such as the one flooding Yosemite's Hetch-Hetchy Valley, should be removed and the natural landscapes reclaimed.

Many existing parks need expansion to protect vulnerable areas, watersheds, wildlife migration routes, and park-quality lands adjoining them. Grand Canyon, Mount McKinley, Redwoods and some other parks encompass only a portion of the resource needing protection. Mineral King, a wildlife refuge almost totally surrounded by Sequoia National Park, should be added to the park. Legislation now pending would do that and settle the long controversy over Disney's plans.

Parks such as Bryce Canyon and Capitol Reef will be little more than parkways through stripped landscapes if their boundaries aren't protected against strip mining for the power projects planned for "Utah National Sacrifice Area." Recreation areas adjoining some existing parks would, in addition to serving as buffer zones, allow the Park Service to permit recreational activities incompatible with wilderness parks, thus taking some pressure (from local residents, especially) off of the Service.

New Parks

National Park Service studies and recommendations on proposed parks should be disinterested and professional, but the Service was essentially under orders from the Ford administration to oppose all non-historical park proposals outside Alaska, regardless of their merits—and regardless that the park system comprises less than one percent of our nation's land.

Although (and because) most of the US population is in the East, most of the natural parks are in the West. Congress has recently begun establishing national seashores and lakeshores and recreation areas in remaining nearly-natural lands and waters near population centers. It is sometimes argued that the Park Service shouldn't administer recreation areas near cities—especially because of the costs—but the few that already exist are very popular. The executive branch touted the program to "bring parks to the people" in the early 1970s and recommended 14 urban parks for starters; but it later opposed the concept, arguing that it is inflationary, and anyway, a local responsibility. But it seems that only the federal government is capable of creating the large parks needed to save these areas, to take a load off existing parks and to provide outdoor experiences for those unable to travel far. The Department of Housing and Urban Development had an Open Space program, but Nixon abolished it. Carter should revive it to help serve urban recreation needs. *National Parks for the Future,* the Conservation Foundation's study of park problems, recommends that land ruined by activities like strip mining, and hence cheap, be purchased by the government and reclaimed by public service employees for future parklands.

The Bureau of Outdoor Recreation was created to oversee a comprehensive national plan for parklands and to identify gaps and channel monies from the Land and Water Conservation Fund to fill them. But it has been a disappointment to conservationists and its report on needed parklands has been suppressed. A 1972 Park Service study identifying natural and historical values not represented in the National Park System had no official status in the Ford administration. The report says the System should "protect and exhibit the best examples of the nation's different kinds of landscapes, riverscapes, shore and undersea environments, the processes which formed them, and the life communities that grow and dwell therein," as well as "the important landmarks of our history." But many of the country's diverse environments, including the tallgrass prairie and the riverbottom hardwood forest, are today endangered.

Agricultural and grazing lands of the Midwest were once a wild prairie inhabited by millions of buffalo, pronghorn antelope, and prairie dogs. The grasses and wildflowers ranged from the shortgrass plains in the rain shadow of the Rockies to grasses that grew taller than humans on the humid eastern edge. Prairie parks, wilderness areas, and other preserves are needed to protect and restore samples of diverse prairies such as the tallgrass prairie, northern plains, Nebraska's Sand Hills and other mixed-grass prairies, the coastal prairie of Texas, and the Central Valley of California—once a poppy-covered plain.

The tallgrass prairie once covered parts of eleven states, but is now almost gone. The three remaining areas that have national park potential are in the Flint Hills of Kansas

In Alaska, we have an opportunity to preserve an American Serengeti; our last large free-ranging animal herds, with a great Neolithic culture, need huge parks and wilderness preserves to survive. Photo by Wilbur Mills from Earth and the Great Weather *(Friends of the Earth).*

and northern Oklahoma, and have survived by the grace of rocky soil that hindered plowing. But these remnants are being eaten away today by grazing, plowing, freeways, power lines, dams, and subdivisions. The Park Service is studying the remaining tallgrass, but high land prices, fierce local opposition, and a lack of appreciation for grasslands have so far prevented establishment of a Tallgrass Prairie National Park.

The rush to build the Alaskan pipeline has made the environmentalists' "doomsayer" predictions appear conservative in retrospect, but it did trigger a one-time opportunity to preserve many of that state's areas of park caliber. The Ford administration urged that 32 million acres be managed by the Park Service with another 51 million acres established as national forests, wildlife refuges, and wild rivers. Environmentalists, having learned the futility of trying to protect and manage less-than-whole ecosystems, are working for the inclusion into the National Park System of approximately twice the acreage that the administration proposed, with a total of 107 million acres proposed for parks, monuments, wildlife refuges, and wild rivers. Conservationists' proposals are drawn along natural boundaries where possible in an effort to protect whole ecosystems, watersheds, and wildlife habitats. The Ford administration's proposals are generally smaller, and in the Wrangell Mountains, leave the forested lowlands to be administered

for "multiple-use" by the Forest Service. Environmentalists oppose this approach, especially in light of the extreme mismanagement of existing national forests in Alaska.

The National Interest Lands in Alaska (often referred to as the "d-2" lands because of the section in the Alaska Native Claims Settlement Act of 1971 authorizing their selection) provide an opportunity to double the size of the National Park System, but Congress has shown little interest in holding hearings. Proposed areas whose protection is not ratified by 1978 will be reopened to resource exploiters. The uniqueness of Alaska may require new preservation concepts, and efforts are being made to work with native groups to preserve traditional cultures.

Numerous new national monuments should be established and some existing ones—including Death Valley, Channel Islands, Glacier Bay, and Katmai—should be expanded and elevated to national park status. The practice of transferring the most spectacular Forest Service lands to the Park Service (where they would *usually* receive better protection) has waned, but deserves revival. The Wheeler Peak area of Humboldt National Forest in Nevada, for example, should be set aside with surrounding desert as the Great Basin Desert National Park.

Remaining free-flowing rivers need to be given the protection of the Wild and Scenic Rivers Act, including the

More areas were deleted in 1975 from the U.N. list of National Parks and equivalent reserves for failure to meet standards of protection than were established in 1974.

Some feel that parks should be intermittently closed for a year—as they are in Canada—just to let the fragile environment rest a bit.

—LESTER BROWN, PATRICIA McGRATH, AND BRUCE STOKES

New River and the Stanislaus, which is threatened by a dam. More national trails should be created for those still wishing to see the country on foot, and existing ones such as the Appalachian Trail need further protection.

The coastline is a precious national resource that must be preserved, if for no other reason, because of its important role in the web of life. Only four percent of the nation's shoreline is accessible to the public, and there is a struggle now to save remnants of the seashores recommended for protection by an ignored Park Service study completed two decades ago. Island Trusts (on the Martha's Vineyard model) should be established to control development and ensure public access to islands that are primarily in private hands, like those around Acadia National Park.

To understand the necessity of preserving these special places, we need only look at Lake Tahoe and Glen Canyon, two of the earth's natural masterpieces. Both are being ruined, one by gambling and overpopulation, the other by needless dam construction. The reclamation of these two magic places would symbolize our national dedication to the concept of preservation.

Historic Preservation and Public Involvement

The Park Service has taken increasing responsibility for preserving historic sites, including aiding state and local efforts. It maintains the National Register, a listing of important historical resources, and provides professional services to other agencies and the states. But historic preservation is at present a low priority item and lacks proper funding and direction.

While administration of historic sites of national significance should remain with the Park Service, historic preservation grants and technical assistance need to be consolidated within one agency, either a major branch of the Park Service, part of the independent Advisory Council on Historic Preservation, or a cabinet-level Office of Preserva-

tion. The Historic Preservation Fund, recently increased by Congress, should be fully funded by Interior. Legislation is needed to offer legal protection for buildings and sites on the National Register and for natural areas designated as National Landmarks.

Archaeological interests need more representation on the Advisory Council on Historic Preservation. The Interior Secretary's Advisory Board on National Parks, Historic Sites, Buildings and Monuments should be an important source of public participation, but it usually rubber-stamps Park Service policies. Minorities, environmentalists and young people are under-represented on the Board—a situation that can be corrected as vacancies occur.

World Heritage Trust

The World Heritage Trust expands the national park concept to an international level, recognizing that exceptional natural, cultural, and historic resources are of global importance. The US should continue to support this fledgling United Nations program. The criteria for inclusion in the Trust are being established, and more than 20 nations have joined the effort. It is expected that the World Heritage Trust will offer financial, training, and public information assistance to qualifying areas.

The US must dedicate itself to a reverence for the natural world that created and sustains us, and to the preservation of its natural, cultural, and historical heritage. Existing units of the splendid National Park and Wilderness Preservation Systems must be kept inviolate for future generations. New areas need to be added to these systems and the World Heritage Trust in order to preserve the miraculous living diversity of planet Earth. All remaining wild areas must be left as wilderness. In the words of Edward Abbey: "Wilderness is not a luxury but a necessity of the human spirit, and as vital to our lives as water and good bread. A civilization which destroys what little remains of the wild, the spare, the original, is cutting itself off from its origins and betraying the principle of civilization."

Recommended Actions

☐ The President should reverse the policy of the Nixon and Ford administrations, releasing funds for the acquisition of new parklands that they impounded, and fully funding the Land and Water Conservation and the Historic Preservation funds.

☐ The President should put pressure on Congress to accelerate the selection of "national interest lands" in Alaska—land for national parks and monuments, forests, wildlife refuges, and wild rivers—and support conservationists' proposals.

☐ The President should announce support of the principle that all types of ecosystem in the US should be represented in the National Park System, and in furtherance of that principle, he should support the acquisition of tallgrass prairie in Kansas and riverbottom hardwood forest in South Carolina's Congaree Swamp.

☐ The President should recommend enlargement of parks that are too small to accomplish their primary purposes, notably Grand Canyon, Mount McKinley, and Redwood National Parks.

☐ The US delegation at the United Nations should work to assure the continued and complete cooperation of the US with the World Heritage Trust, Man and the Biosphere, and similar international efforts.

☐ Congress should prod the land management agencies (and itself) to hasten the completion of the Wilderness Preservation System.

☐ Congress should forbid hunting and mining in all existing units of the National Park System; *subsistence* hunting should be permitted in some of the proposed preserves in Alaska.

☐ Congress should add Mineral King to Sequoia National Park, by which it is almost totally surrounded and of which it should always have been a part.

☐ Place more emphasis on preserving historic sites.

☐ Congress should create an agency or charge an existing one with responsibility for continuing study of ways to dismantle unwanted dams and restore reservoir areas, to restore strip-mined land, and in general, to return devastated lands to something like a natural state.

☐ The National Park Service must:
☐ Standardize rules governing concessions, taking care that its contracts benefit the public and the government no less than they benefit concessioners ☐ Move artificial attractions, extraneous activities, commercial developments, and other non-essential facilities outside park boundaries ☐ Refrain from building new roads or upgrading existing ones ☐ Extend shuttlebus services and discourage private motor vehicles ☐ Use "built-in frictions" instead of high fees to regulate the number of visitors. ☐ Recommend to the President and Congress ways to establish (or reestablish) public mass transit from nearby population centers and transportation hubs to the parks ☐ Encourage bicycle use on shuttlebus roads within parks ☐ Ban privately-owned off-road vehicles of all kinds ☐ Reduce highly developed and high-cost campsites, and restore low-cost, primitive campsites

☐ Exclude developments from prime wild animal habitat ☐ Eradicate non-native species of animal and plant life wherever practicable and reintroduce native species that have been unnaturally displaced ☐ Create national recreation areas and other types of buffer zones around wilderness parks ☐ Protect *all* de facto wilderness in units of the National Park System and recommend that they be formally protected as Wilderness.

☐ Appoint minorities, environmentalists, and young people to the Secretary's Advisory Board.

☐ Appropriate subcommittees of the House and Senate should, if necessary, propose any legislation necessary to assure that the Park Service vigorously pursues the foregoing objectives—unimpeded by the Department of the Interior.

Drawing by Bill Oetinger.

Ideas are the keystone. They leave their mark on the landscape just as surely as chain saws and bulldozers. Machines, after all, are only the agents of a set of ethical precepts sanctioned by the members of a particular society. The most serious form of pollution is mind *pollution. Environmental reform ultimately depends on changing values. The responsibility of higher education is clear.*

—RODERICK NASH

Education—As if Learning Mattered

In 1977 America has an educational establishment capable of confounding the principles of government that gave us such a good start 200 years ago and capable, too, of promoting the destruction of what remains of the North American environment. Students are quite lost from view amid the intricate network of policies, credentials, and standardized programs. They learn, more by their experience than their textbooks, that convenience is the goal and insensitivity the means. Remedial help for the educational establishment requires embarrassingly simple programs the point of which is to put students and teachers in touch with each other, with environments, and with good tools. Humane values and environmental values are learned through close, unhurried contact with people and the land. This requires labor-intensive teaching, low on prepared curricula and paper, high on dialog with people and places. And the structure of the curriculum for a student must make room for skills of the hand as well as the mind, turning labor into craftsmanship, counselling students to enter an age of intermediate technology with competence, critical awareness, and the skill of self-government. Current problems of schools with control, finance, racial animosity, and learning deficiencies all hinge for their solution on decentralization, humanization, and the development of ecologically sound operation—all of which bring student and teacher into the foreground and closer together. Spelling, the art of asking good questions, and the interdependence of a community and a river are all best taught at close range.

Education

The lesson that has been most mysteriously lost and forgotten during the growth of the educational establishment is that children learn. The behavioral prize the primates have been puzzling over and improving on for the better part of 100 million years is learning. Pre-tests, tracking, behavioral objectives, and endless curriculum packages are not nearly as important in the learning process of children as are the behaviors of their elders and peers and the opportunities in their environment. When close contact with elders, peers, and environment is disrupted, children *still* learn—they learn distrust, even terror, and acquire the ability to insulate themselves from their environment.

In light of this long heritage of increasing ability to learn, some of our educational bureaucracy is simply foolish, even amusing. Some slivers of programs and grants have worked to bring students, teachers, and environments closer and to promote learning. But most of the establishment encrustation stands in the way of close personal and environmental contact by design, habit, and sheer size. Children survive in this system by learning how to get by as unimportant individuals in masses tended by administrators, free of responsibility for decisions, insulated from their own capacities, from each other, and from their environment.

It is hardly surprising that problems of support, control, racial hatred, and general apathy flourish. The system is inefficient in traditional economic terms, in its environmental relationships, and especially in terms of the resulting quality of education. The linear passage to higher education, counselled as the only way to get decent jobs, has proved increasingly ineffective and anticlimactic—just a repetition of the high school experience. Its one benefit may be that it has flooded the universities with students expecting teachers and finding only researchers—an embarrassing situation for those schools with articulate student organizations. Grades, held on to tenaciously as the only means to evaluate masses of students, have been soaring to keep the lid on student dissatisfaction, while it is commonly admitted that the quality of student writing has been declining at an equivalent rate.

In 1976 I walk the same half mile that led me to elementary school in 1952, only now I continue past the school yard to catch a bus to the university, where I've been undergraduate, graduate student, and now instructor. This walk encourages reflection over long years of being a student and teacher. I am more sure than ever that the education that matters derives from close contact with other people and with environments—education, to build on Alan Gussow's phrase, that provides a sense of humanity and a sense of place. In these years when we are beginning to understand that Schumacher's economics matters, it is clear that education itself is best as an intermediate technology. It is most efficient, in the quality of student experience, when it is labor-intensive. And its structure and content must support one another.

Walking by my old first grade classroom, I visualize fragments of what our educational system must be. Teachers will be expected to work with few students, but to know them well. In the early years loads should be especially light, and at the secondary level no teacher should be expected to work with more than about 60 students during a week. Advising will be a shared function of all a student's teachers. Dialog with the student and written evaluation will become much more useful than grades in marking educational progress.

Schools will be communities of learning, stressing a common purpose for all their members. All personnel will be involved with instruction and advising of students in addition to their support tasks. This will follow naturally from the need for schools to become self-maintaining, with all members involved in maintenance work. But the point here is that students will learn from laborers, in the traditional sense, as well as more typical instructors—they will learn from janitors, cooks, nurses, secretaries, even administrators. No longer will these people be separated from the learning process.

Schools will be as self-sufficient in use of resources as possible, stimulating self-sufficiency in the local community as well. Energy and materials will come from recycling within the school program and from local sources. The time that such an effort will take will not be lost from the educational program, rather it will be a major part of it. All students, teachers, and other personnel will be working to lessen the environmental impact and increase the self-sufficiency of the school and its community—and this may be the single most important learning activity of all.

While campuses and buildings will remain the focal points of school operation, connections to the outside will be increasingly important. The old school building I pass every morning would seem to many to be ready for demolition. There's nothing educationally streamlined about it.

About 99 percent of the people who speak of "education" mean two things by it: (1) a process which is separate from the rest of life, best done when we are not doing anything else, and best of all in places where nothing else is done, and (2) a process in which some people try to get other people to learn what someone else has decided would be good for them.

—JOHN HOLT

Yet a first grade classmate of mine who has returned to this building to teach is running a truly visionary program. Classroom instruction for his junior high students is supplemented by the maintenance of a recycling program on which the entire local community depends and several wilderness outings a year that bring his students into contact with environments and with their own capabilities. One lesson here is that the old buildings do not have to come down—it is the programs being run in those buildings that determine their educational value. Another is that no building, not the most modern architect's dream of the Ultimate School, is sufficient without program extensions into the local community and outside environments.

Schools will be involved locally in political, economic, and social realities. Apprenticeships in trades, services, government, community maintenance, and wilderness preservation will form an essential part of the instructional program. And communities will greatly increase the efficiency of school structures by using them throughout the year both for instruction and for community functions. Community control of schools will be strong precisely because of the degree of involvement of the students in community programs.

District organization will give way to community boards that advise schools in order to maintain an integrated program throughout a student's education, keeping school faculties in touch with each other's curricula. And higher level advisory groups will facilitate school interaction and exchange programs within broad regions. Such regions might well be political entities with a mandate to gain regional self-sufficiency and insure maintenance of environmental and economic health; their boundaries might well coincide with those of major watersheds. Within such regions a prime lesson for both communities and their schools—urban, suburban, and rural—will be interdependence and cooperation. School support, beyond each school's own capability for self-support, will be provided at the regional level as an integral part of the region's self-maintaining, steady-state economy.

New to the curricula of these schools will be thermodynamics, wilderness, political skills, and skills of the hand. Thermodynamics, the principles of energy and order, will be the basis of all science teaching and will be extended to the practical application of technology assessment. Wilderness, real contact with environments apart from man, will be experienced at several points during a student's program, both as an end in itself and as a means to a new perspective of man's role on earth—custodial, not regal. Political skills, the principles of self-government, will be resurrected from the anonymity into which "Citizenship" has fallen and will be learned through apprenticeship and application in the local community. And academics, which will primarily involve the skills of reading, writing, mathematics, and critical thinking, will be given no more weight in a student's program than skills of the hand—the crafts of building, designing, repairing, maintaining.

Graduation will be as contingent upon readiness to support oneself with manual work as it will be on ability to read and write and maintain learning. The expectation will

Drawing by Ann Kelley

not at all automatically be continuance of education in college. It will be more desirable to enter the community productively and only return to formalized learning when a particular desire emerges. Colleges will be open for continued learning and research, but the pace of research will be slower and the role of critical assessment, applied wisdom, more important.

The preparation and credentialling of teachers and other school personnel will be based on a trial period working with a master teacher. Education degrees will not be sought. Instead, teaching skills will be developed primarily through trial teaching and a community board will evaluate performance throughout the teacher's career. Schools and departments of education at the college level will continue to provide a platform from which to analyze teaching methods and programs—but all faculty of such institutions will be required to teach elementary or secondary students concurrently, to prevent isolation from the learning process, from real school problems, and from community control.

Powerful Inertia

I am reminded every day how distant a goal such a system is, how powerful the inertia of the present system is. At the university I see class upon class in which a majority of students are turning up for exams only, begging for higher grades, and never questioning the subject matter beyond what is necessary to answer a multiple-choice question on a mark-sense form. Degrees are probably nearer to being simply sold than at any time since the Revolution in this country. And a kind of panic scramble for the professional and applied programs is commencing as more and more students discover the purely academic degree has no job-generating powers.

The greatest part of the inertia derives from the ten-

dency of teachers to teach in the manner in which they were taught. There is also the general assumption, given the present system and economy, that we have a substantial teacher surplus. This works in favor of maintaining older teachers and sending new ones looking for other employment. All of which contradicts the desire of most teachers to work with smaller student loads, knowing the chances of doing a better job are at least greater with smaller numbers. I try to take some solace each time I pass my old elementary school and see how radically different its program is today, run by one of its own graduates.

Reforms Beyond Lesson Plans

Curriculum reform by itself is not a hopeful approach to instituting the new system. It is an easy first step to take, but it rarely leads anywhere, once new materials are in use. There are many examples to be found today of ecologically oriented curricula being taught within traditional school operations, so that the message of the texts is daily contradicted on the grounds, in the lunchroom, perhaps even in the use of the course materials themselves. What is wanted is a first step that leads on to others by beginning to alter teacher behavior.

The most effective catalyst is a program that affects the daily operation of schools, affecting all members of the school community and nudging the school toward involvement with the outside community. I believe the most helpful approach is through a program of school self-sufficiency. It will always be attractive economically, and especially so in the light of growing energy consciousness. Federal and state funding incentives could be used to reward schools that can demonstrate:

* that teachers and students, working together with the maintenance staff, have developed an energy conserva-

Photos by Elihu Blotnick, from Saltwater Flats *(BBM Associates).*

tion and materials recycling program in which all participate;

* that maintenance staff members are giving instruction
and supervision on maintenance tasks within the school;

* and that a teacher-student delegation is developing local
community contacts to obtain land for school agricultural use.

Such programs should be monitored as they develop and
receive additional funds when they demonstrate significant
increases in self-sufficiency. Even these steps will threaten
some faculty and administrators. If school maintenance becomes a cooperative effort of faculty and students, however, there will be noticeable benefits in that elusive educational phenomenon, "school spirit." That, along with increased support from a local community receiving the
economic benefits of the school's efforts, should be
enough to carry the day and perpetuate the program.

A benefit of employing students and teachers in school
maintenance is that the school community becomes much
more conscious of itself. And as energy and materials are
monitored, an insight critical to all further developments
should be realized—teacher-student interaction need not
be energy intensive and does not require mountains of
materials. Often the best education is built on dialog alone.
It is hoped that this will lead teachers toward the development of "lean curricula," curricula that *emphasize* the
teacher-student interaction and reduce capital and energy
investments in the classroom. Federal and state funds for
"lean curriculum" workshops, led by master teachers,
should stimulate a move away from the elaborate wares of
the educational publishing houses and begin to put
teachers back in touch with their own creativity. The more
it becomes clear that an unhurried student-teacher relationship is the most productive path to real learning, the
more schools will begin to look beyond the myth of the
teacher surplus. At this point something like a National

Teacher Corps program should help the schools bring in
new personnel on apprenticeships under master teachers.

Once the janitorial and dietary staffs begin to be used for
advice and instruction in the school self-maintenance program, they should continue to share a responsibility for
instruction. It may be a slow evolution, but the idea of a
fully participating educational community ought to
emerge. The more school operation becomes an acknowledged part of the educational program, the more the experience and skills of all personnel will be sought. Some
funding incentives for schools that demonstrate an integration of all personnel into instructional and advisory roles
would help, but an attitudinal change is involved that will
undoubtedly take time no matter what the incentive.

If school-community cooperation on recycling and resource acquisition matures, it will lead to greater community control. The emphasis on self-sufficiency should
stimulate a review of existing school structures and building plans. A revolutionary use of state or federal funds
would help here to nudge districts off dead center: reward
rehabilitation programs utilizing school personnel rather
than traditional building projects. Repairing and refurbish-
ing older buildings will require the assistance of skilled
laborers. Funding should be made contingent upon
employing these laborers as instructional assistants, thus
providing apprenticeships to students within the curriculum. The obvious hope, here, is to further the introduction of a skills curriculum to parallel the academic curriculum.

As community and school become more interdependent
in a recycling and maintenance effort, it would be a logical
step for the school to make more and more use of people
in the community to supplement its programs and for the
community to make greater use of the school facilities and
personnel on a year-round basis. It is essential that this
kind of cooperation develop. Very few of the reforms dis-

cussed here can proceed at all far without community support and agreement. A school attempting too much change on its own is bound to run into fear and misunderstanding.

Regionalism in School and Government

The evolution of districts into watershed regional school consortia has little hope unless there is much progress toward regional governments themselves. Incentives can be offered to inter-school programs that disregard current district lines and tie together schools in a region. But real change in school control at this level will depend on hoped-for changes in the political organization and economy of whole regions. It is clear that the current pattern of separate urban and suburban districts and of patchwork solutions to imbalances, such as busing for racial integration, is not working. The search for better solutions is most likely to lead to regional funding and inter-school

programs that achieve integration in educational experiences, not simply by moving bodies. It may be that the severity of current problems will be a greater stimulus to change than anything else could be.

If the requirement that schools work with communities on resources and recycling is met, then the stage is set for some important curriculum additions. Without community involvement these changes would have far less effect. The best strategy would be to begin funding curriculum development only after progress has been made in community programs. First, citizenship education needs to be resurrected through instruction and practice in the skill of government. Students and teachers should be encouraged to serve in an advisory capacity or directly on local governing bodies as part of the instructional program. Such a use of state and federal funds to stimulate a renaissance in local government might be politically very popular.

The involvement of local artisans in the school mainte-

Drawing by Ann Kelley.

Intellectual disciplines and categories of knowledge tend to flow into one another unless prevented by artificial barriers. Rather than impeding such flows, universities should recognize and encourage them.

—JOSEPH MEEKER

nance program should also be capitalized upon in the school curriculum. People with skills should be encouraged to enter the teaching program, with incentives again being offered those schools that begin to teach such skills on a par with academics. Scholarship monies, in particular, could be awarded to students graduating with hand skills who will begin a productive role in the community and postpone consideration of college. This balancing of curriculum content will, I hope, develop alongside a general renovation of the respect and support awarded to hand labor as our energy-glutted economy turns toward intermediate technology. It is certainly unlikely that the schools alone can lead such a movement, but they can support it in both their curriculum and their operation.

Clear roles for government incentives in more traditional curriculum development have been left unmentioned until now because structural changes in schools are so much more important and will take so much longer. But it is still to be hoped that funds will be used to support the incorporation of thermodynamic principles in all levels of curricula. In teacher workshops and in-service training programs, it should be stressed that teaching the principles of energy and order does not require great amounts of energy and materials. All such workshops should be planned to support the idea of "lean curriculum" development mentioned earlier. The precise placement of funds, avoiding materials-intensive projects and singling out light educational technology, can do much to foster this development.

The federal and state governments can play essential roles in the development of wilderness education at all levels. The reservation of park and wilderness sites for wilderness curricula is one step, in addition to providing support to schools that ensure that all children have wilderness experience at some time during their program. The National Park Service, for example, should be instructed to take more seriously than ever its educational function and turn more and more to school programs.

The best that can be done for colleges and universities is to offer incentives for the same self-sufficiency programs as the lower schools. Moves toward faculty-student maintenance would be the best preparation for the change

in students coming from high schools during the first years of this development. Continued change in incoming students may be expected to stimulate colleges and universities to keep pace. They are not the most important focus for change, however, and will have to be shaped to their own needs and expectations primarily by students that come out of the evolving elementary and secondary systems.

Those most likely to feel threatened by the evolution of the system described here are established teachers, professors, and administrators. It is difficult to see how the changes can be anything but invigorating for the students, other school personnel, and communities involved. All of these will be discovering ways to take a greater share in the educational system. Teachers and administrators may see their territory threatened. The best hope for gaining their confidence and involvement lies in the prospect of reduced student loads and a less shaky economic picture for the schools. An interim contribution to their understanding and patience with this grand design would be a program of one-year apprenticeships outside the field of education. Teachers and administrators would be supported for a year, with the requirement that they learn some skill quite unrelated to their normal duties. Ideally, all teachers would be required to do this about once in every five years, but perhaps at least a beginning could be made by putting established teachers in touch with the increasingly labor-intensive economy—and giving them, at the same time, a new perspective on their own capabilities and the meaning of teaching.

Georg Borgstrom replies to questions of what to do given the current environment-energy situation with the simple response: "Become acquainted with the means of your survival." As this becomes increasingly clear because of economic and societal change, teachers will find that developing a system of labor-intensive education will work to their benefit and actually help them accommodate the changes in society around them.

Great encouragement can be taken from the fact that most of the reforms and programs mentioned here are currently in use in schools scattered all over this country. They are not all to be found in one place as yet, but agricultural self-sufficiency, recycling, maintenance apprenticeships, community control, thermodynamic and wilderness education—all these *can* be found today. Labor-intensive operation and the accompanying increase in the stature of work and hand labor are still in the distance, but trends in the economy will continue to point in their direction and should help educators who have come this far to make the necessary connections. Also helping will be the already growing dissatisfaction among many, particularly the young, with mass-produced "uncrafted" articles. Even now there is an increasing market for hand skills and products.

In 2076 we can have an educational system suited to perpetuating self-government and a life-giving environment. What is required now is a program to unify the technology and the functioning of schools with the message of self-sufficiency they must teach. Schools can cost less, both environmentally and economically, and teach more if they rediscover the learning potential in the simple teacher-student relationship. The road to this labor-intensive education leads from the involvement of all teachers and students in the maintenance of their schools to an electorate educated with the skills of the hand, of government, and of learning itself. Children learn, and they can certainly learn the means of their own survival.

Recommended Actions

All levels of government should encourage, by all means at their disposal, schools and schooling appropriate to a post-industrial society. In particular, they should encourage:

☐ Decentralization and community control of schools, with maximum interaction between community and school.

☐ Ecologically sound school operation, including a recycling program extending beyond the school into the community.

☐ Maximum self-maintenance and self-sufficiency, involving all students and all school personnel.

☐ Labor-intensive teaching, with more teachers devoting more attention to fewer students per teacher.

☐ Recognition that all school personnel have useful skills, and consequently, that all should be recognized as instructor-advisors in their areas of competence.

☐ Development of "lean curricula" relying more on student-teacher rapport and less on capital equipment.

☐ Within the traditional curriculum, emphasis on reading, writing, mathematics, and critical thinking.

☐ The addition to curricula of thermodynamics, wilderness experience, political skills, and skills of the hand.

☐ Year-round use of school buildings for community as well as educational functions, and maximum rehabilitation of existing structures to minimize the building of new ones.

If children do not learn the ropes faster in our society, and even now they learn them faster than we think, it is in part because they do not have to, are not expected to, and do not expect themselves to, and in part because they know that they could not do anything with the knowledge if they had it.

—JOHN HOLT

Decentralization:
Making Small Places Work Again

Americans should all be able to live and earn their livelihoods in the kind of environments they prefer, from open country to central cities. In our early history, most work opportunities were agricultural or agriculture-related. People who would have preferred city life stayed on the land instead because there were no really large cities and because employment opportunities in the city-towns of the day were limited. With the rise of manufacturing, cities mushroomed as the focal points of industrial activity, and with the industrialization of agriculture, machines displaced more and more farm workers who had no choice but to go where the industrial jobs were. From a nation that was almost entirely rural, we became a nation whose people are nearly three-fourths city dwellers. Many of these people prefer city life; for them, we need only make our cities more livable. But many city dwellers would prefer life in small towns or the countryside; for them, we need to create non-urban residential and employment options. We need to decentralize—not totally, but enough to achieve balance. The decentralist impulse will be reinforced as the energy-intensiveness of large-scale US mechanized agriculture becomes insupportable and as the depletion of nonrenewable natural resources causes the contraction of heavy manufacturing. The choice is not between centralization and decentralization; the choice is between intelligently planned decentralization and random decentralization under the compulsion of inexorable social change.

Decentralization

America in 1976 is characterized by centralization of population and of power, both economic and political, and the uneven distribution of human and environmental features that contribute to the quality of life.

The most tangible expression of our centralized society is the geographic distribution of our population. In 1970, 73 percent of the American population lived in metropolitan areas; the remaining 27 percent were classified as "rural." The trend of population movement to the cities, the exodus from farms and small towns, the decline of family farms, have become clichés of American life in the last hundred years. Very recent indications that a population reversal is under way—back to Appalachia, the Ozarks, and other rural and small town areas—are being analyzed cautiously, ex post facto, with little speculation about cause.

Most Americans accept the presumed economies of scale associated with centralization and specialization. Making large quantities of widgets permits cheaper widgets; they are also likely to be standardized and of less practical use. We may be given the illusion of variety by polka dots, stripes, sugar-coating, and slick advertising.

The degree of population concentration in urban areas is frequently claimed to be the underlying factor that makes possible the extraordinary character of our society. Economic opportunities, together with industrial complexes, are concentrated in cities; social and cultural activities are regarded as an urban phenomenon; public transportation systems, which serve large centers at minimal cost, serve rural areas and small towns hardly at all.

Production of durable consumer goods and even food is being increasingly automated, certified, mechanized, and centralized before being shipped back to local retailers in forms so standardized that a "fresh" tomato in Possum Gap's chain grocery store may have the same shape and water content as one in Los Angeles, thousands of miles away. Utility companies pull huge blocks of power thousands of miles to urban areas. Television and radio broadcast from urban centers, and when local stations are given time for local programming, they lack the resources to use it; instead, they rely on canned re-runs of network videotapes. In the end, true community withers on the vine.

Is it myth, or fact, that only a few hands are pulling the strings that make us dance our daily rounds? We have been governed by the idea that the most worthwhile activities take place in large cities; we have accepted the assumption that the best talent of a small community will leave it, and that those who stay are by definition second-rate; and we so lack confidence in ourselves that we believe good ideas come only from experts and from the milieu of central cities. These social clichés have led to a self-fulfilling prophecy of community powerlessness that succumbs to outside control.

Centralization has an apparently inexorable effect: we deplore its consequences, and yet we feel powerless to fight it. But like many monolithic problems, it is less formidable when broken into parts. We need to be concerned less with what the system does to us and concerned more with ways we can restructure our lives as individuals within local communities.

What kinds of alternatives to our present centralization are we aiming for?

Some degree of population decentralization is a basic necessity. Too many people are living in urban settlements. Decentralization of people must also involve decentralization of the economic system that their jobs depend on. A revitalized agricultural economy, the regional dispersion of industrial activity, and a revitalization of small-scale business and community-oriented craftsmanship are three necessary and related developments.

Technological innovations can make possible greater self-sufficiency for individuals and for human settlements of all kinds. New developments in agricultural and industrial technology and in the utilization of energy sources have thus far not been explored with the aim of decentralization; they have served centralization alone. A decentralized society, embodying true alternative lifestyles, would involve revitalized community bonds and would harness communication technologies to replace needless physical mobility. A less restlessly mobile society could be well served by better communications instead of motion.

Ultimately, we need to work for the decentralization of economic and political decision-making power. We should consciously seek greater control over our own futures and our own communities. Concentrations of power and economic monopolies or near-monopolies are antithetical to decentralization, whether they affect our television fare, our postal service, our hamburgers and breakfast cereals, or the construction of our houses.

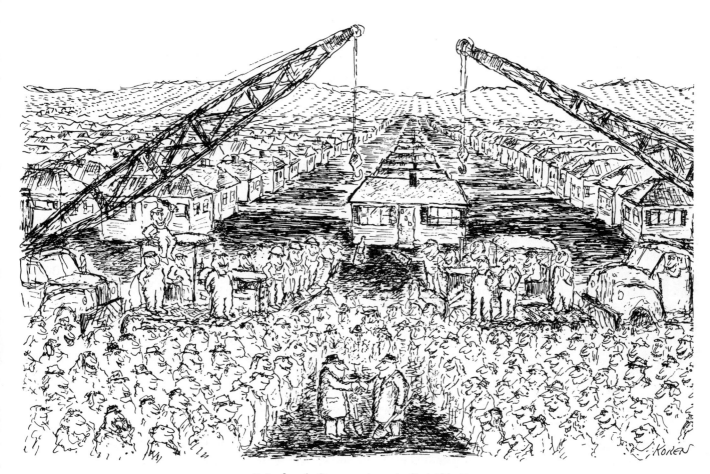

"At last! One nation, indivisible."

Decentralization Means Variety

A decentralized future includes not merely the revitalization of small communities and rural areas, but also the creation of true diversity—real choice among types of human settlement with the advantages of each type maximized. The quality of life features that have been concentrated in one type of settlement or another should be dispersed among all types. It is commonly recognized, for instance, that open space should not be a unique feature of rural areas but should be introduced into other forms of settlement, and equally, that social and cultural events of high quality should not be an exclusive prerogative of urban centers.

Decentralization, then, should involve the more even distribution of desirable kinds of human activity. Aspects of different settlement forms that are intrinsic to settlements by virtue of their size need to be distinguished from other aspects that are merely historically associated with settlements of a certain size. Given modern transportation and communication potentials, for example, there is nothing to prevent residents of small towns from having access to high quality artistic and musical events.

In part, we need decentralization of our thought pro-

cesses to accommodate the acceptance of greater variety. No one could hope to—or would wish to—reduce the US landscape to homogeneity through uniform distribution of population. But we need to recognize the varied histories, sizes, and functions of our diverse communities, and to design policies that loosen the bonds of over-centralization. A desirable diversity of settlement types might be visualized in terms of ten settlement categories. Significantly, many current classifications lump all varieties of settlement under either "urban" or "rural."

1) *Megalopolis.* This represents dense population concentrations of great size, with economic and cultural variety, multiple centers, and area-wide political structures. It is questionable whether such dense and immense concentrations provide significant advantages to their residents, overall, but such settlement forms are clearly developing.

2) *Cities.* Characterized by large population concentrations, cities have diverse economic bases and a diversity of lifestyles. While they benefit from some economies of scale, they suffer from some diseconomies. Evidence suggests that cities historically do not "replicate" themselves, but rather draw excess population from other areas. Cities grew as trade centers, manufacturing centers, and as centers of financial concentration.

Today, perhaps more so than at any time in the past, millions of Americans sense that gigantism, bureaucratism, and the centralization of power have denied them any control over their social and personal lives.

For more than two decades, millions of Americans have "voted with their feet" against this insidious usurpation of public sovereignty by leaving the cities for suburbs and rural towns where they feel they can understand and exercise some degree of control over the social levers that shape their lives. More recently, sizable numbers of people within the cities have created their own neighborhood institutions, tenants associations, food coops, and cultural centers—a civic world of their own that has already begun to partly replace the official world to which they have been so ruthlessly subordinated.

Whether in the cities, suburbs, or rural areas, these millions are endeavoring to reduce their environments to a comprehensible human scale. They are trying to create a world they can cope with as individuals, a world they correctly identify with the freedom and gentler rhythms of a less mobilized, less massified, and more libertarian society.

The human scale is not only eminently desirable to satisfy our basic human impulses, but indispensable to the integrity of the world of life—including human life. Proper maintenance of the soil not only depends upon advances in our knowledge of soil chemistry and soil fertility; it also requires a more personalized approach to agriculture.

If differences in the quality and performance of soil are to receive more attention, American farming must be reduced to a human scale. It will become necessary to bring agriculture within the scope of the individual, so that the farmer and the soil can develop together, each responding as fully as possible to the needs of the other.

The same is true for the management of livestock. Today our food animals are being manipulated like a lifeless industrial resource. Normally, large numbers of animals are collected in the smallest possible space and are allowed only as much movement as is necessary for survival. Our meat animals have been placed on a diet composed for the most part of medicated feed high in carbohydrates. Before they are slaughtered, these obese, rapidly matured creatures seldom spend more than six months on the range and six months on feedlots, where they are kept on concentrated rations and gain about two pounds daily. Our dairy herds are handled like machines; our poultry flocks, like hothouse tomatoes. The need to restore the time-honored intimacy between man and his livestock is just as pronounced as the need to bring agriculture within the horizon of the individual farmer.

Advances in technology itself have largely overcome the industrial problems that were once invoked to justify the huge concentrations of people and facilities in a few urban areas. Non-polluting means of rapid transportation, electric power, and electronic devices have eliminated nearly all the problems of transportation, communication, and social isolation tha burdened humanity in past eras. We can

3) *Suburbs.* These have functioned principally as residential centers, although service facilities and "clean" industries have recently moved in. The classic suburb is highly dependent on the city, however, for the financial resources that make possible its comparatively low population density.

4) *Micro-cities.* These settlements lie between large cities and small towns in size, in self-sufficiency and function, and in sense of community. They may serve as significant trade centers and support centers for surrounding settlements.

These four settlement types might all be called urban. Forms that are usually encompassed within the catch-all category of rural include a similar variety. Agricultural engineer G.B. Gunlogson is one of a number of people who have promoted the use of "countryside" as a phrase more descriptive of a variety of dispersed settlement patterns. Countryside blends various economic functions that arise more out of local community requirements than out of national or outsiders' needs. A significant portion of our countryside today is devoted to the service of people who are merely passing through on highways; in a decentralized society, such facilities would be turned to the service of local needs.

5) *Small towns.* Most people consider a small town to be any community under 25,000 in population and over perhaps 100. In our work with the Small Towns Institute, we have preferred to use a different criterion: the existence of a sense of community. While a sense of community is possible within larger communities—in city neighborhoods, for example—it is certainly harder to achieve. In the past, many small towns had a high degree of economic self-sufficiency and political autonomy, both of which contributed to a distinct sense of community. Small towns most often grew as service centers for agricultural areas, or grew as places where nearby natural resources were processed.

6) *Dispersed cities.* Geographer John Fraser Hart has

now communicate with one another over a distance of thousands of miles in a matter of seconds, and we can travel to the most remote areas of the world in a brief span of time. The obstacles created by time and space are essentially gone. Similarly, size need no longer be a problem. Technologists have developed remarkable small-scale alternatives to many of the giant facilities that still dominate modern industry.

Thus, almost without fully realizing it, we have been preparing the technological conditions for a new type of human community—one that can be gently tailored to the ecosystem in which it is located. It is no longer fanciful to think of humanity's future environment in terms of decentralized, moderate-size cities that combine industry with agriculture, not only in the same civic entity but in the occupational activities of the same individual. The "urbanized farmer" or the "agrarianized townsman" need not be a contradiction in terms.

But this rounded type of community (what I have often described as an "ecocommunity") with its appropriate "ecotechnologies" presupposes far-reaching changes in human sensibility. This delicate ecocommunity, viewed merely as the product of physical and logistical changes, would have a tentative future if it were not fashioned by acutely conscious individuals who enjoy a trusting intimacy with each other and are free to fully participate in the governance of the community and its development. Decentralization thus becomes meaningful from an ecological standpoint only if it forms the arena for the widest possible public involvement in every aspect of community affairs, indeed, if it fosters the recovery of the community as a family, not merely as a well-engineered or "well-planned" geographical entity.

For an age that has literally removed mountains, spanned immense gorges, diverted massive waterways, and rebuilt entire nations in the aftermath of war to call this decentralized image of the future human community a mere "utopia" is a libel on human ingenuity and creativity. And if "utopian" this image be, perhaps this critical era in history cannot afford to be anything but utopian. Yet as gigantism dwarfs the human spirit to antlike proportions and induces a terrifying human passivity, as centralization reaches such grotesque proportions that it denies people any sense of control over their destiny, as town and country become polarized against each other in a staggering ecological disequilibrium, as technology is mindlessly employed to undermine the very biogeochemical cycles indispensable for life on this planet—as all of these developments occur at a headlong tempo that is virtually beyond the comprehension of the most informed experts, we must seriously ask: who, in fact, are the mad "utopians" who have lost all contact with the reality of our times and who are the authentic realists?

—Murray Bookchin

suggested that neighboring small towns sometimes function together as a dispersed city. Some specialization among towns creates the overall diversity of economic and population structure characteristic of a city.

7) *Farms.* Use of the land as a productive resource is the basic feature of farming life. Farms are thus residential units associated with the use of the land for agriculture or animal husbandry.

8) *Non-farm rural settlement.* Uses of land by non-farm populations are primarily residential. Non-farm residents may be farm laborers or work in nearby towns and cities.

9) *Hamlets.* We've used this term to refer to a form of settlement that has hardly existed in the US but is common in parts of Europe. Clusters of three or more houses are identified as a village. Larger hamlets may have a café, a small food store, a school, or a dry goods shop. Their past function was as small-scale, concentrated residential areas for farmers and rural craftsmen.

10) *Communal groups.* The defining characteristics of communal groups, which exist as microcosms within rural areas and even within cities, are primarily ideological. Concepts of economic and political self-sufficiency and limitations on settlement size are frequently components of the communal ideology.

11) *Non-settled land.* All thinking people recognize the necessity of closing some portions of our land area to human settlement. Decentralization does not imply that we should end up with the same number of people living on each square mile of the US; instead, decentralization policies must be accompanied by a clear commitment to preserve portions of our landscape from settlement.

Centralization has been reflected in population patterns, economic and political power, and the uneven distribution of factors enhancing the quality of life. Generally speaking, decentralization must involve less concentration in and dependency on megalopolises, cities, and suburbs.

In order to achieve an orderly process of decentralization in the US—of population and of political, economic,

Photo by Eileen Christelow/Jeroboam, Inc.

and social activities—there must be sweeping changes in the way we apply laws on everything from taxation to environmental protection.

Current laws and administrative regulations favor a continued concentration of power in corporate monopolies, financial institutions, and government bureaucracies. Recent emigration from cities and repopulation of "rural" areas will not necessarily lead to functional communities. We still have many laws that assure the transfer of monopoly economics to the countryside. Administrative regulations and propaganda force rural and small town dwellers to create urban-scale problems so that urban bureaucrats will move in with urban solutions.

Public Policy for Decentralization

To meet the challenge of functional decentralization, we must enact federal and state programs that make monopoly unprofitable and that promote the vitality of individual, group, and community activities. The following six-point program suggests changes that would favor decentralization both of political power and of population.

1. Land Reform

In America, the problem is not only to get land into the hands of individuals who will use it productively in a community context, but also to get it *out* of the hands of monopolies (including government monopolies) without destroying the economic structure that will make individual land ownership possible.

The 160-acre limitation law for irrigated land should be strictly enforced. Legal provisions should be made to allow local planning agencies to enforce other land limitation laws appropriate to regional conditions. For example, 640 acres per person (one section) might be an appropriate limitation in Iowa, while 22,040 acres (one township) might be applicable in parts of Texas. Developers might be limited to speculation on only 160 acres in any one township, thus preventing a single individual or corporation from monopolizing land in areas under development pressure. Railroads that are no longer fulfilling the respon-

sibilities assumed under their original land grants should have the grants revoked; the land returned to public ownership should be opened for or withdrawn from settlement, as appropriate.

With the exception of lands genuinely needed for public purposes, such as wilderness, recreation areas, and wildlife preserves, the vast government-owned lands managed by the Bureau of Land Management and the US Forest Service should be opened for homesteading and subsistence farming. Much of this land is now leased to mining companies, corporate farms, and other large corporations, yielding little benefit to the public.

Mineral rights held separately from the land should be taxed to the owners of such rights. Government-held mineral rights should be placed in the hands of farmers and homesteaders so the inroads of strip mining can be checked by those who live in the community.

2. **Financing for a Small Scale**

Land reform would make more land available and benefit both existing farmers and future homesteaders by re-

ducing land prices. A central problem would remain: how to get land ownership into the hands of the young, the alienated, the urban poor, and the rural sharecropper.

Much could be done by revitalizing the old homestead laws and enforcing them better. Government could start with its own lands, avoiding the costs of compensation that would be necessary when new forms of land limitation are applied to private lands.

Low-interest loans could be made available to poor people to purchase land from owners of excess acres, such as those in California's Central Valley. Loans at 2 percent interest would be cheaper than welfare costs, not to mention the costs of relieving urban blight and other related problems. Similar financing could be made available to enable young people to start very small businesses (a natural foods store, for example) or to buy out existing businesses in small towns.

3. **Restrictive Laws**

A great deterrent to people seeking self-sufficiency with small-scale enterprises are the restrictive laws and regula-

Small-scale operations, no matter how numerous, are always less likely to be harmful to the natural environment than large-scale ones, simply because their individual force is small in relation to the recuperative forces of nature. There is wisdom in smallness if only on account of the smallness and patchiness of human knowledge, which relies on experiment far more than on understanding. The greatest danger invariably arises from the ruthless application, on a vast scale, of partial knowledge such as we are currently witnessing in the application of nuclear energy, of the new chemistry in agriculture, of transportation technology, and countless other things.

Why is it so difficult for the rich to help the poor? The all-pervading disease of the modern world is the total imbalance between city and countryside, an imbalance in terms of wealth, power, culture, attraction, and hope. The former has become over-extended and the latter has atrophied. The city has become the universal magnet, while rural life has lost its savour. Yet it remains an unalterable truth that, just as a sound mind depends on a sound body, so the health of the cities depends on the health of the rural areas. The cities, with all their wealth, are merely secondary producers, while primary production, the precondition of all economic life, takes place in the countryside. The prevailing lack of balance, based on the age-old exploitation of countryman and raw material producer, today threatens all countries throughout the world, the rich even more than the poor. To restore a proper balance between city and rural life is perhaps the greatest task in front of modern man. It is not simply a matter of raising agricultural yields so as to avoid world hunger. There is no answer to the evils of mass unemployment and mass migration into cities, unless the whole level of rural life can be raised, and this requires the development of an agro-industrial culture, so that each district, each community, can offer a colourful variety of occupations to its members.

—E.F. SCHUMACHER

tions that are gradually strangling things of human scale in our society. National and state health and safety codes, for example, tend to dictate the specific technology that can be used to achieve health and safety goals. Most of these regulations merely have the effect of promoting specific products and have little to do with health or safety. Some communities ban composting, prohibit the conduct of small businesses in homes (even if they meet zoning requirements), enforce expensive building codes that are imposed on some buildings and not others. One man in Washington State was arrested for building a log cabin because it was not designed by an architect; another was fined for having too many fire extinguishers. In a typical case, fire codes required a building owner to install a fire escape that safety codes condemned as a safety hazard.

Even environmental laws are administered in ecologically unsound ways. Water pollution is encouraged because health codes don't allow composting toilets that produce usable fertilizer; small steam-operated lumber mills are closed down for polluting the air while big firms with tall stacks are permitted to "dilute" their smoke in the upper atmosphere, producing acid rains; farmers are fined for having dusty roads in their fields and are forced to spray oil on otherwise productive soil. To be good, environmental laws must be ecologically sound.

4. Technology and Quality

The decentralization process must take account of the need to bring technology into harmony with people. This means we must encourage technological skills that begin with craftsmanship and culminate in quality.

Decentralization is not merely a logistical or physical solution to concentration and gigantism. Indeed, it is above all a certain sensibility, a way in which people view each other and the natural world. At the very heart of this sensibility is the concept of human scale.

—MURRAY BOOKCHIN

The federal government is taking onto itself more and more power for local matters for everything from family planning to criminal justice to health service. Clearly, national issues are not being addressed in a straightforward way while everyone on the other side of the Potomac starts meddling in local and state affairs because of the lack of faith in the ability of people to govern themselves. Decentralization of power—that is important to me. All those things that can be left at a lower level of political organization ought to be.

—GOVERNOR JERRY BROWN

Centralization robs individuals of diversity, transferring many of their roles to specialists. The process is manifest in gadgetry that we are taught to use but not to understand. As with malfunction lights on auto dashboards, we are not permitted to know that something needs attention until it is too late. With a home appliance that's "sealed for life," there's no way for consumers to extend that life by providing needed maintenance and repair.

Since most people have only a shadow of the knowledge needed for a more self-sufficient life today, we need new programs in schools and colleges to enable those who want to participate in the decentralization process to do so. Courses on Being a Good Consumer and How to Shop for the Best Buys should be replaced, or at least supplemented, by practical courses in carpentry, mechanics (including foundry work and blacksmithing), ceramic technologies, and horticulture. These courses should focus on such self-sufficient and community-oriented skills as small-scale (including by-hand) milling of lumber; designing efficient small-scale mechanical technologies, and making castings and forgings; growing and preserving food.

5. Research on Appropriate Technology

While it is obvious that most Americans have been alienated from the technology of our society, a major factor in this situation has been the public funds poured into the development of large-scale technologies rather than into more efficient small-scale ones. In agriculture, education, transportation, and other fields, research has led to larger scale technologies and increasingly centralized management.

For more than 60 years, agricultural colleges have focused on development of foods that would conform to mechanized harvesting techniques while neglecting research on plants that would produce yields high in quality and volume on small plots of land. In transportation, research favors the increased profitability of vehicle sales rather than more efficient use of fuel and land devoted to transportation facilities. This results in the concentration of technology, marketing, financial capabilities, and even land resources in the hands of monopoly businesses and federal agencies.

Tax structures should favor products manufactured locally and marketed to local consumers. This proposal could be implemented for some products by a tax based on the distance between finished products and their markets. Research funds in agriculture should be allocated to small groups of individuals working on energy-efficient technologies rather than production "efficiencies."

6. Regionally Oriented Industry

With the development of small-scale technologies ap-

Our attitudes toward the future of mankind and the human environment vary considerably with our point of view. Those of us in international organizations are likely to assume a globalist viewpoint. To a globalist, environmental and human problems often appear to be without solution, or their solution involves such massive inputs of money, energy, raw materials, education, and so forth, that any effort seems puny. But only a few environmental problems are really global in nature—and even they usually have solutions which can be applied rather easily at the local level. For example, if we are really threatening the stability of the ozone layer by using aerosol spray cans, it is a simple matter to give them up. They add virtually nothing to the quality of living for any individual, and those who manufacture them can make just as much money doing something else. Similarly, nobody is going to be much affected if the SST never flies again. The future of whales is a global problem, but its solution involves only a change in attitude of comparatively few people in a few countries—and some redeployment of economic effort.

Most conservation problems exist on particular pieces of ground, occupied or cared for by a particular group of people. Attempts to solve them at a global, or even national level often strike far from the mark, because they fail to take into account the attitudes or motivations of the people concerned.

During the past few decades people have been encouraged to look to their nation's capital, or worse yet, to the United Nations, for solutions to problems that had always been considered, in the past, to be local affairs. But the tendency to depend upon the national government for decisions on the management of local resources inevitably creates delay, confusion, and often ends up with the wrong solution for each local community through trying to reach the right solution for all. Thus providing water for a nation's population—as viewed from the top—can mean the need to build giant dams and canal systems, costing hundreds of millions of dollars, and taking many years. At the local level providing water may mean only developing some roof-top collectors, storage tanks, and giving some attention to the management of vegetation on the local hills and valleys. It might take a little money, some labor, and a few months of effort to improve the situation. But who will make that local effort if the responsibility lies with the government, and particularly if the government is likely to over-ride such a local initiative? Similarly, the provision of electricity, viewed from the top, may seem to require the installation of a massive, high-risk, nuclear plant, and an environmentally disruptive national grid of power lines. It could also mean, at the local level, the installation of a windmill, or diverting a small stream through an axial flow generator.

Human societies can be divided into two categories, with some in transition from one to the other. These are *ecosystem people* and *biosphere people*.

Ecosystem people are those who depend almost entirely upon a local ecosystem, or a few closely related ecosystems. Virtually all of the foods they eat, or the materials

propriate to local ecological conditions, it would be more efficient (as well as profitable) to decentralize industry. Federal and state governments should consider tax incentives for decentralized industries. The "distance tax" would be one example. Decentralization would result in more local employment opportunities, the stimulation of local investment in industry, and a wide diversity of production facilities. A decentralized industry could ride out crises that would shut down concentrated businesses. Existing conglomerate industry would find it more profitable to disperse its plants as more and more workers showed a preference for countryside environments.

To design public policies working toward decentralization presents something of a paradox in our over-centralized age. We have tended to let centralized government do more for us, rather than less. Many of our policy suggestions are in accordance with an emphasis on the use of existing centralized systems to achieve a decentralized society, but individuals must work hard at the local level for decentralization. The following principles would aid decentralization; they are the basis on which actions in your town, city, or region may be built.

1. See that governments at all levels make strong commitments to decentralization.
2. Where goals can be accomplished locally, make a strong effort to do so with local personnel, funding, and authorization.
3. When you need outside expertise or monetary help, ask for the minimum possible amounts; don't embark on any project without some local matching effort.
4. Make sure legislative requirements allow for variations of scale; don't require a $3 million water treatment plant for a town of 350 people, as was done in a recent case featured on TV's "Sixty Minutes."
5. Seek diverse, innovative solutions to local problems; let

they use, come from that ecosystem—although there will be some limited trade with other ecosystem groups. Because of their total dependence on a local system, developed usually over many generations, they live in balance with it. Without this balance they would destroy it, and cease to exist, since no other resources are available. The balance is assured by religious belief and social custom—everything is geared to the rhythms of nature—to phases of the moon, changes of seasons, flowering and fruiting of plants, movements and reproduction of animals. Such people have an intricate knowledge of their environment—the uses of plants for food, fiber, medicine. Every species, every thing, in their environment has some meaning or significance. Recent studies have shown that most such people did not live impoverished lives. Instead they tended to have adequate food, good health, abundant leisure—many of the features of the good life that others today strive for and rarely achieve. Once everybody on earth was in this category. Now only a few so-called "primitive" peoples, living more or less in isolation, survive.

Biosphere people are those who can draw on the resources of many ecosystems, or the entire biosphere, through networks of trade and communication. Their dependence on any one ecosystem is partial, since they can rely on others if any one fails. Drawing as they do on planetary resources, they can bring great amounts of energy and materials to bear on any one ecosystem—they can devastate it, degrade it, totally destroy it and then move on. All of those who are now tied in to the global network of technological society are biosphere people. They are the people who preach conservation, but often do not practice it.

We must aim at selective decentralization. Authority to solve local problems should always be held at the local level. Development should be localized, at a human scale, and intended to solve human problems.... Nothing should be done by the province that can be done better by the village. Nothing should be referred to the nation that can be solved by the province. Those most likely to be directly affected by development decisions should have the most active role in reaching those decisions. No development decision should be made without full exploration of its effects upon human society and the natural environment. This does not mean that the local, the small scale, should prevail in all activities. Transportation networks need national coordination. Copper mines, smelters, refineries will require massive inputs of energy and labor—they can't be supplied by a few wind generators. Equally, however, one does not need a gigawatt power plant to meet the energy needs of farms and villages. In fact supplying energy needs in such a way inevitably creates the feeling of alienation and dependence that results when one has no understanding of or control over one's means for survival.

—RAYMOND DASMANN

---

solutions grow out of the nature of your community, its particular situation and skills; find out yourself how other towns are coping; don't rely on overworked officials to investigate innovative techniques.

6. Don't be afraid to force centralized authority to conform to your local requirements instead of the other way around; some towns and cities have successfully pressured national franchises into conformity with local building styles rather than passively accepting standardized design and 50-foot-high signs.

7. Support decentralized institutions in your community; sell to, or buy from, the local farmers' market; patronize businesses that represent local enterprise.

If centralization in our society has come about because of governmental and industrial policies that profit from it, there is no assurance that a short-term political reversal is going to keep massification from happening again.

Worldwide, the centralist process has become a part of governments ranging from dictatorial to democratic, from communist to capitalist.

The most essential element of decentralization is to get the ownership or control of national resources—the land, minerals, energy, agriculture, finance, everything—into as many hands as possible. Government ownership obviously doesn't bring maximum benefits to the people. Governments already own minerals and land rights, but much of this is leased to giant conglomerates while small farmers (and smaller corporations) are frozen out. Eliminating individuals from economic participation has been a major element of many government programs, from urban renewal to agricultural research.

We can work for new legislation as suggested in this chapter, but we must also implement the decentralist society by building practical communities in a decentralist pattern.

The noncommercial urban area comprises about 4.5 percent of all US land. Assuming that the average present development can be represented by a "mixed sprawl" condition, then the switch from current urban land use to one of a high-density planned nature would free about 50 million acres of urban land. This land could be used to slowly decentralize and relocate some of the nation's industrial facilities, thus allowing for shorter trips to work. Such land could also be used to develop community recreation areas, thereby reducing recreational travel needs while focusing individual concern on local environmental quality.

—BRUCE HANNON

Groups of people can easily buy large land holdings cheap. (In Washington State, European multinational investors recently bought thousands of acres of potential agricultural land for less than $100 per acre; it had been for sale for years.) Collective buyers can become individual owners or hold land in a trust. Eventually, decentralists should acquire scattered ownerships within 25 miles or so to prevent large corporations from moving in on decentralized communities and raising taxes.

Decentralist communities have one advantage over corporate landholders: people can vote, and they can eventually control local government for the benefit of the community and local enterprise.

Economic practices are extremely important in establishing a stable society. Using low-energy technologies, recycling wastes in the local ecosystem, using appropriate "soft" technologies to supplement labor-intensive productivity, a small community can produce food, goods, and services at only a fraction of the costs of food and some other commodities that are produced nationally and transported long distances. Large companies cannot compete with farmers' markets or small local industries—provided that local goods are marketed only to the community and not leaked to outside consumers, thereby exceeding the ecosystem's capacity to provide basic resources. Export your ideas and designs, and educate people who will replicate the decentralist process in their own communities, but don't try to expand production beyond the locality's capacity to support the system.

An essential element of decentralization policy is the maintenance of a steady population. Centralization has come about partly because local citizens produce more than enough children to provide continuity to the next generation. This has been happening for hundreds of years in most of the world's peasant and agricultural societies. Excess children end up in cities where the amount of people overwhelms the amount of useful work to be done.

Non-producers gradually build up employment hierarchies of centralist jobs: inspectors, bureaucrats, investigators, record-keepers, government agents—occupations that are either unnecessary or minimal in a true community.

Many recent surveys indicate that Americans are eager to move from large cities to small towns and rural areas, lacking only the assurance of economic opportunity. Public consciousness is increasingly in tune with small-scale, diverse solutions. What sorts of individuals and institutions would experience difficulties in a decentralized society? The experience of New York City suggests that cities and their residents would suffer most from a decentralization movement. The physical and social facilities representing our current over-investment in urban areas will not be easily wound down. The danger is that the wealthy may be the only ones who can afford to decentralize, and the poor will remain. Continued investment in urban areas will surely be necessary to ease the transition to smaller population concentrations, and legislation favoring economic decentralization *must* ensure opportunities for the urban poor. Programs favoring the reuse and recycling of physical facilities in urban areas through conservation and preservation rather than extensive building programs are also a vital strategy. More urban open space can be a result of less severe population pressures. One long-range result of decentralization is sure to be more livable cities as well as more vital small towns and rural areas.

A centralized society not only requires institutions that hold centralized power, it also requires citizens who accede to the demands of that power. There are indications that Americans are becoming wary of centralization. We all know people who are accepting reduced economic rewards but taking advantage of simple opportunities on a small scale and prizing quality of life and a sense of community as parts of the pay-off. Decentralization won't succeed without firm individual and community commitment to the benefits of small-scale as well as large-scale institutions.

Recommended Actions

☐ The President should commit himself to decentralist policies, as should governors, county officials, mayors, neighborhood leaders, heads of families, and individuals.

☐ Lawmakers at all levels should amend or repeal laws that have the effect of encouraging the concentration of population, political influence, or economic power.

☐ Federal homestead laws should be reënacted with tighter enforcement provisions, and public land unsuited to such public purposes as recreation or wildlife preservation should be opened to homesteading and subsistence farming.

☐ Anti-monopoly laws should be vigorously enforced.

☐ Health, safety, and building codes, and similar administrative regulations, should be amended to eliminate arbitrary stifling of individual initiative.

☐ Schools, colleges, and institutions offering adult education should develop courses promoting individual self-sufficiency such as carpentry, organic gardening, handicrafts, accounting for the small shopkeeper, and elementary mechanics.

☐ Incentives to decentralize (and *dis*incentives to centralize) should be built into the tax structure.

☐ Low-interest government loans should be offered to people wishing to buy land or small businesses in small towns.

☐ The law limiting to 160 acres the amount of land irrigated by federal waterworks that can be owned by one landholder should be rigorously enforced; and as the law provides, holders of excess acreage should be required to sell it at pre-irrigation prices.

☐ Federal research-and-development funding should be diverted from "high" technology (especially nuclear fission and fusion) to "low" or "intermediate" technology that is applicable everywhere.

☐ Railroads still holding original land grants should be required either to sell the land and apply the proceeds to the improvement of rail service or to cede such lands back to the federal government; where appropriate, land returned to public ownership should be open to homesteading.

☐ Municipal officials should be encouraged to study ways in which decentralization can be made to work to the advantage of cities and not to their disadvantage.

☐ The urban poor and rural sharecroppers should have highest priority in the homesteading and low-cost loan programs.

Drawing by Warren Miller; © The New Yorker Magazine, Inc.

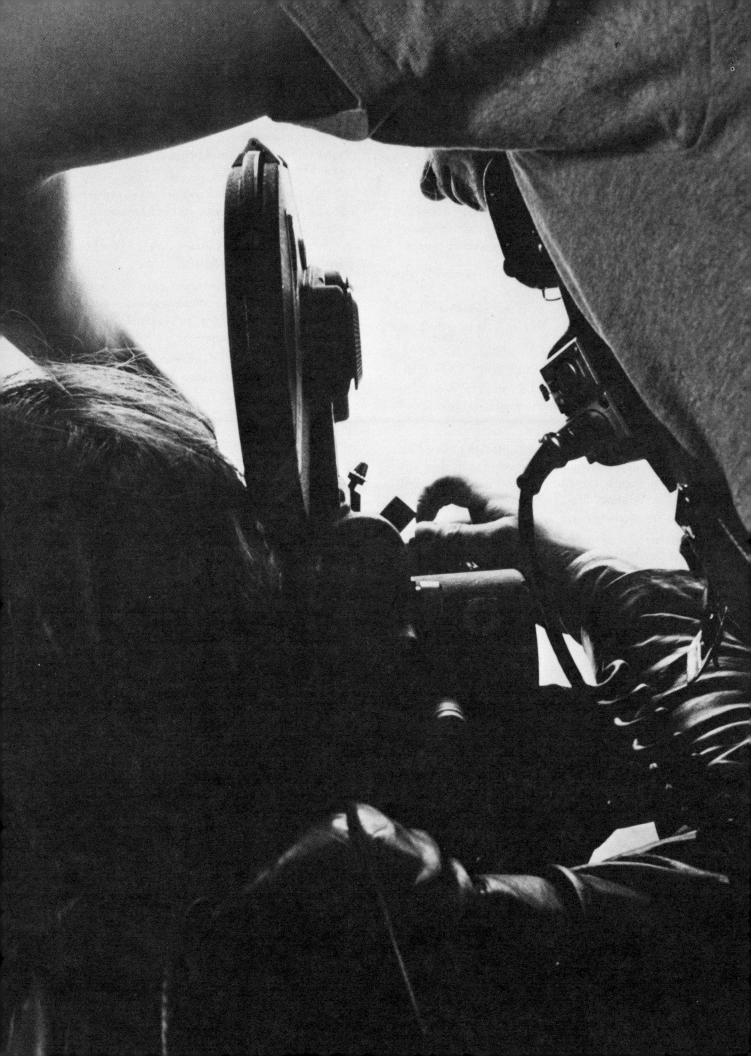

The Media's Conflict of Interests

It is impossible to effect needed social change if the need, the events, and the views for and against aren't reported in the news. If the news media—television, radio, the newspapers and news magazines—fail to report on an event or an idea, the life of communities goes on as if it had not occurred. A free press is vital to the life of a free people, but the media are increasingly guilty of reporting a diminishing amount of the most lively and important of our country's business. The reasons are many. Government interference is usually obvious, always (when recognized) protested against, and frequently driven back. More insidious are the media's own threats to responsible journalism. With fewer newspapers in business every year; television (the most effective medium, if the intellectually thinnest) dominated by show business values; and the remaining outlets being owned by fewer and fewer individuals and corporations, fewer opinions are being expressed, fewer stories are being covered, and there is a growing conspiracy of silence—of which retributions against reporters who do their jobs too well form no small part. The major news organizations fear social ideas and actions, and distort and black out news at the behest of the advertisers who support them. The public's need to know is approaching a tragic confrontation with the press's right to operate without government controls.

The Media

The premise of democracy is that a people can govern themselves. The condition for this audacious assumption is that the people will have the information they need to make wise political decisions. Democracy, the philosopher Richard McKeon has pointed out, is a community based on communication. Judge Learned Hand has said that we have staked our all on the rational dialogue of an informed electorate.

It follows that the press is a fundamental social institution. It is the chief medium of communication among the people and between the people and their elected representatives in government. (By "press," I mean, in this context, and in what follows, newspapers and broadcasting.)

The founding fathers recognized the pivotal importance of communication in a self-governing society. Their First Amendment to the Constitution said Congress shall make no law abridging the freedom of the press. They were under no illusion that a press free from government restraint would automatically be a responsible press. But they knew from recent experience that there would be little chance at all for a press to perform responsibly unless it was protected from government interference.

Now, over the years and without a great deal of close and sustained attention being paid to it, a curious thing has happened to freedom of expression, to the people's access to the ideas and the information they need for the shaping of their political judgment, and to the quality of public affairs journalism. Today, in some respects the most interesting and formidable threat to consistently responsible journalism comes not so much from government as from the mass media themselves.

The actions of government are not insignificant. Indeed, they are serious and disturbing. In broadcast journalism, government regulations now reach to the content of news and public affairs programming. In both broadcasting and the newspapers, some of the courts, including the highest, have been underrating—sometimes on very questionable grounds—one of the indispensable conditions of professional journalism, the confidentiality of the relationship

Reprinted with permission from The Center Magazine, *a publication of The Center for the Study of Democratic Institutions, Santa Barbara, California.*

between the reporter and his sources of information. That this confidential relationship raises competing civil liberties considerations, that it can be abused by an unscrupulous reporter or his source—e.g., to mount an anonymous and cowardly attack on another person—that it can defeat the right of litigants to compel the production of testimony in a trial does not change the fact that confidentiality itself is irreplaceable in a journalism that is truth-seeking and truth-telling.

Less formally, but no less harshly, Richard Nixon demonstrated how easy it was to use the power of his office to punish editors and reporters who insisted on poking around in his intricate deals with Bebe Rebozo. The Internal Revenue Service was quick to respond with tax audits, not of Mr. Nixon's financial affairs, but of those of the offending newspaper people. And the Federal Bureau of Investigation was no less eager to oblige when the White House asked it to run a check on the Columbia Broadcasting System reporter Daniel Schorr, who had been embarrassing the President with awkward questions and sharp comments and so needed to be intimidated.

But the threats to freedom of expression from government are sharp and acute. They are easily, quickly, and dramatically identified as First Amendment issues by an outraged press. The threats from the media, on the other hand, tend—not surprisingly—to be underreported, if not unnoticed, in the press, with the predictable result that they are often dimly perceived and only faintly understood by the public.

Three years ago, Stephen R. Barnett, a professor of law at the University of California at Berkeley, commented, in an article in *The Nation*, on the fact that the media tend to look the other way on important issues in which they—and perforce the public—are involved.

"One hears much about reporters' subpoenas and the threat they pose to the public's right to know, but considerably less about other controversies involving the media, the government, and the First Amendment," wrote Professor Barnett. "The whole subject of media concentration somehow eludes the nation's newspapers and TV stations. Two years ago, for example, when Congress made its own contribution to newspaper monopoly by passing the Newspaper Preservation Act, the publishers' lobbying campaign was backed up by studied blandness in the nation's press. . . .Last summer, when the industry took another major step toward monopoly by killing major newspapers in Boston, Washington, and Newark, the help provided by the Justice Department was overlooked in the media. At present, the leading nonstory is the proposal of the Federal Communications Commission to break up common ownership of newspapers and broadcast stations

San Francisco Examiner newsroom; photo by Peeter Vilms/Jeroboam, Inc.

in cities throughout the country—an uncommonly important and controversial issue that may be unrivaled for the thoroughness with which the media have blacked it out."

Two facts about the media bear most heavily on the performance of working journalists and on the quality of their public affairs reporting. They are the big-business nature of the media and the increasing concentration of their ownership in fewer and fewer hands. Neither of these developments was foreseen by the founding fathers. Both of them jeopardize the freedom and diversity of expression and therefore they make problematic the possibility of realistic and wise decision-making by the American people.

"A free press," Walter Lippmann said in an American Press Institute interview eleven years ago, "exists only where newspaper readers have access to other newspapers which are competitors and rivals so that editorial comment and news reports can—regularly and promptly—be compared, verified, and validated. A press monopoly is incompatible with the free press."

To be sure, the American press, almost from its start, was commercial. The bills had to be paid, and by 1750, according to one historian of American journalism, Frank

Luther Mott, "the most successful printers were able to fill three to five pages solidly with the announcements of merchants and traders of many kinds." But there was diversity in the American press. Circulation of individual papers was numbered in the hundreds (with many readers per copy), and the possibility of starting yet another paper was always a feasible option for anyone who thought the public interest was not being properly served by the existing press.

Today, the business of the media is very big and very profitable. The compulsion to grow bigger and more profitable, while understandable—though often unattractive—in, say, the oil, steel, and automotive industries, introduces a profound conflict of interests in the media and invites hypocrisy in media owners whose function, as A. J. Liebling once noted, is "to inform the public, but whose role is to make money."

"It is startling (or would be, except we are used to it)," wrote Charles Rembar, a lawyer, in the April, 1973, *Atlantic*, "that the means by which the citizens of a democracy get their news—information that they must have in order to run their country—is a form of private property."

The Television Bureau of Advertising predicts that the television stations and networks will take in a record $6.4

billion in 1976. When a network or station sets a new revenue record in any given year, that is good news. The bad news is that it must break that record the following year or tell the investors why.

The Drive to Monopoly

One of the effects of the profit imperative in mass communication is the relentless drive by owners to achieve as much monopoly as the law will allow. The best short description and most astute analysis of how this works and consequently what happens to the freedom and diversity of expression is to be found in Liebling's book, *The Press*:

"The profit system implies a pursuit of maximum profit for the shareholders' sake, distasteful though it may be. That it is theoretically possible to make money by competition in the newspaper field is therefore immaterial, since there is a great deal more money to be made by (a) selling out and pocketing a capital gain; (b) buying the other fellow out and then sweating the serfs. . . .

"The point is, that even when two, or several, competing newspapers in a town are both, or all, making money, it is vastly to the advantage of one to buy out the others, establish a monopoly in selling advertising, and benefit from the 'operating economies' of one plant, one staff, and exactly as much news coverage as the publisher chooses to give. The advertisers must have him anyway, and the readers have no other pabulum. He will get all the income for a fraction of the outlay, so he can afford to pay a price for his competitor's paper far beyond what it might be worth to a buyer from outside, who would continue to operate it competitively. . . .

"What you have in a one-paper town is a privately owned public utility that is constitutionally exempt from public regulation, which would be a violation of freedom of the press. As to the freedom of the individual journalist in such a town, it corresponds exactly with what the publisher will allow him. He can't go over to the opposition [paper] because there isn't any. If he leaves, he ends his usefulness to the town, and probably to the state and region in which it is situated, because he takes with him the story that caused his difference with the management, and in a distant place it will have no value. . . .

"Diversity—and the competition that it causes—does not insure good news coverage or a fair champion for every point of view, but it increases the chances."

In 1955, Robert Hutchins, addressing a meeting of the American Society of Newspaper Editors, told them that "if the soliloquy [of the publisher] is that of one of the richest men in town, it is more than likely that it will sound the same political note as other soliloquies in other towns,

rendered by other rich men. . . .In the absence of some new technological revolution the number of papers per community in this country seems unlikely to increase. . . .As monopoly continues to spread, the ancient check of competition can of course no longer be relied on."

Eight years earlier, Mr. Hutchins' Commission on the Freedom of the Press had concluded a three-year study of the media with this warning:

"Protection against government is now not enough to guarantee that a man who has something to say shall have a chance to say it. The owners and managers of the press determine which persons, which facts, which versions of the facts, and which ideas shall reach the public. . . . Through concentration of ownership the variety of sources of news and opinion is limited. At the same time the insistence of the citizen's need has increased. . . . The service of news, as distinct from the utterance of opinion, acquires a new importance. The need of the citizen for adequate and uncontaminated mental food is such that he is under a duty to get it. Thus his interest also acquires the stature of a right.

"To protect the press is no longer automatically to protect the citizen or the community. The freedom of the press can remain a right of those who publish only if it incorporates into itself the right of the citizen and the public interest. . . . The voice of the press, so far as by a drift toward monopoly it tends to become exclusive in its wisdom and observation, deprives other voices of a hearing and the public of their contribution. . . .

"The outstanding fact about the communications industry today is that the number of its units has declined. . . . If modern society requires great agencies of mass communication, if these concentrations become so powerful that they are a threat to democracy, if democracy cannot solve the problem simply by breaking them up—then those agencies must control themselves or be controlled by government. . . . [In the latter event, we will have lost our] chief safeguard against totalitarianism, and at the same time take a long step toward it."

The concentration of media ownership, despite this warning, has continued to increase. Ninety-six per cent of the daily-newspaper cities now have only one publisher.

In 1910, there were 2,400 daily newspapers in the United States owned by 2,387 individual publishers (sixty-two of these dailies were owned by thirteen publisher groups)—all serving a population of one hundred million people. By 1976, the population had more than doubled—it is now 220,000,000 people—but the number of daily newspapers has dropped to 1,775. Even more significantly, 1,012 of these 1,775 newspapers are now controlled by 172 newspaper-chain owners. Today these chain publishers and single-newspaper publishers are only about forty per cent of the number of publishers in 1910.

But today there are close to nine thousand commercial and educational television and radio stations (699 commercial television stations; 231 educational television stations; 7,205 commercial AM and FM radio stations; and 802 educational FM radio stations). Would not this seem to guarantee adequate diversity in the broadcast media? Not according to Morton Mintz and Jerry Cohen. In their book, *America, Inc.,* published five years ago, they said, "There is no stronger supporting evidence than that dealing with the intense concentration [of media ownership] existing in certain states, regions, and cities.

"In the twenty-five top markets," they write, "there are a total of ninety-seven VHF [television] stations. In addition to the fifteen owned and operated by C.B.S., N.B.C., and A.B.C., newspapers as of early 1960 were operating thirty-four. Of the thirty-four, twenty-six are affiliates of one of the networks. . . .

"Consider communities outside of metropolitan areas and which have populations of between five thousand and fifty thousand. In each of sixty-eight such communities where there is one daily newspaper and one AM station, the paper has an interest in the station. In twenty-eight similar communities where there are two stations, the single newspaper has an interest in one of them.

"Now consider communities in metropolitan areas with populations of 175,000 to two million or more. In eight such communities, a newspaper owns fifty to one hundred per cent of the only radio station. In six similar communities, where there are two stations, the paper owns a majority interest in one of them. . . .

"All fifteen of the network-owned VHF television stations are in the nation's twenty-five largest markets including New York, Chicago, and Los Angeles. The eleven largest cities do not have even one VHF station that is not in the hands of a network, a newspaper, a newspaper chain, an owner of a group of stations, or an industrial or financial conglomerate."

A Justice Department study of a few years ago "showed that in each of fifty major urban markets a single owner controlled two or more broadcast media and/or at least one TV station plus one daily newspaper. In several such markets a newspaper chain or dominant newspaper owned network-affiliated TV, AM, and FM stations."

Federal Communications Commission records show that 231 of the nation's daily newspapers are owned by broadcasting licensees in the same city.

These statistics were valid as of five years ago. But there is no reason to believe that the pattern of media ownership has changed in any significant degree from the picture as reported by Mintz and Cohen in 1971.

And, of course, even a less concentrated ownership of the media would not necessarily diminish the threat to a free and open press. If, instead of the Knight-Ridder group, an independent publisher had purchased the Wichita, Kansas, *Eagle & Beacon* a few years ago, the purchase price would still have been $42.5 million. It is unlikely that anyone who could write a check for that amount would be composing a different soliloquy than that of the richest man in town. The same can be said for the concern that bought the Fort Worth *Star-Telegram* and three broadcasting stations for seventy million dollars. And it can be said, too, for the Australian publisher who picked up the San Antonio *Express & News* for eighteen million dollars.

If one turns to the television industry, the figures are equally impressive. Depending on the market in which a station is located, its price tag can run into the tens of millions of dollars.

When Public Affairs Interfere

Theoretically it is possible for the communications industry, committed though it is to ever-increasing corporate profits, to report all the public affairs issues of the day in adequate depth and to reflect the diversity of viewpoints and interests of the American people, not necessarily totally, not necessarily to the satisfaction of everyone, but in some decently comprehensive way. But the record is not reassuring. The following are a few pieces of evidence, selected from a much larger number on the basis of their representativeness. They illustrate what happens when the business side of journalism dominates the media.

* In February of this year, Sears, Roebuck and Company, the world's largest retailer (annual sales exceed thirteen billion dollars), and the nation's third largest advertiser, went on trial in Chicago before an administrative law judge of the Federal Trade Commission. The charges were that Sears had systematically engaged in bait-and-switch selling tactics. Sears employs thirty thousand people in the Chicago area and 417,000 nationwide. It has more than twenty-one million credit accounts in the United States. The hearings lasted eleven days. Eighteen former Sears employees from thirteen states, and twenty-five consumer witnesses from eleven states testified to Sears' sleazy sales tactics. Michael Hirsh, a Chicago public television producer, writing in the July/August, 1976, *Columbia Journalism Review*, reports that the Chicago *Tribune* (circulation 747,000), which receives five million dollars in advertising from Sears each year, "carried not one line about the case from the date

the trial began . . . until it ended." The *Tribune* filed a four-paragraph story a week after the trial, a "condensed replay of a report filed by David Elsner of the *Wall Street Journal's* Chicago bureau." Coverage by the other two Chicago dailies was only a little bit better.

* Michael Frome was fired in 1974 as conservation editor of *Field & Stream* magazine after he began to rate United States representatives and senators according to their voting records on environmental issues, after he reported questionable land transactions conducted in New Mexico by the state office of the Bureau of Land Management of the Department of the Interior (a report that his editors chose not to publish), and after he filed a criticism of the Forest Service's new Environmental Program for the Future. *Field & Stream* is owned by C.B.S., Inc. "Today," wrote Mr. Frome in the July/August, 1975, *Center Magazine*, "when every company appears to be owned by some other company, it is virtually impossible to say anything of importance without stepping on somebody's toes and irritating the financial nerve, directly or indirectly. . . . Can there be any single element of the American scene that more insidiously threatens our liberties and freedom of speech?"

* Last spring, Michael Krawetz, a reporter-at-large and columnist for the Newburgh (New York) *News*, was fired by the newspaper after Frank Miles, the absentee general manager of the Thomson Newspaper chain (owner of the New York paper), received a letter from the chairman of the Republican Committee of the Town of Newburgh threatening a boycott of all Republican advertising in the paper. "I was fired," said Krawetz, "because I reported all of the bad news going on inside Newburgh. Newburgh is a dying city. I reported how the politicians had helped bring it down. I was fired for writing the truth about Newburgh, and when the going got tough—the truth was beginning to emerge—the politicians began blackmailing my newspaper to silence me. . . . Their pressure tactics on that weak newspaper worked." When Miles was asked for a comment by *Editor & Publisher*, he said, "There will be no comment from me. I advise you to leave this matter alone. . . ."

* In a petition, dated July 1, 1974, and filed before the Federal Communications Commission in Washington, Tracy Westen, a law professor at the University of California at Los Angeles, cites the case of television newsman Richard N. B. Wheatley who was fired in 1974 by KTSM-TV (El Paso, Texas) after Wheatley had filed a misdemeanor complaint against the mayor of El Paso and a city councilman for allegedly violating a new Texas "open meetings" law by holding closed meetings and denying access to the public and the press. Wheatley

claims that commercial pressure was brought to bear on the station by some of its advertisers.

* In Denver, a consumer affairs television reporter, Dave Minshall, was reassigned to political reporting by station KOA-TV after the station received complaints from an advertising agency handling the accounts of some of KOA's clients.

* In Washington, D.C., George Allen's consumer affairs television program, "Caution," was canceled by WTOP-TV, but he doubts that pressure took the crude form of a telephone call from an advertiser or an agency to the station. "It's just that they all think alike," he said. "They all belong to the same economic church. . . . The pressures put on by regular advertisers like General Motors or General Foods are . . . subtle. That pressure translates into the omissions of good reporting."

* Ten years ago, Fred Friendly quit C.B.S. television when the network executives refused to air the Senate Foreign Relations Committee's hearings on American foreign policy in Vietnam and insisted on broadcasting a fifth rerun of "I Love Lucy" and an eighth rerun of "The Real McCoys." Mr. Friendly said the network would not have suffered a net loss that year if they had dropped the reruns for a few days; it would only have made a little less profit. When C.B.S. officials were confronted by that argument in a discussion here at the Center, they replied that, for C.B.S. shareholders, no decrease in net profits is acceptable.

* In Wilmington, Delaware, the newspapers which are the properties of Christiana Securities, a multi-billion-dollar holding company, were forbidden on one occasion to comment on a proposed Shell Oil refinery in the area. The incident is recounted in *America, Inc.*

* The same book relates how William P. Steven was fired as editor of the Houston *Chronicle*, then owned by Houston Endowment, Inc., a company that holds important interests in thirty-two business and banking operations, including a majority interest in twenty-five of them. According to Ben Bagdikian, a press critic cited by Mintz and Cohen, Steven was "by standards common in Houston, 'pretty radical: he supported higher education, Lyndon Johnson, and civil rights.'" John T. Jones, Jr., the corporate official who brought him the news that he had been fired, said, " 'Bill, you had a vision. They don't want a vision; they want a voice.' "

The Big Story That Hasn't Been Done

There are other signs, other indications of weakness in the media, conspicuous "omissions of good reporting."

I have yet to see, for example, any television network

Photo by Kerry Richardson.

documentaries that would clarify the public's understanding of how oil, gas, coal, and electricity prices are established in the fuel industry. I have seen nothing that would lead to a public understanding of the phenomenon of vertical integration in the same industry. Nor have I seen anything on television comparable to the article that appeared almost two years ago in *The Nation* by Louis B. Schwartz, a professor of law and economics at the University of Pennsylvania. Professor Schwartz examined the relationship between big American multinational oil companies and the Organization of Petroleum Exporting Countries (OPEC), and what must be done in this country if consumption of oil is to be cut and conservation of oil resources increased.

In this connection, it may be simply coincidence that Exxon has been a major sponsor of the National Broadcasting Company's "Nightly News" program, and that Gulf, Mobil, Shell, Texaco, and Union are heavy advertisers on all three networks.

It is not that the networks impose a blackout on all news reflecting unfavorably on, say, the oil companies. They cannot ignore a Santa Barbara oil blowout, or an an-

nouncement by the oil companies or an energy czar that the price of gasoline will go up by six cents next week. It is simply that they refrain from enlightening their viewers, through investigative reporting, as to why and how these things happen.

Without a clear understanding of how the political and economic forces interact and produce the phenomena of high unemployment, swollen profits, and ever-increasing prices, citizens—and today they get most of their news through television—are left with the impression that it would be foolish to direct their rage and resentment at any particular target. The implication is that nobody is really at fault, that all of us are caught up in a baffling system beyond anybody's comprehension, control, and responsibility. Lacking an understanding, citizens lack the means to form a politically potent public opinion, one which can be focused and sustained until the needed reforms are accomplished. A public opinion lacking content and based almost solely on diffused rage is really not so much a public opinion as a public mood; as such, it poses no threat to entrenched power.

Of course, the "omissions of good reporting" are not confined to television. Jules Witcover, a highly respected Washington newspaper reporter, said of the 1975 A. J. Liebling Counter-Convention (an annual meeting set up a few years ago by working journalists to offset the annual business-oriented convention of the American Newspaper Publishers Association) that "the most disappointing panel was one on self-censorship. . . . The discussion never got seriously into the questions of why newspapers do not print certain stories. . . . Such a convention ought to confront hard questions that seldom are aired elsewhere, and especially not in newsrooms. . . ."

Erwin Knoll, editor of *The Progressive* magazine, said of the first A. J. Liebling Counter-Convention that the chief complaints of the journalists included "the squandering of their talents on mass media preoccupied with peddling trivia; the boundless capacity of the press to ignore (or distort) the realities with which Americans need to be confronted; the faithful subservience of the media to the power elites of which they are a part."

Morton Mintz recalls that, as a Washington *Post* reporter, he had written a large number of stories involving business crimes. "Often these crimes have been most serious," he said. "One group has involved false and misleading advertising of prescription drugs, which while deceiving the physician can exploit, injure, and even kill the helpless patient. Even when prosecutions have resulted in conviction, most news media—including *Time* and *Newsweek*, the [television] networks, and *The New York Times*—have failed repeatedly to recognize the importance of adequate

Drawing by Ann Kelley.

reporting and have ignored the cases or treated them trivially.

"Unlike a human being," wrote Mintz, "a corporation, which at law is also a 'person,' cannot be jailed. . . . It must be dealt with in the here and now or not at all. Yet the same news media that meticulously record the misdeeds of human wretches, commonly bringing obloquy to their children, go on and on letting giant corporations elude the therapeutic benefits of public shame that fair reporting might bring. The situation is disgraceful. What holds a greater potential to make it worse than to allow control of news media by these same corporations? 'Publicity and openness, honest and complete—that is the prime condition for the health of every society,' Aleksandr Solzhenitsyn said. Will concentration give us that?"

As did Professor Barnett, Mintz and Cohen note in their book that "with few exceptions, newspaper and other media ignored or played down" the hearings held in 1967 and 1968 by Senator Philip Hart's Subcommittee on Antitrust and Monopoly on what was first called the Failing Newspaper Act and then retitled the Newspaper Preservation Act. The new law waives parts of the Sherman Antitrust Act by permitting two newspapers in the same community to set up joint operating arrangements if one of the papers is in danger of "failing." Mintz and Cohen think that this tends to subvert the First Amendment because it makes it legal for established publishers to engage in monopolistic practices against which weekly newspapers and other potential rivals cannot compete.

Whether the authors are right or wrong in their analysis of the Newspaper Preservation Act, the Senate subcommittee hearings filled eight volumes of evidence and argument for and against the waiver of antitrust enforcement. But the newspaper and television industries left the American people in almost complete ignorance of this serious issue.

The public's understanding of the Federal Election Campaign Act in particular and electoral reform in general has also been impaired, in great part because of television journalism's neglect to fulfill its informing function. While it is common knowledge that political candidates must raise enormous sums of money to run for office, and, therefore, unless they are independently wealthy, they must obligate themselves and, as it were, mortgage their political consciences to powerful special interests, I know of no television network or station that has explained in any satisfying and illuminating detail how much of a candidate's money must be spent to purchase television time and newspaper space for advertising, and what the arguments have been in the political-science community for at least minimal amounts of free time and space in the media which would remove much, if not most, of the bribe and extortion factor from American politics.

Television as Prostitute

The "omissions of good reporting" are not the only way by which the media-as-industry are served and the public-as-citizens disserved. Chief Judge David L. Bazelon of the United States Court of Appeals for the District of Columbia Circuit (where most F.C.C. litigation ends up) reviewed some of the other ways in a speech two years ago to the Federal Communications Bar Association in Washington.

"Many of us members of the bench and bar," Judge Bazelon said, "would be willing to walk more than an extra mile" to uphold the traditional view of the First Amendment and help broadcasters resist all government attempts to interfere with their "wide legitimate discretion." But the broadcasters are not making their defense easy. They must, he said, admit their shortcomings, "their abuse of the immense power of television for the private profit of a few, to the serious detriment of the nation at large.

"The broadcast media know—or should know—when their programming is simply and only mass appeal pabulum designed to titillate a sufficiently large majority to enable the broadcasters to sell the most advertising," said the judge.

"They know when they are presenting only one side of a major public issue, when they are shading the facts to present their own point of view, and when they are ignoring the concerns of the community.

"They know the impact of their programs on children, they know about the marketing of human emotions and of the prurient interest in violence and sex. They know when they subvert the professionalism of their own news teams in order to reach the demographic audiences which will attract advertisers. They know that wide exposure of subjects ranging from the names of rape victims to the private grief of a mother on the death of her son constitute unconscionable invasions of privacy. And they know when they are over-commercializing their programming to amortize the inflated cost of the broadcast license.

"In sum," Judge Bazelon said, "I think they know the times they may have prostituted the tremendous potential of television as a human communication tool. They know this and they know what should be done about it. The programming executives and their advertiser clients must stop their single-minded purpose to achieve higher ratings, more advertising, and greater profits, and stop to consider what greater purposes television should serve. And they must do it soon if we are to preserve our First Amendment values for telecommunications."

And, of course, no examination of the curious results that occur when social institutions, such as the communications media, are affected with public interest but must heed business and financial imperatives would be complete without mention of the time, effort, and money lavished on television's anchor-persons, the people who read the news stories on camera. Salaries in the hundreds of

thousands of dollars per year are paid these people, the amount corresponding almost exactly with that percentage of the potential audience—i.e., viewers of the television commercials—they can deliver to the station or the network for which they work.

One of the tests of on-camera announcer personalities at the C.B.S.-owned television station, KNX, in Los Angeles, involved a questionnaire and the wiring of people in a sample audience with a galvanic skin-reaction device which works much like a polygraph and measures a person's emotional response to what he or she is seeing on the TV screen. Patrick Emory, one of KNX's anchorpersons, did poorly on this test and, after he was fired, KNX's vice-president and general manager, Chris Desmond, explained that "it was research, only one of a number of variables used in making the decision."

When Barbara Walters left N.B.C. and joined the American Broadcasting Company for a five-year, one-million-dollar-a-year contract to serve as co-anchorperson with Harry Reasoner on A.B.C.'s evening news, here is how Richard Salant, president of C.B.S. News and one of the industry's more conscientious, public-affairs-oriented persons, reacted:

"A million dollars is a grotesque amount of money. I'm really depressed as hell. If Barbara Walters is a five-million-dollar woman, then Walter Cronkite is a sixteen-million dollar man. This isn't journalism—this is a minstrel show. Is Barbara a journalist or is she Cher. . . . If this kind of circus atmosphere continues, and I have to join in it, I'll quit first. . . . It's some damn fool kind of show business, sports business, movie-star business. I hate it. This isn't what we are supposed to do."

But Richard Salant does not have to join the circus atmosphere; he has been in it from the start. His conscience *does* hurt, it *is* more sensitive than that of most upper-echelon television officials, he *was* one of the few high-ranking newsmen to work for and recommend the founding of the National News Council (of which he is now a member). But the fact is that Richard Salant is a part of the "minstrel show." The Walter Cronkites, Harry Reasoners, David Brinkleys, and John Chancellors are all three-to-four-hundred-thousand-dollar-a-year men. N.B.C.'s Tom Snyder, according to trade journals, receives five hundred thousand dollars for anchoring the New York station's evening news and hosting the "Tomorrow" program. These people are in these brackets because they deliver to their respective networks enough of the potential viewing audience to attract sponsors and their money. A.B.C. did not start a new game or, overnight, turn television journalism into "some damn fool kind of show business" by hiring Barbara Walters away from the National Broadcasting Company. A.B.C. merely upped the ante in what has always been a high-stakes game.

What is instructive in all of this is that it shows us, again, that business and financial gain are at the heart of mass communications in America, and that public affairs journalism and the public interest are somewhere else.

One of Mr. Salant's colleagues at C.B.S., Eric Sevareid, recognized this long ago and, apparently, long ago came to terms with it. In an exchange of views with another television newsman, Martin Agronsky, on a television program sponsored in the late nineteen-fifties by the Fund for the Republic, Mr. Sevareid said: "The bigger our information media, the less courage and freedom of expression they allow. Bigness means weakness." (He obviously would have grave difficulty agreeing with those who tell us today that it would be dangerous to break up the concentration of media ownership because big media are necessary as a countervailing power against big government.)

"Courage in the realm of ideas goes in inverse ratio to size of the establishment," said Mr. Sevareid. "The investment in any given item that is produced—whether it is a TV program or a Hollywood movie or a big mass magazine—is so enormous that they must find a great denominator in terms of audience, whether it is the lowest common denominator or not. The risk is too great. This is not true of the small-capital media, like the stage or book publishing or small magazines."

Agronsky: "A large corporation would not hesitate a moment to spend twice as much money to sponsor a Bob Hope entertainment than it would spend on an hour-long news and public affairs program. It is not that they are priced out by the initial cost [of the public affairs program]: they are priced out by what they regard as the value received: in other words, the audience and the ratings that they can get. . . . They are guided entirely by the return on the investment."

Sevareid: "They are businessmen."

And so, we must add, are television executives.

In Diversity Lives Freedom

It would be surprising, given the newspaper and television industries' corporate-commercial nature and their symbiotic relationship with the business and financial communities, if they were to have achieved a good record in the matter of open channels; that is, in providing adequate access for the information and ideas on which a democratic society lives.

Marquis Childs, after he had completed a study of press freedom for the Ford Foundation, concluded that the lack of diversity of voices in the media and the people's feeling that they have no access to the media are two of the major problems facing both publishers and station owners.

Julius Duscha recalls a comment made by the late William Baggs when he was editor of the Miami *News.* Mr. Baggs said that if Jesus Christ reappeared and walked down Miami's Flagler Street proclaiming the Second Coming, he would probably not get space in the papers unless he hired a press agent and had his publicity man call a press conference to proclaim the glad tidings. And to get the story out of Miami and onto the wire services, it would be necessary, said Mr. Baggs, for one of the Miami papers to get a special angle so it could copyright its story and thus make the wire services take notice of it as something obviously extraordinary. Duscha's comment: "That . . . is a hell of a way to have to get access to a press which claims it reflects the community it serves."

Last year, a black man in Wooster, Ohio, and two Wooster College students phoned A.B.C. radio news headquarters in New York, saying they were holding a hostage and would not release him until the network provided them with free air time to voice certain grievances. As it turned out, fourteen hours later, there had been no hostage. The three were arrested for trying to extort something of value—i.e., air time. Bail was set at one hundred thousand dollars each. Absurd theater? Perhaps. But it did force a troubling question to the surface: Just how many people "out there"—poor, lonely, hopeless—feel that what is being reported by the newspapers and television bears little or no relationship to the reality of their lives, a reality that must be communicated if it is ever to change?

In 1970, the National Commission on the Causes and Prevention of Violence said in its final report:

"The news media can play a significant role in lessening the potential for violence by functioning as a faithful conduit for intergroup communication, providing a true marketplace of ideas, providing full access to the day's intelligence, and reducing the incentives to confrontation that sometimes erupts in violence. . . .

"It should become habitual editorial policy to display fairly and clearly the opinions, analyses, and solutions offered by a wide variety of people, expert and nonexpert, covering the spectrum, regardless of the proprietor's personal position.

"Too many news organizations fear social ideas and social action. As a result, they stimulate, dissatisfy, and arouse anxiety, only to fall silent or limit themselves to irrelevant clichés when thoughtful solutions are required. Alternative solutions to our most urgent social problems, based on the work of our most imaginative social thinkers, and written with the clarity that only a good journalist can produce, ought to be standard practice. . . .

"We strongly recommend that the news media examine carefully the problems posed when equivalent access to the media is denied."

The Commission's language was similar to that of the Commission on the Freedom of the Press, which said, in 1947: "It is vital to a free society that an idea should not be stifled by the circumstances of its birth. The press cannot and should not be expected to print everybody's ideas. But the giant units can and should assume the duty of publishing significant ideas contrary to their own, as a matter of objective reporting, distinct from their proper function of advocacy. . . . All the important viewpoints and interests in the society should be represented in its agencies of mass communication. Those who have these viewpoints and interests cannot count on explaining them to their fellow citizens through newspapers or radio stations of their own."

A dramatic example of what can happen to access—and justice—when a publisher dominates a region was furnished a few years ago by William Loeb, owner of the Manchester (New Hampshire) *Union Leader*. In the early nineteen-seventies, the newspaper began an attack on Thomas N. Bonner, the new president of the University of New Hampshire. According to an account in *The Chronicle of Higher Education*, Bonner was accused by Loeb's paper of coddling Communists, undermining patriotism, disseminating pornography, and squandering the taxpayers' money. One university official said, "I have never seen a more vehement attack on one person." *Foster's Democrat*, a Dover, New Hampshire, newspaper, said that Bonner had been the victim of "one of the most unending and malevolent hate campaigns ever witnessed in our or any other state."

Although Bonner had planned to devote his first years as president to a study of the university's needs, the newspaper's incessant attacks forced him to change his mind. He spent the first two years making five hundred speeches throughout the state, trying to explain to the people the function, needs, and problems of the university. He also sent a weekly newsletter to 7,500 opinion leaders in New Hampshire.

In the end, Bonner collapsed from exhaustion, spent four months recuperating in a hospital, and finally left New Hampshire for the smaller and quieter campus of Union College in Schenectady, New York.

Another case, this one reaching all the way to the Supreme Court, involved Florida's right-to-reply law. The law had required Florida newspapers to publish with equal prominence the replies of political candidates assailed in print. A union official, Pat L. Tornillo, Jr., had been a candidate for the Florida House of Representatives. The

Miami *Herald* attacked him editorially, called him "Czar Tornillo," asserting he had practiced "shakedown statesmanship" by leading a teachers' strike, and said that it would border on madness if voters sent him to the state legislature. The paper refused to print his reply.

Although the Court unanimously found the right-to-reply law unconstitutional, Chief Justice Warren Burger seemed sympathetic to people in Tornillo's position, people who feel shut out of "the marketplace of ideas" by the press, and he reviewed the arguments for greater public access to the press.

In the end, Chief Justice Burger said that a newspaper's editorial judgment, whether fair or unfair, is always protected by the First Amendment. He expressed a desire for a responsible press but noted that "press responsibility is not mandated by the Constitution and, like many other virtues, it cannot be legislated."

The importance of *Tornillo* is not limited, however, to the decision itself. It is a cogent and forceful reminder—to the media as well as the public—that a serious access problem and a question of justice remain. The problem was well framed earlier by the Florida Supreme Court, which had upheld the right-to-reply statute:

"The right of the public to know all sides of controversy and from such information to be able to make an enlightened choice is being jeopardized by a growing concentration of the ownership of the mass media into fewer hands, resulting ultimately in a form of private censorship. Through consolidation, syndication, acquisition of radio and television stations, and the demise of vast numbers of newspapers, competition is rapidly vanishing and news corporations are acquiring monopolistic influence over huge areas of the country.

"Freedom of expression was retained by the people through the First Amendment for all the people and not for a select few. The First Amendment did not create a privileged class, which through a monopoly of instruments of the newspaper industry would be able to deny to the people the freedom of expression which the First Amendment guarantees."

Walter Pincus, writing in *The New Republic*, chastised his fellow journalists for failing to give this issue the "serious reflection" it merits and for their unconcern about "growing media monopolies" and the need to get "all points of view" to the people.

Law Professor Jerome Barron, a counsel for Tornillo, claims that since the Supreme Court's 1964 decision on libel (*New York Times v. Sullivan*), the press has been encouraged to make irresponsible attacks on public individuals. Unless some new approach is developed "to require opportunities for the public figure to reply to a defamatory attack," says Barron, "the [1964 Sullivan] decision will merely serve to equip the press with some new and rather heavy artillery which can crush as well as stimulate debate."

Arthur S. Miller, professor of constitutional law at George Washington University, defended the Florida statute. He said, "freedom of the press really means the public's right to know, something not furthered by the Miami *Herald's* private censorship."

Miller quoted a March 13, 1974, editorial in the Washington *Post* which had asserted that "the national commitment to robust, uninhibited political debate encompasses the liberty to criticize, to exaggerate, to vilify, and even to defame."

No one, said Professor Miller, has freedom to defame. "It is one thing to use the Sullivan doctrine as a defense to a libel action, but quite another to maintain that a newspaper can defame at will."

Miller also noted that "an industry ever-increasingly dominated by a few—the daily press tends more and more to be local monopolies—does not hesitate to invoke government aid. The Newspaper Preservation Act of 1970 got no press opposition—quite the contrary—when it immunized certain activities from the antitrust laws. The media barons, including leading pillars of liberal thought, want it both ways. They want government aid, both in the exemption from the antitrust laws and also in being able to hide behind the Supreme Court's substantial diminution of the libel laws. But they do not want to allow attacked people a right of reply."

The More Stubborn Kind of Truth

One of the "practical" arguments against liberalizing the public's access to the mass communications media is that this would open the floodgates to an exotic variety of kooks and quacks peddling every political and social nostrum that can be conjured up by the fevered imagination of troubled human minds. The traffic problem alone for such a medicine show would cripple the operations of most media, it is argued.

But there are ways to filter the material and manage the traffic and not be too quick to make judgments. More to the point, it is not ideas and opinions that necessarily constitute the most important or the most sensitive and controversial of the access material. It is factual information that is the more troublesome, because more stubborn, kind of truth. It is here that private censorship tends to be swift and punishment ruthless. Michael Frome was not fired from *Field & Stream* because he voiced unpopular opinions. He was fired after he reported factual truths about how certain congressmen voted on specific en-

vironmental issues, and after he reported the fact that certain government agencies were letting valuable land slip out of the public domain into private hands, with inadequate records and no public review.

In her book, *Between Past and Future*, Hannah Arendt distinguishes between rational truth and factual truth and the different kinds of threat each poses to the person of power, political or economic.

"No former time tolerated so many diverse opinions on religious or philosophical matters," she writes, "[but] factual truth, if it happens to oppose a given group's profit or pleasure, is greeted today with greater hostility than ever before. . . . What seems even more disturbing is that to the extent to which unwelcome factual truths are tolerated in free countries, they are often, consciously or unconsciously, transformed into opinions. . . .

"Freedom of opinion is a farce unless factual information is guaranteed and the facts themselves are not in dispute. . . . Factual truth informs political thought just as rational truth informs philosophical speculation."

The importance of access to factual truths in the communications media was underlined by Charles Rembar in his *Atlantic* article. Rembar grants the importance of access to diverse beliefs and opinions, but, he says, "There is something else crucial to the First Amendment. It is communication of fact. Not opinion, not belief, not ideas, but fact; not release of what is inside one's head, but transmission of external data. Even though it has up to now played so small a part in the history of free speech, even though it was scarcely in the minds of those who drafted the Bill of Rights, it is crucial to that document's purposes. . . .

"Factual information was the subject of the case of the Pentagon Papers. . . . It is the stated goal of journalists who resist grand jury subpoenas. Facts are the prize, on both sides of the fight. The subpoenas are not concerned with secret sources of opinion. Neither are the reporters, who want to dig out facts. Again, a former C.I.A. man, Victor Marchetti, seeks to publish a book about what went on in the C.I.A. The C.I.A. and, so far, the courts, do not think he ought to, without a check on whether he is divulging 'classified information.' Nobody suggests he may not publish his opinion of the C.I.A."

As a verification of the critical importance of access to the mass media for factual information in general and for the facts about America's intervention in Vietnam in particular, Abe Rosenthal of *The New York Times* said of his paper's publication of the Pentagon Papers: "For the first time in history citizens were able to read and judge and draw their conclusions from a documentary case study of how one American government after another, in concealment from its public, went to war. . . ."

Photo by Mitchell Payne/Jeroboam, Inc.

Toward Freer Information

Remedial alternatives to the present state of the nation's mass media—all looking toward a freer flow of information and ideas, greater diversity of viewpoints, and more vigorous media competition to bring to the public that "popular information" which James Madison saw as indispensable to "popular government"—fall into four main categories:

* Deconcentration of ownership of the media.
* Facilitation of the entry of new, competitive media in the life of the national community.
* Opening up existing communication channels, expanding the public's access to them.
* Developing the ethical and legal grounds for asserting the individual journalist's claim to a protected professional status vis-à-vis not only the government but also the institution that employs him or her.

Before listing and commenting on the possibilities within each of these categories, it will be necessary to re-

view some of the constitutional considerations involved. In each of the categories, government can and must play an important part. The question is how far the government may go without violating the First Amendment, i.e., without abridging the freedom of the press.

The most useful and balanced discussion I have found on this question is in Thomas I. Emerson's book, *The System of Freedom of Expression* (Vintage paperback), especially the chapter he devotes to the affirmative promotion of freedom of expression.

Emerson, who is now retired from his law professorship at Yale University, points out, as have other commentators in the last thirty years, that it is no longer enough to protect the freedom of the press from government interference in order to guarantee freedom of expression. Today, "the overpowering monopoly over the means of communication acquired by the mass media" constitutes the "most significant threat" to our system of freedom of expression.

At the same time, "modern government, by virtue of its size, resources, control of information, and links to the mass media, plays a more dominant and narrowing role in the system. . . . [Too,] costs of all methods of communication steadily rise beyond the means of the individual or the ordinary group. The result is that the system is choked with communications based upon the conventional wisdom and becomes incapable of performing its basic function.

"Search for the truth is handicapped because much of the argument is never heard or heard only weakly. Political decisions are distorted because the views of some citizens never reach other citizens, and feedback to the government is feeble.

"The possibility of orderly social change is greatly diminished because those persons with the most urgent grievances come to believe the system is unworkable and merely shields the existing order.

"Under these circumstances," Emerson writes, "it becomes essential, if the system is to survive, that a search be made for ways to use the law and legal institutions in an affirmative program to restore the system to effective working order.

"In general, the government must affirmatively make available the opportunity for expression as well as protect it from encroachment. This means that positive measures must be taken to assure the ability to speak despite economic or other barriers. It also means that greater attention must be given to the right of the citizen to hear varying points of view and the right to have access to information upon which such points of view can be intelligently based. Thus, equally with the right and the ability to speak, such an approach would stress the right to hear and the right to know."

For this reason, Emerson thinks, the traditional First Amendment tests (bad tendency, incitement, clear and present danger, balancing of opposing interests, etc.) are not applicable. Rather, "the problem must be resolved in terms of whether there has been an 'abridgement' of freedom of expression [presumably by either government or the media] and the tests must be framed in terms of accommodation of interests within the system, nondiscrimination, promotion."

According to Emerson, the affirmative power of the First Amendment can be invoked in two forms. In one, it is self-executing and enforceable by the courts as a constitutional mandate, as, for example, when a local board of education is compelled, as a matter of First Amendment principle, to make a building available for a public meeting. The second form would have the affirmative power of the First Amendment manifested as the basis for legislation. It might be federal legislation "enacted directly by virtue of the First Amendment, or federal legislation enacted under Section 5 of the Fourteenth Amendment, which makes the First Amendment applicable to the states."

Emerson is fully aware of what he calls the "grave administrative and procedural problems" posed by any effort to employ governmental authority to facilitate operation of the system of freedom of expression. "The attempt to use governmental power to achieve some limited objective, while at the same time keeping the power under control, is always a risky enterprise. Nowhere is this truer than in the area of freedom of expression. Nevertheless, there is no alternative. The weaknesses of the existing system are so profound that failure to act is the more dangerous course. Moreover, the government is already deeply involved at many points—some of great importance—as in its regulation of radio and television. The same kind of movement may be found in other areas of individual rights today, such as the development of the affirmative aspects of the equal protection clause.

"The only prudent course, then," according to Emerson, "is to formulate principles and devise techniques that use social power to facilitate freedom of expression while holding the instrument of that power in check. The initial responsibility of the government is to maintain the basic conditions that a system of freedom of expression requires in order, not just to exist, but to flourish.

"The crucial need is that the society act with vigor and imagination to give affirmative support to the system of freedom of expression. This is especially important in the very broadest areas of affirmative action—the maintenance of fundamental economic, political, and social conditions necessary for a system of freedom of expression to survive at all."

Emerson believes that the kinds of regulation that are unavoidable with regard to radio and television (because of the technical limitations inherent in those media) are unconstitutional when applied to the newspaper. "A limited right of access to the press can be safely enforced," he thinks. This would include the "right of reply to libelous matter" and "perhaps the right to buy noncommercial advertising space. . . . But any effort to solve the broader problems of a monopoly press by forcing newspapers to cover all 'newsworthy' events and print all viewpoints, under the watchful eyes of petty public officials, is likely to undermine such independence as the press now shows without achieving any real diversity."

It is in the second of my four remedial areas listed above—facilitation of the entry of new, competitive media—where Emerson thinks the preferable course of government action lies. "Such a goal cannot be reached by mere enforcement of the antitrust laws. It will undoubtedly be necessary to go to the economic roots of the problem and either by government subsidies or other devices

create an open market with a new form of economic base."

The Right to Know

The affirmative interpretation of the First Amendment rests in great part on the argument that the amendment's guarantee was written principally to protect the citizens' right to know rather than the publishers' right to publish.

In the Supreme Court's Red Lion decision (1969), which affirmed the government's (F.C.C.'s) constitutional right to compel broadcasters to give "adequate coverage to public issues" and to see that the "coverage [is] fair in that it accurately reflects the opposing views," Justice Byron White, speaking for the Court, said: "It is the right of the viewers and listeners, not the right of the broadcasters, which is paramount.... It is the right of the public to receive suitable access to social, political, aesthetic, moral, and other ideas and experiences which is crucial here."

The court cited the technologically imposed scarcity of broadcast facilities and said that "only a tiny fraction of those with resources and intelligence can hope to communicate by radio at the same time if intelligible communication is to be had, even if the entire radio spectrum is utilized in the present state of commercially acceptable technology."

Justice White said that "a license permits broadcasting, but the licensee has no constitutional right to be the one who holds the license or to monopolize a radio frequency to the exclusion of his fellow citizens. There is nothing in the First Amendment which prevents the government from requiring a licensee to share his frequency with others and to conduct himself as a proxy or fiduciary with obligations to present those views and voices which are representative of his community and which would otherwise, by necessity, be barred from the airwaves. ... It is the purpose of the First Amendment to preserve an uninhibited marketplace of ideas in which truth will

ultimately prevail, rather than to countenance monopolization of that market, whether it be by the government itself or a private licensee."

An earlier Court decision—that of *Associated Press v. United States* in 1945—embodied a strong statement of the government's right, precisely under the First Amendment, to prevent the press itself from interfering with the free flow of ideas. The Associated Press had sought to impose restrictions upon a newspaper wishing to use its wire service because that newspaper was a competitor of other papers already receiving the service.

"It would be strange indeed," said Justice Hugo Black, for the Court, "if the grave concern for freedom of the press which prompted adoption of the First Amendment should be read as a command that the government was without power to protect that freedom. The First Amendment, far from providing an argument against application of the Sherman [Antitrust] Act, here provides powerful reasons to the contrary. That Amendment rests on the assumption that the widest possible dissemination of information from diverse and antagonistic sources is essential to the welfare of the public, that a free press is a condition of a free society.

"Surely a command that the government itself shall not impede the free flow of ideas does not afford nongovernmental combinations a refuge if they impose restraints upon that constitutionally guaranteed freedom. Freedom to publish means freedom for all and not for some. Freedom to publish is guaranteed by the Constitution, but freedom to combine to keep others from publishing is not. Freedom of the press from governmental interference under the First Amendment does not sanction repression of that freedom by private interests. The First Amendment affords not the slightest support for the contention that a combination to restrain trade in news and views has any constitutional immunity."

Deconcentration of Media Ownership

1. Enforcement of F.C.C. rules against cross-ownership of broadcasting and print media in the same city (a) now, in cities where it already exists; (b) prospectively, to prevent future cross-ownership acquisitions; and (c) in cases where present ownership is being transferred to new owners.

Although the F.C.C. has an order banning prospective cross-ownerships and requiring the breakup of cross-ownerships in more than a dozen cities, the Commission, last May, renewed the radio and television licenses of one such ownership—WIBW—in Topeka, Kansas, over the objection of the Department of Justice. The Department said that the stations' licensee, Stauffer Publications, Inc., had a monopoly of local advertising and news dissemination that was "repugnant to antitrust principles" and "inimical to the public interest." Stauffer owns the only newspaper in Topeka, its television station is said to have seventy-five per cent of the television circulation, and its radio station twenty-five per cent of the aural circulation. Although the F.C.C.'s latest rules on cross-ownership (adopted last January) still bar the creation of new daily newspaper-broadcast cross-ownerships in the same community, the Commission said it will now require divestiture only in cases that it considers are "egregious" monopolies—apparently where the only station and the only newspaper in a community are commonly owned.

2. Legislation barring non-media ownership of media, and media ownership of non-media interests.

The F.C.C. presently limits the percentage of a television medium's stock that can be acquired by non-media interests, but it has not enforced its rule uniformly. Some institutional investors already hold more than the three-per-cent ceiling laid down for mutual funds and the one-per-cent limit for insurance companies. The F.C.C. has announced it intends to raise both the mutual fund and insurance company ownership limits to five per cent (a figure already in effect for banks), to waive the five-per-cent limit for banks which "involuntarily" receive large blocks of television company stock in trust, and to end its requirement that big investors must file disclaimer of active ownership. Bernard P. Gallagher, publisher of *The Gallagher Report*, a newsletter for sales, advertising, and media executives, thinks these liberalized F.C.C. rules are "dangerous" because of the "muscle" that institutional investors exercise in mergers and acquisitions. But, given the sensitive public-interest nature of the media, why should business and financial institutions be allowed to own any part of a newspaper or broadcasting station?

3. A constitutional testing of the Newspaper Preservation Act of 1970.

To the extent that the law makes it virtually impossible for a third newspaper to enter a community, it is constitutionally questionable. The law permits the two newspapers in a single community to share production facilities, set advertising rates, and share revenues according to the relative economic strength of the two papers.

4. Challenging of the application of the Newspaper Preservation Act in specific cities.

Forty-six newspapers in twenty-three cities now engage in joint operations. Some critics contend that in at least one city neither of the two newspapers was in danger of failing—a necessary condition for invoking this law—and that editorial and news policies and practices have not, in fact, been kept separate, as required by the law.

5. Development of antitrust doctrine and theory which might find that the public interest is seriously harmed not only by monopoly in the marketplace but also by monopoly of the means of disseminating public information, ideas, beliefs, and judgments.

6. Barring the acquisition of cable television facilities by commercial broadcasters and newspapers in the same city.

Facilitation of the Entry of New Media in the Life of the Community

1. Governmental and nongovernmental subsidies to help new media—publications, radio and UHF television stations, cable television—get started and become self-supporting.

Presumably the public interest is now being served by governmental subsidies of the oil industry (to extract fuel resources), the farmers (to maintain the production of food and fiber), the railroads (to service industries), the airlines (to insure adequate travel facilities). The public interest would also be served by governmental subsidies of additional mass communication media to promote a freer and fuller flow of the information and ideas that animate a democratic society.

2. Greater federal subsidization of the Corporation for Public Broadcasting, the federal money coming, in part, from a "tax" on the revenues of commercial television and radio stations and networks.

There should be no federal control of content. Control should be limited to the mandating of a specified amount of air time to be set aside for public affairs and public information programming on public broadcast television stations. The television industry is enjoying record-breaking profits in 1976, and most of the network time is already sold out for 1977. These are public airwaves, the people's airwaves, on which the industry is fattening itself. If it does not voluntarily give a percentage of these profits to support a noncommercial broadcasting service, a governmental assessment is in order.

3. Federal support of municipal "open access" cable television.

The City of Milwaukee has been conducting year-long deliberations over just such a city-owned media facility.

4. Federal and/or private-subscription funding of a Public Information Service in daily-newspaper format.

This would be an expansion of the Corporation for Public Broadcasting precedent, an extension of that precedent to the newspaper medium. Such a newspaper would be insulated from the commercial pressures that now influence the performance of the press in the baneful ways already described. It would also have to be insulated, of course, from interference by government officials. Staffed by professional reporters and editors, such a paper could become a yardstick by which the public could measure the performance of the commercial media. As such, it would introduce a vigorous and healthy competitive factor in the newsgathering and distribution system of the nation's media.

5. Federal and private support for technological exploration to devise more efficient and economical ways to operate newspapers.

The percentage of a newspaper's space set aside for news and public affairs material is often pathetically low, as is the percentage of the paper's budget spent on news and editorial services. More than 1,200 of the nation's 1,775 newspapers have no correspondent in Washington reporting on the actions of United States representatives and senators in their districts and states. Not all of this is due to an inordinate concern on the part of owners for return on their investment. Much is due to the necessarily labor-intensive nature of producing and distributing newspapers, but much is also due—at least until recent years—to the technologically conservative and unimaginative character of newspaper executives.

6. Reservation of new VHF "drop-ins" for public-interest groups.

The Institute for Telecommunications Sciences of the Department of Commerce will study the feasibility of "dropping in" as many as eighty-three new VHF television stations in the nation's top one hundred markets. Knoxville, Tennessee, will be the site of the first feasibility study. If these new stations can be dropped in without disturbing the pictures and signals from existing stations, this can be a historic breakthrough for greater diversity of television programming. If, however, public interest groups and nonprofit organizations are not given—as a matter of public policy—most-favored-applicant treatment, if they are not given the first opportunity to acquire these new stations, the stations will be licensed, for the most part, to the same commercial and business interests that now dominate the mass communications media in the country, and with the same predictable consequences.

"Freedom of the press is guaranteed only to those who own one," said Howard Gossage. Photo by Roger Lubin/ Jeroboam, Inc.

Opening Up Existing Media Channels

1. Enforcement of Fairness Doctrine by the Federal Communications ommission.

The doctrine requires broadcasters to discharge their public trusteeship by alloting a portion of their broadcast time to reporting and discussing important public issues and to do so in a way that fairly reflects opposing viewpoints on those issues. The doctrine also requires that if one political candidate receives air time, his or her rivals must be given equal time; that individuals attacked on the air be given the opportunity to reply; and that political candidates opposed to those endorsed by a radio or television station, or those attacked editorially by a station, be given the right to present their views.

The "access" implications of the Fairness Doctrine are restricted to the above definition. Anne Branscomb, writing in *Aspen Notebook on Government and Media,* says that under the Fairness Doctrine "no right accrues to any individual or group to obtain access to a broadcast channel, and the F.C.C. has consistently held that the doctrine protects the right of the public to be informed rather than the right of any individual to speak." The exceptions to this are as cited above—i.e., individuals attacked on the air, political candidates entitled to equal time, and candidates editorially opposed by a particular broadcasting station.

"Citizen access under the Fairness Doctrine," writes Ms. Branscomb, "is issue-oriented rather than person- or group-oriented. 'Equal time' is not required for a response [to a position on any given issue], nor is the broadcasting of these messages at any particular time of day. All questions concerning determination of issues, spokesmen, timing, and over-all balance have been resolved in favor of licensee discretion. The over-all performance of a licensee is important in determining whether fairness has been achieved on a specific issue."

Since Ms. Branscomb wrote this, however, the F.C.C. ruled (last June) that a West Virginia radio station, WHAR, had failed to cover adequately the strip-mining issue, a matter of grave concern to people living in the area served by the station, and had thus failed to live up to its Fairness Doctrine obligation to provide coverage of issues of public importance. The Commission did not, that is, wait for WHAR'S license-renewal application to make its judgment.

The F.C.C. said that the broadcaster cannot rely on the fact that prior to this complaint, it had not received any requests for strip mining-related programming, since it is the station's obligation to make an affirmative effort to program on issues of concern to its community. In addition, the station must show that there has been some attempt to inform the public of the nature of the controversy, not only that such a controversy exists.

The F.C.C. also reached to the content of network programming in a case involving N.B.C.'s handling of a documentary program on private pension plans in the United States. The Commission held with the petitioner (Accuracy in Media, Inc.) that N.B.C. had presented only one side of this issue. N.B.C. won an appeal in the United States Court of Appeals in the District of Columbia Circuit, and the petitioner said it intends to appeal to the Supreme Court. Chief Judge David I. Bazelon of the Appeals Court filed a dissenting opinion in which he wryly observed that N.B.C. had won only by convincing the majority of the judges that its "Pensions" broadcasts did not "raise a controversial issue of public importance." He said the fear now is that "this litigation strategy will back up into the journalistic process itself and lead to the [broadcasters'] manipulation of programming in a manner designed to avoid the Fairness Doctrine through contortions in the subject matter of the program. If this occurs, we would be faced with the ironic consequence of the court's action having a greater chilling effect on broadcasters than a forthright, open application of the Fairness Doctrine."

2. Evolving the Fairness Doctrine into a representative access formulation.

Philosophy Professor Phil Jacklin of California State University at San Jose described this formulation in some detail in his article, "Access to the Media," in the May/June, 1975, issue of *The Center Magazine.* According to Professor Jacklin, representative access would have a distinct advantage over regulation of message content (just what would constitute a "balanced" presentation of the private-pension controversy, for example?) in that it says nothing about content but only regulation of access. His plan would neither prohibit "monopolization of access by any message source or group of sources." Each "dominant message source" would be required by law to make available ten per cent of all message capacity (time and/or space) for citizen access. Access would be allocated to registered citizens by lot. It would be permissible for individuals to make access contributions to designated representative persons or groups. . . ." Access designation will, in effect, be votes—expressions of concerns and priorities—with respect to what is communicated. Everyone will participate in message selection. Communication will reflect the needs, values, and priorities of all citizens. . . . Surely, in such a sensitive field as communication, it is better to regulate access than to rely on government paternalism in the regulation of message content. As always, free speech in a marketplace of ideas is our best hope."

3. Enforcement of F.C.C. rules and standards at license-renewal time.

It is an open secret that, for the most part, the three-year renewals of broadcasters' licenses is a rubber-stamp operation. A few years ago, then-F.C.C. Commissioner Nicholas Johnson cited an impressive amount of evidence demonstrating that most of the stations in a particular state were making a mockery of their obligation to operate in the public interest; and yet few, if any, of them were called to account by the Commission at renewal time.

4. Public hearings involving broadcasters and audience for the ascertainment of community needs.

This is being done fitfully, often ritualistically, rather than realistically. It should be done regularly and not only on the eve of license-renewal deadlines but at intervals throughout the three-year licensing period.

Developing the Ethical and Legal Bases of the Journalist's Professional Status

Freedom is an essential condition for both responsibility and professional integrity. The problem for the journalist who aspires to high ethical and professional conduct is that his freedom is always qualified and inescapably vulnerable.

The working journalist has only as much freedom as his employer chooses to give him. The First Amendment guarantees the journalist protection from the government's abridgement of his right to report and publish. To date, it has offered no protection from an employer's arbitrary denial of that freedom. And yet, the professional integrity of the journalistic function itself demands it.

It would seem that it is precisely at the point where the individual journalist gathers, organizes, and prepares his information for the public that the First Amendment protection must, above all, be firm, whether the threat to suppress that information comes from government, industry, or the publishers and station owners themselves.

And yet, the publishers and station owners are also journalists and therefore their freedom, too, including the freedom to decide what to publish or broadcast and what

not to publish or broadcast, must be protected under the First Amendment guarantees. It is difficult to see how a law compelling media owners to retain individual journalists and to publish or broadcast their work would not, at the same time, violate the owners' constitutionally protected freedom.

Still, the personal dimension in the work of the individual reporter is, in a way, an irremovable and sovereign element. It is the reporter—not his publisher or station owner—who has confronted the truths that are in his report. And even as one acknowledges that the reporter's truths may be only parts of a larger web of related truths, under what circumstances can he permit his truths to vanish or be reshaped by another who has not experienced them, and still describe his work as professional?

In addition to these constitutional and personal elements in the journalistic function, there is the social element: citizens must depend upon their journalists to provide the information they need to make self-government work and to achieve the end of a political community, that is, justice.

It is here where the journalist may properly lay claim to the status of a professional. His professional aspirations and responsibilities are to be found in what he contributes to and what is required by the citizens of a democracy.

This was clearly seen by the former C.B.S. news correspondent Daniel Schorr. Perhaps at least as portentous as his confrontation with the Ethics Committee of the House of Representatives were the professional implications of his relationship with C.B.S. The network suspended him, with pay, after he passed to *The Village Voice* a secret House committee report on U.S. intelligence activities.

In a speech to the Individual Rights and Responsibilities section of the American Bar Association, Schorr said:

"If government should not control news, then no one should. The First Amendment says only that Congress shall make no law abridging the freedom of the press and speech. Perhaps it is time for an unofficial First Amendment that says no enterprise shall make rules abridging individual freedoms of speech and press.

"I am not suggesting that reporters have any right to decide what their employers will publish or broadcast. What I am talking about is the extent to which a journalist—part of a large news enterprise, subject to its disciplines when engaged in its process—still retains personal freedom of expression outside it. . . . A newspaper reporter who takes elsewhere a story that his editor has decided—perhaps for valid reasons—not to print may be severely disciplined, or even fired. That has happened.

"When did freedom of the press evolve into a franchise to be exercised through large enterprises? . . . I would suggest that the First Amendment is not only the news

establishment's First Amendment, but it is every journalist's and every American's individual right and, what's more, individual responsibility."

A newly formed Citizens' Committee Concerned with Freedom of the Press sharpened this point in a statement on the Schorr case. The committee includes the historian Henry Steele Commager and professors Burke Marshall and Thomas Emerson of Yale, Richard Falk of Princeton, Matthew Meselson of Harvard, and Salvador E. Luria of Massachusetts Institute of Technology, along with Leonard Woodcock, president of the United Auto Workers.

It was formed, Professor Marshall said, to support Schorr and to monitor other cases where freedom of the press is threatened. The committee is concerned with threats from all sources:

"We are determined as citizens to insure that our right to know be decided not only by conflict between the press and the institutions of government—including the Congress and the courts as well as the executive—but also by citizen participation in that conflict to see that the people's paramount right to information necessary to the democratic process is preserved against encroachment either by

government or by the press itself."

The American Society of Journalists and Authors invoked a similar rationale in its defense of Michael Frome, and added a note on the professional journalist's need for freedom. After Frome was fired by *Field & Stream,* the Society held a public meeting and Patrick M. McGrady, its president, issued this statement:

"We journalists and authors are especially concerned that our right to tell and the public's right to know are being increasingly suppressed as heavy-handed, secretive conglomerates aggrandize their power. We are fully aware that this is a complex problem with no easy solutions. We do not desire to impoverish or weaken any medium, but rather to strengthen the media generally by protecting our intellectual and expressive freedoms."

The Society specifically asked Congress and the F.C.C. (the F.C.C., because the conglomerate owner of *Field & Stream* is C.B.S., Inc.) to investigate the circumstances surrounding Frome's firing and to focus on the threat posed by conglomerate enterprises to the work and the integrity of the journalists they employ.

Can the individual reporter or editor be protected in the

performance of his professional duties to society—whether inside or outside his principal place of employment—without violating the rights of his employers?

Is it too much to expect that a professional contract or working agreement can be drawn up and a professional journalists' association organized to use that contract for measuring the performance of both the journalists and their employers? The agreement would have to spell out working conditions of the journalists, due-process protections against arbitrary actions by the journalists' employers, a fact-finding mechanism by which the professional association would be empowered to make independent investigations of professionals' complaints, and routine publication of their findings.

•

All the remedies I have recommended, except that which asks for strict enforcement of the F.C.C.'s Fairness Doctrine, have one thing in common: they keep government at arm's length from the content of newspapers and broadcasting. They seek, instead, to promote maximum diversity of media ownership, maximum competition in the task of informing the American citizens of public affairs and issues, and maximum protection for journalists so that they may, in fact, perform as professionals without fear of reprisals from any source. When such diversity, competition, and protection are achieved, there will be no need for a Fairness Doctrine of any kind.

I am under no illusion as to the probability that some of these remedial recommendations may be realized soon. The same forces that persuaded Congress to pass the Newspaper Preservation Act—forces in both the newspaper industry and Congress itself—are still at work. The same forces in government that have permitted special monopolistic privileges in both the newspaper and broadcasting industries, that have permitted the latter to flout their solemn public interest obligations as stewards of the people's airwaves, are still at work.

Congressmen need the media, and the media need the good will and benign attentiveness of Congress if only to keep reformers at bay. It is a cozy mutual protection arrangement. Under the circumstances neither will seriously disturb the other. And it is not likely that American public opinion will demand reform, since that public opinion is to a great extent dependent upon what the media choose to disclose about these problems.

The emergence of ombudsmen in some newspapers, the work of the National News Council and some state press councils, the mid-career university fellowships for journalists, the vigilance of *The Columbia Journalism Review*, some of the schools and departments of journalism—all these have helped, in varying degrees, to preserve at least some awareness of the gap between duty and performance.

But hopes for permanent reform must lie in the courts rather than Congress or the industry, at least for now.

Public interest law firms have an opportunity to proceed from *Red Lion* ("It is the right of the viewers and listeners, not the right of the broadcasters, which is paramount. . . .") and *Associated Press v. United States* ("Freedom to publish means freedom for all and not for some. . . . Freedom of the press from governmental interference under the First Amendment does not sanction repression of that freedom by private interests") and to build on these doctrines the legal arguments that will bring into the courts for judicial scrutiny the existing system and practices of the mass communication media.

It is from such scrutiny, and from the effort of journalists themselves to define the professional nature and requirements of public affairs reporting, that we might expect society, in Thomas Emerson's words, to "act with vigor and imagination," especially in the very broadest areas of affirmative action—the maintenance of those "fundamental economic, political, and social conditions" that are needed "if a system of freedom of expression is to survive at all."

American journalism has marvelous technical resources at its disposal. It has some newspapers—notably *The New York Times* and Los Angeles *Times*—which reflect and exemplify very high professional standards. And it has a host of workers who do manage to perform professionally often enough, despite the external and internal limitations that are imposed on them, to convince me that reformist initiatives would be greeted by journalists with unabashed joy. But, as Professor Emerson said, one must go to "the economic roots of the problem" and "create an open market with a new form of economic base." And what a nascence of public affairs journalism that could produce!

Is there a doubt whether a common government can embrace so large a sphere?
Let experience solve it. . . . It is well worth a fair and full experiment.
—GEORGE WASHINGTON

Only One World: The United Nations And Foreign Policy

The United Nations Charter enshrines the principle of absolute national sovereignty, which is another way of saying it enshrines anarchy. For absolute sovereignty and anarchy both consist, essentially, in refusing to acknowledge any authority higher than one's own. Despite its congenital defects and the contempt in which many hold it, however, the United Nations has many important achievements to its credit. It has encouraged decolonialization; it has, in many cases, secured more humane treatment of individuals and minorities by their own national governments; it has helped eradicate diseases and has relieved the plight of disaster victims; it has convoked a series of conferences, beginning with the 1972 Stockholm Conference on the Human Environment, that compelled all nations to confront vital problems; and it has prevented or shortened wars. Indeed, we cannot be certain that without the UN's moderating influence, World War III would not have broken out. When all is said and done, however, the UN depends wholly upon voluntary cooperation by member-states whose assertions of absolute national sovereignty amount to a warning that cooperation may be withheld at any time. There is a move afoot within the UN to amend and strengthen its Charter. The official US reaction to date has been negative. This is a national disgrace. Had not the similarly defective Articles of Confederation been succeeded by the US Constitution in 1789, we would not have survived as a nation long enough to celebrate our bicentennial.

One World

The United Nations is a great but obsolescent institution that does not fit the world it was designed to protect. From the beginning, in 1945, it has always been precariously balanced on several mistaken and impractical assumptions:

1. That its major task of peacekeeping can rest on the unanimous action of the great powers (the permanent members of the Security Council);
2. That the most serious problems facing mankind are international disputes;
3. That an annual meeting of diplomats, with equal votes for all nations, the majority of them small and powerless (the General Assembly), can deal effectively with international and world affairs;
4. That important international disputes will be submitted to a World Court, even though all parties must first consent, and that without enforcement power anywhere in the whole international system, a World Court's decisions will be obeyed;
5. That recommendations from such faulty and weakly constructed institutions can substantially affect the actions of major powers, or manage the vital problems of mankind;
6. That while unregulated national sovereignty is obviously the chief stumbling-block to world peace and sane planetary management, it is both sacred and monolithic; that it cannot be regulated, or divided between internal and world affairs, without loss of the individual citizen's freedom and influence.

Nevertheless, while laboring under all these plainly false assumptions, the United Nations has important accomplishments to its credit.

* It has prevented, concluded, or stalemated several minor wars, which might have become major, as in the Congo, Cyprus, and the Middle East. In so doing, it has invented and proved viable the international peacekeeping force, demonstrating that fears about language difficulties and struggles over command were groundless.
* It has encouraged, and in some cases presided over, the elimination of colonial domination throughout the world, so that only in a few places outside the communist dictatorships are populations of size and conscious discontent living under the domination of alien masters.
* It has set higher standards for government treatment of the individual and of minorities through its Human Rights Declaration, so that such ancient evils as slavery, torture, and systematic racial discrimination are no longer openly practised in most of the world.
* Through its specialized agencies, it has carried on philanthropic enterprises of unprecedented scope and success. This year, for example, the UN expects to announce the complete and final eradication of smallpox, now making its last stand in the highlands of Ethiopia. Thus ends an agelong scourge whose threat no national effort could ever completely remove. Earthquake, famine, and the distress caused by war, persecution, and economic dislocation have all been mitigated by United Nations action.
* It has proposed a "New Economic Order" with a fair prospect of some result. In September 1975, the Seventh Special Session of the General Assembly produced in 16 days a resolution on international economic cooperation that is a potentially historic accommodation of the previously opposed viewpoints of the rich and the poor countries. The attitude of the United States in this session was notably cooperative. The General Assembly then accepted and implemented this resolution, reorienting the UN Development Program to reach poorer populations in developing countries. This recent Assembly also set up procedures to make new arrangements for world trade that will be favorable to poor countries, to reduce world unemployment, and to prevent corrupt practices by transnational corporations.
* Most significant of all, in the last decade the United Nations has set up a series of special conferences to deal with rising dangers to mankind, and indeed to all life on this planet, dangers that are fully as menacing and lethal as war. Of these conferences, the most successful, and an example for those that have followed, was the Conference on the Human Environment in Stockholm, June 1972.

Where previously environment was of minor importance to most governments, today there are few important nations that do not have government ministries or agencies to handle environmental problems. This influence, however, has been dimmed by the fact that the new UN Environment Programme (UNEP) has never been properly funded and has been much pressured to turn its small funds to the ends of development rather than to its appropriate tasks of preservation, restoration, and monitoring of the earth's water, air, soil, minerals, plants, and animals.

Internationalism does not mean the end of individual nations. Orchestras don't mean the end of violins. —GOLDA MEIR

Throughout the poor countries there is already a gaping abyss between conservation laws and their enforcement. This reflects not only poor communications between governments and the rural poor, but also the clash between the exigencies of conservation and the individual's pressing, undeniable needs.

People hungry for land are not apt to leave forest or pasturelands unplowed, regardless of what ecological soundness dictates. Farmers hungry for bread are not likely to defer production this year to enhance soil quality for the next generation. Those with no other means than wood to cook their dinner cannot be expected to leave nearby trees unmolested even if they are labeled "reserved" by the government. And people brutalized by exploitive economic and social systems will probably not treat the land any more gently and respectfully than they are treated themselves.

Unfortunately, there are no quick solutions to the dismal cycles of poverty, ecological decay, and rapid population growth. To be sure, conservation ethics and problems need to be treated daily as "news" by the media and as part of basic curriculum in educational systems. Regulations protecting essential forests and mountain slopes also need to be strictly enforced. But these measures will never succeed until the populace has the technical and financial means to cooperate, and this means reaching the masses with ecologically sound agricultural advice and with credit facilities; maximizing rural employment on farms and in small-scale industries; and breaking down the social, legal, and economic structures that deny the poor basic opportunities for advancement. It means creating participatory institutions, whether through local government, cooperatives, or communes, that give the poor a sense of responsibility for and control over their destiny. That these prerequisites of ecological recovery are identical to the tactics of a more general war against poverty and hunger should come as no surprise.

Among a large share of the world's poor, words like "conservation" and "environmental protection," if they are known at all, strike a negative note. They are associated with denial and repression rather than with the improved quality of life that those who use them have in mind. Clearly, the movement to save a habitable environment will never succeed if its historical emphasis on protection and preservation is not balanced by progress in production and the satisfaction of basic human needs. Forestry departments will never effectively police forest reserves if they do not more successfully increase tree planting and wood production for local uses in forests, plantations, and the countryside. Soil conservation agencies will not stop the spread of cultivation to steep slopes if agricultural policies do not also increase production and employment on the better farmlands and improve the distribution of land ownership and production gains. The wildlife refuges and undisturbed natural ecosystems necessary in the interests of biological diversity, scientific study, and esthetics will never last if social conditions and productivity in adjacent areas are desperately low.

Conservation means protecting trees from the ax where necessary or desirable, but it also means far more—for the principal aspiration of the world's poorest half is to climb from the depths of severe social deprivation, not to save the environment for its own sake. Those concerned with global ecological deterioration and its consequences have no choice but to throw themselves into the maelstrom that is the politics of social change. —ERIK ECKHOLM

Under UNEP's aegis, however, concern for the polluted Mediterranean finally produced protocols signed by 12 countries, at Barcelonia, in February 1976, to clean up and prohibit pollution and dumping—UNEP's first great success. Meanwhile, the heedless rush to environmental disaster has been slowed in many other areas.

Other UN conferences on world problems of equal gravity have been the Population Conference at Bucharest, the Food Conference at Rome, and the ongoing Law of the Sea Conference that began at Geneva in 1958. The effects of 1975's conference at Mexico City for the International Women's Year and 1976's Conference on Human Settlements at Vancouver are still to be evaluated. Coming in the next few years are potentially vital conferences on the world's water supplies, the problem of its expanding deserts, and (perhaps) how to halt nuclear proliferation and the arms race.

At a glance, it can be seen that the range of problems

*America must offer the world a positive program. It must never accept, as a
final fact, the division between East and West. It must understand that the
only rational attitude is One World—that the only sane goal is world
government.*

—JAN MASARYK

presented at these world conferences are the world's real
business. They simply dwarf the sputtering belligerence,
the name calling, the generally disregarded resolutions
(whether censorious or bland) of the General Assembly. In
the light of perils to the whole of humanity and the livabil-
ity of planet Earth, most of the Assembly's headline-
making agenda looks to be taken up with old, mutually-
damaging regional feuds. Much of the oratory is based on
the shibboleths of home foreign offices rather than hope of
persuasion or reasonable presentation of promising alternatives.

As a matter of fact, only a few resolutions produce divisions. Scores are passed by consensus or without objection. Most of these are also void of fertile new ideas. They

endorse what everyone endorses, and condemn the man-
eating sharks that everyone condemns. Often, it seems that
the best thing the Assembly does each year is to authorize
debate on real problems—somewhere else.

Of late, the majority of General Assembly delegates
have begun to feel vaguely that something is wrong with
the United Nations. In August 1975 and again in February
1976, a Special Committee on Charter Review and
Strengthening the Role of the Organization has held a
series of meetings. So far, nothing of substance has been
produced. The Third World would like to get rid of the
great-power veto, but it has not even begun to come to
grips with the changes necessary—in the General Assembly and World Court, particularly—that could enable the

We are paying a heavy price for having accepted, "as the
best we could get" at San Francisco, a form of world organization which falls far short of the minimum needed.
The United Nations can act decisively only when it can
obtain unanimity among heavily armed nations which inherently have acute conflicts of interest. There is only the
remotest chance of ever getting such unity. Civilization—
perhaps the very existence of the human race—depends
upon our being willing and able to convert the U.N.
promptly from a futile league into a world federal government adequate to maintain peace.

The value of open discussion which can reach no definitive end is grossly exaggerated. Blunt talk under such circumstances is more likely to exacerbate feelings than to
relieve tensions. Men in a New England town meeting
tend to speak and act responsibly because all are conscious
that their deliberations may lead to a decision by which *all*
the participants will be equally bound. This element is
completely lacking in the General Assembly of the United
Nations.

Similarly, discussion within our nations in open forums,
on and off the air, operates under awareness that the debates can influence legislative bodies empowered to enact

statutory law which is enforceable. This makes a very great
difference in the attitudes of the disputants toward debate.

We apply the term "law" to international agreements
which are unenforced and unenforceable. We call a world
arbitration tribunal a "court," though it lacks compulsory
jurisdiction and there is no provision for the enforcement
of its decisions. The very name of our world organization
contains a specious word. Union is implied by "united,"
and there is not even a vestige of merged sovereignty in
the so-called United Nations. As one contemplates the
international scene, the impression mounts that here above
all other places is the arena where it is most important to
follow the advice of Justice Holmes that we "think *things,*
not *words.*"

Aversion to the idea of world government arises mainly
from two false assumptions. The first is that national governments would be abolished, or entirely subordinated, in
the creation of a world state. The second is that nationality
would thereby be wiped out. Both fears are baseless. We
do not need to end nationalism; we need only modify the
present absolute nature of national sovereignty.

The unqualified status of nationalism must be ended, but
nations can and should retain complete control over all

We have repeatedly expressed our opinion in favor of the development of an international organization or some kind of world government which gives full autonomy to its various national units and which at the same time removes the causes for war and national conflict.

—PANDIT NEHRU

great powers to consider giving the veto up. The only certain result is that the committee will continue, for it has not even started to fulfill its mandate.

The US State Department seems to be mired in inaction and indifference, which it expresses in opaque statements such as "It is not a violation of our duty to think charter review is a bad idea."

Internal and external uneasiness about the UN's future has also spread to the Secretariat and the Secretary-General, who feel obliged in almost every public speech to remind their hearers that the United Nations is not a world government, and to assert stoutly that it should not be, since the principle of absolute national sovereignty (which guarantees world anarchy) must never, never be given up.

Like the Player Queen in Hamlet, they do "protest too much." Being for the most part intelligent men with some experience in public administration on behalf of successful governments, they must know quite well what the United Nations lacks: the power to make, adjudicate, and enforce world law. They simply despair of making the world's peoples and their national governments willing to provide such power. So like the good international civil servants that they are, they do their best with what they have and do not agitate for more or better.

But what powers the United Nations has, like those of the League of Nations before it, will obviously only postpone, not avert, disaster. Not all of today's threats to human life will materialize, but only one needs to. Without

matters that are exclusively national in scope or character.

The suggestion that the federal form of government seems best suited to the world's need is not a call for a world constitution patterned closely on that of the United States or on any one of the other existing federal systems; it is merely pointing out the remarkable applicability of the principle.

Specifically, the powers of central governments in existing federal systems fall within five categories: citizenship, defense, currency, trade and communications *among* the parts, and a common judicial system. Each citizen of a member state is also a citizen of the whole. The common government assumes responsibility for the security of all and therefore controls all military establishments, armaments, and the like. Each federal union has a common currency; each regulates interstate trade and communications. A supreme court with subsidiary circuit and district courts is maintained for the adjudication of disputes among the parts; the union has power to compel all to use these courts rather than to resort to violence. It is probable that a world government would need no more extensive powers than these; conversely, it will be dangerous to attempt to operate a world authority with any less power.

There is little danger that we shall give a world government too much power. To seek for the minimum adequate powers, and then to provide for these and no more, is certain to be one of the guiding principles of a world constitutional convention. There is far greater danger that we shall transfer too little power to a world government in the first instance, and thus force it to begin its work under the same handicap which now vitiates the United Nations and which doomed the League.

No mysterious, freakish realm is entered as we try to deal with world problems on a global scale. There the same kind of human beings operate and the same types of conflict threaten harmonious relations which we have learned to control or prevent elsewhere. In other areas of life we create and uphold political agencies with authority and power to determine what solutions shall be tried from among those suggested by the experts; we must establish and maintain in essentially the same way an international equivalent of our municipal, state, and national governments. *The world must be governed.*

—VERNON NASH

Most numerous now are adherents of the specialized-function approach to world problems. A host of issues, highly publicized in recent years, such as environmental pollution, control of multinational corporations, overpopulation, food scarcity, shortages and maldistribution of energy and other depletable resources, and exploitation of the seabed have led to growing clamor for separate world authorities to cope with these intractable subjects. The tendency of these single-problem specialists is to go their isolated ways. And while their pseudo-parliaments of experts perform the careful technical work of a government department preparing important legislation under a parliamentary system, their proposals must go to as many as one hundred thirty-eight governments and must wait months, years, or sometimes forever for ratifications. For enforcement they must rely on the various governments, whose performances may vary from good to bad to none at all. And like the United Nations itself, each of these specialized agencies or authorities must go hat in hand to beg its funding from the member governments. Another nagging problem with such dispersion is that the small, impoverished nations can ill afford the costly disparate representation in these numerous pseudo-parliaments and their growing bureaucracies. This method not only perpetuates the present showy, often wasteful, galaxy of specialized agencies but also has the effect of fragmenting the public pressure needed to attain any substantial transfer of governmental power to the United Nations. Advocates of increasing use of this approach may succeed in getting a little something—to be touted as a mighty triumph—but the overall situation will continue to deteriorate. This piecemeal granting of would-be authority over each separate world problem, commended as the easier approach, has proved a failure. Even a village would find it next to impossible to function if it had first to establish a separate administration over every local concern. Proponents of this method are advocating procedures at the world level they would never tolerate in their own locality.

Today's problems are too large and too pressing to be dealt with by the gradual development of the Charter through amendment and judicial interpretation, as in the case of the United States Constitution. World government—federal and democratic in its own structure—needs to be created fully mature and can profit by the long experience of existing federal practice. Fortunately it can also begin with assets never before available. For example, the vast research capacity of the United Nations and the array of scientific and technical specialists it is able to mobilize have already pin-pointed many of the problems, amassed the information, and indicated possible solutions. It is the power to act that now must be combined with all this knowledge.

—EDITH WYNNER

---

determined, enlightened, and united planetary management, the odds on civilized survival are not good.

Obligations in the Face of Disaster

What then is the obligation of the people and leaders of the nation that is still the single most powerful member of the United Nations?

Here is a nation that has just celebrated 200 years of *e pluribus unum.* Have we so little Latin that we have forgotten that our national motto means "out of many, one"?

What should it take to apply to the world the principles of "liberty and union, now and forever, one and inseparable"—principles that have worked so long, and on the whole so well, for us?

We cannot start by asking what other nations would agree to. The first thing to ask is what we of the USA would agree to. *We would not agree to a simple reproduction of today's US-type governmental institutions in the United Nations.* We would not agree even if other nations would accept the US system, which is highly questionable. The twentieth century has seen too much abuse of the one-man-leader principle for us to accept a world Executive as strong as our President. We ourselves have just had a close brush with an attempt by a President to destroy his political opposition and put himself above the law. Moreover, attempts to transfer our system to nations of different political experience, in Latin America, for instance, have not been notably successful.

The world as a whole would be more likely to accept the parliamentary system—a prime minister and other ministers rising out of the majority party in the legislative body—and so, it seems probable, would we. As to a world legislative body, we certainly would not agree to be bound by laws enacted by any body resembling the present unrealistic one-nation-one-vote General Assembly. We would require a body much more representative of population and, certainly at first, of economic contribution. We would require that its powers be strictly confined to matters of worldwide effect and concern. It follows then that

STRONG: Let us just look at the way man himself has developed. We've seen and talked about the Rift Valley. But as man has evolved over this approximately three million years that we know he's inhabited the earth, his loyalties have been gradually enlarged. His willingness to cooperate within larger and larger frameworks has been demonstrated by the fact that he has moved and his loyalties have moved from the family to the tribe to the village to the town to the city to the city-state and now to the nation-state. And each time—this hasn't been because he's suddenly been struck with a wave of idealism; it's because his growing self-interest has required it.

As man has advanced technologically and industrially, the interdependencies of man on man have grown. And if he's going to take advantage of the technological civilization, he's got to enlarge the circle within which he cooperates with other people.

Now, the interesting point here, that as man's loyalties have grown, up to the point of the nation-state, for example, he hasn't had to completely shed his loyalty to his family. You're loyal to your home town. You're loyal to your state. You're loyal to the United States of America. There's no real conflict between this hierarchy of loyalties.

But now we've got to take the ultimate leap, all of us. We've now got to give our loyalty, as well, to planet earth. And this doesn't mean that we give up our loyalty to all the other groupings to which we owe our loyalty. It simply means that we have to modify them. We have to make room for that new dimension of loyalty to planet earth.

MOYERS: Maurice, there is blood being shed in Northern Ireland right now, in the Middle East right now. There are conflict-creating tension and animosities all over the earth that fly in the face of that leap, because we don't see ourselves as citizens of planet earth. What gives you any hope that this fine statement of a goal that you've set forth has any practical possibilities of realization?

STRONG: It has the practical possibilities simply because it's the only guaranty of survival. We simply must make that leap. There is no alternative to making it, and man all through history has shown that when there is no alternative, he can rise above these petty jealousies.

You know, the changes in man's loyalties that I've described haven't come about easily. They haven't changed the basic nature of man. Man is still aggressive; he's competitive. But when his self-interest does force it, he is prepared to be cooperative.

Now, we may not make it. Perhaps our petty greeds, our petty loyalties, our narrowness of vision, they may possibly consume us. We may not make it. But we certainly won't make it unless we act on the basis that when the chips are down, we will have the guts, we will have the enlightenment, we will have the wisdom to do what is best and what is necessary for us.

—BILL MOYERS' JOURNAL

the representative unit should be world geographic regions, not nations. Each region should have at least two representatives, voting as individuals and elected at different times. Such a regional Assembly of Peoples might be added to the present General Assembly of Nations, thus producing the familiar institution of a two-house legislative body.

"International disputes" could not be brought into such a legislative body for politicized tugging and hauling. They would have to be submitted to the jurisdiction of a system of regional, appellate, and superior world courts. Final decisions would be enforceable on individuals, avoiding any attempt at enforcement on nations, just as courts inside nations enforce law on individuals and so never have to make war on cities, provinces, or states.

We would require a World Bill of Rights, guaranteeing all the freedoms we now have and protecting the agreed-upon reserved rights of individuals and of local and national governments from infringement by world institutions or their officers.

For some time, we would cautiously insist on maintaining a fairly high level of national armament. Meanwhile, there would be a *pooling* of some armament to make a modest stockpile for reinforcing world law and world court settlements. But as soon as the new world institutions had proved their ability to operate within their guidelines, our nation and others would naturally begin to cut down on the excesses of overkill that now absorb so much of our national income, disarming eventually to the level required to maintain domestic order.

This is certainly the only way, short of general catastrophe, in which disarmament can come about. People will not give up national power, which they trust (however mistakenly) to protect them, until they have come to trust a worldwide power that has proved it can and will protect them.

If such a thorough revision of the UN Charter is to be attained—and nothing much short of it is likely to be adequate to the crises ahead—what should the United States be doing now?

Recommended Actions

☐ The US should cease its opposition to Charter review in the Special Committee on the Charter and bring in a bold, constructive plan such as that outlined earlier. The Special Committee has had two sessions and accomplished nothing, waiting for leadership. The US representative should fill the vacuum at once with a plan that will command worldwide attention. No matter if it is denounced in many quarters. That is the beginning of action and the end of drift.

☐ The US should set an example of adequate funding for the UN Environment Programme, urging all other nations to do likewise and using its influence to keep UNEP funds from being diverted to purposes other than environmental preservation.

☐ Foreign aid (non-military) and international development loans (IDA) should be maintained at present levels to raise the standard of living of poor countries throughout the world and help finance environmental and population control programs.

☐ The "New Economic Order" should receive US cooperation as promised at the Special Session of the General Assembly in September 1975. It would be shortsighted to withhold cooperation because of the present atmosphere of hostility toward the Third World (and the UN itself) engendered by the ill-advised Zionism resolution. That resolution was counterproductive, and many of the nations that supported it may well change their position in the future.

☐ The United States should use all its influence to obtain a strong treaty and Law of the Sea. The world heritage of the oceans, their marine life, and the wealth of the deep sea bottoms should be protected for all mankind and for future generations. The US's unilateral extension to 200 miles of its national rights offshore is justified for the protection of its coastal waters and fish stocks, but the US should offer to bring its position into conformity with an adequate Law of the Sea treaty.

☐ The United States should support UN action following the World Food Conference, especially the new UN specialized agency designed to increase the production of food in poorer countries, provided that these programs use environmentally sound agricultural practices. This means less dependence on chemical fertilizers and mechanized agribusiness methods and more reliance on natural soil-enrichment and better tools and training for individual rural workers.

☐ The United States should support efforts throughout the world to control excess population. This nation should make zero population growth its own policy for at least the next few decades.

☐ Whatever the outcome of the Human Settlements Conference at Vancouver, the US should act to reverse the decay of its own cities and to halt excessive urban growth both here and abroad by improving the quality and opportunities of rural life. We should not accept as inevitable the fantastic evils of doubling the present world population, nor the internal migration trends that swamp the cities and destroy the countryside.

☐ The United States should support efforts to improve the status, education, health, and working conditions of women—in much of the world an under-privileged half of the human race. Through subsistence farming, women provide a large part of the labor for the world's food production, and everywhere their equipment, literacy, living standards, and right to family planning, self-determination, and respect should be brought into the modern age.

☐ Finally, the United States should shake off the indifference toward the UN shown by recent administrations. It is true that our former majority support has slipped away. But if we continue the spirit of economic cooperation shown in the Special Session of 1975, our influence will be swiftly restored. As President Kennedy said, "If we did not have the United Nations, we would have to invent it." But if we do not quickly reassume our former leadership, with some meaningful and far-reaching reforms, we will wake up some day to find that we do not have the United Nations. It will be late in the day then to invent it. Perhaps *too* late to save any of the things that have been most precious to us.

1. A global village such as ours cannot exist peacefully for very long if there are continually widening gaps between rich and poor nations and worsening maldistribution of access to and consumption of resources. The environmental problems of the globe can only be addressed in the context of greater equity and justice in sharing both benefits and costs of economic activity.

2. Foreign aid must be considered in the context of the balance of trade and payments. If the provisions of foreign aid do not *reduce the imbalance of payments between rich and poor* then, nothing has been accomplished, unless all that is desired is for the wealthy to be able to think that they are doing something for the less fortunate. Global environmental problems thus involve a consideration of the roles (especially with respect to influencing the policies of individual nations) of OECD, GATT, UNCTAD and the general economic and trade relations.

3. The analysis of problems and the development or adaption of solutions to those problems must be *site and cultural specific*. Too often developing countries try to use technical, economic or political solutions for problems analysed for other climates or cultures or the analysis is done for them by experts from different climates and cultures. If solutions are not especially designed to fit the climatological and physical realities and the cultural conditions (from literacy levels and economic situation to cultural patterns of behaviour) then those "solutions" generally become problems.

4. Foreign aid, especially "tied" aid, and trade can introduce "technological momentum" which can irreversibly start nations on the road to energy and capital expensive systems. Part of the site and culture specific analysis of problems should include PROC: product, resource, operating costs. That is, the "lifetime costing" in the broad sense must be carried out, including not only initial costs and obvious operating costs such as energy and replacement parts, but also costs such as requirements for space, travel, technical expertise, water, etc.

5. The current policies governing immigration to overdeveloped countries are currently established on a basis that robs developing countries of the highly trained human resources they need most urgently. In addition, most developed countries have a balance of "people" surplus with developing countries because of the personal wealth, education and skills immigrants bring with them. Foreign aid in the form of dollars or goods cannot compensate for the loss of human resources. Nor can the loss of those human resources be compensated by volunteer programmes.

6. There are at least two sets of problems: a) those of *overdevelopment*: the excessive consumption of resources and production of wastes which require technological and social solutions to existing overdevelopment problems and b) those of *underdevelopment* which, with respect to environmental concerns, involve avoiding problems which do not yet exist. Avoiding the first set of problems in the first place is quite distinct from the solving of those problems. The development or maintenance of political/economic systems which do not produce environmental problems due to the use of technology would be preferred to acceptance of political/economic systems which have a technological imperative requiring that further technological development (of pollution control technology) is necessary. This is economically, energetically and environmentally the expensive way to proceed.

7. Within the USA, not only is it necessary that the population growth rate be controlled but the consumption of energy and resources must also be reduced if the impact of that population is to be reduced. Preoccupation with population size without adequate consideration of the rates of resources and energy consumption (and production of wastes) will only convince the developing world of the shallowness of the USA's concerns about global problems.

8. It should be emphasized that there are now enough physical, economic and electronic links between nations that isolation as a solution to environmental problems is almost impossible. Pesticides and persistant organics (e.g. PCBs) do not respect borders. Overdeveloped countries must have access to resources of developing countries even if they do respect the need for increased prices and conservation (recycling). Increased travel makes health a global issue for diseases spread rapidly. The electronic links transmit more subtle problems of values, expectations and wants (as opposed to needs). Global impacts such as those possible from increasing CO_2 concentrations, or levels of atmospheric particulates from industry and agriculture, aerosols (especially fluorocarbon propellants) and from the operation of SSTs make isolation an unreasonable solution to environmental problems. Migration of fish and wildlife is another critical link.

Opening of the United Nations Environmental Programme's Governing Council, Geneva, 1973. U.N. photo.

9. Either conservation and environmental protection are accepted consciously and practiced conscientiously, especially by the overdeveloped world, or outside forces (nature or OPEC) will force those changes.

10. Tourism is both a blessing and a curse to developing countries. Tourist dollars bring raising expectations and environmental problems. Opportunities to sell locally made goods can only be developed if heavy expenditures are made for foreign goods necessary to attract and hold foreign tourists (plumbing and cooking facilities, transportation systems and the energy to run them, etc. etc. etc.).

11. The people of the "Fourth World" must be given much more consideration, especially in the "new world" OECD countries (Canada, USA, Australia, NZ) especially as a model for developing nations as far as their indigenous peoples are concerned and as a way to develop some of the necessary sensitivity to resource and environment management and the relation with other cultures.

12. To date the developed countries (or more correctly the developed portions of countries) have gone through a series of resource base changes since the opening of the new world and the industrial revolution. The resource base changes have forced changes on society: change in fur populations in Canada and the fur trade, the exhaustion of nonrenewable resources, both fossil fuels and mineral ores, change in agricultural lands, etc. In all cases, solutions to the resource base changes were sought in someone else's back yard. New supplies of minerals, energy, water, food, agricultural land, furs, etc. were found and exploited. It is no longer possible to follow the "frontier" ethic of despoiling what appears to be there to be wasted because there will always be a new source to be discovered and exploited. *It is now essential that overdeveloped nations in particular seek the solutions to their problems where those problems exist,* not in someone else's back yard. Therefore, conservation and maximum utilization of an area's resources and potential resources would be the first approach to a problem of scarcity rather than the current approach of looking for someone else's resources to exploit first before thinking of any changes in lifestyle, etc.

13. There are a number of technologies which are environmentally superior to current systems. One example of such a system might be the use of ozone for disinfection of water supplies and/or sewage rather than chlorine. It is a superior disinfectant, it produces oxidized rather than chlorinated compounds and so has essentially no longer term adverse environmental effects (this use of ozone does *not* cause air pollution problems). It increases the DO levels of treated effluents; although it requires technology and electricity, it is generated on-site rather than involving the transportation of expensive chemicals. Ozone could be a very strong factor in reducing some of the human settlements problems due to lack of clean water supplies. Combined with the use of methane generators (which produce fuel and preserve most nutrients for fertilizer) ozone disinfection would be particularly effective. —MAURICE F. STRONG

Surely war is civilization's greatest failure.

—LAWRENCE ABBOTT

War and Defense

War is the ultimate destroyer. Preparations for war are economically ruinous and tend not to prevent wars but to cause them. In a condition of international anarchy, war is not merely possible but inevitable. The cure for anarchy at the world level is government at the world level. A world government will be federal in form because only a federation can create unity out of diversity, preserve local autonomy, and govern enormous geographical areas effectively. A world federation can not only abolish war and preparations for war, but can also make easier the solution of other global problems such as overpopulation, the exploitation of oceanic environments, and control of the atom. The elimination of war is an environmental as well as a moral imperative.

Photo by David Douglas Duncan, from War Without Heros
(Harper & Row), by permission of the photographer.

War

War is systematic mass murder, the ugliest manifestation of man's inhumanity to man. Elementary morality demands of us that we work tirelessly to abolish it. And morality aside, war cannot be defended on practical grounds. There can be no victor in World War III; there can only be losers.

Our full military strength cannot be used against another nuclear power without inviting Armageddon. We cannot even use nuclear weapons against a weak non-nuclear power, for small countries have big friends. In the kind of war we still dare to wage, the United States was fought to a standstill by a sixth-rate military power.

We are asked to believe that a burdensome military establishment—which cannot be rationally used in large wars and cannot be effectively used in small ones—is needed to deter Russia. But Russia knows we cannot use our nuclear deterrent unless we are prepared to see tens of millions of Americans killed in the ensuing holocaust.

Such a deterrent is not credible and does not deter. Russia was not deterred in the Baltic, at Berlin, in Czechoslovakia, or in Hungary. Nor did Russia's nuclear deterrent dissuade Eisenhower from sending the Marines into Lebanon, Johnson from escalating the war against North Vietnam, or Nixon from conspiring to overthrow by force a duly elected Marxist president of Chile.

It may be argued that the US nuclear deterrent is not expected to restrain Russia in other parts of the world, but simply to forestall a nuclear attack against the United States itself. This is illogical, for a Soviet leader mad enough to contemplate killing 100 million or so Americans would be mad enough to do it regardless of threatened retaliation. The same must be said of any American mad enough to think of killing 100 million Russians. Deterrents, so-called, do not deter; they merely prolong a precarious balance of terror. Meanwhile, they cost everyone more than anyone can afford.

Politicians who claim that our ponderous military machine is morally or pragmatically justifiable are wrong precisely where it is most necessary to be right.

Preparedness: a Cruel Illusion

Wars would be infrequent indeed if nations were unprepared for them. Preparedness does not diminish, but rather increases, the likelihood and frequency and severity of war. In theory, all nations might voluntarily agree to enhance their true security by disarming. In practice, however, unanimous agreement to disarm is unimaginable and less-than-unanimous agreement will not suffice.

While war remains possible, preparedness seems essential; and while nations prepare for war, war remains inevitable. If ever there was a vicious circle, this is it.

The circle can only be broken by making warfare impossible, so that preparations for war clearly become superfluous. People everywhere would rejoice in dismantling their military machines if they knew they safely could. The key point, then, is whether war can be made impossible, and if so, how?

War *can* be made virtually impossible, obviating the need for military preparedness. Before we enlarge on that, though, there is more to be said about war, preparedness, and their effects on the environment.

The burden of preparedness is immense; were it not perceived as essential to national survival, we would not tolerate it for a moment. President Ford sought 100 billion dollars in fiscal 1977 for the defense establishment, which was more than one-quarter of the total budget.

If preparedness is expensive, war itself is vastly more so. It was President Johnson's attempt to produce both guns and butter without raising taxes—his fight now, pay later policy—that touched off double-digit inflation. Even in a well-managed economy, war and preparedness for war are inherently inflationary; they enlarge consumer purchasing power without producing anything that consumers can buy. The war machine also competes with the civilian economy for raw materials, skilled workers, managerial talent, and capital, thus reinforcing inflationary trends.

A war economy is an economy perennially whipsawed by inflation.

Military hardware is a prodigious consumer of scarce metals and other fast-vanishing resources indispensable to an industrial society. Together with rampant consumerism in wealthy nations, military procurement is a major cause of resource shortages that are reaching crisis proportions.

Even in peacetime, military establishments are ravenous consumers of energy. And wartime energy consumption by military machines beggars the imagination.

Damage to the environment was an incidental byproduct of war in the past, and relatively trivial. But modern warfare is the one activity of man that has *as its primary objective* the deliberate degradation of the environment. The United States warred against the environment in Vietnam, defoliating forests that might hide the enemy and destroying crops and croplands that might feed him. Future wars, if we allow them to happen, will be even more

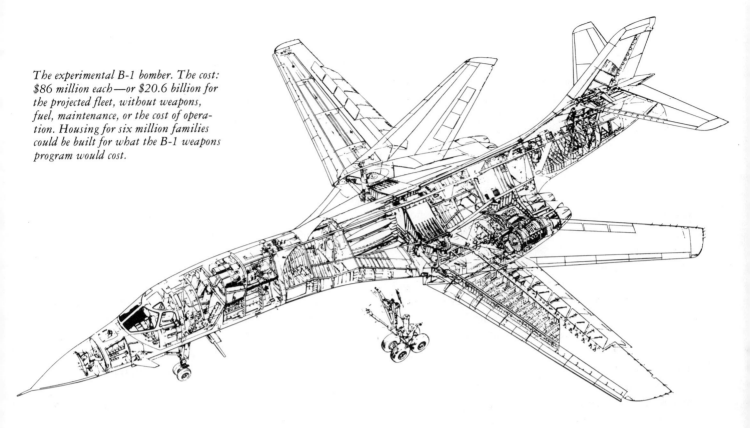

The experimental B-1 bomber. The cost: $86 million each—or $20.6 billion for the projected fleet, without weapons, fuel, maintenance, or the cost of operation. Housing for six million families could be built for what the B-1 weapons program would cost.

ecocidal. Chemical and biological weapons are designed to destroy life-support systems—to poison water supplies, for example. All-out nuclear war might pollute the entire planet with levels of radioactivity that no form of life can endure. Humanity's suicide would be one part of a vaster tragedy. Evolution's promising experiments with terrestrial life would all be snuffed out, dead by our hand.

Anarchy and War
Or Government and Peace?

Every cause of war *between* nations also exists *within* nations. Yet war within nations is rare while war between nations is commonplace. The difference is this: anarchy has been superseded by government *within* nations, but *among* nations, anarchy still reigns supreme.

The need for world government is precisely the same in principle as the need for local, state, and national governments. Until anarchy is superseded by government at the world level, war among nations will remain an ever-present menace.

We have in the United Nations a league or confederation, not a government. The distinction is all-important. The constituent parts of a government are its citizens, and law can normally be non-violently enforced because lawbreakers are individuals or small groups. But a league's

constituent parts are its member states, and when a league's decision is flouted, enforcement necessarily involves coercing a nation-state. There is no non-violent way to do that.

A league is an attempt to square the circle—to keep peace among member states without impinging upon their absolute sovereignty. Since sovereignty is the recognition of no authority higher than one's own, and since national sovereignty's ultimate expression is the asserted right to wage war, every league contains the seeds of its own dissolution. The United Nations does much good where voluntary coöperation is obtainable, but as a keeper of the peace, it is merely the latest in a long line of futile confederations that were designed not to work.

We can have absolute national sovereignty without world peace. Or we can have world peace without absolute national sovereignty. We cannot have both; the two are fundamentally irreconcilable. If peace is our sincere desire, we cannot rationally defend the "sovereign equality of nations."

Sovereign equality is, in any case, a transparent fiction. What real equality is there between Chile and China, Iceland and India, or Romania and Russia? What reality does national sovereignty possess in a world where history's mightiest military power cannot assure the safety of its citizens or its own survival? Any loss of national

Every gun that is made, every warship launched, every rocket fired signifies, in the final sense, a theft from those who hunger and are not fed, those who are cold and are not clothed. This world in arms is not spending money alone. It is spending the sweat of its laborers, the genius of its scientists, the hopes of its children.

—PRESIDENT DWIGHT EISENHOWER

sovereignty required by the creation of a world government will be the loss of a dangerous illusion. Which is a gain.

Sovereignty is *divisible.* Nations can be supreme in some respects and not in others. And sovereignty is *transferable.* Sovereignty over matters of importance to everyone alive can be transferred to a world federation without compromising national sovereignty in matters of strictly national concern.

The divisibility and transferability of sovereignty was a discovery of America's Founding Fathers. Under the Constitution, not yet 200 years old, the first federal union was based upon the sharing of sovereignty by the nation, the state and local governments, and their citizens. Americans, of all people, should find world government easy to accept. For a world government is certain to be a federation—an adaptation to the world's needs of the federal principle invented by our Founding Fathers and first applied here in 1789.

The alternative to world federation is endless war and ceaseless preparations for war. World federation alone can eradicate these evils.

The Path to Peace

Establishing a world federation will not be easy. Indeed, we can make it impossible by failing to try hard enough or soon enough. But there is nothing intrinsically impossible about it if we take reasonable steps one at a time. Here are some of the steps that can lead to a federation of the world.

* The President in particular and opinion-makers in general should use all techniques of education and persuasion to obtain support for world federation by a solid majority of the American people.
* By presidential proclamation, world federation by (or before) 1989, the bicentennial of George Washington's inauguration under the US Constitution, should be made a national goal.
* Intensive, unremitting diplomacy—at home, in the United Nations, and abroad—should aim at winning ac-

ceptance of the principle of world federation and winning agreement to sponsor a world constitutional convention.
* Paralleling diplomatic activity, citizens groups should obtain as many signatures as possible on a petition from the *people* of the United States to the *people* of all other countries urging them to join with us in forming a world republic.
* US delegates to a world constitutional convention should be chosen before the convention is called, giving them time to prepare.
* Before the convention assembles, delegates should intensively study governmental institutions and political philosophies, past and present. Although the US precedent is likely to be more closely followed than any other, a world federation will not be a carbon copy of anything. Its founders must be prepared to innovate.
* Nations that have agreed to sponsor a constitutional convention should convoke it as soon as it becomes clear that a majority of the nations of the world, representing a majority of the world's people, will attend.
* The constitutional convention should be open-ended, adjourning only when it has a draft constitution to propose.

Authors of a draft constitution will be anxious not to offend any major powers. They will surely do their best to make the constitution acceptable to the United States. It will not be a perfect instrument, but like the US Constitution, it will be perfectable by amendment.

And like the US Constitution before it, which took effect when nine of the original 13 states ratified it, a world constitution will doubtless provide for less-than-universal participation at the outset, if necessary. Ratification procedures are certain to be designed in such a way, however, that a federation will not be inaugurated unless it incorporates most of the people and most of the nations of the world. Even from the beginning, the federation will be more powerful than any nation or combination of nations that choose to stay outside. Conscious of its power, the federation can afford to woo self-excluded nations with friendliness and generosity, untainted by anxiety.

Today mankind does not ask the right questions to survive as a species. The right questions are not concerning new technologies. Men have already proved they can work in groups to solve any technological problem. But men have not demonstrated a capability to organize the people of the planet to take the necessary steps to insure survival.

Once we ask the right questions there is no reason why we can't find the right answers.

In the past, defensive wars have been the only means to bring men together to work for a common survival. Today the problem is not to make people non-aggressive, for then they would do nothing. The problem is to activate people to work for the survival of mankind as a species. And in accepting such world-orientation there is no real conflict between patriotism and internationalism. Pollution cannot

be tackled alone from either a provincial or a national standpoint. The atmosphere and the ocean envelope the whole earth. The environmental crisis may thus provide a rallying point since it makes the difference between national and international attitudes unimportant.

Even though everyone cannot have a large family, all people, young and old, must be continually exposed to children to see and experience the promise of future generations. Start with the family and learn to love that. Then extend this love to local community, language, religion, country. If all individuals do this worldwide, they will also learn to love the whole human family so much as to be willing to die so that it may survive.

—MARGARET MEAD

The U.N.'s provisions for enforcement (as we continue to stress) are an attempt to apply the vigilante-band system on the world level. To expect "posses" of national contingents to be assembled *ad hoc* after each outrage overlooks an essential factor. Whenever armed cowboys of a ranchers' association joined to run down a gang of cattle rustlers, they knew that the outlaws sought by them were merely a small number of men with light arms. The U.N. Charter requires a willingness to go to war; great masses of men with weapons of incredible destructiveness must hurl themselves against other masses of men who are similarly armed. The difference in degree is sufficient to become a difference in kind.

The whole war system must be eliminated before na-

tions can be greatly improved internally. It is not enough to be able to win total wars; the attempt to keep prepared to do so can ruin us, even if we should be fortunate enough to avoid actual conflict.

It is plain beyond a doubt that a league or confederation (any loose association of fully sovereign states) simply cannot prevent war. In consequence a swift contempt develops for leagues, or—what is even worse—the public becomes entirely indifferent to them. Since no one can be led to trust such a system, each nation insists on keeping the power to defend itself. This very armed might in turn sabotages the league. There is little, if any, hope of avoiding war under the U.N. as presently constituted.

—VERNON NASH

A balance of power is inherently unstable. The kind of imbalance represented by a world federation versus a relatively few hold-out nations is far more stable than a precarious balance that all parties are laboring to imbalance. Still, an incomplete federation should not rest until it is whole. Only when there is no external threat to any government can all governments buckle down to their real missions: to do, as Lincoln said, what people cannot do at all or cannot do as well for themselves.

An Agenda for Immediate Action

What can be done *immediately*? Assuming a President and a political party sincerely committed to ending war and preparations for war, these things can be done at once:

* The President, speaking before both houses of Congress with worldwide TV and radio coverage, can dedicate

himself and his administration to world peace through world federation.
* Congressional leaders can introduce a join resolution of House and Senate declaring that world federation is our national goal.
* The President and Congress coöperatively can establish a commission of constitutional scholars and others to study governmental institutions and political philosophies, past, present, and theoretically possible. The commission's work will help US delegates prepare for a world constitutional convention.
* The President, with the concurrence of Congress, can announce a 5 percent per year *reduction* in the US "preparedness" budget. This can be done with great economic and social benefit, and the risk will be slight so long as we retain overkill capacity. You cannot kill people more than once, and piling overkill on top of overkill is expensively insane.

Statesmen cry "peace, peace," but there is no peace because they will not accept the slightest restraint on their ability to roam and fend at will in the world or to do anything they conceive to be in their own national interest, even though what they are doing may be contrary to every known canon of justice and decency.

If these hopes [that the collective wisdom of humankind will find an effective outlet in the United Nations] are to materialize, the General Assembly's duties and authority will have to be codified. Here, we are confronted with a structural problem. However egalitarian the one-nation, one-vote method of representation may seem in theory, what happens in practice is that the General Assembly is the victim of its disproportions. There is nothing democratic about a structure that enables, say, three nations with a combined population of three million to have three times the voting strength of a nation with a population of 200 million.

These disparities have kept the General Assembly from becoming the source of world law and, indeed, have converted that body into an arena for magnifying the world's troubles.

The UN today places its emphasis, not on principles of peace and justice among nations, but on the ability of nations to retain absolute, unfettered sovereignty and complete freedom of action in the world arena. Thus, the UN is blocked from becoming greater than the sum of its parts. It is an extension of the international anarchy it was ostensibly designed to replace.

We will best strengthen our position in the UN and in the world when we become fully committed to the regeneration and full development of the UN as a functioning mechanism of world law.

The United Nations cannot survive as a cockpit in which to choose up sides or to trade insults and abuse. It must be vested with objective standards for establishing justice in the relations among nations. Most important of all, it must represent peoples, not just governments.

—NORMAN COUSINS

Our billions of dollars per year saved out of military budgets can be allocated to peace efforts, to foreign aid aimed at making nations self-sufficient in food, and to American citizens whose income is below the poverty level. If we divert money from the arms race to such unchallengeably humane programs, the United States will recapture the moral leadership it has frittered away since World War II.

Disarmament will not come suddenly enough to take defense contractors by surprise. They will have ample opportunity to phase their companies out of war production and into civilian markets bit by bit, over a period of years. If dislocations nevertheless occur, the affected companies and their employees must be helped. The companies can be given preferential tax treatment, for example, and preference in the award of government contracts during a transition period. The various programs to assist the unemployed will be available to displaced war workers, and special programs should not be necessary. The gradual transition from a wartime to a peacetime economy ought to be at least as manageable as the transition following the sudden end of World War II. An end to armaments will be an unmixed blessing.

A New World Without Foreigners

A world from which war, fear of war, and preparations for war have been eliminated will be an altogether new world, totally outside our experience and hard to imagine. Some of the greatest changes will be psychological. When all four billion human inhabitants of the planet feel confident that they will not die in war and that their loved ones won't either, an incalculable weight will be lifted off humanity's heart.

Military adventurism will be a thing of the past. We can rest assured that our governments will not involve us in entanglements we need be ashamed of. A sense of guilt will gradually dissolve as our last foreign excursions fade into history. Love of country can flower into authentic, non-jingoistic patriotism.

There will be no foreigners in a world federation. The basis for xenophobia will be removed. We will live in an opener world where travel and communication are freer. International friendships will multiply, and feelings of separatism will fade. The ancient dream of universal brother- and sisterhood will begin to take on reality.

Today, autocratic governments maintain themselves by pretending to be their nations' only bulwark against external threats, real or imaginary. A world federation will eliminate real threats and reveal imaginary ones for what they are. Even if a world federation is not empowered to push autocratically-governed countries closer to democracy, autocracies will wither on the vine.

The growing gap between rich and poor nations is an

An American tank, left from the battle for Peleliu Island (September 1944), one of the most Hellish, insane, and unnecessary of World War II. Booby traps set during the battle remain defending jungle caves, 30 years after the defenders died and the winners passed on. Photo by Robert Wenkam, from Micronesia: Island Wilderness *(Friends of the Earth).*

explosive issue, and it is hard to see how it can be resolved without resort to war in our present anarchic world. The gap will not magically disappear within a world federation. But if the federation and the nations comprising it dedicate themselves to narrowing the gap, the poorer nations will probably be content to seek gradual, non-violent solutions.

Many of the benefits of federation are economic. The most obvious of these is the reduction to near nothing of worldwide expenditures for preparedness, which now amount to 300 billion dollars per year (of which US citizens are saddled with one-third). With a monopoly of military force, the world federation will need very little of it. So nearly the entire 300 billion dollars can be diverted to humane purposes.

Military expenditures, as previously noted, are inherently inflationary. Diversion of 300 billion dollars per year into other economic channels will help curb the inflation that is now pandemic.

Even if a world federation is not given direct authority over international economic matters, it will provide a relatively non-competitive atmosphere in which monetary reforms and other economic activity can be more rationally pursued. Problems involving multinational corporations will be more easily solved.

World federation will produce many environmental benefits. It will end the deliberate destruction of ecosystems not only in war, but also in weapons tests, training maneuvers, and the like—an improvement hard to overstate. World federation will also moderate the resource drain and pollution problems.

Pollutants do not respect boundaries, and many forms of pollution cannot be attacked effectively on a nation-by-

So long as peace rests merely upon the continued willingness of potential war makers to behave themselves, the world has made no progress toward lasting peace. Anarchy is still the chief attribute of our international relations.

—VERNON NASH

nation basis. A world federation can attack pollution problems more systematically, and will be the logical instrument to control the exploitation and pollution of the oceans, our common heritage.

Overpopulation is an intractable environmental problem in a world of sovereign nations who suspect that population control is a plot to weaken them in relation to potential enemies. Nations within a world federation will soon learn that they have nothing to fear from one another, and overpopulation is one of many problems that can be approached with far greater expectation of success in a less nationalistic, less competitive atmosphere.

At some point, overpopulation tends to be self-limiting through increased death rates. The self-limiting process would be ghastly, but life would go on. Another environmental threat, on the other hand, might turn Earth into a dead planet. Control of the atom might be easier within the political framework of a world federation. Getting the nuclear genie back into its bottle may come to be seen as the most compelling of all reasons for the establishment of a federation of the world.

World federation is not a panacea. Serious problems will persist. But the changes world federation makes, or makes possible, will be wholly salutary.

Historical Footnote

A world federalist movement flourished in the United States (and throughout the western world) during the 1940s. Why did it wither? And what reason is there to suppose it can be revived?

Ironically, the federalist movement split into factions. "Minimalists" believed federalists should advocate a world organization with powers limited to the enforcement of disarmament and the suppression of violence; they favored high-level lobbying in Washington. "Maximalists" believed a world federation should be empowered to promote justice as well as suppress violence, and that it would need legislative, executive, and judicial powers comparable to those of governments at other levels; they felt that grassroots support was a necessary precondition of effective lobbying.

Minimalists triumphed in a struggle for control of United World Federalists, in part at least because most "big names" in the movement were minimalists. It was a costly victory; most rank-and-file members evidently leaned toward the maximalist position, for UWF membership promptly plummeted. The organization never regained its lost momentum. Its continued existence, however, impeded the formation of a more dynamic federalist movement.

At about the time UWF eviscerated itself, other events created a climate unfavorable to federalism. Notable among them were the cold war, McCarthyism, Russia's ending of the US atomic monopoly, the Korean War, and the start-up of the United Nations (which, despite the manifest inadequacy of its peace-keeping machinery, siphoned off support from world federation). Even a strong and unified federalist movement would have had trouble holding its own.

There is no guarantee that the federalist movement can be revitalized, but there are grounds for hope. The frailty of the UN's peace-keeping apparatus has been amply demonstrated for a quarter-century. The cold war has thawed considerably. The burden of armaments grows ever more intolerable, and the arms race grows ever more dangerous. The flimsy facade of "credibility" has been stripped away, and must be replaced by something better. Above all, an anarchic world of competing national sovereignties is obviously ill-equipped to control the atom, and failure to control the atom could spell the end of life on earth. The longer federation is delayed, the more urgently it will be needed.

At its peak, the federalist movement won endorsements from hundreds of Members of Congress and hundreds of statesmen abroad. But federation was never unequivocally advocated by a US President. With presidential leadership, support for world federation would swiftly surpass in breadth and depth the promising movement of the forties.

We have ended general lawlessness in human relationships except at the international level. This failure is the one *fundamental* explanation for the frequent recurrence of war. Every other element listed among the major causes of war exists in each community—factors such as greed, prejudice, and ruthless will for power. Yet mob riots which get beyond the control of municipal police are rare, and civil wars within most countries are even more infrequent. Why should wars among nations be a normal, recurring pattern whereas civil wars are exceptional? Lack of enforceable world law is the answer.

What is more paradoxical than a league—designed to keep the peace—which, by its design, can do so only by making war? The ends of the United Nations would be defeated by the only means it can employ to secure these ends. Economic sanctions also punish innocent and guilty alike. The Charter as it stands is unworkable and immoral.

However much civilized countries may wish to expend their energies and wealth on constructive ends rather than on armaments, they feel compelled by world conditions (over which they have no control) to build bombs rather than bridges, jet fighters instead of tractors, and so on. The strongest nations can maintain their relatively greater measure of sovereignty only by ruinous expenditures of blood and treasure. In heaven's name, what kind of freedom is that for sensible men?

If a world government is given sole authority and responsibility for maintaining the peace of the world, and if nations are permitted to retain only such small forces with light arms as are judged by the world authority to be required for the maintenance of internal order within each country, then the military forces of a world government can likewise be reduced to comparably small numbers as soon as all nations have joined. A nuclear world union will doubtless maintain whatever forces may seem to be required by the strength of the countries which chose to remain outside. Once universality has been reached, the military establishment of the world union need only be large enough to provide adequate insurance against possible rebellion. The use of strictly civilian policing methods, backed by mobilizations of militia as needed, can stop preparedness for revolutions or for international war before they reach unmanageable proportions.

A careful study of human history reveals that the assumption that war is inherent in human nature—and therefore eternal—is shallow and faulty, that it is only a superficial impression. Far from being inexplicable or inevitable, we can invariably determine the situations that predispose to war, and the conditions which lead to war.

The real cause of all wars has always been the same. They have occurred with the mathematical regularity of a natural law at clearly determined moments as the result of clearly definable conditions.

If we try to detect the mechanism visibly in operation, the single cause ever-present at the outbreak of each and every conflict known to human history, if we attempt to reduce the seemingly innumerable causes of war to a common denominator, two clear and unmistakable observations emerge:

1. Wars between groups of men forming social units always take place when these units—tribes, dynasties, churches, cities, nations—exercise unrestricted sovereign power.
2. Wars between these social units cease the moment sovereign power is transferred from them to a larger or higher unit.

From these observations we can deduce a social law with the characteristics of an axiom that applies to and explains each and every war in the history of all time.

War takes place whenever and wherever non-integrated social units of equal sovereignty come into contact.

War between given social units of equal sovereignty is the permanent symptom of each successive phase of civilization. Wars always ceased when a higher unit established its own sovereignty, absorbing the sovereignties of the conflicting smaller social groups. After such transfers of sovereignty, a period of peace followed, which lasted only until the new social units came into contact. Then a new series of wars began.

Just as there is one and only one cause for wars between men on this earth, so history shows that peace—not peace in an absolute and utopian sense, but concrete peace between given social groups warring with each other at given times—has always been established in one way and only in one way.

Peace between fighting groups of men was never possible and wars succeeded one another until some sovereignty, some sovereign source of law, some sovereign power was set up *over* and *above* the clashing social units, integrating the warring units into a higher sovereignty.

Once the mechanics and the fundamental causes of wars—of all wars—are realized, the futility and childishness of the passionate debates about armament and disarmament must be apparent to all.

If human society were organized so that relations between groups and units in contact were regulated by democratically controlled law and legal institutions, then modern science could go ahead, devise and produce the most devastating weapons, and there would be no war. But if we allow sovereign rights to reside in the separate units and groups without regulating their relations by law, then we can prohibit every weapon, even a penknife, and people will beat out each other's brains with clubs.

War is the result of contact between nonintegrated sovereign units, whether such units be families, tribes, villages, estates, cities, provinces, dynasties, religions, classes, nations, regions or continents.

We also know that today, the conflict is between the scattered units of nation-states. During the past hundred years, all major wars have been waged between nations. This division among men is the only condition which, in our age, can create—and undoubtedly will create—other wars.

The task therefore is to prevent wars between the nations—international wars.

Logical thinking and historical empiricism agree that there *is* a way to solve this problem and prevent wars between the nations once and for all. But with equal clarity they also reveal that there is *one* way and one way alone to achieve this end: The integration of the scattered conflicting national sovereignties into one unified, higher sovereignty, capable of creating a legal order within which all peoples may enjoy equal security, equal obligations and equal rights under law.

The significant thing about the present crisis is that the nation-states, even the most powerful, even the United States of America, Great Britain and the Soviet Union, are no longer strong enough, no longer powerful enough to fulfill the purpose for which they were created.

They cannot prevent disasters like the first and second world wars. They cannot protect their peoples against the devastation of international war.

However sincerely the American, British and Russian governments sought to keep out of the war, they were forced into it in spite of themselves. Millions of their citizens have died, hundreds of billions of dollars of their national wealth have been wasted, for sheer survival. They had to fight for their lives.

If the sovereignty of the United States of America, the sovereignty of Great Britain and the sovereignty of the Soviet Union do not suffice to protect their citizens, then we need not even talk about the fiction of sovereignty in Latvia, Luxembourg or Rumania.

Democratic sovereignty of the people can be correctly expressed and effectively instituted only if local affairs are handled by local government, national affairs by national government, and international, world affairs, by international, world government.

Only if the people, in whom rests all sovereign power, delegate parts of their sovereignty to institutions created for and capable of dealing with specific problems, can we say that we have a democratic form of government. Only through such separation of sovereignties, through the organization of independent institutions, deriving their authority from the sovereignty of the community, can we have a social order in which men may live in peace with each other, endowed with equal rights and equal obligations before law. Only in a world order based on such separation of sovereignties can individual freedom be real.

Poles and Russians, Hungarians and Rumanians, Serbs and Bulgars, have disliked and distrusted each other and have been waging wars in Europe against each other for centuries. But these very same Poles and Russians, Hungarians and Rumanians, Serbs and Bulgars, once having left their countries and settled in the United States of America, cease fighting and are perfectly capable of living and working side by side without waging wars against each other.

Why is this?

The biological, racial, religious, historic, temperamental and character differences between them remain exactly the same.

The change in one factor alone produced the miracle.

In Europe, sovereign power is vested in these nationalities and in their nation-states. In the United States of America, sovereign power resides, not in any one of these nationalities, but stands above them in the Union, under which individuals, irrespective of existing differences between them, are equal before the law.

It seems, therefore, crystal-clear that friction, conflicts and wars between people are caused, not by their national, racial, religious, social and cultural differences, but by the *single fact* that these differences are galvanized in separate sovereignties which have no way to settle the conflicts resulting from their differences except through violent clashes.

Just as peace, freedom and equality of the citizens of a nation require within their state specific institutions and authorities separate from and standing above municipal or local authorities, and the direct delegation of sovereign power by the people to these higher, national, government authorities—so peace, freedom and equality of men on this earth, between the nation-states, require specific institutions, authorities separate from and standing above national authorities, as well as the direct delegation of sovereign power by the people to these higher world government authorities, to deal with those problems of human relations that reach beyond the national state structure.

—EMERY REVES

Recommended Actions

☐ The President should dedicate himself and his administration to world federation.

☐ The House and Senate should declare that world federation is a national goal.

☐ The administration should establish a commission of constitutional scholars to analyze governmental institutions that might be applicable to a world federation.

☐ The President, Congress concurring, should announce a unilateral 5 percent per year reduction in military expenditures to prove good faith and capture the imagination of the world.

☐ Opinion-makers from the President down should educate and persuade until a majority of Americans clearly favors world federation.

☐ All diplomatic channels should be used to foster support of world federation in other countries.

☐ A petition bearing as many signatures as possible should invite the people of other countries to join the people of the United States in creating a world republic.

☐ US delegates to a world constitutional convention should be chosen ahead of time so they can prepare carefully for their assignment.

☐ As soon as it becomes clear that a world constitutional convention will be well enough attended, sponsoring nations should announce the time and place of the convention.

☐ The world constitutional convention should remain in session until it has a draft constitution to propose.

☐ The proposed constitution should be ratified or rejected on its merits.

☐ If the proposed constitution is not adopted, a new constitutional convention should be called.

☐ If a federation begins with less-than-universal membership, the United States should urge non-member nations to join the rest of humanity in a true federation of all the world.

Readings in Environmental Law

The law makes possible environmental victories that could not be won through political action, mobilization of public opinion, or any other means. An outstanding example is the Alaska pipeline case. In the context of the energy crisis, environmentalists' attempts to block construction of the pipeline were popular neither with politicians nor the public. Nevertheless, because the law was on their side, environmentalists won in court. That Congress cynically passed a law permitting pipeline construction to proceed anyway doesn't alter the fact that the law is a supremely important tool for environmental protection. Most other chapters in this book argue that there ought to be laws about this and that, so a parallel chapter on environmental law would tend to be highly duplicative. Instead, we offer here a number of writings on various facets of environmental law.

The Future of Environmental Law

In the last five or six years we have witnessed the creation of a vast body of environmental law. During this brief and exciting era we have seen many environmental laws passed at the federal, state, and municipal levels. Judicial environmental precedents have been cascading down from the bench in a torrent. So many environmental rules and regulations have been issued by the various agencies that lawyers have been unable to keep up with them. Vast bureaucracies have been created to administer these new environmental laws. Millions, yea billions, of dollars have been spent on the newly enacted schemes.

The structure of law that has been created in the last half decade is indeed impressive, from the National Environmental Policy Act and the Clean Air Act right down to the actions of small towns like Petaluma, California. The question we must now ask ourselves upon assessing the future of this great body of law is whether it is adequate to deal with identified environmental problems.

A question like this cannot be answered with certainty. One can only guess. Standing here today, however, I would guess that we are closer to the beginning than we are to the end of the creation era of environmental law. I believe the creation of major new environmental laws will continue for at least another decade or two before we will be able to say that we have created a body of law adequate to deal with environmental problems.

I say this because I believe the law created so far does not in fact deal adequately with several fundamental problems. I contend that we have not yet come to grips through the law with certain problems of overwhelming importance. These problems are of such a magnitude that formulating adequate legal responses to them will be a long trial and error process.

1) *Ambient Problem.* The first environmental problem which I bring to your attention, and with which I contend that environmental law has not dealt adequately, is what I will call the "ambient problem." The ambient problem is the problem of the condition of humanity's media or ambiance—the air one breathes, the food one ingests, the water one drinks, the light spectrum that bathes us, the panorama before our eyes, and the sound waves beating against our ears. It is a fundamental fact that we are biological organisms whose form is the result of an evolutionary process that occurred in a specific ambience. As such, we require that specific ambience for survival and can tolerate only limited alterations thereof. Despite this fundamental fact, we have unwittingly altered the ambient conditions in which we live. We have added a whole list of new chemicals to our medium—sulphates, nitrates, oxidants, etc. We have allowed chlorinated hydrocarbons to become a part of our fatty tissues. We have turned loose a pandora's box of polychlorinated-biphynals, fluorides, cadmium, asbestos, vinyl chlorides, and on and on the list goes. As a consequence, we have inflicted upon ourselves a whole host of major and minor ills and problems. This in short is the "ambient problem."

The most important thing that can be said of the laws we have passed to deal with the ambient problem, such as the Clean Air Act, the Water Pollution Control Act, and the Federal Insecticide Act, is that they do not deal adequately with the ambient problem. True, these laws have had their successes, but the ambient problem remains.

What is wrong?

For myself, I have come to the conclusion that the approach of the existing laws relies too heavily on complicated technical-legal schemes administered by bureaucrats. This approach has its uses, but it must be supplemented by another approach. One possible supplemental approach that appeals to me is one that has been much talked about in the environmental area, but which has not really been tried: the constitutional right. If we are to solve the ambient problem, then perhaps each of us needs a constitutional right for the protection and preservation of our ambient environment. The procedural scheme to implement such a right would, of course, be crucial to its efficacy. In order to make the constitutional right effective, for example, there would have to be a strong presumption in favor of the natural environment. Thus, if there is any doubt about a chemical, then it could not be broadly distributed through the market.

Can it happen? Can we really enact such a constitutional amendment? Proponents of the Women's Equal Rights Amendment have just learned that amending the Constitution is very difficult. Nevertheless, if the public comes to believe the problem is as serious as I believe it to be, then such an amendment would be feasible. A consensus against cancer and for a constitutional right can form and those with vested interests in uninvited additives will simply have to accept it.

United Nations photo.

2) *The Population Problem.* The next problem the law has not responded to is the population problem. Three months ago *Science* magazine carried a review of the world population and food situation by Lester Brown. Despite the wonders of the miraculous green revolution, Brown reports that the world's food supply has not kept up with population growth and that we are facing an imminent crisis. As Brown puts it, the world is now living hand-to-mouth. The world is essentially without a food reserve; it has no reserve land to put into production; almost every country is now a net importer of food; North America is the only substantial exporter; the world fish catch appears to be past its peak and is falling. Yet despite these and other grim facts, world population continues to rise.

It seems clear that the population problems cannot be solved simply by increased food production efforts. Institutional and legal innovations are required to limit populations. The *San Francisco Chronicle* on January 2, 1976, carried a startling story from the Punjab which may be a straw in the wind. The Punjab is in the process of enacting a law to require the compulsory sterilization of everyone between 15 and 45 with more than 3 children. When asked if people would complain about a loss of basic human rights, a Punjabi health official said such complaints had been received earlier about compulsory smallpox vaccinations, but that everyone eventually accepted such vaccinations as necessary for the good of all. He predicted that compulsory sterilization would be likewise so accepted and that it would soon become standard procedure throughout India.

Such a drastic direct population control will not, I hope,

be required in the US, where we have one of the world's lowest birth rates. However, we cannot escape the population problem simply by maintaining a low birthrate. As we are sitting on virtually 80% of the world's surplus food production, we must choose to whom we are to sell it: this raises a large number of difficult "distribution" issues. Is the food to go to the highest bidder—that is to the emerging OPEC countries, to Japan and to Western Europe? Or is it to be an instrument of foreign policy, perhaps even, as some suggest, a weapon? Thus, is the food to go to Russia as a reward and to be withheld from her as a punishment? Or is food to be an instrument of humanitarian altruism, distributed to those in need in Bangladesh, the Sahel, and Ethiopia?

Distribution questions do not just apply to food supplies directly, but embrace the whole agricultural support system. As a consequence, we face a series of environmental issues we cannot escape. To what extent should we preserve agricultural lands and how do we do it? Should we allow the use of scarce fertilizer stocks on our lawns? Should we destroy a national forest in South Carolina to mine phosphates for fertilizer? To what degree should grains that could be consumed directly by the poor of the world be fed to livestock? What weight do we give to domestic inflation and domestic food prices in dealing with these problems?

And, if the problems of distribution were not difficult enough, we also face another type of "population" problem. It seems clear that no matter how we solve distribution problems, many hundreds of millions in the world are going to be deprived. We must assume that many of the deprived will not accept their fate, but will act. If the food does not come to them, they will go to the food. We must realize that the world's transportation and communication facilities have created a situation of amazing potential. World communications have spread a vision of plenty in our country to the less fortunate of other countries. Rising expectations and cheap transportation are creating a situation whereby tens, perhaps hundreds, of millions will have both the desire and means to come to our country. The poor of Mexico are demonstrating quite clearly that our border is no barrier. And while we can always absorb a few million more, can we absorb the potential hundreds of millions that may choose to come?

The malnourished of the world, now perhaps a billion in number, may soon accelerate the great current of migration from hunger to the food of North America. At this point the law will face a terrible challenge: how to preserve the basis of our exportable surplus for the long term in the face of short-term misery and need.

3) *Development Problem.* The third problem I bring to

you is the development problem. The epitome of the development problem is the appearance in fifteen short years of San Jose, as a pock on the skin of the planet. New cities have occurred throughout history, but the rapidity and destructiveness of contemporary development is a new planetary phenomenon and a cause for alarm. Right now the very process is at work in Kuwait where a Persian Gulf Los Angeles is being created with amazing rapidity. Anchorage and Fairbanks' populations are now being boomed at a tremendous rate by the pipeline. The growth of such places as Houston, Texas, is legendary. Such explosive development, I think it is fair to say, is almost always an environmental and resource-conservation disaster. Contemporary development explosions result in air pollution, water pollution, the destruction of farmland, urban sprawl, and the extravagant wastage of energy and other resources.

There has to be a better way. I don't know what it is, but I do know that the Department of Housing and Urban Development has not found it. When I look at the bureaucrats' handiwork, whether in planning, land-use controls, or government development, I find their solutions inadequate and sometimes worse than unrestrained Houston's. This is a challenge of grand proportions that has not been met.

4) *Renewable Resource Problem.* The fourth problem is that of the destruction of our renewable resources. At this very moment we are depleting our fishing stocks, we are wasting our soil resources, and we are fast reaching the end of our timber stocks. Sadly, of all the environmental problems, this is the one we have been aware of the longest. At the turn of the century, this country went through a great wave of conservation concern and reform. We created a Forest Service, a Fish and Wildlife Service, a Soil Conservation Service, and other conservation agencies. However, through abuse and overuse, we continued to lose ground. The reason for failure, I suggest, must lie in part in the nature of our earlier solution to the problem.

Our twenty-thousand-man Forest Service now lets million-acre, fifty-year concessions to industry. Our Interior Department wrecks the salmon resources of the Pacific Northwest with dams to make electricity to make aluminum beer cans. Our Soil Conservation Service has become an agency which promotes the destruction of free-flowing streams. In brief, our solutions were administrative and bureaucratic and they have turned on us and bitten us.

What is the answer to this problem? I believe Professor Christopher Stone has told us: the fish, the trees, the living soil we depend on must have standing for judicial protection. They must have a legal status, which can be protected in the law.

Photo by Arthur Tress.

This of course is not the whole of the answer. We must think long and hard about who the guardian *ad litem* for these living resources should be.

- It cannot be the worker who fells the tree;
- It cannot be the politician who counts votes;
- It cannot be the bureaucrat who will not risk his job;
- It cannot be the technical expert whose income derives from any of those others I have just mentioned.

Who then is it to be?

At this point I have no solution save *everyman*—a universal guardianship of everyone and anyone, regardless of race, religion, color, species, or planet of origin, to step forward to protect the living resources of the earth.

5) *Non-renewable Resource Problem.* The fifth problem I bring to you is that of the wastage of our *non*renewable resources. Of these, the most important, of course, is the earth's reserve of hydrocarbons.

As best I can tell, our society remains deeply committed to the most rapid destruction possible of the earth's hydrocarbons. The supply of hydrocarbons, however, is finite and it is not at all clear that there will or can be a substitute. What is more, the world for many generations will need those hydrocarbons for health, happiness, and survival.

As far as I can tell, there is no justification whatsoever

for our profligate use of hydrocarbons. The retreat from the automobile must begin at once, and all possible steps must be taken to bring our use of hydrocarbons down to a more modest and rational level.

Many things can and must be done. A very minor step would be an additional 50¢ a gallon tax on gasoline to put its price over $1.00. Each year thereafter I would continue to raise the gasoline tax. Such a measure would create the incentive necessary for far less use of gasoline. Of course people must be given time to adjust. There are many ways to attack the problem, but we must get started at once.

6) *Catastrophe Problem.* The sixth problem which environmental law has not dealt with adequately, is the emerging problem of man-made catastrophes which can result from the use of Faustian technologies. By Faustian technologies I mean such things as nuclear power, followed by such wonders as recombinant DNA, laser death rays, and what have you. With the deployment of these technologies, we are now facing the prospect of accidents and sabotage on a grand scale. We have nearly had two nuclear blowdowns in this country already and there are rumors that the Russians have in fact had a blowdown.

So far we have dealt with this prospective problem by ignoring it. In the case of atomic energy, we have even passed a law to excuse reactor manufacturers and operators from liability. With the first large catastrophe, however, our present head-in-the-sand approach will end. Our liberal democracy will at that point be strained to the breaking point. Frankly, I don't know of a solution which permits both the broad use of Faustian technologies and our traditional liberties. The day after we lose Detroit, you and I may lose a good bit of our personal freedom. Monitoring may become a way of life. We may be unable to enter any metropolitan area, or to move about within one, without passing through numerous control points. We may be periodically seized and searched to a degree far greater than we now are at airports.

The only alternative I see is for us to devise ways to severely limit and control the Faustian technologies. We must develop institutions that guide technology's development in such a way as to lessen, not heighten, the possibility of catastrophe. In short, we must control technology or control people. There is no other alternative except to risk catastrophe.

7) *The Problem of Other Species.* As a seventh problem, I bring to you and lay in your lap the problem of those other species who share our planet with us. So far we have not solved the problem of a decent and adequate environment for our co-tenants on this planet. We have, apparently, no adequate place for our brother the brown bear or for our sister the blue whale. The very ecosystems they depend on

are relentlessly destroyed. Even the symbol of our nation, the bald eagle, is all but gone.

Our approach to this problem has been manifold. We have created national parks, wilderness areas, wildlife refuges; we have established fish and game departments; we have established hunting controls; we have passed endangered species acts. There is nothing wrong with these efforts, except perhaps that we have not taken them far enough. Thus, our National Forest Wilderness System remains after many decades a paltry 13 to 14 million acres. Out of the billion-plus acres of this nation, that is truly a pathetic figure.

I think of the bald eagle as our miner's canary whose demise brings us warning that all is not right around us. We still suffer from an earlier arrogance that no species really matters except ourselves. This conceit may be our fatal mistake. The disappearance of other species may foreshadow our own disappearance.

8) *International Problem.* Eighth! Most of the problems I have raised with you are not America's alone. We share them with the world. It has been said before, but it is worth saying again: We have not solved the problem of international cooperation. Treaties, UN organizations, world courts, and what have you, are now insufficient to their tasks. We have only begun. I would not presume to tell you how we can do better, but I will presume to say we have not done well. We simply *must* do better.

We *must* prevent the destruction of such things as the Amazon forests, the ocean ecosystem, and East Africa's wildlife.

9) *The Problem of Future Generations.* And last, most of the problems which I have raised relate not only to ourselves but also relate to future generations—to our children and grandchildren and beyond. Having just adopted a little girl, I have this very much on my mind. We are clearly living too much in the present, too much for ourselves. We are not thinking sufficiently of our estate, the legacy we will leave.

What are we bequeathing? Exhausted resources, polluted lakes, destroyed rivers, wrecked soil? Are we endangering the basis of life on the planet—by broadcasting carcinogens and mutagens which risk the health and genetic stock of the future?

Our democracy is defective because we give the future no vote; our economy is defective because we exclude the future from the market; our law is imperfect because we exclude the future from the courts. Let us at least keep the future in our plans and give our successors a chance to survive. Let us construct rights for the future and duties for the present to the future.

—JAMES MOORMAN

The Evolution of Law

United States environmental law evolved from existing doctrines to a remarkable extent and is administered by familiar institutions. Common law notions of trespass, nuisance, and eminent domain provided the focus for those first lawyers who happened also to be conservationists.

I intend to seek to identify where the political changes of recent years have left the legal system, what reforms would help, how we can expect the law to evolve, and one or two ideas our system might adapt from others.

Most legislation either prohibits or promotes. This country's principal environmental legislation, however—the National Environmental Policy Act (NEPA)—seeks a process more than a result. Such process legislation doesn't dictate a particular decision, it mandates that decisions must be reached in particular ways. The assumption underlying process legislation is that good results usually flow from good procedures.

Prohibition makes sense when one is certain of assumptions (or is confirmed in one's prejudices). Process legislation appeals when one is uncertain about assumptions and needs a process to test them. Our principal prohibition statutes are the Air and Water Quality Acts and the Marine Mammals Protection Act. Each says what it doesn't like, prohibits more of it, and authorizes regulations to improve things.

In contrast, NEPA requires not good decisions but the process of careful consideration in an open forum. Statutes patterned on NEPA have been adopted by no less than 24 states.

The central device of federal and state environmental policy acts is the impact statement. The laws require that an environmental impact statement, evaluating a proposed government action and its alternatives, be drawn up whenever the proposed action has important potential consequences. To the extent that impact statements are prepared defensively by officials already committed to a proposed project, the statements help only by providing ammunition for private groups opposed to certain government projects. That has proven to be immensely important, however.

The NEPA process is especially beneficial in situations of uncertainty. Looking back to the early 1970s, many environmental concerns did rest on uncertain bases. As more becomes clear, however, it may be time to cease testing assumptions and to enact prohibitions. It isn't useful to continue marshaling facts after conclusions become inescapable. The bottle and poptop can makers, for example, are happy for their industry to be studied as long as anyone likes—even at considerable cost to themselves. They are happy about delay because the time for restriction or prohibition of their throwaway trash is long overdue.

As NEPA matures, it becomes more common to find impact statements that are in technical compliance but are woefully inadequate in terms of true consideration of issues. Because the first generation of NEPA litigation proceeded simplistically—either you mentioned every contingency, in which case you were all right, or you didn't, in which case it was back to a fresh start—writers of impact statements often aim a paragraph at every possible environmental consequence and give in-depth consideration to very few. Such treatment may reveal soft spots to environmental activists, but it does little if anything to improve government agencies' decision-making processes.

Still, NEPA enjoys a flexibility and applicability that prohibition legislation cannot. When new threats are perceived, environmental assessments can be made without new hearings and legislation.

After watching the successes built around the environmental impact statement, those who believe environmentalism has gone too far are clamoring for *economic* impact statements. Unfortunately, current thinking about the cost of environmental protection is so badly askew that the accepted dichotomy is environment versus economics, and environmentalists tend to oppose economic impact statements. But the bad environmental choice is usually a bad economic choice as well, a general principle that helped environmentalists defeat dams in Grand Canyon and the American SST. Too many environmentalists shun economic analysis, feeling they should respond to "higher values." Impact statements could be used to educate snobs of all persuasions.

Following the Tax Model

There is currently some pressure to create new federal courts specializing in environmental issues. These would be modeled after the federal tax and claims courts. Some environmentalists have argued that their cases are necessarily complex and specialized, and that most judges cannot be expected to handle them adequately. Many non-environmentalists favor the idea in the belief that environmental cases are clogging the courts. The latter rationale reflects a desire to shove these concerns off into a corner.

Interest in special environmental courts waned after a Justice Department study showed that less than one-half of one percent of the federal courts' caseload dealt with environmental matters. The courts are clogged all right, but mostly with things other than NEPA.

Specialized masters to assist regular courts make more sense. What is complex about environmental cases is not the law but the facts, particularly scientific data, underlying the dispute. Special masters (or "friends of the court") with technical expertise could expand the general level of environmental awareness without the restriction of responsibility to an elite, specialized bar and judiciary.

To Protect the Right to Court

Environmentalists' one-half of one percent of the federal courts' caseload will get even smaller unless recent rulings hampering effective action can be corrected by legislation. The problems are Supreme Court rulings that (1) restrict the compensation of parties engaged in public interest litigation, and (2) reduce the practicality of class action lawsuits.

The end to reimbursement of plaintiffs in public interest litigation came as a bitter aftertaste to the Alaska pipeline fight. In *Alyeska Pipeline Service Company vs. The Wilderness Society, et al,* The Wilderness Society, the Environmental Defense Fund, and Friends of the Earth sued to block the Alaska pipeline. The conservationists won in the courts, but Congress repealed their victory by rewriting the law and declaring via statute that pipeline construction didn't violate NEPA. Afterwards, the plaintiffs applied for their legal expenses, based on a line of cases authorizing payments to "private attorneys general." The idea behind this doctrine is that plaintiffs who uphold the law save the government the costs of enforcement and deserve compensation.

In line with these precedents, the Court of Appeals awarded attorneys' fees to the conservation groups; the pipeline construction company was ordered to pay $100,000. The Supreme Court reversed, holding that to force one side in a dispute to bear the other's expenses was so contrary to American tradition that each instance must be specifically authorized by the legislature.

In overturning the series of cases that established the private attorneys general theory, the Supreme Court relied on an 1853 statute—since eliminated—promulgating the American rule that each side pays its own expenses. The Court held that long-accepted exceptions to that rule were

interpretations of the 1853 statute—although cases involving the exceptions failed to mention the statute or demonstrate any awareness of its existence. A dissenting opinion argued that the private attorneys general doctrine was an exercise of the court's inherent power to do equity, and that the Supreme Court itself had never previously regarded awards of attorneys' fees to be the exclusive province of Congress.

Alyeska hurt people outside the environmental movement: almost all public interest litigation on behalf of minorities, the poor, and consumers relied in part at least on the hope that a successful result need not be an expensive one.

Several statutes specifically provide for awards of legal expenses, and *Alyeska* will not affect cases brought under them. Federal air, water, and noise pollution laws give courts the option of awarding legal expenses, showing that Congress expected private enforcement to play a major role in their implementation.

Two peculiar features of environmental practice justify special consideration of funding methods. First, most environmental cases seek injunctions, not damages; the lawsuits seek to stop threatened actions, not to be compensated for their consequences. If the court grants the injunction sought, the bulldozer goes away and there are no damages to collect; if the court denies the injunction, the bulldozer goes ahead and the damage is irreversible. The lawsuit usually dries up and blows away rather quickly in either case, and no damages are recovered from which to defray costs. Consequently, contingent fee arrangements, which let lawyers collect only when and if the client does, are refused by all but stupid or idealistic attorneys.

The second peculiarity of environmental cases is that they are changing in ways that require more data, more experts, and thus more money. In the early 1970s, the typical case forced consideration of environmental consequences upon defendants who contended that the law couldn't possibly be aimed at them. Typically, the defendant's case was extremely weak; failure to comply reflected arrogance as much as anything else. But now the "easy" cases are over. As compliance gets better, the cases get tougher. Omissions must be ferreted out; mistakes must be found; our experts must challenge theirs. Cases emerge from the law library and get into the field, at enormous additional expense.

The *Alyeska* decision will inevitably choke off much public interest litigation by environmentalists and others. Realistically, too, it is likely to skew the growth of environmental law, causing plaintiffs to frame their cases in ways that arguably bring them within one of the few statutes allowing attorneys' fees. This is common practice, but a tactic likely to convert an otherwise good case into a loser.

There can be no mistaking the remedy for *Alyeska*—legislation. Immediately after the decision, a number of bills were introduced providing for expenses under specific statutes felt to be suitable for private enforcement. Some suggested blanket legislation authorizing payment in all cases brought to uphold important congressional policies. Private enforcement under the private attorneys general theory is not a perfect mechanism. A legal ombudsman, a formula allocating some fraction of the cost of promoting a project to the project's opponents, or public subsidy of the enormous costs of discovery [i.e., "compulsory disclosure, as of facts or documents"] in modern environmental cases might work better. But some remedy must be found, and quickly.

Class Action Suits

In similarly damaging precedents, recent Supreme Court cases all but eliminated the usefulness of class action suits to environmentalists. Generally, a class action allows multiple plaintiffs with similar injuries from a common cause to sue and share in a common recovery of damages.

In *Zahn vs. International Paper Company,* four lakeshore property owners sued for themselves and a class of 200 others, alleging that paper plant pollution had damaged their properties' value. The property of each of four named plaintiffs had suffered at least ten thousand dollars' damage, the minimum necessary to confer federal jurisdiction. The Supreme Court ordered dismissal of the class action, holding that not only the four named plaintiffs but every member of the class must be shown to have suffered at least ten thousand dollars' damage.

Environmental issues typically arise because the benefits of proposed actions are concentrated among a few with power to decide and the burdens are widely dispersed among many people who have no influence on the decision. It is because the benefits are concentrated and the burdens are shared that environmental controls have relied so largely on regulation and prohibition. Dispersed burdens could be aggregated by the many victims in class action suits and the overall net cost demonstrated. As a practical matter, the class action often provided the only way to defray the enormous costs of modern research, discovery, and proof. Finally, of course, class actions lightened the load on the courts, avoiding the constant retrials of the same basic facts by multiple claimants.

The Supreme Court has continued to chip away at the class action. A 1974 case required mailings to all indentifiable class members even though that class—all odd-lot

stock traders—numbered more than two million and the cost of pursuing the dispute was thereby pegged above two hundred thousand dollars.

The class action was one of the few effective remedies against the systematic little illegalities that threaten to nib-

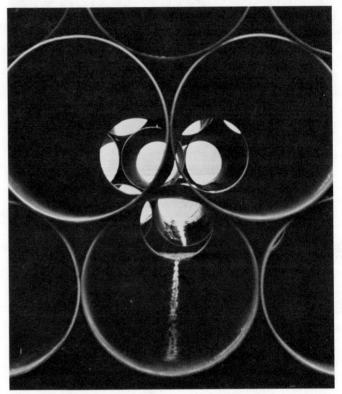

Pipe for the Alaska pipeline, the worst environmental defeat since Glen Canyon dam. Photo by Tom Turner.

ble the underrepresented to death. Class actions afforded an ideal method of bringing together the costs of pollution in a single action. The remedy should be revived.

Revitalized Institutions

Institutions besides the courts must enter the business of generating public information regularly and systematically. In early 1975, the Securities and Exchange Commission (SEC) held hearings to determine whether corporate disclosure rules should extend to environmental and social programs as well as financial data. The SEC hearings were prompted by a NEPA lawsuit brought by the Natural Resources Defense Council.

The SEC is only 40 years old, but during that time, an enormous body of law and regulatory practice has grown up to standardize the preparation of financial information by American corporations. Most of the work of preparing and presenting this information falls upon the corporations controlling the raw data. Those corporations therefore develop internal expertise in financial disclosure. As a result, a large volume of periodic, systematic reports, in a standardized form approved by the SEC, is available to the public. The SEC watchdogs the preparation of reports and punishes violators.

Environmentalists should work to extend the scope of mandatory public disclosure regulated by a wider variety of institutions. Courts have jurisdiction over everybody, but they don't have continuing close relationships such as the SEC enjoys with the business community, the Interstate Commerce Commission with transportation industries, the Food and Drug Administration with pharmaceutical companies. The coziness that often develops between the regulated and the regulators is often criticized, but the potential for effective public disclosure through regulatory institutions is tremendous. If, as Brandeis said, "sunlight is the best disinfectant," just getting information to the public should be the first step. Refinements can be left to the future.

A Geneva Convention for the Environment?

If domestic environmental law is largely derivative, the international arena invites creative efforts toward shared concepts and strong institutions.

The kind of international behavior most similar to our treatment of the environment is war. Is, then, the base from which enforceable standards can evolve the Geneva Convention?

The major instances of international settlement of environmental problems—or more precisely, of compensation for damage already done—have involved special forums set up to settle specific disputes. Since the 1930s, at least, bilateral compacts have assessed damage and compensated victims. Canada and the United States settled a smelter pollution dispute through such a device, and the French and Spanish arbitrated a river-diversion case. These forums were not courts, with continuity and power to compel. They were created by and dependent for their continued existence on the problems they sought to resolve.

Decisions by the International Court of Justice or under the rules of the International Arbitration Association would be preferable, if only for the opportunity to build expert staff. Environmental cases have been submitted in both places, but at present, no international forum can compel its own jurisdiction. The opponents must stop squabbling long enough to agree on a forum. If you strip compulsory jurisdiction and the law of injunction from US environmental law, you are left with very little. That little

is what one starts and ends with internationally.

In the US, environmental damage to individuals either goes uncompensated or must be compensated by the tort system. Success requires proof that the defendant did specified things that directly resulted in specified injury to the plaintiff. Proof is obviously easier when the victim gets hit by an automobile than when an asbestos worker turns out to have cancer or an urbanite suffers from emphysema. Statistics say that city living increases the risk of emphysema, but which of any number of polluting factories should pay?

The Japanese, often more practical than we, have been experimenting with a remedy since 1973. In that year, their Diet enacted a system for the compensation of victims of industrial pollution. Under the law, Japan is divided into zones. Sufferers in zones where statistics indicate that pollutants led to an increased incidence of disease can be certified to receive compensation for medical expenses and lost wages. Funds for compensation come from graduated emission charges and a tonnage tax on cars.

Such a system permits compensation on the basis of scientific probability rather than legal evidence of causality. Usually, this is the best evidence that victims can muster. In dealing with cancer and other environmental diseases whose lengthy latency periods make their origins uncertain, no one can offer proof on the basis of traditional notions of causality.

Many environmentalists react negatively to schemes that allow polluters to weigh the costs of control against the expense of fines or compensation to victims. Compensation schemes like that adopted in Japan seem to constitute a license to pollute—often viewed as a license to kill, which in a sense it is. Nevertheless, such schemes deserve support—not to replace our tort system but to provide an alternative. To the extent that costs of pollution can be shifted from the public to those responsible for it, the incentive to find remedies increases.

In our country, to consider recourse to the legal system at all requires a certain optimism about the time available for change. Legislation takes too long, and the courts take longer. A step backward for each two steps ahead is standard. For the judicial system to contribute as much to environmental breakthroughs in the next decade as it has in this, proportionately more resources will be necessary as cases get tougher.

The principal value of the legal process lies in its ability to test for uncertain facts—not perfectly, but better than torture or other methods popular at one time or another. Like old age, the legal process looks better when you consider the alternative.

—MARK HORLINGS

Man and Nature
Meet in Court

It is this note of the *unthinkable* that I want to dwell upon for a moment. Throughout legal history, each successive extension of rights to some new entity has been, theretofore, a bit unthinkable. We are inclined to suppose the rightlessness of rightless "things" to be a decree of Nature, not a legal convention acting in support of some status quo. It is thus that we defer considering the choices involved in all their moral, social, and economic dimensions.

Now, to say that the natural environment should have rights is not to say anything as silly as that no one should be allowed to cut down a tree. We say human beings have rights, but—at least as of the time of this writing—they can be executed. Corporations have rights, but they cannot plead the fifth amendment; *In re Gault* gave 15-year-olds certain rights in juvenile proceedings, but it did not give them the right to vote. Thus, to say that the environment should have rights is not to say that it should have every right we can imagine, or even the same body of rights as human beings have. Nor is it to say that everything in the environment should have the same rights as every other thing in the environment.

It is not inevitable, nor is it wise, that natural objects should have no rights to seek redress in their own behalf. It is no answer to say that streams and forests cannot have standing because streams and forests cannot speak. Corporations cannot speak either; nor can states, estates, infants, incompetents, municipalities or universities. Lawyers speak for them, as they customarily do for the ordinary citizen with legal problems.

In a system which spoke of the environment "having legal rights," judges would, I suspect, be inclined to interpret rules such as those of burden of proof far more liberally from the point of the environment. There is, too, the fact that the vocabulary and expressions that are available to us influence and even steer our thought. Consider the effect that was had by introducing into the law terms like "motive," "intent," and "due process." These terms work a subtle shift into the rhetoric of explanation available to judges; with them, new ways of thinking and new insights come to be explored and developed. In such fashion, judges who could unabashedly refer to the "legal rights of

the environment" would be encouraged to develop a viable body of law—in part simply through the availability and force of the expression. Besides, such a manner of speaking by courts would contribute to popular notions, and a society that spoke of the "legal rights of the environment" would be inclined to legislate more environment-protecting rules by formal enactment.

If my sense of these influences is correct, then a society in which it is stated, however vaguely, that "rivers have legal rights" would evolve a different legal system than one which did not employ that expression, even if the two of them had, at the start, the very same "legal rules" in other respects.

The problems we have to confront are increasingly the world-wide crises of a global organism: not pollution of a stream, but pollution of the atmosphere and of the ocean. Increasingly, the death that occupies each human's imagination is not his own, but that of the entire life cycle of the planet earth, to which each of us is as but a cell to a body.

To shift from such a lofty fancy as the planetarization of consciousness to the operation of our municipal legal system is to come down to earth hard. Before the forces that

Graphic courtesy
Les Amis de la Terre.

are at work, our highest court is but a frail and feeble—a distinctly human—institution. Yet, the Court may be at its best not in its work of handing down decrees, but at the very task that is called for: of summoning up from the human spirit the kindest and most generous and worthy ideas that abound there, giving them shape and reality and legitimacy. Witness the School Desegregation Cases which, more importantly than to integrate the schools (as-

suming they did), awakened us to moral needs which, when made visible, could not be denied. And so here, too, in the case of the environment, the Supreme Court may find itself in a position to award "rights" in a way that will contribute to a change in popular consciousness. It would be a modest move, to be sure, but one in furtherance of a large goal: the future of the planet as we know it.

—CHRISTOPHER B. STONE

The Inanimate in Litigation

The critical question of "standing" would be simplified and also put neatly in focus if we fashioned a federal rule that allowed environmental issues to be litigated before federal agencies or federal courts in the name of the inanimate object about to be despoiled, defaced, or invaded by roads and bulldozers and where injury is the subject of public outrage. Contemporary public concern for protecting nature's ecological equilibrium should lead to the conferral of standing upon environmental objects to sue for their own preservation. See Stone, Should Trees Have Standing? Toward Legal Rights for Natural Objects, 45 S. Cal. L. Rev. 450 (1972). This suit would therefore be more properly labeled as *Mineral King v. Morton.*

Inanimate objects are sometimes parties in litigation. A ship has a legal personality, a fiction found useful for maritime purposes. The corporation sole—a creature of ecclesiastical law—is an acceptable adversary and large fortunes ride on its cases. The ordinary corporation is a "person" for purposes of the adjudicatory processes, whether it represents proprietary, spiritual, aesthetic, or charitable causes.

So it should be as respects valleys, alpine meadows, rivers, lakes, estuaries, beaches, ridges, groves of trees, swampland, or even air that feels the destructive pressures of modern technology and modern life. The river, for example, is the living symbol of all the life it sustains or nourishes—fish, aquatic insects, water ouzels, otter, fisher, deer, elk, bear, and all other animals, including man, who are dependent on it or who enjoy it for its sight, its sound, or its life. The river as plaintiff speaks for the ecological unit of life that is part of it. Those people who have a meaningful relation to that body of water—whether it be a fisherman, a canoeist, a zoologist, or a logger—must be able to speak for the values which the river represents and which are threatened with destruction.

Mineral King is doubtless like other wonders of the Sierra Nevada such as Tuolumne Meadows and the John Muir Trail. Those who hike it, fish it, hunt it, camp in it, or frequent it, or visit it merely to sit in solitude and wonderment are legitimate spokesmen for it, whether they may be a few or many. Those who have that intimate relation with the inanimate object about to be injured, polluted, or otherwise despoiled are its legitimate spokesmen.

. . . The problem is to make certain that the inanimate objects, which are the very core of America's beauty, have spokesmen before they are destroyed. It is, of course, true that most of them are under the control of a federal or state agency. The standards given those agencies are usually expressed in terms of the "public interest." Yet "public interest" has so many differing shades of meaning as to be quite meaningless on the environmental front.

Yet the pressures on agencies for favorable action one way or the other are enormous. The suggestion that Congress can stop action which is undesirable is true in theory; yet even Congress is too remote to give meaningful direction and its machinery is too ponderous to use very often. The federal agencies of which I speak are not venal or corrupt. But they are notoriously under the control of powerful interests who manipulate them through advisory committees, or friendly working relations, or who have that natural affinity with the agency which in time develops between the regulator and the regulated.

The Forest Service—one of the federal agencies behind the scheme to despoil Mineral King—has been notorious for its alignment with lumber companies, although its mandate from Congress directs it to consider the various aspects of multiple use in its supervision of the national forests.

The voice of the inanimate object, therefore, should not be stilled. That does not mean that the judiciary takes over the managerial functions from the federal agency. It merely means that before these priceless bits of Americana (such as a valley, an alpine meadow, a river, or a lake) are forever lost or are so transformed as to be reduced to the eventual rubble of our urban environment, the voice of the existing beneficiaries of these environmental wonders should be heard.

Perhaps they will not win. Perhaps the bulldozers of "progress" will plow under all the aesthetic wonders of this beautiful land. That is not the present question. The sole question is, who has standing to be heard?

Those who hike the Appalachian Trail into Sunfish Pond, New Jersey, and camp or sleep there, or run the Allagash in Maine, or climb the Guadalupes in West Texas, or who canoe and portage the Quetico Superior in Minnesota, certainly should have standing to defend those natural wonders before courts or agencies, though they live 3,000 miles away. Those who merely are caught up in environmental news or propaganda and flock to defend these waters or areas may be treated differently. That is why these environmental issues should be tendered by the inanimate object itself. Then there will be assurances that all of the forms of life which it represents will stand before

William O. Douglas (right) and David Brower.

the court—the pileated woodpecker as well as the coyote and bear, the lemmings as well as the trout in the streams. Those inarticulate members of the ecological group cannot speak. But those people who have so frequented the place as to know its values and wonders will be able to speak for the entire ecological community.

—WILLIAM O. DOUGLAS

Getting the Government to Obey Its Own Laws

Today, the central problem of litigating environmental causes with the United States Government is that of litigating with a *discretionary* government, a government of men, rather than a government of laws. On questions affecting the environment, our executive branch has assumed for itself a discretion not merited by law, indeed has exalted its discretion *over* the law, which it has relegated to the background role of legitimizing presumptive delegations of discretion to itself.

This situation imposes three tasks on a lawyer who would litigate environmental questions with the government. His first and fundamental task is that of establishing the proposition that the government decision he is concerned with is, in fact, governed by law. This task presents itself to the lawyer because the government continually attempts to convert the substantive statutory mandates that govern it into mere discretionary guidelines.

The lawyer's second task is that of establishing that the government decision in question can be reviewed through the judicial process. This task arises because the government uses special ploys, *not available to other litigants,* to avoid the review in court of its environmental decisions.

The lawyer's third task is to force the executive branch to obey any decision he wins against the government in court. And this task arises because the government, even when ordered by a court to obey the law, will sometimes continue on its course of evading the law.

Government of Techniques for Turning Statutory Mandates into Grants of Discretion

How does the executive branch convert statutory mandates that should govern its conduct into loose discretionary licenses? One way is by issuing so-called "administrative interpretations" in the form of general counsels' opinions, secretarys' opinions, attorney generals' opinions, and the like. There is a general rule that when a court is faced with an ambiguous statute, it should give deference to the interpretation of the agency charged with the administration of that statute. The government seems to believe that this rule means that it simply can change the law by issuing an opinion.

The trans-Alaska pipeline case provides a clear example of how the executive branch abuses administrative interpretation. Under the Mineral Leasing Act of 1920, Congress authorized the Secretary of the Interior to grant pipeline rights-of-way across public lands the width of the pipe, plus 25 feet on both sides. Section 28 of the act read in part, as follows: "Rights-of-way through the public lands . . . may be granted by the Secretary of the Interior for pipeline purposes . . . to the extent of the ground occupied by the said pipeline and twenty five feet on each side of the same. . . ."

Now this is clear enough. However, to make sure that no additional lands were to be available under other authorities, the statute went on to say: "*Provided further,* that no right-of-way shall hereafter be granted over said lands . . . except under and subject to the provisions, limitations, and conditions of this section. . . ." (*Italics added*)

As it happens, the trans-Alaska pipeline is so big that the 54 feet it could have had under the above statute is insufficient. The oil companies need 100 feet for their pipeline, another 100 feet or so for a road, and miscellaneous other land for river crossings, radio stations, air fields, gravel pits, and so on.

The Interior Department searched its archives and found some old administrative interpretations. One 1931 Attorney General's Opinion in particular encouraged the department. It said that the width limitation could be ignored for a pump station. You can't have pipelines without pump stations, the attorney general had said. Furthermore, he went on to reason, Congress could not have intended to prevent new pipelines. Therefore, the attorney general concluded, you can permit the use of additional land for pump stations. The Department of the Interior decided that the logic and reasoning of the pump-station opinion could be applied to all the extra-land needs of the trans-Alaska pipeline. The secretary thus determined that he could ignore the width limitation set out in the law altogether. The government fought for its discretion on this ground for three years. I am pleased to say that not one judge of the Washington, D.C., Court of Appeals would accept the secretary's logic.

Another technique of the executive branch for avoiding mandates is "ratification," by which it tells some committee of Congress that the executive branch has violated, or that it desires to violate, the law. When Congress does nothing about the violation, the executive branch then claims that Congress has ratified the violation and that, presto, the law

is thus amended. A ratification can best be achieved when some agency submits the information to a friendly appropriation committee. The claim of ratification comes when the Congress appropriates money for the agency. Another way to achieve a "ratification" even without the cooperation of some committee is by obtaining authorization for a project, which is then claimed to be inconsistent with the particular statutory mandate annoying the government. Thus, the executive branch can claim a repeal by implication, even though Congress was not informed of the possibility of repeal and nowhere indicated that it intended a repeal.

A wonderful example of the techniques of ratification can be found in the Rainbow Bridge case. A few years ago, Congress passed the Colorado River Storage Act authorizing several dams on the Colorado River, the best known being that at Glen Canyon. There was a fight in Congress at the time as to whether the dams' waters would be allowed to flood certain national parks, in particular Dinosaur National Monument and Rainbow Bridge National Monument. After a bitter fight, Congress included Section 3 in the act, which states: ". . . It is the intention of Congress that no dam or reservoir constructed under the authorization of this Act shall be within any National Park or Monument." That seems pretty clear, doesn't it?

In order for the Bureau of Reclamation to build Glen Canyon Dam to the height it desired and also to prevent water from backing into Rainbow Bridge National Monument, a small retaining dam would have had to be built below the monument on Bridge Creek. However, officials of the Bureau of Reclamation and the members of the appropriations committees of Congress apparently thought that such a retaining dam was a waste of money, so the funds for it were never appropriated. What about Section

"YOU GOTTA CREDIT TH' SUPREME COURT – THEY KNOW A CRIME AGAINST NATURE WHEN THEY SEE IT!"

Drawing by Dwayne Powell, by courtesy of The News and Observer.

3? you ask. The bureau simply ignored it, on the grounds that (1) they had told the Congressional appropriations committees about the problem, (2) Congress had failed to appropriate money for the retaining dam, and (3) Congress had thus silently ratified the flooding of Rainbow Bridge. The bureau shored up this argument with a second, similar argument: that when Congress passed legislation authorizing other dams on the Colorado River, it must have assumed, for certain technical reasons, that Lake Powell would reach a level that would flood the monument. Thus, the bureau reasoned, Congress must have repealed Section 3 by implication.

A third way the government converts the law to mush is by changing the language of statutes as they are reflected in regulations. In 1897, Congress passed a law governing the national forests known as the Organic Act, one provision of which requires that trees ". . . before being sold, shall be marked *and* designated. . . ." Marking is done with a marking hammer. The forester traditionally went through the woods and marked the trees with a hammer to indicate which trees were to be cut.

The Forest Service, however, wanted broad discretion to decide how timber should be cut. In particular, it wanted discretion to permit wide clear-cuts. The process of marking individual trees, however, is not consistent with clear-cutting, where the ground is simply scalped for acres and acres. In short, marking is a nuisance the Forest Service wishes to dispense with. To get around the marking requirement, the service decided to change an "and" to an "or." Thus, while the national forest Organic Act reads "mark *and* designate," the Forest Service regulation covering the point reads "mark *or* designate." There is a very interesting decision from the Northern District of West Virginia, *West Virginia Division of the Izaak Walton League of America v. Earl L. Butz,* that rejected the regulation and other "liberal" Forest Service interpretations of its Organic Act. I commend it to you as a lesson in how to catch the government up on creative regulation writing.

There are many more devices by which the executive branch guts the law. Let me mention just one more: simply missing deadlines and letting timetables slip, otherwise known as foot dragging. An example of this was revealed to me recently in regard to the new Marine Mammal Protection Act of 1972. Certain provisions of that act exempted tuna fishermen for two years from the act's requirements that they obtain permits before taking porpoises in the act of tuna fishing. Another provision, however, provided that the Department of Commerce was to issue interim regulations for the two-year period "to reduce to the lowest practicable level the taking of marine mammals incidental to commercial fishing operations." These provi-

Logging above Redwood National Park. Photo by Bruce Colman.

sions were intended to combat certain tuna-fishing practices that have caused hundreds of thousands of porpoise fatalities.

After several of the initial 24 months passed without any regulations having been issued, a group of citizens concerned about porpoises sued to obtain regulations. Finally, on January 22, 1974, 13 months late, the Commerce Department issued regulations to go into effect in April. The effect of the delay was to allow two unregulated fishing seasons to pass, totally nullifying the department's lawfully mandated duty. The suit, *Project Jonah v. Frederick B. Dent,* in the U.S. District Court for the District of Columbia, resulted in no ruling or opinion and will probably now be dismissed as moot.

The examples I have discussed of executive disrespect for statutory mandates are from my own experience in environmental litigation. I have had other such experiences, and I have read many case reports where government officials have substituted their discretion for the law for one reason or another. The best known are the cases under the National Environmental Policy Act, which simply involve the gross failure of the government to prepare an environmental impact statement. Many cases involve blatant failures to enforce permit requirements or to protect lands and waters clearly mandated for protection. These failures occur so often and are so often justified as being matters of executive discretion that I believe it is fair to say that the lawyer's first task in dealing with the government on an environmental decision is to track down and counter its various rationalizations for substituting its discretion for the law.

Procedural Techniques by Which Government Avoids Review

When the lawyer has done this, however, he is not through. He has a second task, which is to meet a number of special ploys, not available to other litigants, that the government will use for avoiding judicial review.

The first of these ploys is the doctrine of sovereign immunity. When I went to the Land and Natural Resources Division of the Justice Department to practice law several years ago, I was informed early on that the first line of defense in any lawsuit defended by that division was to raise the doctrine of sovereign immunity by motion to dismiss. This doctrine holds that the government can only be sued with its own consent. The memoranda of the lands division once almost invariably asserted that such consent had not been given in whatever the case in question happened to be. Happily, the courts seem now to pay less attention to this ploy than they did in the past. The Congress obviously intended by the Administrative Procedure Act, as well as a number of other statutes, that the actions of government officials be subject to judicial review. The doctrine of sovereign immunity, which derives from the notion that the king can do no wrong, is clearly out of place in a modern democracy based on law.

The government, however, still asserts the doctrine, arguing that courts should not, as they put it, "stop government in its tracks." Occasionally they con a court into accepting the doctrine. A case where the Sierra Club was the victim of the royal majesty of our sovereign is *Sierra Club v. Hickel,* in which a decision to turn a wildlife refuge over to a power company in a land exchange was held to be unreviewable on the ground of sovereign immunity.

The second ploy of the government to avoid review is to challenge plaintiffs' standing to sue. If, like myself, you were raised to believe that an active participation in civic matters is a virtue, be prepared for a shock. Your government prefers to tell its citizens that they have insufficient interest in their government's decisions to obtain any test of the legality of those decisions. Apathy and docility are what the executive branch prefers.

The next ploy of the government is to obtain the laxest possible standard of review. Under the Administrative Procedure Act, the government already has an enormous advantage. Plaintiffs can overturn their decisions generally only if they are arbitrary, capricious, or represent an abuse of discretion. This, however, is not good enough for the government, which often baldly asserts that decisions are based on nonreviewable discretion.

Failing to win complete nonreviewability, the government will then indulge in a series of arguments to win a rubberstamp review. There are many varieties of this ploy and, as I could spend my entire time on them, I will limit myself to just one example. The arbitrary and capricious standard applies to government decisions. The government, however, attempts to have this standard applied to questions of whether it has complied with procedural prerequisites to its decision. One of the most important such prerequisites is the environmental impact statement required by NEPA. Happily, many courts have held that the EIS mechanism should be reviewed strictly as a matter of law.

Another ploy of the government to avoid review is to test plaintiffs on the question of the exhaustion of administrative remedies. No matter how exhaustively your client has debated a subject with a government agency, the executive branch often has additional socalled "remedies" for your client yet to hurdle.

For example, the Forest Service takes the position that before you can sue with regard to one of its decisions you must file an appeal with a forest supervisor, work your way up to the regional forester, then to the chief of the Forest Service and finally to the Secretary of Agriculture. Thus the Forest Service requires four appeals before they will acknowledge that your client is entitled to sue.

Who is kidding whom? This is all unnecessary. Even one review by an agency can be justified *only* if there is a real opportunity for reversal. A four-step appeal cannot be justified under any circumstance. The system is simply used to exhaust plaintiffs, not remedies.

What else do they throw at you? I don't have to tell you about the resistance to discovery under the doctrine of executive privilege. It has been in the press so pervasively that you must all be aware of it. It is just another special privilege asserted by the government to avoid review. There are others, but you have the picture.

It may sound as though I am complaining because the government fights hard in a lawsuit. Not so. I am only pointing out that the government attempts to avoid review of any kind through special ploys not available to the ordinary litigant, such as executive privilege or sovereign immunity. The purpose is to avoid accountability under the

'LOWER!'

Drawing by Dwayne Powell, by courtesy of The News and Observer.

law. Your second task in litigating with the government over an environmental matter is to anticipate and be prepared for these ploys.

Federal Evasions of Court Orders

Now, once you have fended off the various maneuvers of the government to avoid the law and judicial review under the law, and you have won your case, your fight with discretion may not be over.

You may find that the government just won't obey the court order you have won. I don't mean by this merely that the government will appeal, seek stays, or seek a bill from Congress. Of course it will do that. Rather, I am referring to another way they resist a decree. To explain what I mean, I will relate to you the example of the Sierra Club's nondegradation case, *Sierra Club v. Ruckelshaus.*

In this case, Sierra Club won a nondegradation interpretation of the Federal Clean Air Act. Under the Clean Air Act, the Environmental Protection Agency (EPA) is required to promulgate National Ambient Air Quality Standards. Once EPA has promulgated the ambient standards, the states thereafter are required to promulgate enforcement plans to achieve and maintain the standards. The act requires EPA review of all enforcement plans to insure they will, in fact, enforce the standards. EPA is required to disallow a plan or part thereof if found inadequate and can promulgate its own plan or part thereof if a state does not correct an inadequate plan.

As it happens, and depending on where you are, actual air quality is often better than the ambient standards promulgated by EPA. The nondegradation principle is that

ambient standards can only be used to clean up air of poorer quality than that defined by the standards and cannot be used as a license to pollute air of a better quality. EPA originally accepted this principle and, in fact, so stated in the very body of the Ambient Air Quality Standards. However, when EPA issued its instructions to the states for preparation of the enforcement plans, it reversed itself and announced that degradation would be permissible.

The Sierra Club sued and won the point in the district court on a preliminary injunction on May 30, 1972. The parties stipulated that the order should be considered final for purposes of appeal. Then the district court was upheld twice, first by the court of appeals, and finally by the Supreme Court, each time without opinion.

The court ordered EPA to do two things. First, EPA was ordered to disallow state plans that did not embody the nondegradation principle. EPA complied with this part of the order on November 9, 1972. Second, the court ordered EPA to promulgate final regulations setting forth nondegradation principles for state enforcement plans by November 30, 1972. EPA to this day has not complied with this second requirement. EPA's requests for stays were denied three times by the district court and the court of appeals between May 30 and November 30, 1972. Nevertheless, EPA made no effort to issue proposed regulations that would meet the November 30 deadline. EPA avoided noncompliance at the last minute when the solicitor general went to Chief Justice Burger on November 29 and obtained a stay that remained in force until the Supreme Court affirmed the lower courts on June 11, 1973.

What EPA did after the Supreme Court ruled against it was very interesting indeed. A month after the ruling, EPA issued four alternative sets of proposed regulations to implement the court's order. In our judgment none of the proposals even come close to implementing nondegradation. Furthermore, if you take the *Federal Register* at face value, they are not even intended to. The proposed regulations were prefaced, *inter alia,* with this statement. I quote the *Federal Register* of July 16, 1973, Vol. 28, p. 18986: "In EPA's view, there has been no *definitive judicial resolution* of the issue whether the Clean Air Act requires prevention of significant deterioration of air quality. When the issue was presented to the Supreme Court, the court was equally divided. The court's action had the effect of permitting to stand the judgment of the Court of Appeals for the District of Columbia Circuit, which was entered in the procedural context of the issuance of a preliminary injunction."

I must interrupt to remind you that the government had in fact stipulated that the preliminary injunction would be considered a final decree. The statement goes on to say: "In the absence of a definitive judicial decision on the issue, the Administrator adheres to the view that Section 110 of the Clean Air Act requires EPA to approve state implementation plans that will attain and maintain the national ambient air quality standards, and that the Act does not require EPA or the states to prevent significant deterioration of air quality. The proposed alternative regulations set forth herein would establish a mechanism for preventing significant deterioration pursuant to the preliminary injunction issued by the District Court."

Now this is ambiguous, but what I fear they mean is that they believe they do not have to, and are not going to, enforce nondegradation. All they are doing, in their view, is issuing some regulations in order to comply, technically, with a court order, after which, I believe they are saying, they are not required to take further positive action.

At about the time this statement appeared in the *Federal Register,* the White House was saying, with regard to the legal proceedings of Archibald Cox to obtain the Water-

gate tapes, that the President would only be bound by a definitive ruling of the Supreme Court. There were many speculations in the press as to what sort of an order of the Supreme Court the President would have considered definitive. We at least know now that a 4-4 affirmation is not, in EPA's view, definitive. In any event, EPA has never made its statement "inoperative," and we conclude that EPA has chosen to use the rule-making proceeding as a vehicle of resistance to, rather than implementation of, the court's order. To this day, 14 months after the court's deadline, we have not yet seen final regulations. We see before us years more of litigation over the regulations, once they are issued. And if we ever obtain good regulations, we believe we will have to sue to enforce them. Thus, EPA simply will not comply in any meaningful way unless kept under litigation pressure for years to come.

We have been discussing how a lawyer must prepare to respond to the government's drive to act in a discretionary fashion, to avoid review, and to avoid compliance with court orders. Is there any way, you may ask, to solve this problem on an institutional basis, rather than in *ad hoc* litigation?

There is only one way. That is for government officials to create a climate in which political pressures are not allowed to overwhelm all other elements of federal decision-making. To base decisions on discretion, while ignoring the written law, weakens the rule of law. Obviously, only a few people can put the decision-makers in their pocket. In a nation as large and diverse as ours, the consequences of lawless government are resentment, disillusion, bitterness, suspicion, and division. It is all before us today. The only way out of this swamp is for the government itself to scrupulously abide by the rule of law. Only if we can be sure that the government respects the rule of law can we have respect for and confidence in the government.

—JAMES W. MOORMAN

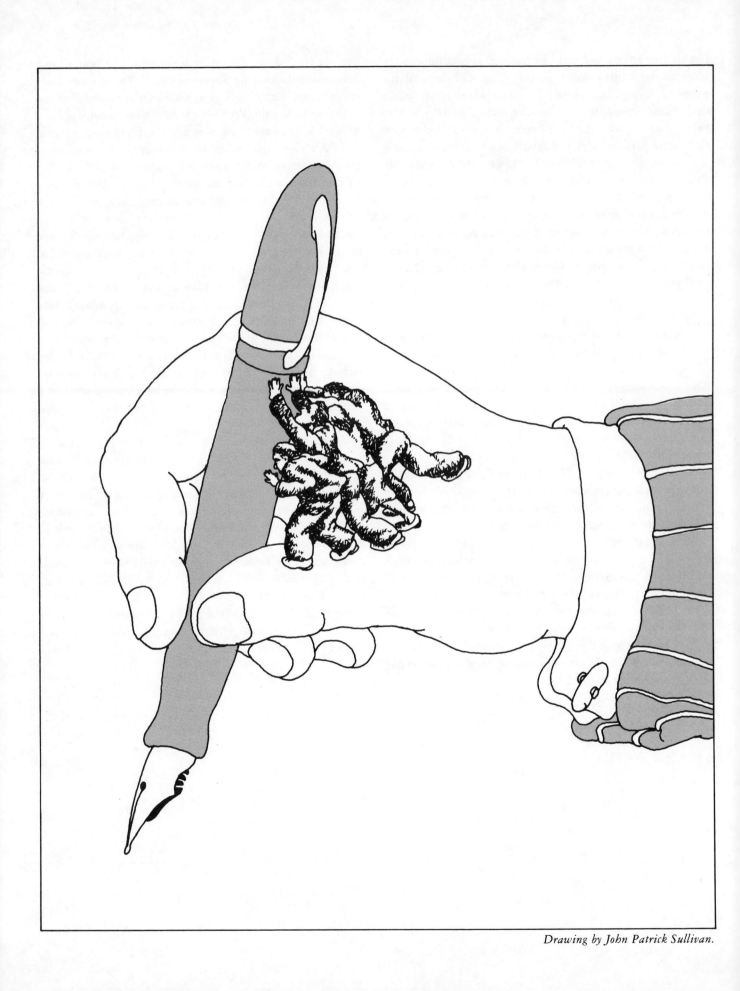

Drawing by John Patrick Sullivan.

A Citizens' Appendix:

How to Get Laws Introduced and Passed

The most insidious destroyer of democratic government is non-participation. People feel strongly about issues, but say to themselves: "I am powerless. What can I do to influence public policy?" This attitude has been a problem for centuries. Plutarch chronicles Solon as saying: "He shall be disfranchised who in times of faction takes neither side." Major societal problems will not be cured until there is much more universal participation in the political process. Laws *can* be influenced by people, working singly or in groups on public issues. Mastery of the complex machinery of the political process, however, is a necessary prerequisite. In order to effectively influence legislation, citizens must know when and how to apply pressure on their elected representatives.

I know no safe depository of the ultimate powers of the society but the people themselves; and if we think them not enlightened enough to exercise their control with a wholesome discretion, the remedy is not to take it from them, but to inform their discretion.

—THOMAS JEFFERSON

The only sure bulwark of continuing liberty is a government strong enough to protect the interests of the people, and a people strong enough and well enough informed to maintain its sovereign control over its government.

—FRANKLIN D. ROOSEVELT

How to Get Laws Passed

If a Representative or Senator were to answer truthfully the question, "What is the most important issue you are involved in?" the answer would probably be, "My own reelection." Survival, especially for members of the House who are elected every two years, is of paramount importance. It dwarfs all other issues. Even Senators who only need to campaign every six years are well aware of the political maxim that one doesn't ignore the wishes of one's district for long and survive.

Primarily, it is this overriding concern with reelection that gives citizens power to influence the laws that will be formulated. Unfortunately, most people do not use their power to influence legislation, and thus Congressmen hear most frequently from paid industry lobbyists. (We will use "Congressmen" to mean both Representatives and Senators unless it makes a difference, in which case, we will distinguish between them.) In addition to the major corporations that employ fulltime lobbyists, the Washington staffs of trade groups have for years served as conduits to explain to legislators what their members want. It is only relatively recently that public interest groups have employed Washington staffs to act in this capacity. The fact that so much consumer and environmental legislation has been passed within the last ten years speaks well for the effectiveness of these public interest lobbyists. Such measures as the Fair Campaign Practices Act, the Clean Air Act, the Eastern Wilderness Act, and numerous land protection bills would not have been passed in effective form without public-interest lobbying pressure.

If you do not live in Washington and yet you want to be effective influencing legislation, it is almost imperative that you join a national public interest group that is concerned with your issue and has an effective lobbying office in Washington. Enacting a bill into law is a long, tortuous process. For people outside of Washington to initiate ideas that ultimately become law, it is usually necessary to have a Washington liaison who can personally meet with legislators, be available for quick consultation, and keep the local individual or group aware of latest developments. The Washington staffs of consumer and environmental groups act as this contact for their members in the same way trade groups have acted for decades. Because legislative developments can move so quickly and because political savvy about the complex world of Capitol Hill is gradually built up over the years, the importance of affiliation with an effective national lobbying group cannot be overstated.

Another service that national groups provide is a legislative newsletter. Almost all groups have a publication that discusses the latest developments in legislation, who key Congressmen are, and how to influence them. The newsletter is an extremely important lobbying tool because local newspapers and TV do not provide in-depth analysis of legislation in Congress until it has either passed or failed. Potential amendments, for instance, are rarely discussed in the local press, even though an amendment may change the whole thrust of a bill. Thus, the legislative newsletter provides valuable information in addition to stimulating widespread interest in the issue.

The techniques that follow are basic lobbying strategies that you can employ to influence legislation.

To be effective, the first thing you must do is become knowledgeable about the issue. Once you have expertise, you have something very much needed by the overworked staffers on Capitol Hill—accurate information. Becoming knowledgeable is not the herculean effort it may seem; it becomes fairly simple if you get assistance from your Congressman.

First, find out if any legislation has been introduced or if hearings have been held on the issue. There is a service available to Congressmen called the Bill Status Office. The staff of the legislator merely telephones a Capitol Hill extension to learn from the computerized service what bills have been offered on a subject, whether hearings have been held, whether the bills have passed either house, etc. For a more detailed analysis of the subject and a more complete explanation of the bills, legislators can call on the Congressional Research Service. This service is located in the Library of Congress and provides legislators with detailed information on any subject. Capitol Hill staffers can call the Congressional Research Service with a problem and a few days later receive a carefully prepared paper citing the pro and con arguments.

If your Congressman is willing, and most are, you can make use of these services to find out quickly if legislation has been submitted on your issue and what the points of contention are. Simply write your Congressman and ask him to ask the Bill Status Office to determine whether any bills have been submitted on your topic, whether hearings have been held, and what has happened to the bills. If you would like a more detailed analysis of the bills, ask him to request that the Congressional Research Service, instead of the Bill Status Office, determine what bills have been submitted. Request background information on the pro and con arguments and citations of any relevant government studies that have been done on your issue. The National Academy of Sciences, for instance, does studies on almost every conceivable topic. Studies by government agencies provide background information that gives you expertise and can be used later on in the legislative battle.

Once you have received your Congressman's response, you can begin assembling the material you will need to become knowledgeable about the issue. Get the bills, any committee reports, and hearing records. Study them. Be sure to cite bills by their number, prefixed by HR for House of Representatives and S for the Senate. If the bill has been reported out of committee, ask that the committee report be included with the bill. This report gives a section-by-section analysis of major points in the bill and also explains the pro and con arguments advanced in committee debate.

The bills and committee reports can be obtained by writing to the House Document Room, Washington, D.C. 20515 or the Senate Document Room, Washington, D.C. 20510. Hearing records must be obtained from the committee that held the hearing, not from the Document Room.

Studying this material and doing independent research at your library will give you a good start. But what if there have been no bills introduced in your area of interest, or all the bills in existence embody bad principles? The answer, of course, is to write a bill of your own.

Introducing a Bill

Congressmen have at their disposal an Office of Legislative Counsel that drafts bills and amendments for Congressmen and committees. The Office will take bill drafts and outlines from a Congressman and put them into legal language suitable for introduction. It is partly because of the availability of this Office that so much legislation is now introduced. If you have an idea you want to expand into a bill, it is a relatively simple matter to contact your Congressman, get him to send your idea to the Office of Legislative Counsel, and then convince him to introduce the resulting bill. While some members of Congress refuse to introduce a lot of legislation, most are very willing to introduce well-thought-out bills for their constituents. The legislation that is introduced in this manner, however, usually ends up in the great burial ground of the Congressional committees and is never heard of again. It is relatively easy to get a bill introduced. To get it introduced in a way that will give it a good chance to become law is more difficult.

Old hands on Capitol Hill know that *who* introduces a bill and *which committee* the bill is referred to often determine whether or not the bill will become law. Only rarely will a bill become law if it is introduced by someone who is not a member of the committee that considers it. In fact, to give the bill the best chance, it is necessary to have someone introduce it who is a member of the *sub*committee that will consider it. In other words, there must usually be a champion of the bill working for it at both the subcommittee and committee levels.

Before asking a Congressman to introduce your bill, try to determine which committee and subcommittee it would logically be referred to. Get a copy of the volume entitled *Constitution, Jefferson's Manual, and Rules of the House of Representatives* from the Superintendent of Documents, Government Printing Office, Washington, D.C. 20402. This book is published every session and describes the jurisdictions of House Committees. Unfortunately, it is not free; it costs $9.30 in paperback. A similar volume that describes Senate committee jurisdictions, *Senate Procedure, Precedents and Practices,* is available from the Government Printing Office for $8.10 in paperback.

Once you have determined which committee the bill will be referred to, get the *Congressional Directory* or some similar reference book from the library and find out who the members of that committee are.

The next step is to determine which member will be the most receptive to your viewpoint and the most influential on the committee. First, choose a member of the majority party. Minority members rarely have enough clout to get controversial legislation out of committee. Consider seriously a committee member who may be neutral on your issue but who comes from your state. Usually you would choose your own Congressman because you would be able to use reelection pressures to get the bill pushed.

Another major factor in choosing a member to introduce your bill is that some members become specialists in certain areas. These members often consider themselves to be more nationally oriented, and because they are proud of their knowledge and reputation, will introduce bills concerning their specialty for citizens who are not their own constituents. Getting one of these specialists to introduce your bill means that you capitalize on the respect and influence that this member has.

Gerald McMurray, the Staff Director of the Housing Subcommittee of the House Banking and Currency Committee, stresses how influential specialists are: "If I had a bill in the housing area, for instance changing the block grant program, I would want the Housing Subcommittee Chairman Thomas Ludlow Ashley to introduce it because he is known as the one man in Congress who knows almost

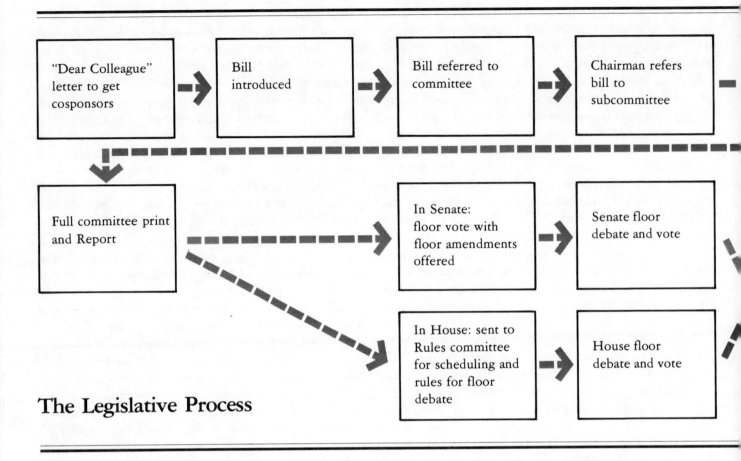

The Legislative Process

everything about our federal housing program. I'd expect a bill he introduced to have a good chance of passing because of the respect with which other members view his knowledge. The advice I would give someone who wants to get a bill enacted into law is, 'Try to get a specialist, a member respected by the other Congressmen for his knowledge, to introduce it.'"

One easy way to get help in deciding who should introduce your bill is to contact the Washington staff of the environmental, consumer, or other public interest group that is most concerned with your issue. The staffs of these groups are familiar with the leanings of most Congressmen who are sympathetic to their views and are generally able to give good advice on who would be the most influential member of the committee.

Once you have found an effective member to introduce your bill, write to him proposing your idea. Include a draft of your bill and any supporting material you have been able to gather, such as scientific studies by government agencies, magazine or newspaper articles, statements by public officials, etc. The more polished and complete your package seems, the greater the likelihood that your bill will be introduced. Offer to get more background material and to explain your bill more fully if the staff wishes to telephone

you. Include your telephone number. Finally, to maximize your chances, try to get endorsements from other people and groups for your bill.

Once a Congressman has agreed to introduce your bill, find out the name of the staff person in his office who will be handling the legislation. It is very important to become friendly with the Congressman's staff person assigned to your issue. It is this staffer who does the day-to-day work on the issue, and his opinion is respected by the Congressman. The only caveat is that congressional staffers, like the legislators themselves, are overworked. It is necessary to keep in telephone contact with them and to help them perform many tasks, such as assembling witness lists for hearings, preparing speeches, etc. On the other hand, there is a serious danger of alienating them if they are bothered too frequently. There is a fine line between keeping a staffer informed and bothering him.

Your relationship with the Capitol Hill staff is a professional, mutually beneficial one. Remain businesslike even in the face of delay. The staffer's schedule (or his boss's) will often force a delay. Unless procrastination has become chronic, remember that it is one of the facts of legislative life, and don't let it upset your relationship with the Hill staffer.

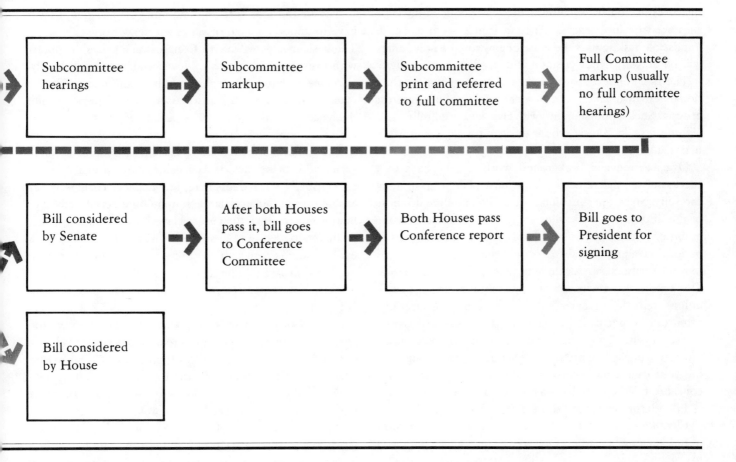

Once the mechanics of getting the bill introduced are completed, the process of expediting its passage through both Houses begins. At this point, traditional lobbying techniques must be used, so a digression to explain these techniques is necessary.

Lobbying

The key to lobbying is the efficient use of limited time and scarce resources. An understanding of the ramifications of the congressional committee system is essential to this concentration of lobbying effort.

Most basic work on legislation is done in the subcommittees and committees of Congress. The committee system is a timesaver. By working in only one or two areas throughout their congressional tenure, Congressmen do not have to learn basic facts every time they work on a new piece of legislation. To become an effective lobbyist, it is important to realize how influential the committee system is. It is not unusual for a member to stand up on the House floor when legislation is being considered and say; "I am against this amendment. We thoroughly discussed this issue during our committee debate and decided not to amend the legislation in this way." Sometimes he will even add, "I don't think you should vote for this because, if we are

going to have committees in Congress, you should rely on their judgment in these matters."

Congressmen do rely on committee judgments. Usually, 90 percent of the issues in the bill are permanently resolved in committee. Of course, there are many exceptions. Some bills are completely revised on the floor. And some issues become so controversial that interest is high and many amendments are offered. But in general, the basic work is done at the subcommittee and committee levels, and only the most controversial sections of the bill are amended on the floor. Lobbyists wise in the ways of Capitol Hill realize this and concentrate their efforts on the committees. Extra effort expended on the relatively small number of committee members pays tremendous dividends when the time comes for a floor vote. For example, if you are successful in getting the committee to adopt your position, the committee's authority and prestige will help defend that position from attack on the floor. Even though you will use the following techniques at all stages in the political process, the bulk of your effort should be directed at getting a good bill reported out of committee.

Lobbying falls into two general categories: working with Congressmen's constituents and working with the media.

Organizing a Congressman's constituents to exert effective pressure on his opinion is the way public interest issues are won in Congress. At first, it may seem to be an impossible task; but as the issue begins to take hold, allies will be drawn to your position and it will become easier.

The first thing to do is to get the endorsements of national environmental, consumer, and public interest groups. Such endorsements will give you credibility and will impress upon local groups that your issue is important nationally.

Organization and background work are the keys to a successful legislative battle. You must plan your strategy carefully. Since the subcommittee and committee do most of the nitty-gritty work, they should be the focus of your attention. Contact the major local groups and branches of national groups in the districts of committee and subcommittee members and ask them to take a stand on the issue. Don't stop with environmental or consumer groups; labor unions, religious organizations, and fraternal organizations often can be persuaded to take stands on national issues. These groups sometimes have more impact than public interest groups. The broader the scope of groups supporting your cause, the more seriously the Congressman will consider it. When you have a broad coalition of support, it is difficult for him to say "those do-gooders are at it again."

Identify and recruit an interested person in each committee member's district. One way to find such a person is to ask the local branches of the national public interest groups for their recommendations. Material can then be sent to the person to disseminate to other interested people and groups. This contact person must be kept up to date on all developments and technical aspects of the legislation because he will also serve as your contact with the local press. Background papers, material suitable for use in pamphlets, etc., must be sent to this contact. He will be responsible for publicizing the issue, contacting local groups, organizing a letter-writing campaign, setting up a telephone network if possible, and coordinating the effort in the member's district.

Having an effective contact person in each district can often mean the difference between success and failure. Rafe Pomerance, a Friends of the Earth staffer and the Legislative Coordinator for the National Clean Air Coalition, describes one instance: "We knew Congressman Dingell was going to offer an amendment in committee to gut the automobile emissions standards section of the Clean Air Act. But, because we had established contact people in each member's district, we were able to generate an outpouring of sentiment against the issue in five key districts. These five members changed their votes, and that proved to be the margin we needed to defeat the amendment."

One of the jobs that you and your contact people will have to undertake is to organize a letter-writing campaign. The basic means by which a Congressman keeps in contact with his district is the mail. Never underestimate the importance of letters. Telephone calls to the local office or even to Washington are often useful, but letters provide the basic demonstration of interest and expression of opinion concerning an issue.

The volume of mail a Congressman or Senator receives varies with many factors. Legislators from primarily rural areas usually receive less mail, but a speech or newspaper article may stimulate a large volume on a certain day. No matter how many letters are received, each one is opened, read, catalogued, and answered. Thus, there is a tally in every Congressman's office of voter interest and sentiment on different issues. The legislator is told daily, or at least weekly, how voter interest is running. He is told again before a vote.

Every Congressman knows that voters are often too apathetic to express their preferences in writing. When a person does take the trouble to write, the Congressman assumes that the writer's position must also be held by a large number of other people in the district. In other words, he feels that every letter represents the sentiments of 50, 100, or even 500 voters in his district. A letter-writing campaign, therefore, is an important lobbying tool. There are certain techniques of letter writing that you should use and recommend to co-workers:

1. Always be courteous. You can disagree with a Congressman's position, but never be discourteous in doing so.
2. Try to keep the letter to one typewritten page. Complex letters are often put aside to be answered later and may lose their effectiveness. If you have more material than will fit onto one page, include extra background pages, but label them clearly as background and put your name and address on them in a corner. These pages will probably be routed to the staff person handling the issue and so will have more impact.
3. Do not write about more than one issue in each letter. That only confuses the staff and dilutes your impact.
4. It is better not to use a form letter provided by an environmental, labor, consumer, or other organization. It only takes minutes to write a few sentences of your own, and such a letter is much more effective. Try to add a few sentences about the issue's impact on the legislator's district.
5. If you write to a Congressman who is not your own, send a copy to your legislator and clearly indicate that

Photo by Elihu Blotnik/BBM Associates.

you have done so on the bottom of your page. Otherwise, your letter may be routed to your own Congressman as a courtesy, and the legislator you want to influence will be bypassed.

6. If you are writing to criticize or praise a bill, be as specific as possible. If you do not know the bill number, try to describe the bill by its precise name, such as the "Eastern Wilderness Bill."

7. If you are writing about an amendment, try to include the bill number, who will offer the amendment, and what the amendment will do.

8. If possible, include in your letter some reference to the Congressman's past actions on your issue or some other related issue. Including this kind of reference shows that you are aware of his past record and that you are following the issue closely. If you write to the legislator and ask to be included on his newsletter list, you can become more aware of his attitudes.

9. Ask your Congressman to vote a specific way, support a specific amendment, or take a specific action. Otherwise you will get a "motherhood" response. He

will say in a general way: "Of course I am in favor of clean air, adequate health care, or whatever you want." Then he may vote the wrong way. In order to be effective, you must be specific so you can hold him accountable for his actions.

10. It is always wise to try to meet the Congressman before you write to him. Then you can refer to your meeting in the first few sentences of your letter. Call his district office to ask for his schedule of office hours and public meetings.

Working With the Media

Since, initially, the congressional committee will be the basic unit you are working with, a good beginning is to go to your local library and get *The Ayer Directory of Newspapers, Magazines, and Trade Publications* or *Bacon's Publicity Checker* from the reference section. These books list the major newspapers throughout the United States. From one of them, you can extract a press list of the major newspapers in the district of each of the members of your committee. Such a list will prove very valuable as the campaign heats up. The next thing to acquire is the League of Conservation Voters charts of the voting records of Senators and Congressmen. By looking over these charts, you can deduce the political leanings of members of your committee. The charts can be obtained for $2.00 each from the League at 317 Pennsylvania Ave. SE, Washington, DC 20003.

The *Congressional Record* is also an important element in the legislative process. Reading it can be an enlightening experience, but it can also be used as a public relations tool. Congressmen can publish in the *Record* speeches, reprints of newspaper and magazine articles, etc., up to two *Record* pages in length. Then they can have these sections reprinted (subject, of course, to the approval of any copyright holders) at nominal cost. These *Congressional Record* reprints can then be sent to their constituents, to the press, or to anyone else the member wishes to receive them. If the member assents, it is possible for a group to pay the printing costs for these reprints and thus get reprints to send to its members. Sending out *Congressional Record* reprints is a good way to engender interest in an issue.

Letters to the editor of the newspapers in key members' districts are also good tools to stimulate interest in your issue. Send a copy of your letter to your Congressman at the same time that you send it to the newspaper. Then he will see it even if the newspaper does not print it. If it is printed, you will have an opportunity to write a follow-up letter to your Representative, including the printed letter. Be sure to ask the member to take some specific action, whether it be to ask the chairman to hold hearings, to support an amendment, or whatever you wish at the stage in the legislative process your bill is in.

Calling up editors and reporters of the local media in key Congressmen's districts to ask them to cover the issue is also a good way to influence legislation. Local newspapers and radio stations are usually much more willing to cover issues relevant to their Congressman or Senator than the national press, especially if you stress the local implications. Moreover, studies show that the local media are more influential in affecting people's opinions than the national media. Members of Congress are aware of this and pay particular attention to what is reported back home.

One of the best ways to influence a Congressman is not used as much as it should be. This is the use of praise when he makes a speech, offers an amendment, or takes a stand that is praiseworthy. Politicians hear a lot of criticism from the press and from constituents, but only rarely do they get praised. If a Congressman does something that is good for your cause or good for the environment in general, send him a letter thanking him. Either enclose a copy of the letter with a note to the local press, or even better, write a press release and send it to the newspapers in the Congressman's district. Praise him for his stand. Chances are good that the local media will pick up your press release and praise him also. If that happens, the Congressman will be very grateful for the favorable publicity in his home district where it can help him get reelected. The praise may encourage him to devote more time to your issue or even to become a specialist in it. After Senator Warren Magnuson wrote several consumer bills that became law, he was acclaimed in the press and by consumer groups. The praise had a salutary effect. Gradually he turned his committee, the Senate Commerce Committee, from a business-oriented group into a consumer panel. In 1968, he even made his successes as a consumer advocate the main theme of his reelection campaign.

Praising legislators publicly for their good works is a way to encourage them to do more good. But it is also a way to insure that your viewpoint will be taken seriously in future matters, since it conditions the Congressman to view you as an ally.

There are myriad ways to influence the media. The following is a partial list:

1. Assemble a press list and learn to write a good press release by studying books from your public library on press relations techniques and talking to reporters on your local papers.
2. Appear on local radio and TV talk shows and also get experts from local universities and organizations to appear.
3. Write feature stories and submit them to local magazines.
4. Try to get editorial support from local TV and radio stations. Contact the station managers and ask them to take a stand supporting your viewpoint. Have sufficient background material available. If you are successful, ask the station for a copy of the editorial and send it to the legislators.
5. Try to get local TV stations to do a documentary about your issue.
6. Contact other organizations in your key congressional districts and urge them to publicly support your position. Their support can be announced by a press release to the local media and by their newsletters to their members. Make sure they notify their Congressmen and Senators of their position. It is very important not to forget to contact labor unions and other powerful groups that are principally concerned with your issue. These groups can be very influential with the local media and broaden your support.

Photo by Patrick Miller.

7. Form local coalitions in key congressional districts. Formation of such a coalition is a newsworthy event and will be picked up by the local papers if they are properly briefed. Such a local angle on a national issue can help make it more relevant for the local press.

8. Visit local politicians and local political organizations such as the Young Democrats and Young Republicans. Ask them to make a statement on your issue and publicize it. It is a good idea when contacting local politicians and political organizations that do not have large staffs to include a sample statement they can release under their own name by slightly rewriting it. Other actions politicians could take include writing an article on the subject, appearing on local TV and radio shows, organizing other politicians, or testifying at congressional committee hearings. It is generally quite easy to get ambitious young politicians to take these actions because they will get publicity that will help in their future careers.

9. If there are public figures who have championed your issue in another part of the country, write to them. Ask them if they are going to be visiting your area in the future and if they would mind being interviewed by the press and making a statement on your issue. For instance, Pete Seeger, in his travels around the country giving concerts, is often interviewed on the subject of water pollution because he has become a spokesman for cleaning up New York's waterways. If it is explained that a key Congressman or Senator lives in the district, the public figure will often be willing to be interviewed because of the chance to influence public policy.

10. If you hear negative ads about your issue on television or radio, contact station managers about the possibility of getting free time to respond under the Fairness Doctrine. The station is only required to *sell* you time if the opposition bought time. In some cases, however, the station will decide that if you cannot pay for time, they will offer you some free, as a public service.

Until fairly recently, public interest issues were not publicized very much. Now everyone realizes the value of publicity to mobilize sentiment about an issue. Using your press list and organizing the constituents of key Congressmen are the two most effective ways to influence legislation. But lobbying techniques, to be useful, must be employed at different times in the legislative process. Thus, you must become familiar with the process by which a bill becomes a law.

At almost every step in the legislative process, it is possible to lobby for your viewpoint. Just as a bill is introduced, if not before, cosponsors are sought by the member introducing it. You can help by writing to urge Congressmen or Senators to cosponsor the legislation. The mechanics of getting cosponsors is similar in both Houses. In the Senate, the member sends out a "Dear Colleague" letter to all other Senators describing the bill and asking for cosponsors. Then the names of the cosponsors appear on succeeding prints of the bill. The House rules differ slightly although the "Dear Colleague" letter is the same. In the House, only 25 members may cosponsor a bill. The difference is theoretical, however, because other members who are in favor of the bill merely introduce identical bills. Getting a large number of cosponsors is important because the more cosponsors a bill has, the easier it is to get hearings on the bill. The chairman of the subcommittee or committee considering the bill has almost absolute power to determine if hearings will be held. Naturally, he feels more pressure to call hearings if there are 50 cosponsors rather than five.

Once a bill has been introduced, it is referred to the committee that has jurisdiction over that issue. Then the bill is usually referred to a subcommittee for detailed consideration. It is possible, however, that the chairman of the full committee will not refer the bill to a subcommittee but instead will rule that the bill be taken up by the full committee.

When the bill is referred, the chairman of the committee or subcommittee decides if hearings will be held right away. If he sets a date for hearings, it is the job both of the staff of the Congressman who introduced the bill and of the subcommittee staff to organize a witness list. Depending on the complexity and scope of the bill, hearings can be set for 1, 2, 3, or even more days. Various kinds of witnesses are called: scientists, representatives of trade groups, public interest groups, government representatives, industry, and anyone with interest in the subject. They deliver testimony and answer questions from the subcommittee members. It is relatively easy to become a witness at a hearing. The staff person handling the witness list tries to get a broad representation of various points of view and so is anxious to find diverse individuals who are interested and knowledgeable.

Since most committees have very little money to pay travel expenses to Washington, they use two ways to get testimony from people unable to come to Washington on their own. The more common method is for people living far away to submit written testimony. Such testimony is included in the hearing record and is considered by the staff and legislators when making judgments about the bill. The other alternative is used, logically, when most of the witnesses would live outside of Washington but in close proximity to each other. This usually occurs when land bills are under consideration, or bills that would only affect one region. Field hearings are then held locally, congressional staff and legislators going to the area to take testimony.

Hearings are the basic medium of communication with the subcommittee, and their importance cannot be overstated. In addition to preparing testimony of your own and either submitting it in writing or delivering it in person, you should try to convince other groups and individuals who agree with your viewpoint to submit testimony. Congressmen or Senators not on the committee can testify, as can other politicians and public figures. Testimony from such individuals is valuable both because it is more frequently covered in the media and because legislators, obviously, pay close attention to influential people in their own profession. Try to convince other Congressmen and Senators and some local politicians to testify supporting your position.

Obviously, the hearing is an ideal occasion to release a statement to the press. Since members of the press usually attend important hearings, you can hand out a press release there that will often get picked up in a general story about

the hearings. If it doesn't, such a release could still spark interest in your viewpoint and serve as background for future stories. Even if you cannot be at the hearing, it is wise to send your release out to your press list so it will arrive before the hearing takes place. At each point in the legislative process, every effort should be made to get your viewpoint into the press.

After the hearing, your bill could lie fallow indefinitely. Once again, lobbying techniques should be used to get a "markup." This term was coined because subcommittee members take a clean copy of a bill and mark it up with amendments. A markup is a working session. The bill is read, page by page, and the subcommittee members offer amendments and vote on them. When they have gone through the bill completely, they decide whether or not to vote out the bill as amended. Voting it out means they send a clean copy of the amended bill to the full committee.

If, after the hearing, no markup is scheduled, you should try to get influential members of the subcommittee, the full committee, and members of Congress in general to contact the subcommittee chairman asking for a markup. Letters to the subcommittee chairman, especially those from people in his district, are influential. Creating a climate of interest about the issue through publicity and through constituent pressure is very important. Once again, at this point in the process, having a liaison at a Washington public interest group can be very valuable. Your Washington contact can talk to staffers on Capitol Hill and determine why there is a logjam. Often, personal contact will spur Hill staffers and Congressmen to take the

FOE staff members (l-r) Tom Garrett, David Brower, and Jerome Waldie testify at the Hathaway confirmation hearings, April 1975. Photo by Carol Parker.

issue more seriously and schedule a markup. In any case, your Washington liaison should be able to determine which lobbying techniques would be most appropriate to help get the markup.

Once a markup is scheduled, it is imperative to determine what amendments will be offered and what counteramendments or strengthening amendments you would like to offer. Your Washington associates can find out, in general, what amendments will be offered. Contact between you and the Washington public interest group staff will have to be on a daily basis to determine strategy. Information will be needed for arguments in support of or against amendments. New amendments will have to be written and Congressmen found to introduce them. Lobbying pressure will have to be intensified. Here the background work that you have done establishing coalitions and contacting groups and influential people in the subcommittee members' districts will begin to pay off. You should be able to generate hundreds of telegrams and letters supporting your position by contacting various groups and individuals in key members' districts.

Work with the press should also be bearing fruit now. If you have generated interest in subcommittee members' districts, you can now follow up with a press release detailing the controversy in the markup. Another way of getting publicity is to have a local group in a key subcommittee member's district release a statement to the press. You want to create both constituent and media pressure to show that there is a ground swell of support for your position.

Once the subcommittee markup is over, even if you have been successful in getting strengthening amendments passed and debilitating amendments defeated, you will have to start over again when the bill is sent to the full committee.

The full committee can start the whole process again by calling a new set of hearings on the legislation as sent from the subcommittee and taking testimony from different people. In fact, this rarely happens. Usually the full committee goes directly to a markup of the subcommittee legislation. Depending on the members of the committee and the interest generated in the legislation, the full committee markup can be a pro forma ratification of the subcommittee work or a full-scale revision of the bill. Once again, the same lobbying techniques that were used to get a markup and to influence the subcommittee members will be used on members of the full committee.

Assuming that you have managed to get a good bill reported from the full committee, the next step differs between the two houses of Congress. In the Senate, the bill is scheduled for floor debate where amendments can be of-

fered. In the House, the bill goes to the Rules Committee, which schedules it for floor action, sets limits on debate, and even determines whether or not amendments will be allowed. Nancy Matthews, legislative assistant to Congressman Richard Ottinger, explains how much power this committee has: "The Rules Committee is much more than a traffic cop regulating the flow of legislation. By limiting debate in different ways, the Rules Committee makes policy decisions which affect the floor vote. They can even kill a bill by refusing to give it a rule."

If the Rules Committee bottles up your bill, traditional lobbying techniques must once again be employed to convince the committee members that there is a need for the legislation. Organizational and constituent pressure from the members' districts and publicity about the committee's action have been effective in dislodging legislation from this committee in the past.

Once a bill has been scheduled for floor action, lobbying goes on at a fever pitch. Information on the bill must be disseminated as widely as possible. Try to get a story published in newspapers such as the *Washington Post* or *The New York Times*. Publicity at this time is very valuable. A couple of weeks before the 1974 Strip Mining Bill was to be voted on in the House, a public interest coalition notified Congresswoman Patsy Mink that the Chamber of Commerce had received air time on various radio stations for a tape criticizing the bill. Representative Mink then wrote to a large number of broadcasters asking if they would present her rebuttal to the Chamber of Commerce tape. Less than a week before the vote, Congresswoman Mink's rebuttal was broadcast by 70 or 80 radio stations. This last minute publicity was probably a factor in the legislation's passing the House.

In addition to publicity, letters and mailgrams must arrive from all over the country. If you have done your background work well, long before the vote you will have placed stories in the newsletters of the major consumer and environmental organizations asking for supporting letters to Congressmen. As the vote approaches, you should contact the regional representatives of the major environmental and consumer groups asking their help in generating mail and Western Union mailgrams.

There is a last minute flurry of activity before the floor vote. Members of Congress who are knowledgeable and influential must be found to give speeches in support of the bill on the floor. You or the Washington public interest group staff might be pressed into service writing these floor speeches if the member's staff is too busy. Arguments against weakening amendments must be provided to key legislators. Strengthening amendments must be written and influential legislators must be persuaded to offer them.

The vote is the culmination of months of effort. Then, if your bill passes, the procedure begins all over again in the other house. Even after both houses have passed the legislation, the bill must go to a Conference Committee to iron out differences between the House and Senate versions. The Conference Committee is composed of members of the House and Senate committees that have worked on the legislation. The same lobbying techniques used to influence committee consideration can be used again to influence the Conference. Moreover, since the members are the same ones you worked with at the committee level, you should have a fairly good rapport with them.

When the Conference has reported out a compromise version of the bill, it once again goes to the floor of both houses. Approval, however, is a virtual certainty. Conference Reports are hardly ever defeated. Then the bill goes to the President for his signature.

The lobbying techniques described above may seem to be difficult and time-consuming. They are not. You may not need to apply pressure at every step in the process. Often a bill will take on a life of its own and sail through almost unopposed. Even with controversial legislation, allies will be drawn to your position and the work can be spread among various groups and individuals.

The important point to remember is that a single person can succeed in getting legislation enacted. A case in point is Dr. Abe Bergman of Seattle, a pediatrician with a social conscience. In 1966, Dr. Bergman boiled over because he was seeing children with severe burns from flammable clothing. He persuaded Senator Magnuson to accompany him on a tour of the burn ward at a local hospital. Magnuson promptly introduced a bill providing that standards be set to make children's sleepwear flame resistant. But Dr. Bergman did not stop with the introduction of the bill. He helped Magnuson's staff prepare a witness list and testified himself. As the legislation progressed, he continued to keep in contact with the staff and was available to assist in preparing background material. The legislation was enacted into law in 1967.

Then Dr. Bergman discovered that laws are not always enforced. The law provided that the Secretary of Commerce set the standards to make the sleepwear flame resistant. But the Secretary did not set the standards. Years passed and once again Dr. Bergman decided to act. He persuaded some people he knew at a local television station to make a TV documentary on the children's burn problem. As Dr. Bergman puts it: "If you are a public interest lobbyist and you don't have any money, you have got to use the media. The television documentary produced 3,000 letters in one day to the Secretary of Commerce. Senator Magnuson then made sure the Secretary saw the documentary, and the week after he saw it he signed the regulations."

Since the enactment of the Flammable Fabrics Act, Dr. Bergman has initiated the Poison Prevention Packaging Act, which became law in 1970, and the bill establishing a National Health Service Corps, which was signed into law on December 31, 1970. He is working on other proposals for legislation.

Dr. Bergman is one example of a successful citizen lobbyist. Another could be you.

Photo by Daniel Gridley

A Professor's Crusade

His classmates in an Iowa farm town inscribed a motto under Paul Taylor's photograph in the high school annual.

"I can," it said, "and I will."

Today he is 80 years old. He moves with the exaggerated caution of the very old. He suffers from glaucoma, but his eyes still blaze with a fury that hasn't diminished in 30 years.

"The land monopolists have controlled enforcement of the reclamation law and torn the law to ribbons," he says.

At this point he becomes Dr. Paul S. Taylor, one of the nation's most distinguished economists and professor emeritus of the University of California, a man whose life of scholarship turned more than 30 years ago into a crusade that he can and probably will complete.

To Taylor, the issue is fundamental. From the fall of the Roman Empire to the collapse of the Saigon government, the answer to a nation's inner strength lies in the question of who controls the land.

"This generation raised on the streets doesn't understand," he once remarked. "They are unaware of the social and political significance of widespread distribution of land ownership."

Efforts by earlier generations in this country culminated in the National Reclamation Act of 1902, which was intended to break up the West's huge ranches by providing cheap federal irrigation that would create family farms. With its controls over monopoly and speculation, it's still the law.

Taylor has repeated this message to anyone who would listen.

Since 1949 his name has appeared on more than 40 law review articles, letters to editors, statements before Congress, scholarly reports and speeches. The message is always the same:

Enforce the reclamation law so farmers can buy into the lands of irrigation projects.

Unable to wipe the law off the books, the big landowners have a problem, Taylor says.

"They are still in an uncertain, perhaps even precarious position, violating the law," he says.

Taylor shows up every weekday at 9 a.m. in Room 380 of Barrows Hall on the Berkeley campus. The small office is crammed with thousands of documents organized into files, bound in numbered volumes or stacked in boxes on the floor.

Asked a question about reclamation, he goes directly to the right pile and produces the necessary document in a flash. It startles his colleagues. One of them said:

"Behind the facade of an old man lies the brain of a computer."

George Ballis, executive director of National Land for People, credits Taylor with keeping alive the reclamation issue.

"In retrospect, if he wasn't waging that lonely fight through the law journals and congressional committees, maybe we wouldn't have anything to fight over now. He was so persistent."

In a sense, Paul Taylor *is* history. Born in Iowa before the turn of the century, he spent his teenage summers working on an uncle's farm. He recalls that his grandfather "broke the sod on a farm near Madison with a yoke of oxen."

At the University of Wisconsin he studied under labor economist John Commons. Taylor says Commons was deeply concerned with the application of knowledge.

"The question behind studying was always, 'What do you do about these problems?'"

He quit school to join the Marines as a captain in World War I, when he was gassed at Chateau Thierry.

To recuperate, Taylor sought California's mild weather and enrolled at UC to complete his doctoral studies. He

spent 1926 to 1934 studying Mexican migratory labor, and in the Depression years was a logical choice as consultant on rural affairs to the California Emergency Relief Administration.

In 1937 word reached Taylor of a human disaster in Nipomo, where thousands of migrant laborers had flocked to harvest the pea crop. They were stranded without food or shelter in San Luis Obispo County after wet weather destroyed the crop.

Assigned to report on the situation, Taylor wanted the help of a photographer. Her name was Dorothea Lange.

Photography wasn't considered then a proper tool for social research. Miss Lange was listed as a secretary.

Taylor's report on Nipomo was the first to recognize the impact of mass migration from the ruined lands of the Dust Bowl. Asked for better statistics, Taylor replied testily that plenty of numbers would become available if the full tragedy were allowed to unfold without immediate action.

The report was handcarried to Washington by Taylor's superior, Dr. Laurence Hewes, who showed it to Eleanor Roosevelt, Henry Wallace and anybody who would look.

Photo by George Ballis

Photo by Robert Schaeffer

The photos were more convincing than all the statistics put together, and the result was a federal crash program to provide food, medical care and housing to Dust Bowl refugees.

After their marriage, Taylor and Lange toured the nation in 1939 to produce "An American Exodus," a powerful book about the Depression's victims.

Not until 1943, as an Interior Department consultant, did Taylor discover the 160-acre limitation on ownership of land receiving federal irrigation.

The limitation was part of the 1902 law. So was a live-on-the-land residency rule for water recipients. Taylor found that most federal reclamation projects were controlled by big farmers and absentee investors. He was shocked. He still is.

He reserves special anger for the Bureau of Reclamation, charged by Congress to enforce the law.

"They took oaths of office," says Taylor. "Why the hell don't they obey them?"

Years of research, analysis and heavy scholarship followed. After retiring in 1962 as chairman of the economics department, Taylor began to devote full time to the land issue.

Taylor argues that land ownership patterns are directly related to the quality of rural life and the health of society itself. Small farms produce schools, churches, community organizations and a wealth of satisfying experiences for individuals, he says. Big farms, he contends, create an impoverished class of farmworkers.

These relationships were documented on journeys to Portugal, Brazil, Venezuela, Columbia and Peru, where Taylor studied land patterns. He was sent as a consultant to Vietnam in 1957 and again, twice, in 1967.

His simple advice about Vietnam was received with about as much official enthusiasm as his comments on the

160-acre limitation. He said the absence of meaningful land reform in South Vietnam was one of the prime reasons why the Saigon government, dominated by landlords, lacked peasant support.

His investigations of reclamation projects in the United States have left him deeply troubled.

"I have never learned so much about how my society operates—on the executive, legislative and judicial levels—as I have learned on the issue of reclamation law," he says.

It's an indictment.

The loneliness of Taylor's crusade continued after the death in 1965 of Dorothea Lange, who had long been regarded as the nation's most distinguished photographer of rural problems.

Taylor continued his work. In the past year alone, he has published three articles in law reviews, issued a scholarly statement to a Senate committee and spoken at an Oakland

Photo by Robert Schaeffer

conference. Letters and inquiries flow from his office. He maintains his own library of reference materials, assisting other researchers and lawyers.

He can, and he will.

"If you allow yourself to be knocked out of the ring, then you're probably not coming back," Taylor said in an interview for the UC Oral History Project.

"I think I learned a long time ago that this issue has deep roots. We're dealing with important skirmishes in a battle that's been going on for a hundred years and is going to go on for a lot more.　　　　　　—WILL HEARST

About the Authors

All the contributors to *"Progress As If Survival Mattered"* are dedicated activists, committed to keeping this planet a living place, though they came to their commitments from widely divergent backgrounds.

David R. Brower has been leading conservation battles and writing and editing books and magazine articles for four decades. He served the Sierra Club as executive director from 1952–69 and, as general editor of the Club's book program, created the historic exhibit format series, which included *This Is the American Earth* and *"In Wildness Is the Preservation of the World"*. He founded Friends of the Earth in 1969, and now serves as FOE's president and general editor of FOE Books. Mr. Brower's conservation work has won him numerous awards and honorary degrees. He was the subject of John McPhee's *Encounters With the Archdruid* (1971).

Hugh Nash, son of world federalist author and leader Vernon Nash, was born in 1923 in Kansas City, Missouri. From 1924–36, the Nash family lived in China, where the elder Mr. Nash taught at Yenching University. Hugh Nash holds a BA from Cornell in Political Science (1947) and has been an editor and writer for *World Government News* (1947–51), *Architectural Forum* (1953–64), and the *Sierra Club Bulletin* (1964–69). He joined the Friends of the Earth staff in 1970 as editor of *Not Man Apart* and is now NMA's senior editor.

Stewart M. Ogilvy, born in Winnipeg in 1914, and graduated from Trinity College, Hartford, in 1936, with an SB, has been an editor for the Population Institute since 1972. He has served on the board of directors and as secretary, treasurer, and publications chairman for the World Federalists (1941–47), represented the World Federalists USA on the US Council of the Movement for World Federal Government (1946–47), and has been acting executive director of United World Federalists (1947). He has been vice president of Friends of the Earth and FOE Foundation, a member of the advisory board of the Scenic Hudson Preservation Conference, vice president of Negative Population Growth (1972–73), advisor to Zero Population Growth, and has served on the board of directors of the American Movement for World Government. He was editor of the Sierra Club Atlantic Chapter's *Argonaut* (1957–59) and chairman of that chapter (1960–61). He is a naturalized US citizen and lives in Yonkers, New York.

Amory B. Lovins, physicist, born in Washington, DC, in 1947, and educated at Harvard and Oxford, has been a consultant on energy and physics since 1965. He resigned

his fellowship at Merton College, Oxford, in 1971 to become British Representative of Friends of the Earth and has written six books for FOE and associated organizations: *Eryri: The Mountains of Longing* (with Philip Evans), *Openpit Mining, The Stockholm Conference: Only One Earth, World Energy Strategies, Non-Nuclear Future* (with Dr. John Price), and *Soft Energy Paths.* The last title, his latest, is an expansion to book length of his most influential paper, "Energy Strategy: The Road Not Taken?", which appeared in *Foreign Affairs,* October 1976. He lives half the year in London and travels extensively in Europe and North America to consult with and advise governments, research institutes and industry groups.

Mary Lou Van Deventer, a native of Michigan, came to work for Friends of the Earth in 1974. She served as managing editor of *Not Man Apart* from 1975–77, writing and editing on Alaska, public lands, the recombinant DNA issue, Micronesia, and general issues of pollution and resources. She is currently writing a novel set in a conserver-society future. While with FOE, she was a regular contributor to *Mother Earth News.*

Cynthia Johnston received her BA in Languages and Anthropology from the University of Colorado in 1967. Since then she has been in politics, working for Hubert Humphrey (1968), Edmund Muskie (1971–72), and Jimmy Carter (1976) in their campaigns for the presidency, and for the Democratic National Committee (1967–68), League of Women Voters (1969–70), and Californians for Nuclear Safeguards (1977). She is now a political consultant to the California Teachers Association and is a consultant on labor and community liaison for Friends of the Earth. Her FOE work concentrates on environmentalism's relations with minority groups and includes programs on inner city outings, full employment, and Black people's concerns.

John Hamburger, born in Rochester, New York, in 1948, and holding a BA in Psychology from the University of Chicago, is a freelance editor in the San Francisco area. After holding a variety of jobs from bus driver to laboratory technician, he was a copy reader for Stanford University Press from 1974–75 and a special editor for FOE Books in 1975–76. He currently edits nonfiction, religious, and text books for Harper and Row, Wadsworth Publishing Company, and Mayfield Publishing Company.

Mary Jean Haley is a San Francisco freelancer, born in Nevada, raised in Montana, and graduated from Mills College with a BA in English (1968). She is a former editor for

Clear Creek magazine and the Council on Economic Priorities. Her articles have appeared in *Outside, Rags, New West, New Times, Rolling Stone,* and *CoEvolution Quarterly.*

Joan Gussow, born in Alhambra, California, in 1928, and holding a BA in Zoology and Chemistry from Pomona College (1950), is a consultant, teacher, and author on food, nutrition, and education. She earned her MEd (1974) and EdD (1975), both in Nutrition Education, from Teachers College, Columbia University, where she is now an Associate Professor and chairs the College's program in nutrition and education. She is coauthor (with Herbert Birch, MD, PhD) of *Disadvantaged Children: Health, Nutrition, and School Failure* (1970) and is author of the forthcoming *Who Is Going to Eat the Breakfast of Champions?* She is a consultant to the FDA, USDA, and the Children's Television Workshop, and Senator McGovern's task force on world hunger, and serves as vice president of the Community Nutrition Institute. Her husband, Alan, is a noted artist, editor of *A Sense of Place* (1972), and vice president of FOE.

Anne Wickham was born in Oakland in 1946, earned her BA in Anthropology from Oberlin in 1969, and joined the League of Conservation Voters staff in 1971. When LCV and FOE were legally separated, she moved to the FOE staff as assistant to the wildlife director (1972). In 1977, after a year and a half in the post of wildlife director, she became conservation director of FOE. She has become one of Washington, DC's, most respected lobbyists on wildlife, fisheries, and international ocean issues. She serves on the Oberlin Alumni Board and the Advisory Committee to the Corporation for Public Broadcasting.

Bruce Colman was born in Berkeley, California, in 1949, son of a prominent soil scientist. Mr. Colman received his AB (in English, with Honors) from Trinity College, Hartford, in 1971, and came to work for FOE the same year. From 1972–75 he was an associate editor of *Not Man Apart,* writing on Alaska, wilderness, forestry, oil tankers, parks, and democracy. In 1975, he became the president's assistant for book publishing. His freelance writing has appeared in *Mountain Gazette* and *American Alpine Journal.*

Stephanie Mills was picked by *Mademoiselle* as one of the young women to watch in the 1970s. Born in Berkeley (1948) and reared in Phoenix, she received her BA in Contemporary Thought from Mills College in 1969. Her graduation talk as Class Speaker, decrying the environmental damage caused by modern industry and the population bomb, made front pages all over the country. She was editor of *Earth Times* (1970) and is now editor of *Not Man Apart.* She has contributed to *Clear Creek, CoEvolution Quarterly, Playgirl,* and the *San Francisco Bay Guardian,* and is a member of the boards of directors of Planned Parenthood Federation of America (1970–76), the Association for Voluntary Sterilization, and the Farallones Institute. She attended the UN's conferences on the Human Environment (Stockholm, 1972) and on Habitat (Vancouver, 1976), is authoress of *The Joy of Birth Control,* has lectured widely, and serves on FOE's Advisory Council.

Chuck Williams was born in 1943, and worked from 1962–68 as an instrumentation engineer before volunteering for VISTA (1969–70). He received a BA from Sonoma State College, in Liberal Studies, in 1971, and spent 1970 through early 1977 traveling through America's national parks, studying their needs and problems, photographing them, and building a reputation as one of the conservation movement's most well-informed, insightful, and dynamic national park experts. He has been FOE's National Parks Representative since 1975. He now lives in Skamania, Washington. His writing has been published in *Sierra Club Bulletin, High Country News,* and *Backpacker.*

Mark Terry, educator and author, was born in Seattle in 1947. He was educated at Pomona College, the University of Washington (BA, *cum laude,* in Anthropology, 1969), and Cornell (MAT in Science Education, 1971), where he was a Shell Merit Scholar. He is a member of Phi Betta Kappa and Phi Delta Kappa (the national honor society for education majors). He has taught at high schools in California, Oregon, and New York, and now teaches at Overlake School in Redmond, Washington, while doing graduate work and teaching secondary environmental education at the College of Education, University of Washington. He is author of the seminal *Teaching for Survival* (1971) and, with Paul Witt, of *Energy and Order* (1976), a lesson-plan on energy issues, for teachers of tenth grade.

Clay and *Anne Denman* were instrumental in founding the Small Towns Institute, in 1969. Both are codirectors of the Institute, and Clay doubles as president of its board of directors. Both hold PhDs from the University of California, in Anthropology. Clay has been teaching Anthropology at Central Washington University since 1964, Anne since 1967. He is a professor, she an associate professor. The Institute, which is housed at CWU, provides an information-exchange facility for communities, which enables them to share experiences in solving common problems—like historic preservation, planning for growth or non-growth, financing the arts, finding a role for the elderly. Its magazine is *Small Towns.*

Donald McDonald has been a working journalist and journalism teacher since 1945. A native of Wisconsin, he received his BA and MA (1949) from Marquette University and later served there as Dean of the College of Journalism. He joined the Center for the Study of Democratic

Institutions in 1965 where he edits *The Center Magazine* and *World Issues.* He also lectures on public affairs reporting, at the University of California, Santa Barbara.

Mildred R. Blake, born in Illinois 1897, received her BA from the University of Michigan in 1918 and went to work reporting for newspapers in the midwest, before spending 30 years as an advertising writer (she retired in 1950). From 1945–47 she was cochairman (with Mark Van Doren) of World Federalists, USA. She has served on the board of United World Federalists and the New York branch of UWF. She was the organizing chairman for an advertising campaign for the reform of the United Nations in 1965–66, and joined Friends of the Earth, as representa-

tive to the UN, in 1971, in which capacity she attended the UN Conference on the Human Environment. She retired from her UN post with FOE in 1975, but continues to serve on the Board of Directors.

Ann Roosevelt, Boston-bred, holds a BA from Radcliffe (English, 1966) and an MA from Boston University (Political Science, 1971). She was an assistant editor for Random House (1970–71) and in 1972–73, was assistant science advisor to Senator Edward Kennedy. She joined FOE as legislative director in 1973, specializing in energy issues. Since 1975, she has served as FOE's New England representative, while living in Boston.

Acknowledgements
(Continued from page 4)

Futurist, October 1974), "Forcing the Hand of the De-regulators" (*Just Economics,* October 1975), and "Toward a New Economics."

John Holdren, "The Nuclear Controversy and the Limitations of Decision-making by Experts" (*Bulletin of the Atomic Scientists,* March 1976), and "Too Much Energy, Too Soon" (*The New York Times,* July 23, 1975).

M. King Hubbard, "The Energy Resources of the Earth" (*Scientific American,* September 1971).

Ivan Illich, *Tools for Conviviality* (Harper and Row, 1973).

Mike Jacobs, *One Time Harvest* (*The Onlooker* and the North Dakota Farmers Union, 1975).

F.H. King, *Farmers of Forty Centuries* (1911; recently reprinted by Rodale Press from the original plates).

Lewis Lundborg, "Making a Living in the Third Century" (*Saturday Review,* July 10, 1976).

Donald McDonald, "The Media's Conflict of Interests," *The Center Magazine,* December 1976).

Margaret Mead, "The Energy Crisis—Why Our World Will Never Again Be the Same" (*Redbook Magazine,* April 1974), "This Time There Is No Enemy" (*AAUW Journal,* April 1974), and "The Next Billion Years" (*PSA California Magazine,* May 1974).

Donella Meadows, "Equity, the Free Market, and the Sustainable State."

Joseph Meeker, "Genes and Clever Livers" (*The North American Review,* Fall 1975).

James Moorman, "The Future of Environmental Law" (a speech given February 5, 1976), and "The Law" (*Sierra Club Bulletin,* October 1974).

David Morris and Gil Friend, *Energy, Agriculture, and Neighborhood Food Systems* (Institute for Local Self-reliance, 1975).

Bill Moyers, "Earthwatch from Nairobi" (broadcast by the Educational Broadcasting Corporation, March 20, 1975).

Vernon Nash, *The World Must Be Governed* (Harper and Brothers, 1949).

Natural Resources Defense Council, *Newsletter,* (Summer 1976).

The New York Times, "Issues '76: Energy" (March 30, 1976).

McKinley Olson, *Unacceptable Risk* (Bantam Books, 1976).

William Ophuls, "Technological Limits to Growth Revisited" (*Alternatives,* Winter 1975).

Walter C. Patterson, "Hiroshima Pilgrimage" (*New Scientist,* August 21, 1975).

Russell Peterson, speech on environmental and economic justice and jobs, May 1976.

Emery Reeves, *The Anatomy of Peace* (Harper and Brothers, 1945).

Gordon Robinson, "Forestry As If Trees Mattered" (*Not Man Apart,* Mid-August 1976).

Stephen Schneider, *The Genesis Strategy* (Plenum Press, 1976 and Delta, 1977).

E.F. Schumacher, *Small Is Beautiful* (Harper and Row, 1973).

Bob Schwartz, "American Business Needs You!" (*New Age Journal,* March 1976).

Hans Selye, "Health and the Stress of Our Social Environment."

John Shuttleworth, an editorial in *Mother Earth News* (September 1975).

Thomas C. Southerland and William McCleery, *The Way to Go* (Simon and Schuster, 1973).

Christopher B. Stone, *Should Trees Have Standing? Toward Legal Rights for Natural Objects* (William Kaufman, Inc., Los Altos, California, 1974).

Maurice F. Strong, "Noah, the Flood, and World Government" (*The Humanist,* July/August 1975).

Nicholas Wade, "Nicholas Georgescu-Roegen: Entropy the Measure of Economic Man" (*Science,* Volume 190, pp. 447–450, 31 October 1975, Copyright 1975 by the American Association for the Advancement of Science).

Leonard Woodcock, speech at Environmental and economic justice and jobs conference, May 1976, and "Jobs and Environment—No Conflict" (*Not Man Apart,* January 1976).

Edith Wynner, "Noah, the Flood and World Government," (*The Humanist,* July/August 1975).

Herman E. Daly, Mark Horlings, Donella Meadows, and Gary Soucie contributed original essays to *Progress As If Survival Mattered.* These appear among the readings on economics and law, and, in Mr. Soucie's case, as side bars in several other chapters.

We wish to thank: Ruth Easton, Dan Eisenstein, and Ann Sieck for proofreading; Leonard Rifas for editing cartoons; Marianne Ackerman and Joe Holmes for preliminary photo editing; and especially Jeroboam, Inc., a photographers' collective, in San Francisco, that let us rifle their files for some of the best material we've seen in years.   —B.C.

It is only a little planet
But how beautiful it is.
—ROBINSON JEFFERS

Progress As If Survival Mattered has presented Friends of the Earth's program for creating a conserver society in the US.

These are steps we are working on with every legal means at our disposal, here and abroad: lobbying legislatures; engaging in litigation; testifying before and serving as consultants to the administrative branch of government; and helping business and industry, through our books, through consulting arrangements, through advice solicited and unsolicited, prepare for the era of diminishing resources.

You can help this effort by joining Friends of the Earth.

Membership rates are:

$25/year—Regular
$35/year—Supporting
$60/year—Contributing
$100/year—Sponsor
$250/year—Sustaining
$1000—Life
$5000 or more—Patron.

(Students, retired persons, and those lavishly underfinanced, may join for $12/year.)

All members receive *Not Man Apart* twice a month and are entitled to discounts on FOE books. Members in categories of $35/year and over receive FOE gift books as premiums.

Dues in FOE are not tax-deductible, in order that we may lobby vigorously.

Friends of the Earth Foundation solicits deductible contributions of money or property.

Membership applications in FOE, or donations to FOE Foundation should be addressed to the US head office, in San Francisco:

124 Spear Street
San Francisco CA 94105.